Encyclopedia of Literature and Politics

○○○ *ADVISORY BOARD* ○○○

∘∘∘ *Encyclopedia of* ∘∘∘

Literature *and* Politics

Censorship, Revolution, and Writing
Volume III: S–Z

∘ ∘ ∘

Edited by M. Keith Booker

GREENWOOD PRESS
Westport, Connecticut • London

Library of Congress Cataloging-in-Publication Data

Encyclopedia of literature and politics : censorship, revolution, and writing / edited by M.
    Keith Booker.
        p.   cm.
    Includes bibliographical references and index.
    ISBN 0–313–32928–1 ((set) : alk. paper)—ISBN 0–313–32939–7 ((vol. 1) : alk. paper)—
    ISBN 0–313–32940–0 ((vol. 2) : alk. paper)—ISBN 0–313–33568–0 ((vol. 3) : alk. paper)
    1. Politics and literature—Encyclopedias.   I. Booker, M. Keith.
    PN51.E63   2005
    809'.93358'03—dc22   2005008522

British Library Cataloguing in Publication Data is available.

Library of Congress Catalog Card Number: 2005008522
ISBN 0–313–32928–1 (set)
        0–313–32939–7 (Vol. I)
        0–313–32940–0 (Vol. II)
        0–313–33568–0 (Vol. III)

First published in 2005

Greenwood Press, 88 Post Road West, Westport, CT 06881
An imprint of Greenwood Publishing Group, Inc.
www.greenwood.com

Printed in the United States of America

The paper used in this book complies with the
Permanent Paper Standard issued by the National
Information Standards Organization (Z39.48–1984).

10 9 8 7 6 5 4 3 2 1

For Amy, Adam, Marcus, Dakota, Skylor, and Benjamin

⚬⚬⚬ *Contents* ⚬⚬⚬

○○○ *Preface* ○○○

During the past few decades, literary studies have come to be dominated by approaches that emphasize the social, historical, and political significance of literary works. This development (after the cold-war decades, in which political approaches to literature were out of favor) reemphasizes the close connection that has existed between literature and politics throughout Western history. This three-volume encyclopedia brings together a wide variety of information on the relationship between literature and politics in a conveniently accessible encyclopedia format.

The encyclopedia is international in scope, covering relevant information from the ancient Greeks forward, though with a necessary emphasis on the modern era (after 1900). Indeed, because the topic of the encyclopedia is so broad, it has been necessary to make a number of choices in emphasis. For example, because the encyclopedia is written in English and because English is expected to be the principal language of most readers, the various entries concentrate especially on American and British literature, with the expectation that this literature will be most relevant to the majority of readers. Secondary emphasis has been given to other Anglophone literatures (from Canada, Australia, the Caribbean, and Africa), while it has been possible only to touch on the highlights of other world literatures (from Latin America, Russia and the Soviet Union, China, Europe, and the Middle East).

The more than five hundred entries in the encyclopedia are of a number of basic types. The most numerous entries are biographical ones, which summarize the careers of important authors, critics, and literary theorists, as well as historical figures who have had an impact on the evolving relationship between literature and politics. There are also a number of entries describing important works of literature, as well as crucial critical nonfiction works and literary journals. A number of broader entries survey national literatures or important literary movements (such as Soviet socialist realism, American proletarian fiction, or postcolonial literature), while others cover broad critical categories, such as Marxist criticism, feminist criticism, or postcolonial studies. Finally, additional entries provide coverage of specific themes, concepts, and genres toward the goal of providing a single reference point for a general approach to the relationship between literature and politics. The various entries are cross-referenced using a system of boldfacing; in any entry, the first mention of an item that is also covered in an entry of its own will be given in boldface.

The entries in the encyclopedia have been written by expert scholars who work in the field to which the entries are relevant. In that sense, the information provided is the best that could be obtained. However, the length restrictions inherent in a work such as this one require that the information included here is merely a starting point and should not be taken as complete and comprehensive. In this sense, readers interested in more complete and detailed information should pay serious attention to the suggestions for further reading that are included at the ends of the entries and should consult the suggested sources for further information.

Alphabetical List of Entries

○○○ *Categorical List of Entries* ○○○

Li Ang
Lindsay, Jack
Lippard, George
London, Jack
Lorde, Audre
Lu Xun
Lumpkin, Grace

MacDiarmid, Hugh
Mailer, Norman
Malraux, André
Mandel'shtam, Osip Emil'evich
Mann, Thomas
Mao Dun
Martí, José
Matthiessen, Francis Otto
Mayakovsky, Vladimir Vladimirovich
McKay, Claude
Menchú Tum, Rigoberta
Milosz, Czeslaw
Milton, John
Mir, Pedro
Mo Yan
Momaday, N. Scott
Monette, Paul
Moravia, Alberto
Morris, William. See *News from Nowhere*
Morrison, Toni
Müller, Heiner

Nabokov, Vladimir
Naipaul, V(idiadhar) S(urajprasad)
Neruda, Pablo
Nexø, Martin Andersen
Ngũgĩ wa Thiong'o
Nizan, Paul

O'Casey, Sean
Odets, Clifford
Olsen, Tillie
Ondaatje, Philip Michael
Oodgeroo
Orwell, George
Osofisan, Femi
Ostrovsky, Nikolai Alekseevich
Owen, Wilfred

Page, Myra
Paley, Grace
Pasolini, Pier Paolo
Pavese, Cesare
Pilnyak, Boris Andreyevich
Pinter, Harold
Platonov, Andrei Platonovich
Plenzdorf, Ulrich
Polonsky, Abraham
Pound, Ezra
Prichard, Katharine Susannah
Pushkin, Aleksandr Sergeevich

Revueltas, José
Rickword, Edgell
Ridge, Lola
Robinson, Kim Stanley
Rolland, Romain
Roumain, Jacques
Rushdie, Salman
Russ, Joanna

Sassoon, Siegfried
Schuyler, George S(amuel)
Scott, F. R.
Seghers, Anna
Sembène, Ousmane
Senghor, Léopold Sédar
Serge, Victor
Shakespeare, William
Shaw, (George) Bernard
Shelley, Percy Bysshe
Shen Congwen
Sholokhov, Mikhail
Silko, Leslie Marmon
Sillitoe, Alan
Silone, Ignazio
Sinclair, Upton
Slesinger, Tess
Smedley, Agnes
Solzhenitsyn, Aleksandr Isaevich
Soyinka, Wole
Spenser, Edmund
Stead, Christina
Steinbeck, John
Stevenson, Philip Edward

Stowe, Harriet Beecher
Swift, Jonathan
Swingler, Randall

Taggard, Genevieve
Tagore, Rabindranath
Thompson, Jim
Thoreau, Henry David
Tolstoy, Alexei
Tolstoy, Leo (Lev) Nikolaevich
Toomer, Jean
Traven, B.
Trotsky, Leon
Tsvetayeva, Marina
Turgenev, Ivan Sergeevich

Unamuno, Miguel de

Valenzuela, Luisa
Vallejo, César
Vargas Llosa, Mario
Vizenor, Gerald Robert
Voinovich, Vladimir Nikolaevich

Walker, Margaret
Wang Shuo
Warner, Sylvia Townsend
Weatherwax, Clara
Weiss, Peter
Wells, H. G.
West, Nathanael
West, Rebecca
Whitman, Walt
Wiesel, Elie
Williams, William Carlos
Wolf, Christa
Woolf, Virginia
Wright, Richard

Yeats, William Butler
Yezierska, Anzia

Zamyatin, Evgeny Ivanovich
Zola, Émile

CRITICS AND THEORISTS

Adorno, Theodor Wiesengrund
Althusser, Louis
Anzaldúa, Gloria E.
Arendt, Hannah

Bakhtin, Mikhail Mikhailovich
Barthes, Roland
Baudrillard, Jean
De Beauvoir, Simone Ernestine Lucie Marie
    Bertrand
Benjamin, Walter
Bloch, Ernst
Bourdieu, Pierre
Butler, Judith

Caudwell, Christopher
Certeau, Michel de

Debord, Guy
Deleuze, Gilles
Derrida, Jacques
Du Bois, W.E.B.

Eagleton, Terry
Enzensberger, Hans Magnus

Fanon, Frantz
Foucault, Michel
Fox, Ralph

Gold, Michael
Goldmann, Lucien
Gramsci, Antonio

Habermas, Jürgen
Hall, Stuart
Haraway, Donna J.
Harvey, David

James, C.L.R.
Jameson, Fredric

Kraus, Karl
Kristeva, Julia

Lefebvre, Henri
Lukács, Georg

Macherey, Pierre
Mariátegui, José Carlos
Marx, Karl
McLuhan, Herbert Marshall
Mohanty, Chandra Talpade
Mulvey, Laura

Negri, Antonio

Ohmann, Richard

Reed, John
Robinson, Lillian S.

Said, Edward
San Juan, Epifanio, Jr.
Sartre, Jean-Paul
Sedgwick, Eve Kosofsky
Spivak, Gayatri Chakravorty

Weber, Max
Williams, Raymond
Wollstonecraft, Mary

Zizek, Slavoj

HISTORICAL EVENTS, GROUPS, AND MOVEMENTS

Académie Française
Anticommunism
Apartheid

Black Nationalism
Brecht-Lukács Debate

Chinese Writers' Association
Cold War, The
Comintern. *See* Third International
Communist Party
Cuban Revolution

Easter Rising

Federal Writers' Project
French Revolution

Gastonia Mill Strike
General Strike

Haitian Revolution
Harlem Renaissance

Indigenismo
Industrial Workers of the World (IWW)

John Reed Clubs

McCarthyism. *See* Anticommunism

Nigerian Civil War

Popular Front

Russian Revolution

Soviet Writers' Congress (1934)
Spanish Civil War

Third International

World War I
World War II

HISTORICAL FIGURES

Goldman, Emma

Lenin, Vladimir Ilyich

Mao Zedong

Nkrumah, Kwame

Padmore, George

Stalin, Joseph Vissarionovich

◦ S ◦

SAID, EDWARD (1935–2003). Born in Jerusalem to a Palestinian Christian family in what was then the British protectorate of Palestine, Said spent most of his professional career as a professor at Columbia University, where he was, for decades, an influential academic as well as the most effective advocate for the Palestinian cause in the United States. He was thus important not only as a teacher and scholar, but also as a public intellectual, a role he discussed in *Representations of the Intellectual* (1994).

Said made seminal contributions in the field of literary studies, beginning with his 1964 Harvard University dissertation on **Joseph Conrad** (published in 1966 as *Joseph Conrad and the Fiction of Autobiography*) and extending through his advocacy of a more socially responsible form of poststructuralism in *Beginnings* (1975) and *The World, the Text, and the Critic* (1983). But it was with the publication of *Orientalism* (1978) that Said began to make his most valuable contributions to the field of literary studies. Here, influenced by the discourse theory of **Michel Foucault**, Said argues that Europeans in the nineteenth century often justified their imperial expansion into the rest of the world through a belief in stereotypes that envisioned non-Europeans as lazy, irresponsible, irrational, and sexually promiscuous. Importantly, the major purveyors of these "Orientalist" stereotypes were not politicians but the scholars, anthropologists, and ethnologists charged with studying the Orient. Said's work suggests, moreover, that these Orientalist scholars were not a unique phenomenon. He argues that all human knowledge is filtered through ideological discourses and that Orientalist stereotypes continue to be influential in the contemporary Western world.

Though highly controversial upon publication, the insights of *Orientalism* have largely been vindicated by subsequent scholarship, and the book has become the founding work in the field of colonial discourse analysis. In this and subsequent works, such as *Culture and Imperialism* (1994), Said made crucial contributions to the growing field of **postcolonial studies**. His political perspective was influenced by Marxist theorists such as **Antonio Gramsci** and **Raymond Williams**, though his work often challenged the insights of Marxist theory as well, thus drawing the criticism of Marxists such as Aijaz Ahmad.

Politicized by the Six Days' War of 1967, it was ultimately as a passionate and articulate advocate for the Palestinian people that Said made his most important and lasting contributions to the world around him. He served as a member of the Palestinian parliament-in-exile from 1977 to 1991. In numerous television appearances and editorial pieces, he tirelessly brought the point of view of the disenfranchised Palestinians (otherwise typically ignored in the American media) to the American people. Books such as *Covering Islam* (1981, updated 1997), *The Politics of Dispossession* (1994), *Peace and Its Discontents* (1995), and *The End of the Peace Process* (2000) brought attention to this issue as well. His memoir, *Out of Place*, was published in 1999.

Selected Bibliography: Ahmad, Aijaz. *In Theory: Classes, Nations, Literatures*. London: Verso, 1992; Ashcroft, Bill, and Pal Ahluwalia. *Edward Said: The Paradox of Identity*. New York: Routledge, 1999; Bové, Paul A., ed. *Edward Said and the Work of the Critic: Speaking Truth to Power*. Durham, NC: Duke UP, 2000; Moore-Gilbert, Bart. *Postcolonial Theory: Contexts, Practices, Politics*. London: Verso, 1997; Said, Edward. *Beginnings: Intention and Method*. New York: Basic Books, 1975; Said, Edward. *Covering Islam: How the Media and the Experts Determine How We See the Rest of the World*. New York: Vintage-Random House, 1997; Said, Edward. *Culture and Imperialism*. New York: Vintage-Random House, 1994; Said, Edward. *The Edward Said Reader*. Ed. Moustafa Bayoumi and Andrew Rubin. New York: Vintage-Random House, 2000; Said, Edward. *The End of the Peace Process: Oslo and After*. New York: Pantheon, 2000; Said, Edward. *Joseph Conrad and the Fiction of Autobiography*. Cambridge, MA: Harvard UP, 1966; Said, Edward. *Orientalism*. New York: Vintage-Random House, 1979; Said, Edward. *Out of Place: A Memoir*. New York: Knopf, 1999; Said, Edward. *Peace and Its Discontents: Essays on Palestine in the Middle East Peace Process*. New York: Vintage-Random House, 1995; Said, Edward. *The Politics of Dispossession: The Struggle for Palestinian Self-Determination, 1969–1994*. New York: Pantheon, 1994; Said, Edward. *Representations of the Intellectual*. New York: Pantheon, 1994; Said, Edward. *The World, the Text, and the Critic*. Cambridge, MA: Harvard UP, 1983; Sprinker, Michael, ed. *Edward Said: A Critical Reader*. Oxford and Cambridge: Blackwell, 1992; Veeser, H. Aram. *Edward Said*. New York: Routledge, 2005.

M. Keith Booker

SAN JUAN, EPIFANIO, JR. (1938–). Born in Manila, Philippines, San Juan received his Ph.D. from Harvard University in 1965. He has taught at a number of universities in the United States and abroad, including the University of Connecticut, Tamkang University in Taiwan, and Washington State University. He has also served as a fellow of the Center for the Humanities at Wesleyan University, and director of the Philippines Cultural Studies Center. One of the leading leftist cultural critics in the United States, San Juan has written extensively on race, gender, ethnicity, Marxism, **postcolonial theory**, literature, and his native Philippines. His work is aptly situated in the third-world anticolonial Marxist tradition that includes such landmark intellectuals as Amilcar Cabral, **Frantz Fanon**, and **Aimé Césaire**.

In works such as *Carlos Bulosan and the Imagination of Class Struggle* (1972), *Writing and National Liberation* (1991), *Reading the West/Writing the East* (1992), and *The Philippine Temptation* (1996), San Juan writes with regard to the situation of the Philippines at the close of the last century as its masses face the choice of following "the path of neocolonial barbarism or the path of national-democratic redemption."

As well as intervening in the imperialist ideological construction of U.S. literary study and its canon, these works create critical paradigms and resurrect literary traditions to aid in the development of a Filipino national consciousness informed by a politics of resistance to U.S. imperialism. His interdisciplinary method connects literature to the global and Philippine political economy, embedding his analysis of imaginative literature and critical practice in the historical context of U.S.-Philippines political, economic, and cultural relations. He exemplifies a method of dialectical literary study reasserting the significance of culture in Marxist analysis and of cultural practice within political movements, charting new directions for Asian American cultural and literary studies and Marxist scholarship. Moreover, he introduces a body of Filipino literature traditionally marginalized within third-world and Asian American literary studies. Additionally, these works, in their implicit critiques of postcolonial theory, anticipate San Juan's own critiques of critical practices in the humanities. Welding high theory and grassroots radical practice with a political deftness rarely encountered in academic scholarship, San Juan has challenged the critical paradigms dominant in **cultural studies** and the humanities in such works as *Racial Formations/Critical Transformations: Articulations of Power in Ethnic and Racial Studies in the United States* (1992), *Hegemony and Strategies of Transgression: Essays in Cultural Studies and Comparative Literature* (1995), *Beyond Postcolonial Theory* (1998), and *Racism and Cultural Studies: Critiques of Multiculturalist Ideology and the Politics of Difference* (2002). His work highlights the complicity of dominant academic theory with the ideology of the U.S. racist imperialist state by curtailing investigation of racial and class inequalities. In all, San Juan has fulfilled what he identifies as the responsibility of the critic to identify progressive elements of cultural practice that challenge U.S. imperialist domination and demystify those that further U.S. exploitation—in short, "to reformulate our critique of imperialist ideology in the realm of literary theorizing."

Selected Bibliography: San Juan, E., Jr. *Beyond Postcolonial Theory.* New York: St. Martin's, 1998; San Juan, E., Jr. *Carlos Bulosan and the Imagination of Class Struggle.* Quezon City: U of the Philippines P, 1972; San Juan, E., Jr. *Hegemony and Strategies of Transgression: Essays in Cultural Studies and Comparative Literature.* Albany: SUNY P, 1995; San Juan, E., Jr. *Racism and Cultural Studies: Critiques of Multiculturalist Ideology and the Politics of Difference.* Durham, NC: Duke UP, 2002; San Juan, E., Jr. *Reading the West/Writing the East.* New York: Peter Lang, 1992; San Juan, E., Jr. *Writing and National Liberation.* Quezon City: U of the Philippines P, 1991.

Tim Libretti

SARTRE, JEAN-PAUL (1905–1980), one of the key French intellectual figures of the twentieth century. Associated primarily with existentialism, but also with phenomenology and later with Marxism, Sartre's brilliance is evident not only in his philosophical writings but also in his novels, drama, political essays, literary criticism, biographies, and autobiography. Major literary works include the novel *Nausea* (*La Nausée*, 1938) and such plays as *Les Mouches* (*The Flies,* 1943) and *No Exit* (*In Camera*, 1945). In addition, *The Family Idiot* (*L'Idiot de la famille*, 1971–1973)—Sartre's three-thousand page study of Gustave Flaubert—was, in his own words, a "true novel" that drew on psychoanalysis, sociology, philosophy, and literary theory in its attempt to answer the vast epistemological question, What can we know of a man today?

In the 1930s, Sartre's work focused primarily on questions of the nature of the self, the status of the emotions, and the role of imagination in human consciousness. But it is in *Being and Nothingness* (*L'Être et le néant*, 1943) that Sartre gives his most extended account of the nature of consciousness as pure negativity that negates not only the world but also itself. It is in the *Critique of Dialectical Reason* (*Critique de la raison dialectique*, 1960) that Sartre develops these ideas in their historical perspective, in a work that represents Sartre's most serious and large-scale attempt to come to terms with Marxism. After **World War II**, he had participated in a short-lived attempt to forge a noncommunist left-wing alliance, the Rassemblement democratique revolutionnaire. During the **cold war** in the 1950s, he had drawn closer to communism, but the rapprochement was eventually halted by Sartre's horror at the Soviet repression of the Hungarian Uprising in 1956.

The *Critique* aimed to offer a new perspective on issues such as social conditioning, historical progress, class struggle, the role of the individual in history, scarcity, and revolutionary activity by taking into account the way in which freedom operates within social movements, the way in which human beings interact in group situations, and the complex power struggles that had been analyzed philosophically in *Being and Nothingness*. Indeed, Sartre's analyses of questions of scarcity, praxis and the "practico-inert," and colonialism remain highly relevant today and are currently being rediscovered by political philosophers who had previously pigeonholed Sartre within his early phase, which focused primarily on questions of individual freedom.

Sartre is a philosopher of freedom and paradox. His conception of the relationship between liberty and situation, according to which the human being is always and only free within and with respect to his or her situation, allows him to talk of "the necessity of liberty," to envisage freedom as something to which we are "condemned," and, in the later years of his life, to maintain that we are simultaneously free and predestined. Admired as a liberator of thought and feared as a moral iconoclast in the 1940s, Sartre came to be recognized as France's major philosopher in the 1950s and early 1960s, only to be eclipsed by the vogue for structuralism and then poststructuralism in the 1960s and 1970s. Since his death in 1980, Sartre has once again been taken seriously as a philosopher in Europe and the United States, in particular in the wake of the current revival of interest in questions of ethics and subjectivity.

Selected Bibliography: Aronson, Ronald. *Jean-Paul Sartre: Philosophy in the World*. London: New Left Books, 1980; Flynn, Thomas R. *Sartre, Foucault and Historical Reason*. Chicago: U of Chicago P, 1997; Howells, Christina, ed. *The Cambridge Companion to Sartre*. Cambridge: Cambridge UP, 1992; Levy, Bernard-Henri. *Sartre: The Philosopher of the Twentieth Century*. Trans. Andrew Brown. Cambridge: Polity P, 2003; Sartre, Jean-Paul. *Basic Writings*. Ed. Stephen Priest. London: Routledge, 2001.

Christina Howells

SASSOON, SIEGFRIED (1886–1967), one of the greatest British war poets of the twentieth century and, paradoxically, a significant war protester. From 1914 to 1918, **World War I** ravaged Europe, taking more than 10 million lives, 750,000 of which were British. The poet and novelist Sassoon served as an infantry officer with the British Expeditionary Force on the western front from 1915 to 1918. He was wounded twice and awarded the Military Cross for heroism twice. But perhaps the bravest act of his life took place on June 15, 1917, when he wrote his famous *non serviam*, "A Soldier's Declaration." In it he stated that having seen and endured the suffering of the war, he could no longer be a party to the prolonging of that suffering for ends that he believed evil and unjust, thereby risking his life in protest against the deception practiced on the soldiers by the politicians. Sassoon's protest against the continuation of the war, printed in the London *Times*, shocked the British nation, for Sassoon was not only a war hero but a member of one of the most influential families in the country. However, the British government arranged for the army to declare that Sassoon was suffering from shell shock—now called post-traumatic stress syndrome—and had him committed to a mental institution in order to avoid the publicity of a court-martial. Sassoon could not bear being away from the men in his battalion fighting and dying in France, and so he arranged to be declared "cured" and returned to combat.

Sassoon was born into a privileged family in Kent, England, and was educated at Marlborough College and Cambridge University. He published fourteen small collections of affected poetry between 1906 and 1916, almost all at his own expense, but he found the naturalistic voice that informed his antiwar poetry—*Counter-Attack and Other Poems* (1918) and *The War Poems of Siegfried Sassoon* (1919)—in battle.

After the war, Sassoon went on a speaking tour across the United States, where he lectured against war. He was against war for humanitarian and economic reasons, and because youth were deluded into sacrificing their lives in the name of patriotism. But with time, Sassoon became less interested in politics and more religious—and so did his poetry. Sassoon converted to Catholicism in 1957. Sassoon's main literary achievement was his creation of a new and bitter language of war, through the authentic voice of a combat soldier.

Selected Bibliography: Cohen, Joseph. "The Three Roles of Siegfried Sassoon." *Tulane Studies in English* 7 (1957): 169–85; Moorcraft, Jean. *Sigfried Sassoon: The Makings of a War Poet: A Biography, 1886–1918.* New York: Routledge, 1999; Sternlicht, Sanford. *Siegfried Sassoon.* New York: Twayne, 1993.

Sanford Sternlicht

THE SATANIC VERSES (1988). No other novel in recent years has generated controversy on the scale of **Salman Rushdie**'s *The Satanic Verses* (*SV*). The "Rushdie affair" bares the deep cultural differences between Western culture and Islamic culture. Arguments over the novel have been carried on in voluminous rhetoric in journals and newspapers worldwide and also on the streets, where at least twenty people have died worldwide either during protests against *SV* or simply because they were associated with the publication of the novel, as in the case of *SV*'s Japanese translator.

Because of its subject matter, *SV* might be regarded as an example of **postcolonial literature**, but Rushdie's thoroughly Western attitudes and aesthetics have more in common with **postmodernism**. Narrated in Rushdie's usual jovial tone, the novel starts with its protagonists—all born and raised in Bombay—falling through the morning sky into the English Channel from a jetliner that explodes on its way to London. Gibreel Farishta, an Indian film star of great magnitude for the last fifteen years, falls seriously ill after the fall, resulting in a spiritual awakening that involves vivid dreams. Saladin Chamcha gives up on both his dysfunctional family and India, and comes to England, where he finds work as a voice-over artist. Underwriting much of the novel is the mental anguish associated with familial and cultural reconciliation, and the struggle for self-identification.

Blasphemy occurs for scholars of the Qur'an when Gibreel Farishta dreams, for he dreams of the city Jahilia and the prophet Mahound—a disrespectful name for Muhammad of Western medieval origin. Most of the account of the Hegira, the movement from Mecca to Medina, is paralleled and, by some accounts, parodied. Mahound is an unscrupulous businessman bargaining for followers. Gibreel's dreams reprise the controversial textual variation of the satanic verses, in which Satan, speaking through Gabriel/Gibreel, basically attempts to convince Muhammad that other gods exist. Allah later sets Muhammad straight. Many Islamic scholars deny the satanic episode ever occurred. Islamic clerics contend that Rushdie's intent was to satirize the life of Muhammad. Rushdie maintains that his intent was harmless.

Within months of publication, the book was banned in many countries. Islamic organizations began to demand an end to the novel's publication and sale. Threats were made. On February 14, 1989, Ayatollah Ruhollah Khomeini, imam of Tehran, announced a *fatwa*, or religious order, calling on all Muslims to end the life of the blasphemer Rushdie. The next day, a wealthy Islamic organization offered $3 million (U.S.) to any Muslim, and $1 million to any non-Muslim, who killed Rushdie. Rushdie went into hiding, and outrage poured into the Western papers. Diplomats were recalled, and economic ties with Iran severed. Two weeks later, twelve people were shot by police during anti-Rushdie riots in Bombay. Public figures who supported Rushdie were also threatened with death. Bookstores and publishing houses were firebombed in the United States and the United Kingdom. Western intellectuals, artists, and diplomats wrote to Khomeini for clemency, but to no avail. Rioting, firebombing, and death threats continued for nearly two years. Despite much discussion and negotiation, the fatwa is presently (2005) still in place, having been recently reiterated by Islamic clerics.

Selected Bibliography: Amees, Munawar A. *The Kiss of Judas: Affairs of a Brown Sahib.* Kuala Lumpur, Malaysia: Quill, 1989; Appignanesi, Lisa, and Sara Maitland. *The Rushdie File.* London: Fourth Estate, 1989; Fletcher, M. D., ed. *Reading Rushdie: Perspectives on the Fiction of Salman Rushdie.* Amsterdam, Netherlands: Rodopi, 1995; Kuortti, Joel. *Place of the Sacred: The Rhetoric of the "Satanic Verses" Affair.* New York: Peter Lang, 1997; Mufti, Aamir R. "Reading the Rushdie Affair: 'Islam,' Cultural Politics, Form." *Critical Essays on Salman Rushdie.* Ed. M. Keith Booker. New York: GK Hall, 1999. 51–77.

David Leaton

SCANDINAVIAN LITERATURE. Scandinavia is generally regarded as the five small countries of Denmark, Iceland, Norway, Sweden, and Finland. The region shares cultural, historical, and intellectual similarities, although it is not unified linguistically. Finnish and *Sami* (the language of the Laplanders) are Finno-Ugric languages in the Uralic language family and entirely distinct from the Scandinavian (North Germanic) languages (Danish, Icelandic, Norwegian, and Swedish).

The medieval Icelandic sagas are unique in European letters. These thirteenth-century prose narratives, written in the vernacular (Old Icelandic), are precursors to the modern novel. The well-known family sagas depict the lives of the early settlers of Iceland during the Viking age (ca. 870–1050 C.E.), for example *Laxdœla saga* and *Njáls saga*. Skaldic (or court) poetry also distinguishes medieval Scandinavian letters; the *Prose Edda* (The Younger Edda) was composed by Snorri Sturluson, Iceland's most outstanding man of letters, around 1220, and served as a textbook for skaldic poets. It is heavily influenced by ancient mythological and heroic poems preserved in the *Poetic Edda* (The Elder Edda). In addition to these thirteenth-century Icelandic texts, a rich oral narrative tradition flourished during the Middle Ages, particularly the folk ballad. Scholarly editions of Danish folk ballads alone number over six-hundred songs and rival the ballad heritage of Scotland. *Kalevala*—the Finnish epic poem compiled and published in 1849 by folklorist Elias Lönnrot from ancient oral poetry—has been translated into over forty languages.

The Nordic mythology of the pagan Vikings, recorded in the *Eddas,* gradually merged with Christian beliefs and symbols (the official conversion of the Scandinavian countries took place between the tenth and thirteenth centuries). Following a relatively short period of Catholicism, the Lutheran Reformation of the early sixteenth century brought about a dramatic shift in intellectual life and the inception of indigenous hymn traditions. As in other Protestant countries, Bible translations are milestones in Scandinavian literary history. After the introduction of printing presses and standardization of orthography, "national" literatures began to develop in the Kingdom of Denmark-Norway (a dual kingdom from the late fourteenth century) and in the Kingdom of Sweden (which ruled Finland from 1155).

Thomas Kingo is the major baroque poet of seventeenth-century Scandinavia; his hymns reflect the crosscurrents of Lutheran orthodoxy and Renaissance secularism that typify the century. Discovered in 1869, the eloquent prison memoir *Jammers Minde* (Memories of Woe) of Leonora Christina, the daughter of Denmark's famous King Christian IV, is a remarkable seventeenth-century document that is now a classic in Scandinavian literature. The Age of Enlightenment in Scandinavia is best represented by the Norwegian-Dane Ludvig Holberg, best known for his popular comedies written for the Danish stage in the 1720s and 1730s. Holberg was Scandinavia's first international literary figure and the most influential eighteenth-century man of letters. The early nineteenth century marks the blossoming of a romantic movement in Scandinavian literature, a golden age of arts and letters, which inspired poets Adam Oehlenschläger and N.F.S. Grundtvig (also internationally recognized as a religious and educational reformer), Henrik Wergeland, Easias Tegnér, and J.L. Runeberg. Next to the Bible and **William Shakespeare**, the tales and stories of Hans Christian Andersen are the most widely translated works of world literature. Rising from very humble origins, Andersen came to be celebrated in Europe and America as a novelist, travel writer, and poet during his own lifetime. His collections of *eventyr* (fairy tales), the first published in 1835, revolutionized conventional literary prose by infusing it with a lively colloquial style derived from the author's firsthand knowledge of oral folk traditions. A Danish contemporary of Andersen was the father of modern existentialism, Søren Kierkegaard, who published his principal works between 1843 and 1855. Although Kierkegaard is internationally regarded as a philosopher, his sophisticated literary style and irony have exercised considerable influence on Scandinavian prose.

Ill-fated political alliances during the Napoleonic Wars (the Kingdoms of Denmark and Sweden allied with France) resulted in the shrinking of Scandinavian colonial empires in the early nineteenth century: Finland was ceded from Sweden in 1809 and became an autonomous grand duchy under tsarist Russia (the Republic of Finland was established in 1918); Norway gained independence from Denmark in 1814 (and joined a union with Sweden until 1905). These political developments spurned efforts at defining national identities and literary heritages. The early- and mid-nineteenth centuries mark the heyday of Scandinavian folklorists who recorded folk tales, ballads, and national epics, such Finland's *Kalevala*. In Norway, scholars Peter C. Asbjørnson and J. E. Moe complied the voluminous *Norske Folke-eventyr* (Norwegian Folk Tales, 1841–1844), a major contribution to the comparative study of folklore.

The "modern breakthrough" in Scandinavian letters was heralded by Danish literary critic Georg Brandes in the 1870s and inspired realism and naturalism in Scandinavian prose and drama, as in the works of **Henrik Ibsen** and August Strindberg. Late-nineteenth-century Scandinavia produced a number of fine prose stylists, including J. P. Jacobsen and Herman Bang and the first generation of professional women writers, such as Amalie Skram. **Martin Andersen Nexø** was among a new class of working-class writers who emerged at the turn of the century; Nexø's *Pelle the Conqueror* (*Pelle Erobreren*, 1906–1910) gained him wide popularity outside his native Denmark. Scandinavian literature of the early twentieth century also boasts two of the first women writers to win Nobel Prizes for literature, Selma Lagerlöf and Sigrid Undset. Undset's trilogy *Kristin Lavransdatter* (1920–1922) is one of the few Scandinavian works of fiction to remain in print in English translation. The greatest Scandinavian literary modernist of the first half of the twentieth century is the Norwegian novelist Knut Hamsun, whose prodigious career ended in controversy due to his Nazi sympathies during **World War II**. Other internationally recognized Scandinavian writers of the early and mid-twentieth century include the Icelander Halldór Laxness, the Finns E. F. Sillanpäa and Väinö Linna, the Swedes Vilhelm Moberg and Pär Lagerkvist, and the Danes Johannes V. Jensen and Isak Dinesen (pseudonym of Karen Blixen), whose *Out of Africa* (1937) and collections of tales were originally published in English as well as Danish. A number of important Scandinavian writers have gained recognition in the late twentieth century, including P. O. Enquist, whose novels appear in English translations.

Selected Bibliography: Naess, Harald S., ed. *A History of Norwegian Literature.* Lincoln: U of Nebraska P, 1993; Schoolfield, George C., ed. *A History of Finland's Literature.* Lincoln: U of Nebraska P, 2002; Stecher-Hansen, Marianne, ed. *Danish Writers from the Reformation to Decadence: Dictionary of Literary Biography, Vol. 300.* Detroit: Thomson Gale, 2004; Warme, Lars, ed. *A History of Swedish Literature.* Lincoln: U of Nebraska P, 1996; Zuck, Virpi, ed. *Dictionary of Scandinavian Literature.* Westport, CT: Greenwood, 1990.

Marianne Stecher-Hansen

SCHUYLER, GEORGE S(AMUEL) (1895–1977). George Schuyler was the best-known African American journalist of his day, as well as the first nationally known African American journalist of the twentieth century. For a decade, from the mid-1920s to the end of the Depression, Schuyler was affiliated with various versions of socialist political and social movements, serving as managing editor of A. Philip Randolph's *Messenger,* and writing for various leftist publications while lecturing at the Rand School and Brookwood College.

In 1921, Schuyler joined the Socialist Party and organized its Negro Community Forum. He also attended meetings of the Friends of Negro Freedom, another socialist forum. However, Schuyler would not stay connected to the official Left for very long. An intellectual as well as a social maverick, Schuyler became disaffected with what he considered the Left's total misapprehension of the race issue and the solutions to it. Although committed to the betterment of the conditions of blacks in America, he was also an iconoclast who thought that the idea of a separate and distinct "Negro" culture or history or state was ridiculous. *Black No More* (1931)—his first novel, and the first full-length satirical novel by an African American—played with the consequences of a process that would allow blacks to become white if they liked. The next year, his novel *Slaves Today* fictionalized contemporary African slavery in Liberia and argued against any "back-to-Africa" romanticism; Schuyler had been a long-time critic of Garveyism. Still, it has been argued, Schuyler was interested in some form of Pan-Africanism, as evidenced by his serialized fiction in the *Pittsburgh Courier,* now collected as a two-part novel, *Black Empire* (1991).

Through the 1930s, Schuyler moved further from his earlier socialism toward a Washingtonian version of black self-help in the form of cooperative leagues. He tried to convince the NAACP to support experiments with cooperatives but was unable to do so. His insistence on the centrality of the problem of race in American life led him to join the isolationist America First Committee in 1940, arguing that until America solved her domestic problems, she had no business telling other countries how to run their affairs. By the end of **World War II**, Schuyler was both politically and socially in the conservative camp. Long an editorial writer, investigative reporter, and columnist for the *Pittsburgh Courier*, he gradually alienated its leadership by his commentary. In 1964, he attacked Martin Luther King Jr. on the eve of his being awarded the Nobel Peace Prize, and the *Courier* refused to print the column. By 1966, Schuyler was no longer writing for the paper. In his later years, he served on the board of the John Birch Society.

Selected Bibliography: Schuyler, George S. *Black and Conservative: The Autobiography of George S. Schuyler.* New Rochelle: Arlington House, 1966; Talalay, Kathryn. *Composition in Black and White: The Life of Philippa Schuyler.* New York: Oxford UP, 1995.

Jon-Christian Suggs

SCIENCE FICTION. Science fiction (SF) is a curious in-between genre, neither **realism** nor fantasy: "a form of the fantastic that denies it is fantastic" (Rose 20). The SF scholar Darko Suvin argues that SF is a genre whose "necessary and sufficient conditions are the presence and interaction of estrangement and cognition, and whose main formal device is an imaginative framework alternative to the author's empirical environment" (*Metamorphoses* 7–8). With this, Suvin too highlights science fiction's equidistance from realism and fantasy. His first term, "estrangement," taken from **Bertolt Brecht**, emphasizes the way these texts operate like their modernist contemporaries, "denaturalizing" the world that currently exists, showing its apparently immutable foundations themselves to be contingent and open to modification. Whereas modernist texts accomplish this through formal and linguistic experimentation, SF does so through the portrayal of "other" worlds (the future, other planets and their societies, or our own world with a dramatic new element—a visitor from the future or another place, a natural catastrophe, or a new technology—introduced into it). However, unlike other forms of fantastic literature, such as myth, folk tales, or modern fantasy, works of SF strive to portray this other world as one bound and limited by the same scientific or cognitive laws as our own. Many of the earliest efforts in the genre took great care to show how the imaginary world they were portraying was a reasonable extrapolation from the most cutting-edge scientific knowledge of their time.

The term "science fiction" (following "scientific fiction" and then the even more cumbersome "scientifiction") was coined in the 1920s by the editor Hugo Gernsback to describe the kind of fiction published in his magazine, *Amazing Stories*—the first dedicated exclusively to science fiction. While the works published by Gernsback, as well as his own influential editorials, did a great deal to fix the contours of the modern genre, SF finds its origins in the later part of the nineteenth century. Gernsback's own early description of the genre acknowledges this source: "By 'scientifiction' I mean the Jules Verne, **H. G. Wells**, and Edgar Allan Poe type of story—a charming romance intermingled with scientific fact and prophetic vision." There are earlier important precursors to the genre. Suvin, for example, finds science-fictional elements in the tales of imaginary voyages by, among others, Lucian, Thomas More, François Rabelais, Cyrano de Bergerac, and **Jonathan Swift**, while Paul Alkon argues that Jacques Guttin's 1659 *Epigone* was the first fiction to be set in the future. This genealogy bears out science fiction's own place in the larger mode of the prose romance: like other romance genres—**utopian fiction** being one of the most significant for SF—science fiction is more concerned with the production of imaginary worlds or space than well-rounded characters (the latter being the provenance of the modern realistic novel).

Four nineteenth-century literary developments set the stage for the emergence of modern science fiction, beginning with fantastic tales of the gothic, exemplified by Mary Shelley's *Frankenstein* (1818) and the stories of Poe. The gothic plays the indispensable role of undermining the hold of the then reigning novelistic realism. Second, the latter part of the century witnessed a resurgence of the literary utopia, especially after the publication of Edward Bellamy's ***Looking Backward*** (1888) and William Morris's ***News from Nowhere*** (1890). Third, the new practice of the negative utopia, or **dystopian literature**, which would prove to be very fertile ground for later SF writers, emerged out of a fusion of the utopia and novelistic **naturalism**. Finally, the second half of the century saw the publication of Verne's "*voyages extraordinaire*"—fantastic travel narratives rendered with an exacting adherence to the advanced scientific speculation of the day.

It is in the "scientific romances" of Wells that these various strands come together to produce the first full examples of the genre. Wells's earliest fictions, most significantly *The Time Machine* (1895) and *The War of the Worlds* (1898), set the pattern for later writers. Mark Rose argues that science fiction's paradigmatic encounter of the "human and the nonhuman" expresses itself through "four logically related categories . . . space, time, machine, and monster" (32). Rose's middle two categories are evident in the title of Wells's first work, the story of an unnamed British gentleman's voyage in a machine of his own devising to a far-flung future, where the social classes of Wells's own Britain have hardened into two distinct species, the Morlock and the Eloi. *The War of the Worlds*, on the other hand, focuses on the figures of space and the monster, as it describes the invasion of the English countryside by strange beings from Mars. Wells's work also demonstrated the deep political potential of the genre, as *The Time Machine* uses the genre's allegorical capacity to attack the social inequities of contemporary Great Britain, while *The War of the Worlds* similarly unveils the brutalities of European colonial expansion in Africa. It is this critical dimension that will be one of Wells's most significant legacies.

Following Wells's establishment of the genre, there was a great outpouring of science-fiction visions in a number of different national contexts. This included the work of Russian and Soviet writers, such as Alexander Bogdanov, **Alexei Tolstoy**, **Evgeny Zamyatin**; the Czech **Karel Čapek**, whose play *R.U.R.* (1920) gave the world the SF term "robot;" and the British authors E. M. Forster, Olaf Stapledon, and C. S. Lewis. Many of these writers acknowledge their reliance on Wells's founding fictions, while also expanding in strikingly new directions the formal and imaginative possibilities of the genre.

However, this first wave of SF "modernism" was interrupted in the late 1920s. Two events stand out in this regard. First, the growing intolerance for any kind of literary or artistic experimentation within the Soviet Union effectively halted until the late 1950s all SF production in that nation. Second, and perhaps even more significant, the emergence within the United States of popular "pulp" magazine SF, pioneered by Gernsback, completely transformed the genre's status. While reprinting some of the writers mentioned above and demanding a rigorous application of scientific principles by all his writers, Gernsback's *Amazing Stories* and other early SF magazines also published a good number of quite popular "space operas," including *The Skylark of Space* saga of E. E. "Doc" Smith and the Anthony "Buck" Rogers stories of Philip Francis Nowlan (both began in the August 1928 issue of the magazine), as well as the fantasy adventure stories of Edgar Rice Burroughs, creator of Tarzan and John Carter of Mars. These works offered tales of adventure set in intergalactic space and on exotic worlds, gave their readers simplistic moral visions of the struggle between good and evil, and kept the critical estranging elements of the earlier modernist SF to a minimum. However, perhaps the most significant consequence of Gernsback's work as an editor was to create the first SF "fan" communities, thereby largely confining the genre's public to young men and boys interested in science and technology and producing a particular literary and cultural argot all their own. The majority of work in the genre over the next decades would be restricted to the United States.

The full flourishing of this "realist" age of magazine SF took place under the direction of another editor, John W. Campbell. Campbell's *Astounding Science-Fiction* inaugurated in the late 1930s what is referred to as science fiction's golden age. The writers Campbell brought to prominence—among them, A. E. Van Vogt, Theodore Sturgeon, L. Ron Hubbard, Murray Leinster, Isaac Asimov, and **Robert Heinlein**—remain some of the best known in the genre. Campbell demanded a much more rigorous grounding of SF in actual scientific knowledge (thereby creating the basis for the subgenre of "hard science fiction," first defined in the late 1950s and exemplified by such writers as Arthur C. Clarke and Hal Clement, and today by Gregory Benford and **Kim Stanley Robinson**), as well as a more careful exploration of the implications of their estranging hypotheses. Moreover, these writers expressed a tremendous faith in science, rationality, and technology as "the privileged solution to the world's ills" (Fitting 60), values shared by the genre's audience. Two examples of this are Van Vogt's story "Black Destroyer" (1939)—later reworked into the novel *The Voyage of the Space Beagle* (1950), which was the basis for the SF film *Alien* (1979)—wherein an apparently unstoppable alien menace is finally overcome by humanity's superior knowledge of history; and Asimov's epic *Foundation* trilogy (published in book form in 1951–1953 by combining stories earlier published in *Astounding*), a future history in which a scientific elite plays a vital role in the movement out of an interplanetary dark age.

The years following the conclusion of **World War II** saw the emergence of a new generation of writers—among them, Ray Bradbury, Clarke, James Blish, Walter Miller Jr., Alfred Bester, Fritz Leiber, and Cordwainer Smith—whose confidence in the powers of science and technology was far less sure. The 1950s would also witness the resurgence within the genre of critical and dystopian fictions, exemplified by Bradbury's *Fahrenheit 451* and Frederick Pohl and C. M. Kornbluth's **The Space Merchants** (both 1953). Meanwhile, more and more attention was paid within the genre to the social and psychological impact of modernity and to the development of complex character psychology, giving rise to what would be known as "soft" science fiction. The single most important writer to emerge from this context was **Philip K. Dick**, whose rich and diverse visions of near future worlds would tremendously influence both the later development of the genre and popular culture at large (a number of Dick's works have been adapted for film, beginning with Ridley Scott's *Blade Runner* in 1982, based on *Do Androids Dream of Electric Sheep?*).

The work of Dick and others helped set the stage for the emergence in the 1960s and 1970s of SF's high "modernist" moment (commonly referred to as the "new wave"). These years witnessed a revolution within the genre, as writers became more willing to experiment with form and to tackle subjects previously considered taboo. These works also reflected the growing political turbulence of the time, and would offer brilliant critiques of the bureaucratic state, consumerism, the **Vietnam War**, environmental despoilage, gender and racial inequality, and a host of other issues. As a result, the audience for the genre grew, encompassing many in the burgeoning radical youth movements. Some of the writers who rose to prominence as part of the new wave in the United States were Harlan Ellison, who also edited the landmark *Dangerous Visions* anthologies (1967, 1972), showcasing the work of many of these writers; Frank Herbert, whose novel *Dune* (1965) placed ecological concerns centrally within the genre's purview; Thomas Disch, whose *Camp Concentration*

(1968)—along with **Ursula K. Le Guin**'s *The Word for World Is Forest* (1972) and Joe Haldeman's *The Forever War* (1974)—is one of the great science fiction critiques of the U.S. war machine; and the prolific Robert Silverberg. Science-fictional elements also began to be more prominent in literary fictions, especially among such writers as William Burroughs, Kurt Vonnegut, and Thomas Pynchon.

This moment also witnessed a new flourishing of SF production outside the United States. The British magazine *New Worlds*, especially under the editorship of Michael Moorcock, showcased many of the best of these writers, including Brian Aldiss, who would also write the great modernist history of SF (one that had little patience for the genre's hard realist predecessors), and J. G. Ballard. Meanwhile, John Brunner emerged as an important writer of dystopian fictions with contemporary political concerns, including the sequence *Stand on Zanzibar* (1968), *The Jagged Orbit* (1969), *The Sheep Look Up* (1972), and *Shockwave Rider* (1975). Moreover, some of the most important SF writers of all time emerged during these years from Soviet bloc nations, including Stanislaw Lem (Poland) and the brothers Arkady and Boris Strugatsky (USSR).

Finally, with the new diversity of the genre's audience, there would be an increasing diversification of the genre's producers. Although a handful of women—including C. L. Moore, Judith Merril, Leigh Brackett, and James Tiptree Jr. (Alice Sheldon)—did publish memorable works early on, it would not be until the later 1960s that women writers would take up a new prominence and centrality in the genre, often with works that dealt directly with issues of gender and sexuality; these writers include Anne McCaffrey, Le Guin, **Joanna Russ**, Marge Piercy, Suzy McKee Charnas, and Vonda McIntyre. Le Guin's *The Left Hand of Darkness* (1969) is exemplary in this regard, as it tells of a race whose sexual biology is radically different from our own, and who as a result lack our fixed gender divisions. Samuel R. Delany was another pathbreaking figure, as one of the first African American and later openly gay writers in the field. Delany would be followed by another major African American SF writer, Octavia Butler, whose *Xenogenesis* trilogy (1987–1989) and two *Parable* novels (1993, 1998) became some of the most discussed work in the genre. Writers of this moment, including McCaffrey, Le Guin, Delany, and later Gene Wolfe, also helped revitalize the genre of fantasy, sometimes—especially in the case of Wolfe's far future *The Book of the New Sun* (1980–1983)—blurring altogether the distinctions between fantasy and SF.

The tremendous energies of this moment had largely been spent by the end of the 1970s, and the conservative counter-assault of the 1980s created an environment less hospitable to the kinds of formal experimentations and dangerous visions of SF modernism. The early 1980s also witnessed the next major development in the genre, with the emergence of "cyberpunk fiction." Although Bruce Sterling took on the role of the spokesperson for the movement, it was William Gibson who quickly emerged as its leading author. Gibson's trilogy *Neuromancer* (1984), *Count Zero* (1986), and *Mona Lisa Overdrive* (1988) transformed the genre and brought a new literary critical attention to it. Rejecting the optimism of the Gernsback-Campbell era SF realism and equally cool on the radicalism of the previous modernist SF, cyberpunk proved to be a perfect fit for the political climate of the Reagan-Thatcher era. Moreover, in its celebration of new information technologies, its suspicion of older Fordist and welfare-state policies, and its poaching from and pastiche of a wide range of genres and styles, including noir detective fiction, cyberpunk emerged as an exemplary form of **postmodernism**. Other prominent writers associated with the movement include Pat Cadigan, Rudy Rucker, and Neal Stephenson, the latter's *Snow Crash* (1992) and *The Diamond Age* (1996) representing some of the most interesting SF of the 1990s.

Many of the SF writers who rose to prominence in the late 1980s and 1990s—including Ken MacLeod, Sheri Tepper, Terry Bisson, Orson Scott Card, Butler, Stephenson, Robinson, Greg Egan, Iain M. Banks, and China Miéville—represent a new eclecticism in the genre, as they draw on the resources of hard SF, utopian and dystopian fiction, cyberpunk, and fantasy, among other forms. There has also been a resurgence among many of these writers of the critical political energies that were in abeyance in the heyday of postmodern cyberpunk, and they may yet signal a new stage in the genre's development.

Selected Bibliography: Aldiss, Brian. *Trillion Year Spree: The History of Science Fiction.* New York: Avon, 1986; Alkon, Paul. *Origins of Futuristic Fiction.* Athens: U of Georgia P, 1987; Barr, Marlene S. *Lost in Space: Probing Feminist Science Fiction and Beyond.* Chapel Hill: U of North Carolina P, 1993; Booker, M. Keith, *Monsters, Mushroom Clouds, and the Cold War: American Science Fiction and the Roots of Postmodernism, 1946–1964.* Westport, CT: Greenwood, 2001; Clute, John, and Peter Nicholls, eds. *The Encyclopedia of Science Fiction.* 2nd ed. New York: St. Martin's, 1995; Disch, Thomas. *The Dreams Our Stuff Is Made Of: How Science Fiction Conquered the World.* New York: Simon and Schuster, 1998; Fitting, Peter. "The Modern Anglo-American SF Novel: Utopian Longing and Capitalist Cooptation." *Science Fiction Studies* 6.1 (1979): 59–76; Freedman, Carl. *Critical Theory and Science Fiction.* Hanover, NH: Wesleyan UP, 2000; Jameson, Fredric. "Generic Discontinuities in SF: Brian Aldiss' *Starship.*" *Science Fiction Studies* 1.2 (1973): 57–68; Jameson, Fredric. "Progress versus Utopia; or, Can We Imagine the Future?" *Science Fiction Studies* 9.2 (1982): 147–58; Jameson, Fredric. "Science Fiction as a Spatial Genre: Generic Discontinuities and the Problem of Figuration in Vonda McIntyre's *The Exile Waiting.*" *Science Fiction Studies* 14 (1987): 44–59; Jameson, Fredric. "The Space of Science Fiction: Narrative in A. E. Van Vogt." *Polygraph* 2/3 (1989): 52–65; Moskowitz, Sam. "How Science Fiction Got Its Name." *The Prentice Hall Anthology of Science Fiction and Fantasy.* Ed. Garyn G. Roberts. Upper Saddle River, NJ: Prentice Hall, 2003. 1127–35; Moylan, Tom, and Raffaella Baccolini, eds. *Dark Horizons: Science Fiction and the Dystopian Imagination.* London: Routledge, 2003; Parrinder, Patrick, ed. *Learning from Other Worlds: Estrangement, Cognition, and the Politics of Science Fiction and Utopia.* Durham, NC: Duke UP, 2001; Pringle, David. *Science Fiction: The 100 Best Novels. An English-Language Selection, 1949–1984.* London: Xanadu, 1985; Roberts, Robin. *A New Species: Gender and Science in Science Fiction.* Urbana: U of Illinois P, 1993; Rose, Mark. *Alien Encounters: Anatomy of Science Fiction.* Cambridge, MA: Harvard UP, 1981; Ross, Andrew. *Strange Weather: Culture, Science and Technology in the Age of Limits.* London: Verso, 1991; Slusser, George Edgar, and T. A. Shippey, eds. *Fiction 2000: Cyberpunk and the Future of Narrative.* Athens: U of Georgia P, 1992; Suvin, Darko. *Metamorphoses of Science Fiction: On the Poetics and History of a Literary Genre.* New Haven: Yale UP, 1979; Suvin, Darko. *Positions and Presuppositions in Science Fiction.* Kent, OH: Kent State UP, 1988; Wegner, Phillip E. "The Last Bomb: Historicizing History in Terry Bisson's *Fire on the Mountain* and Gibson and Sterling's *The Difference Engine.*" *Comparatist* 23 (1999): 141–51; Wegner, Phillip E. "Soldierboys for Peace: Cognitive Mapping, Space, and Science Fiction as World Bank Literature." *World Bank Literature.* Ed. Amitava Kumar. Minneapolis: U of Minnesota P, 2003. 280–96; Westfahl, Gary. *The Mechanics of Wonder: The Creation of the Idea of Science Fiction.* Liverpool: Liverpool UP, 1998.

Phillip E. Wegner

SCOTT, F. R. (FRANCIS REGINALD) (1899–1985). Poet, lawyer, scholar, and activist, Scott was key both to the development of modernist poetry in English Canada and to the growth of modern socialist political organizations. Born in Quebec City, his father was an Anglican minister and a well known Canadian poet, who combined a fervent imperialism with radical social views supportive of labor. Based in Montreal, the younger Scott inherited this radicalism, but would combine it instead with the post-imperialist nationalism, which grew in the 1920s and 1930s. He helped to found both the *McGill Fortnightly Review* (1925–1927) and *Preview* (1942–1945), two of the three or four small magazines that established a forum for poetry diverging from fin de siècle norms and open to modern content or experimental form. His own style is direct and unsentimental, and while it often expresses an absurd world with grace and optimism, he is better known for his incisive satires.

Combining the writing of social philosophy with activism, Scott cofounded the League for Social Reconstruction—similar to the American League for Democracy—in 1932 and served as its president from 1935 to 1937. He also took part in shaping the Cooperative Commonwealth Federation—the political party (precursor to the New Democratic Party formed in 1961) that formed North America's first socialist government—in Saskatchewan, and served as the party's national chairman (1942–1950). In later years, he held important positions in the federal government and the United Nations. Moreover, as a lawyer, Scott played a role in winning important civil-rights cases that reached the Supreme Court of Canada in the 1950s and 1960s, including reversing the censorship in Quebec of *Lady Chatterley's Lover*.

Selected Bibliography: Djwa, Sandra. *The Politics of the Imagination: A Life of F. R. Scott*. Toronto: McClelland and Stewart, 1987.

Glenn Willmott

SCOTTISH LITERATURE. Two major themes embodying significant political ideas run through Scottish literature: the quest for social egalitarianism and the desire for national self-determination. After the Union of the Crowns in 1603, when James VI of Scotland became James I of England, and after the Union of the Parliaments in 1707, when Scotland's parliamentary authority was devolved to England, Scotland retained distinctive national structures in law, education, and religion, which maintained the social ideal of egalitarianism—both in particular forms of social practice and as myth. The principle of a generalist education as a birthright rather than a privilege of money or class was fundamental to the thinking and writing of Robert Burns and Walter Scott. Enlightenment and **romanticism**, instead of following chronologically, were combined in these writers. The social democrat Burns and the patrician conservative Scott shared a fundamental belief in the common good. For Burns—writing songs and poems that would be memorized by illiterate people as well as city literati—the social status of human beings was merely a stamp of rank; the real worth resided in the individual's essential humanity. Similarly for Scott, the "common cow-feeder's daughter" Jeanie Deans, in *The Heart of Midlothian* (1818), represents human heroism and is worth at least as much as the aristocratic heroes of either Hanoverian or Highland societal systems in *Waverley* (1814). Burns's song "A Man's a Man" was politically powerful enough to prompt reporters to note that aristocrats, upon attending the reopening of the Scottish parliament in 1997 and hearing it sung as part of the proceedings, were discomfited by its uncompromising political position.

This is a characteristic of Scottish literature more generally, also. Even as early as William Dunbar's poem in praise of the marriage of James IV in 1503, celebrating feudal order and social priorities, the law of nature is greater than that of royal authority, and king and queen are admonished to observe it. Further back still, the poetry associated with the Celtic Christianity of St. Columba and the first kings of Alba (the earliest name for Scotland) recognizes an ideal of kinship and dialogue across differences that reflects the community of different tribes that were beginning to form a national identity. And in the twentieth century, the socialist beliefs of **Hugh MacDiarmid** and **Lewis Grassic Gibbon**, both active in the Scottish literary renaissance of the 1920s and 1930s, were infused by aggressively egalitarian ideals. These ideals run through the works of Scottish writers of the twenty-first century.

Equally, the question of national self-determination is a major theme in Scottish literature, from early epics about the Wars of Independence and their heroes—John Barbour's *The Bruce* (1376) and Blind Harry's *The Wallace* (1460)—to the era of Burns and Scott. In the later nineteenth century, when Scotland was widely known as North Britain, patriotic unionism was generally held to be the national condition, but the 1920s saw a resurgence of belief in the interconnected vitality of cultural and political independence. The political founding of parties committed to national self-determination coincided with literary and critical production revaluing and reasserting Scotland's potential from the perspective of Scotland, rather than from an Anglocentric viewpoint. In this, Scotland's modern literary history parallels postcolonial or postimperial literatures in other parts of the world and, however clear the connections and overlaps might be, is most accurately seen as distinct from English literature.

More specific themes in the literature include evocations of complicity in British imperialism (whether affirmatively, as in the popular fiction of John Buchan or Ian Fleming, or critically, in such doom-laden poets as James "B. V." Thomson or John Davidson, whose nihilistic pessimism was intimately influential on **T. S. Eliot**). Conflicts in religion are most evident in the ambivalent legacy of the Reformation, which attacked corrupt authority and insisted on education as a general democratic right, yet prohibited enlightened questioning and taught learning by rote rather than through Socratic dialogue.

Superstition and folk belief are frequently in tension with political and economic materialism in fiction where neither supernatural nor psychological explanations seem adequate to account for events within—for example, James Hogg's *The Confessions of a Justified Sinner* (1824), Robert Louis Stevenson's *The Master of Ballantrae* (1889), and *Dr. Jekyll and Mr. Hyde* (1886). Matters of language and landscape prioritize local authenticity and the multivocal nature of various peoples, while conflicts of character and community are often found in the writing of the ardent socialist Naomi Mitchison, who nevertheless owned a large estate and valued folk traditions profoundly. There are literary tensions between romance and realism—exaggerated in the excesses of tartanry on one hand and denationalized cosmopolitanism on the other, such as the distinctive but generally non-nationalist writing of Norman Douglas or C. P. Taylor. Similarly, sentimentalism and scabrous pessimism represent two sides of Scottish literature in the late nineteenth and early twentieth centuries, in either the fiction of the Kailyard school ("kailyard" meaning "cabbage patch" or "backyard vegetable garden")—self-sufficient small-town local fiction where characters are presided over by the benevolent minister and the wise dominie, or schoolteacher—or in cruel tragic novels, such as *The House with the Green Shutters* (1901) or *Gillespie* (1914).

There are three generally recognized historical eras of achievement in Scottish literature: the Renaissance and Reformation (with writers such as Robert Henryson, William Dunbar, Gavin Douglas, and Sir David Lyndsay, whose great play *Ane Satyre of the Thrie Estaits*, from 1540, remains one of the most politically engaged, instantly accessible, and entertaining works in Scottish literature); the Enlightenment and romanticism (a period of complex unity, accommodating vernacular, pastoral, and city poets such as Allan Ramsay and Robert Fergusson; radical philosophers such as Adam Ferguson, Adam Smith, and David Hume; as well as Burns and Scott); and the modern renaissance (Hugh MacDiarmid, Lewis Grassic Gibbon, and Neil Gunn) and post–**World War II** revival (including the great generation of Scottish poets Edwin Morgan, Norman MacCaig, George Mackay Brown, Iain Crichton Smith, Robert Garioch, Sorley MacLean).

After the 1979 referendum, in which a majority of Scottish voters were in favor of devolution but had their opinion made ineffective by Westminster rule, Scottish writers were at the forefront of cultural assertion of distinctive identity and the desire for self-determination. Edwin Morgan, Alasdair Gray, James Kelman (whose winning of the Booker Prize in 1996 triggered a volley of anti-Scottish, class-biased comment), Liz Lochhead, and Tom Leonard contributed powerfully to the cultural climate, which produced the overwhelming and undeniable 1997 vote in favor of devolved parliament with "tax-varying" powers.

Scottish literature remains one of the most under-researched areas of literary study. Further work has begun to reveal the complex richness of very early poetry from the times of Saint Columba and the *Gododdin* to the literature of the Wars of Independence; of the complex eighteenth century and Gaelic poetry of the Jacobite risings; of the popular vernacular literature of the late nineteenth century to the connections between literature and work broadcast on radio or television, or on film. Research has uncovered radical city poetry of the nineteenth century, including astonishing poetry by urban, Dundee-based James Young Geddes and the poets included in Tom Leonard's groundbreaking anthology *Radical Renfrew* (1990). The major breakthrough for Scottish socialist theater was *The Cheviot, the Stag and the Black, Black Oil* (1973) by John McGrath and the 7:84 Theatre Company. Scottish literary criticism and reappraisals of Scotland's cultural history have begun to redress a long period of neglect and obfuscation, bringing new light to neglected authors such as Catherine Carswell, Willa Muir, Nan Shepherd, Violet Jacob, Marion Angus, and Veronica Forrest-Thomson, but much remains to be done.

Selected Bibliography: Bold, Alan. *Modern Scottish Literature.* London: Longman, 1983; Craig, Cairns, ed. *The History of Scottish Literature.* 4 vols. Aberdeen: Aberdeen UP, 1986–1987; Gifford, Douglas, et al., eds. *Scottish Literature in English and Scots.* Edinburgh: Edinburgh UP, 2003; Glen, Duncan. *Hugh MacDiarmid and the Scottish Renaissance.* Edinburgh: W.R. Chambers, 1964; Leonard, Tom, ed. *Radical Renfrew: Poetry from the French Revolution to the First World War*. Edinburgh: Polygon, 1990; Morgan, Edwin. *Crossing the Border: Essays on Scottish Literature*. Manchester: Carcanet, 1990; Riach, Alan. *Representing Scotland in Literature, Popular Culture and Iconography*. London: Palgrave Macmillan, 2004; Royle, Trevor. *The Mainstream Companion to Scottish Literature*. Edinburgh: Mainstream, 1993; Walker, Marshall. *Scottish Literature since 1707*. Harlow: Longman, 1996; Watson, Roderick. *The Literature of Scotland*. London: Macmillan, 1986.

Alan Riach

SEDGWICK, EVE KOSOFSKY (1950–). With the exception of **Judith Butler**, no figure has been more important to the emergence of "queer" as a critical concept and as a revisionary principle of self-definition than Eve Kosofsky Sedgwick. Sedgwick's *Between Men: English Literature and Male Homosocial Desire* (1985) and *Epistemology of the Closet* (1990) may best be understood as two volumes of a history of sexuality that made queer theory possible. Although indebted to the genealogical analyses of power, knowledge, and desire by **Michel Foucault**, these books also refashion that history in important ways. First, they contest several of Foucault's historical generalizations, suggesting earlier and other modes of homosexual definition; second, they provide a conceptual apparatus for analyzing the coarse dichotomy of "homosexuality" and "heterosexuality"; third, they intervene in the field of feminist theory by insisting on the differences between gender and sexuality. *Epistemology* intervenes in **gay and lesbian studies** by arguing that the field is best served by turning away from the debate over whether homosexual desire is "essential" or "socially constructed." Sedgwick replaces that binary with another: "minoritizing" versus "universalizing" understandings of gay and lesbian identities. Sedgwick asks, For whom and in what way does the violently exclusive dichotomy organizing subjects into *either* homosexual *or* heterosexual identities matter?

Tendencies (1993) marks the explicit emergence of the concept of "queer" in Sedgwick's work. In part, "queer" names the cultural practices by which identities and desires are constituted, contested, and oppressed within genders as well as between them. The critique of sexual difference—as the primary means of understanding and experiencing identity—that extends to Sedgwick's earliest work finds its most powerful expression here. *Tendencies* explores other means of conceiving identities and, in particular, insists on the indissoluble link between queer and the performative: queer not only *is*, but also *does*. True to its thesis, *Tendencies* is thus marked by experimental modes of self-perception, self-formation, and relationality. The volume concludes with an obituary essay, whose autobiographical engagement with the psychic and social consequences of sickness points to *A Dialogue on Love* (1999)—a pathography, or illness narrative, that Sedgwick writes in the wake of her cancer diagnosis. This book is an account of her therapeutic enterprise to find ways of continuing to live athwart the medicalized identity of the "cancer patient." Sedgwick describes *Dialogue* as a "texture book," as if to anticipate her next collection of essays, *Touching Feeling: Affect, Pedagogy, Performativity* (2003). In this book, Sedgwick gives full expression to her long-standing interest in the enigma of emotion, and in living out what she calls nonlinear and "nondualistic thought." Close attention to affective and textural life sets Sedgwick's work against the regimes of thought and sight that ordinarily and perhaps inevitably dominate critical thinking, especially in the academy. Sedgwick's work seeks not only to theorize but also to exemplify an alternative way of being in the world, which she calls "reparative"—reading and writing that embrace the contingency of truth and authorship and that value unconventional associations. Sedgwick's work embodies reparative practice in many ways, from her poetry and more recent expeditions into weaving and sculpture, to her commitment to AIDS activism, whose emergence and history is for her precisely contiguous with that of queer theory.

Selected Bibliography: Barber, Stephen M., and David L. Clark, eds. *Regarding Sedgwick: Essays on Queer Culture and Critical Theory.* New York: Routledge, 2002; Butler, Judith. *Gender Trouble: Feminism and the Subversion of Identity.* New York: Routledge, 1990; Foucault, Michel. *The History of Sexuality.* Vol. 1. *An Introduction.* Trans. Robert Hurley. New York: Vintage-Random House, 1980; Sedgwick, Eve Kosofsky. *Between Men: English Literature and Male Homosocial Desire.* New York: Columbia UP, 1985; Sedgwick, Eve Kosofsky. *A Dialogue on Love.* Boston: Beacon, 1999; Sedgwick, Eve Kosofsky. *Epistemology of the Closet.* Berkeley: U of California P, 1990; Sedgwick, Eve Kosofsky. *Tendencies.* Durham, NC: Duke UP, 1993; Sedgwick, Eve Kosofsky. *Touching Feeling: Affect, Pedagogy, Performativity.* Durham, NC: Duke UP, 2003.

Stephen M. Barber and David L. Clark

SEGHERS, ANNA (1900–1983). Seghers was one of the great figures of German **modernism** and a major international voice in the cause of socialism and antifascism. Born Netty Reiling and raised in the traditions of Judaism and the Enlightenment in a Rhenish family of art and antiquities dealers, she studied philosophy, sinology, and art history at the University of Heidelberg and earned a doctorate in 1924 with a study of "Jews and Judaism in the Works of Rembrandt." In 1925 she married the Hungarian philosopher László Radványi, director of the Berlin Marxist Workers School. In 1928 she was awarded the Kleist Prize and soon won acclaim as one of Europe's outstanding young avant-garde writers ("the greatest woman artist of her generation on the Continent," according to John Lehmann of the Hogarth Press). In 1928, she also joined the German **Communist Party** and League of Proletarian-Revolutionary Writers, thus affirming her lifelong commitment to working-class and liberation movements around the globe.

When the National Socialists came to power in 1933, Seghers fled via Switzerland to France. In 1941, after departing Marseille on one of the last refugee ships to leave the harbor, she and her husband and children arrived in Mexico and thus escaped the Holocaust that claimed her mother and other members of her family. During thirteen years of exile, Seghers was active in the antifascist movement as a speaker and essayist. While her prose narratives, such as *The Revolt of the Fishermen (Aufstand der Fischer von St. Barbara,* 1928), *The Excursion of the Dead Girls (Der Ausflug der toten Mädchen,* 1946), and *Caribbean Stories (Karibische Geschichten,* 1949/ 1960), chronicle myriad social and political upheavals, she gained international renown with a series of antifascist novels: *The Wayfarers (Die Gefährten,* 1932), *A Price on His Head (Der Kopflohn,* 1934), *The Road of Februar (Der Weg durch den Februar,* 1935), *The Rescue (Die Rettung,* 1937), *The Seventh Cross (Das siebte Kreuz,* 1942), *Transit* (1944), and *The Dead Stay Young (Die Toten bleiben jung,* 1949).

Seghers's close friends and associates included **Georg Lukács** (with whom she notably debated about **modernism** and **realism** in the 1930s), **Bertolt Brecht** (with whom she collaborated on the 1952 Berliner Ensemble production of her radio play *The Trial of Jeanne d'Arc at Rouen in 1431*, first aired in 1937 in response to German and Soviet show trials), Karl Mannheim, **Walter Benjamin**, Ilya Ehrenburg, **Pablo Neruda**, Lev Kopelev, and **Jorge Amado**.

After the war, Seghers settled in East Berlin, where she served as president of the Writers' Union, 1952–1978. Her influence on the literature of the German Democratic Republic (GDR) was immeasurable. Plays by **Heiner Müller** and Volker Braun were inspired by her narratives; **Christa Wolf** and many others were influenced by her prose style. Her own works were immensely successful in the GDR. If sale of her books was boycotted in the Federal Republic at the height of the **cold war**, they found a belated popular reception among West Germans in the wake of the extra-parliamentary student and ecology movements of the 1960s and 1970s. First translated in 1928 (into English since 1929), Seghers's works have been read worldwide.

Selected Bibliography: Fehervary, Helen. *Anna Seghers: The Mythic Dimension.* Ann Arbor: U of Michigan P, 2001; LaBahn, Kathleen J. *Anna Seghers's Exile Literature: The Mexican Years.* Bern: Peter Lang, 1986; Lehmann, John. *New Writing in Europe.* Harmondsworth: Penguin, 1940; Romero, Christiane Zehl. *Anna Seghers: Eine Biographie.* 2 vols. Berlin: Aufbau, 2000, 2003; Stephan, Alexander. *"Communazis": FBI Surveillance of German Emigré Writers.* Trans. Jan van Heurck. New Haven, CT: Yale UP, 2000; Wallace, Ian, ed. *Anna Seghers in Perspective.* Amsterdam: Rodopi, 1998.

Helen Fehervary

SEMBÈNE, OUSMANE (1923–). Senegalese novelist and filmmaker whose many novels and films have distinguished him as one of the most notable writers and filmmakers working on any continent. What sets Sembène apart as well is his unflagging commitment to the common and dispossessed people of his native Senegal and modern Africa in general, a commitment reflected in his recurring dramatization of both the plight and the extraordinary resilience and spirit of "ordinary" Africans. Works such as the film *Faat-Kine* (2000) illustrate, in addition, Sembène's enduring commitment to championing the causes of African women.

Sembène's sympathetic relations with ordinary Senegalese can be traced in part to his own modest beginnings. Born in Ziguinchor in southwestern Senegal, he worked in his youth as a fisherman on the Atlantic Coast and studied at the School of Ceramics in the town of Marsassoum in the Kolda administrative division, not far from Ziguinchor. Having left school at fifteen and moved north to Dakar, he worked as a plumber, mechanic, and bricklayer, and taught himself French. In 1939, he was drafted into the French army and joined the Free French forces in 1942, arriving in liberated France with them in 1944. Returning to France in 1947, Sembène gained employment as a longshoreman in Marseilles and became absorbed in left-wing political thought and active in trade-union work. After breaking his backbone while unloading a ship in Marseilles in 1951, he turned more fully to intellectual life, studying varied books, art, and theatrical productions. His first novel, *The Black Docker* (*Le Docker noir*), informed by his work as a longshoreman, was published in 1956, and in the following year, he published his second novel, *Ô pays, mon beau peuple!* (O My Country, My Good People). Sembène's masterpiece from this period is the renowned historical novel *God's Bits of Wood* (*Les Bouts de bois de Dieu*), which appeared in 1960—the year of Senegalese Independence—and dramatizes a five-month strike in 1947 and 1948 conducted by African workers on the Dakar-Niger railroad.

In the meantime Sembène pursued an interest in filmmaking, believing that he could use the medium to communicate with the vast majority of his Senegalese compatriots who did not read French or have any books. After studying film at the Gorki Studios in Moscow under Soviet director Marc Donskoï, Sembène returned in 1963 to Senegal and made three short movies, including *Borom Sarret*, and in 1966, he made the first full-length film by an African, *La Noire de . . .* (*Black Girl*), which became a 1967 prize winner at the Cannes Film Festival. Several of Sembène's subsequent films were adapted from his own works of fiction, and after 1960, those works frequently addressed the conditions of postcolonial life in Senegal and, by extension, in much of Africa.

The 1965 novella *The Money Order* (*Le Mandat*) narrates the ordeal of an unemployed Senegalese man when he is unable to cash a money order due to his lack of an identity card. Sembène crossed an important frontier when he released *Mandabi* (1968), a film version of *The Money Order* done in Sembène's native Wolof (the most widely spoken indigenous language in Senegal) rather than French. Sembène, like the Kenyan writer **Ngũgĩ wa Thiong'o**, has insisted that his work should reach the large majority of the public that does not read the former colonizer's language, and he is critical of the use of the colonial language for modern African art and education. Thus, while most of Sembène's writings are in French, most of his screenplays have been entirely or partly in Wolof. In addition, Sembène's film *Emitai* (1972) is in Jola, another indigenous Senegalese language, while his most recent film *Mooladé* (2003), made in Burkina Faso, is in Bambara, an indigenous language of Burkina Faso, Mali, southern Mauritania, and eastern Senegal. (*Mooladé*, which won Le Prix d'Un Certain Regard at the 2004 Cannes Film Festival, is another controversial film, confronting the practice of female genital mutilation that is still extensively practiced in Africa.)

Other significant works of fiction by Sembène include *Xala* (1973), *The Last of the Empire* (*Le Dernier de empire,* 1981), and *Niiwam et Taaw* (1992), while other cinematic achievements include *Xala* (1974), *Ceddo* (1976), *Camp de Thiaroye* (1988), and *Guelwaar* (1993). Given the trenchant political criticisms embodied in his work, it is not entirely surprising that Sembène's films routinely met with the disapproval of the censor during the rule of Senegal's first president **Léopold Senghor**, who was himself an important writer. On the other hand, one of the objects of Sembène's own political disapproval has been the class of politicians and entrepreneurs who have facilitated neocolonialism in modern Africa. These middlemen have allowed Western interests to continue to dominate Africa economically and to exploit its people and resources. Perhaps Sembène's indignation at the heedless opportunism of these individuals stems in part from his historical awareness of the role of similar middlemen during the eras of slavery and colonialism in Africa. This awareness underlies Sembène's indictment of corrupt contemporary business practices in

Xala (both novel and film), a satire of Africa's postindependence political situation that corresponds in several key respects to **Frantz Fanon**'s analysis of postcolonial injustice and resistance in *The Wretched of the Earth* (1961).

Sembène's belief in the artist's role as one of giving voice to the nonprivileged majority has prompted him to compare the modern African artist to the griot—the storyteller, musician, historian, and social critic of traditional West African culture. This comparison is indicative of another familiar trait in his work—namely, its concern with reconciling African tradition with the conditions of modernity. Sembène is keenly aware of the debt modern Africans owe to traditional African culture, since it is that culture that sustained Africa and offered a source of inspiration and pride to its people during and after the colonial period. At the same time, he rejects unproductive subservience to the forms and the stories of the past, believing that modern Africans must create their own cultures, inspired by tradition but not enslaved to it.

Selected Bibliography: Cham, Mbye Baboucar. "Ousmane Sembène and the Aesthetics of African Oral Traditions." *African Journal* 13 (1982): 24–40; Cordell, Dennis D. "Ousmane Sembène's *God's Bits of Wood.*" *African Novels in the Classroom.* Ed. Margaret Jean Hay. Boulder, CO: Lynne Rienner, 2000; Murphy, David. *Sembène: Imagining Alternatives in Film and Fiction.* Trenton, NJ: Africa World P, 2001; Petty, Sheila. *A Call to Action: The Films of Ousmane Sembène.* Westport, CT: Greenwood, 1996; Pfaff, Françoise. *The Cinema of Ousmane Sembène: A Pioneer of African Film.* Westport, CT: Greenwood, 1984; Sembène, Ousmane. "Film-makers and African Culture" (uncredited interview with Sembène). *Africa* 71 (1977): 80; Sembène, Ousmane. "Man Is Culture." Sixth Annual Hans Wolff Memorial Lecture (March 1975). Bloomington: African Studies Program, Indiana University, 1979.

Thomas J. Lynn

SENGHOR, LÉOPOLD SÉDAR (1906–2001).

SENGHOR, LÉOPOLD SÉDAR (1906–2001). Born in Joal, Senegal, Senghor is one of the founders of the **negritude** movement along with **Aimé Césaire** from Martinique and Léon-Gontran Damas from French Guyana. Senghor's father was a landowner who claimed both noble Mandingue and Portuguese ascendancies. His mother was of Peul origin. Senghor spent his first seven years in his birthplace under the guidance of his maternal uncle Waly Bakhoum—the Sérères practice a matrilineal system—who initiated him to the native culture that became influential in his writings. His formal education started at age seven: the Catholic school at the Joal Mission (1913–1914), the boarding school at Ngasobil, and then Djilôr. In 1923, he entered the Libermann Seminary in Dakar to study for the priesthood, but later transferred to Lycée Van Vollenhoven, where he passed his baccalaureate in 1928. He went to study in Paris on a scholarship and graduated (1931) from Louis-le-Grand, where he met Georges Pompidou. Later, he earned his *diplôme d'études supérieures* from the Sorbonne and, in 1935, his *agrégation* degree in grammar, the first African to get this honor.

From 1935, he studied African anthropology with renowned teachers such as Paul Rivet, Marcel Mauss, and (especially) the German anthropologist Frobenius, whose influence on the negritude ideology is indisputable. Immersed in African and French cultures, Senghor refuted the notion of Africa as a void in need of redress by way of colonization. He collaborated to various literary magazines, namely *La Revue du Monde noir* (1931), *L'Étudiant noir* (1934), and *Présence africaine* (1947). His *Anthologie de la nouvelle poésie nègre et malgache d'expression française* was the watershed moment in Francophone African literature.

Senghor is the most acclaimed African poet and a winner of many awards. His main collections include *Chants d'ombre* (1945), *Hosties noires* (inspired by Bergson, 1948), *Éthiopiques* (1956), and *Les Élegies mineures* (1979). Although *Éthiopiques* invokes a grandiose black past, it celebrates the various African artistic manifestations: rhythms, sensual femininity, and ancestral wisdom. Senghor's poetry also shows a strong influence of French **surrealism**. In his five essays entitled *Liberté* and in *Ce que je crois* (1988), he dealt with a wide range of topics touching on African cultures and their relationships with other civilizations. He puts faith in humankind by underlying a common goal of brotherhood beyond national, racial, and cultural divides for the triumph of *la civilisation de l'universel*.

Senghor was also an educator and a statesman. He started his teaching career at Lycée Descartes in Tours (1937), then moved to Lycée Marcelin Berthelet in Paris. In 1944, he was appointed professor of African languages at l'École Nationale de la France d'Outre-Mer. The highest achievement was his election at the prestigious French Academy in 1984. A **World War II** veteran, Senghor represented Senegal at the French Assembly from 1945 to 1958. He held several important positions in the French government under presidents Faure and de Gaulle. At Senegal's independence in 1960, he became the first president till his retirement in 1980 at Verson, Normandy, where he died on December 20, 2001.

Selected Bibliography: Biondi, Jean-Pierre. *Senghor, ou, la tentation de l'universel.* Paris: Denoël, 1993; Markovitz, Irving Leonard. *Léopold Sédar Senghor and the Politics of Negritude.* New York: Atheneum, 1969; Spleth, Janice S. *Léopold Sédar Senghor.* Boston: Twayne, 1985; Vaillant, Janet. *Black, French, and African: A Life of Léopold Sédar Senghor.* Cambridge, MA: Harvard UP, 1990.

Kasongo M. Kapanga

SERGE, VICTOR (1890–1947). Born Viktor L'vovich Kibalchich in Brussels, the son of Russian *Narodnaia Volia* sympathizers, Serge was an active participant in, and prolific writer about, some of the most important political struggles of the first part of the twentieth century, including the **Russian Revolution**. From the age of fifteen, Serge became actively involved in revolutionary movements in Belgium and France and, as editor of *L'Anarchie* in Paris, was jailed from 1913 to 1917 for defending anarchists on trial for robbery. He took part in the syndicalist insurrection in Barcelona in 1917 and, after internment in France, arrived in Petrograd in 1919. Here he fought in the civil war and became secretary to the **Third International** and editor of *Communist International.* He also worked for the Comintern in Berlin and Vienna, returning to the Soviet Union in 1926. He was expelled from the **Communist Party** in 1928 as a member of the Left Opposition and exiled to Central Asia in 1933. In 1936, he was deported from the Soviet Union following a campaign on his behalf by French intellectuals. Denied entry into France by the French government, he initially went to Belgium, though he was later admitted to France. Serge was forced to leave France in 1940 following the Nazi occupation and lived in Mexico until his death.

Serge's works, both fiction and nonfiction, merit considerably more attention than they have received. They were inspired by his ardent belief in the necessity for social change and informed by his own experiences. The fact that he was a writer who worked in Soviet Russia in the aftermath of the 1917 revolution, was a victim of the rise of Stalinism, and yet survived to record his experiences renders him almost unique. His relative obscurity can primarily be attributed to the political stance he took, which supported the ideals of the early Russian Revolution but opposed **Stalin**. He was therefore largely ignored by both sides of the **cold war**.

Serge wrote over thirty books, numerous pamphlets, and contributions to many newspapers and journals. He also published poetry. He wrote in French, but his major works have been published in translation. His most notable novels are his autobiographical trilogy *Victory-in-Defeat; Defeat-in-Victory* (written 1926–1931), which charts his early political life, culminating in his work as a Bolshevik in Petrograd in 1921; and *The Case of Comrade Tulayev* (1940–1942), which is set in the Soviet Union in 1938–1939, during the Moscow trials, and explores the fate of Bolsheviks under Stalinist repression. His nonfictional works on Russia include *Year One of the Russian Revolution* (1925–1928)—a chronicle of events surrounding the October 1917 insurrection—and *Destiny of a Revolution* (1937)—an unrelenting attack on the developing Stalinist system. His autobiography *Memoirs of a Revolutionary* (1942–1943) is both the story of a life devoted to fighting social injustice and an eyewitness account of revolutionary upheavals in Europe. These works, together with the wealth of other material he produced, provide a valuable insight into revolutionary movements in the countries in which Serge lived and worked, and are also a testament to his commitment to both revolutionary change and literature. They are an invaluable source for those interested in the history, politics, or literature of the period.

Selected Bibliography: Greeman, Richard. "Victor Serge: The Making of a Novelist (1890–1928)." Diss. Columbia University, 1968; Johnson, Roy. "Victor Serge as Revolutionary Novelist: The First Trilogy." *Literature and History* 5.1 (1979): 58–86; Marshall, Bill. *Victor Serge: The Uses of Dissent.* Oxford: Berg, 1992; Richardson, Al, ed. *Victor Serge: The Century of the Unexpected.* Special issue of *Revolutionary History* 5.3 (1994).

Jackie Shellard

THE SEVENTH CROSS (*DAS SIEBTE KREUZ*, 1942) by **Anna Seghers** is one of the greatest novels of the antifascist resistance against Hitler and an eloquent testimony to the resilience of the human spirit in the modern era. When seven prisoners escape from a concentration camp in the Rhineland in the mid-1930s, the camp administration organizes a manhunt in the Mainz-Frankfurt-Höchst area, and in time, all but one of the fugitives are apprehended. Thus, only the seventh of the hastily cropped trees mounted with crossboards that await the captured men in the camp courtyard stands empty—the seventh "cross." While the fate of the six men confirms the power and brutality of the Nazi regime, young Georg Heisler's escape on a Rhine freighter bound for Holland, aided by more or less unwitting citizens and a largely communist network of political resistance, is inscribed in the collective memory of camp prisoners huddled around a fire kindled from the seven "crosses" felled at the novel's end. If the novel's suspense revolves around the flight of the rather unremarkable Heisler, its essential drama and heroism concern the figures who witness and abet his escape, affected in myriad ways by their encounter with what is the redemptive story of much more than one man. The multiperspectivism and panoramic sweep of the novel afford it epic grandeur in the tradition of Stendhal, **Joseph Conrad**, and **Leo Tolstoy**.

Seghers wrote *The Seventh Cross* in 1938–1939 in exile in Paris. The first chapters appeared in the Moscow-based journal *International Literature* in the summer of 1939, whereupon serialization ceased due to the Hitler-Stalin pact. The onset of war made publication in Western Europe untenable, and in 1940, Seghers sent copies of her manuscript to the United States. In 1942, one year after her escape to Mexico, *The Seventh Cross* was published in English by Little, Brown & Co. in the United States, where it became a best-seller. Appearing at a critical time in the American war effort, the novel was a Book-of-the-Month-Club selection, syndicated nationwide as a comic strip, republished in an armed-services edition, and made into a Hollywood film directed by Fred Zinnemann and starring Spencer Tracy, Hume Cronin, and Jessica Tandy. The first German edition appeared in Mexico in late 1942, followed by Canadian and British editions and translations into Spanish, Swedish, Dutch, Danish, Norwegian, and French. To date, the novel has been published in over forty languages. After its initial success, *The Seventh Cross* fell victim to the **cold war**. While over a million copies were sold in the German Democratic Republic (and large numbers elsewhere in Europe), it was soon forgotten in the Anglo-American world, and not published in West Germany until 1962. The novel has inspired numerous dramatizations as well as Hans Werner Henze's choral *Symphony No. 9*.

Selected Bibliography: Fehervary, Helen. *Anna Seghers: The Mythic Dimension.* Ann Arbor: U of Michigan P, 2001; LaBahn, Kathleen J. *Anna Seghers's Exile Literature: The Mexican Years.* Bern: Peter Lang, 1986; Rosenberg, Dorothy. Afterword to *The Seventh Cross* by Anna Seghers. New York: Monthly Review P, 1987. 347–81; Stephan, Alexander. *Anna Seghers: Das siebte Kreuz—Welt und Wirkung eines Romans.* Berlin: Aufbau Taschenbuch, 1997; Wallace, Ian, ed. *Anna Seghers in Perspective.* Amsterdam: Rodopi, 1998.

Helen Fehervary

SHAKESPEARE, WILLIAM (1564–1616). Perhaps the most widely respected author in world literature, Shakespeare has also been deployed in support of a variety of political positions. In the nineteenth century, for example, Shakespeare's work was employed as a supposed demonstration of British cultural superiority and thus as a justification for British imperialism. On the other hand, at the 1934 **Soviet Writers' Congress**, Shakespeare was consistently paired with **Maxim Gorky** as a model for aspirant writers of **socialist realism**. For the critic Sergei Dimanov, "Shakespeare was a fighter who, standing at the head of his class, sliced his way into life. Those of our writers who have a truly proletarian world-view must study Shakespeare so that our hatred can destroy the enemies of the socialist motherland, so that our love can be the purest, tenderest and kindest, so that our thoughts can take the world by storm and move humankind forward to the radiant future." This is no more than an extreme example of Shakespeare's political pliability. Through the years, Shakespeare's work, selectively interpreted, has been of equal service to fascists, Marxists, royalists, and republicans. In the United Kingdom, as British power and influence has dwindled, it has remained convenient for politicians of all shades to promote him as a national icon.

It is only through selective application of the available evidence that Shakespeare can be politically aligned. In the rural midlands of England, where he was born into a tolerably prosperous merchant family (his father made and marketed gloves), the hottest political issue was religion. The brief but bloody Counter-Reformation under the Catholic Queen Mary I had ended with her death in 1559, and Protestantism was once more the state religion under Elizabeth I. Either covertly or openly, though, Catholic practices continued. The Arden family, to which Shakespeare's mother belonged, was piously of the "old" faith, and there is no doubt that Shakespeare grew up in its shadow. The claim that both he and his father were Catholics, though never substantiated, has not been conclusively silenced. It was a conscious endeavor of the queen herself, and of her most "politic" counselors—the Poloniuses of the state—to "stage" patriotism while rendering politics as unspectacular as possible. The accidental effect was to ease the nation's passage from feudalism to capitalism, a process of which Shakespeare was a minor beneficiary; compared with most of his Stratford neighbors, he was a rich man at the end of his life.

The contemporaneous growth of a professional theater in London was the decisive factor in Shakespeare's life. We do not know what impelled him to join the theater, nor what route he followed in the journey from tiny town to big city, but he was firmly established in London by 1594, when he became a founder-member of a theater company, formed under the patronage of the Lord Chamberlain. It was only through patronage that actors (or poets and artists of any kind) could thrive, and patronage has its own politics. The Lord Chamberlain, Lord Hunsdon, was the Queen's cousin, routinely Protestant and patriotic, and nurtured on xenophobia. To be in with him was to gain access to royal favor. It is implied by negative evidence that Shakespeare handled his contacts with persons of power discreetly. Writing plays in the turbulent last decade of the old, childless (and therefore heirless) queen was a perilous business, as Ben Jonson and others found to their cost. Given the trials and errors of many of his fellow dramatists, it seems fair to conclude that Shakespeare knew when and how to keep his political head down. He peopled his English history plays with earls and dukes whose machinations were often discreditable, without exciting the public anger of their family descendants in the audience, and that, in an era of aristocratic paranoia, ought to be seen as extraordinary. In his tragedies, a consistent theme is the struggle for, and abuse of, power. Taking monarchy for granted as a political system—its shadow is present even in the plays set in republican Rome—he invited his contemporaries to consider the qualities essential in a "good" monarch. Even his comedies, however tangentially, recognize the effect of corruption in high places. But these are the commonplace concerns of Elizabethan and Jacobean drama; they do not imply a radical political vision. Jockeying for position was as much the daily commerce of actors and playwrights as of courtiers, and Shakespeare did it better, and at less personal risk, than most. Even when, as in his own or his company's association with the volatile Earl of Essex, he got his hands burned, he managed to pull them out of the flames very quickly.

Essex, during the final years of Elizabeth's reign, aligned himself with the radical Protestants ("Puritans" is a later misnomer) who, through the 1590s and into the new century, sought to reform the Church of England, to eradicate Catholicism, and incidentally to disempower the queen's aging counselors. The Chorus that opened Act 5 of *Henry V* at its 1599 performance explicitly compared Essex, then fighting in Ireland, with the triumphant Henry V. This, at a time when factionalism at court was fierce, was fighting talk, uncharacteristic of Shakespeare but suggestive of a political engagement with Essex's vision of England as a European power. There may be substance in the suggestion; Shakespeare's plays are rich in a patriotic rhetoric that rises above the conventional.

Patriotism, however, makes for flimsy politics. When James I adopted Shakespeare's company as the King's Men, it was with the intention of controlling London's most successful group of actors. There is no clear evidence of resistance from playwright or players; indeed, unlike the Shakespeare proclaimed by the 1934 Soviet Writers' Congress as a champion of the proletariat, Shakespeare consistently showed little real resistance to official power in either his life or his work. The plays reveal a fastidious disdain for men *en masse*, and although their critique of courtly corruption is perceptive, it is also fundamentally conventional. Shakespeare's political passivity, embodied in his final years of retirement in his home town, is that of a prosperous protobourgeois.

Selected Bibliography: Barroll, J. Leeds. *Politics, Plague, and Shakespeare's Theater: The Stuart Years.* Ithaca: Cornell UP, 1991; Dollimore, Jonathan, and Alan Sinfield, eds. *Political Shakespeare.* Ithaca: Cornell UP, 1985; Goldberg, Jonathan. *James I and the Politics of Literature.* Baltimore: Johns Hopkins UP, 1983; Guy, John, ed. *The Reign of Elizabeth I: Court and Culture in the Last Decade.* Cambridge UP, 1995; Honan, Park. *Shakespeare: A Life.* Oxford UP, 1998; Howard, Jean E. *The Stage and Social Struggle in Early Modern England.* London: Routledge, 1994; Stone, Lawrence. *The Crisis of the Aristocracy, 1558–1641.* Oxford: Clarendon Press, 1965; Thomson, Peter. *Shakespeare's Professional Career.* Cambridge: Cambridge UP, 1992.

Peter Thomson

SHAW, (GEORGE) BERNARD (1856–1950). Perhaps the greatest political playwright in the history of English drama, Shaw's political acuity and his acquisition of the tools of Marxist analysis allowed him to lead his times and articulate the pressure and content of his historical era even as he, himself, altered and affected it. Shaw authored more than fifty plays, often publishing them with lengthy prefaces that explained his political views. Demonstrating the Marxian axiom that the task of philosophers was not merely to understand but to change the world, he embraced the notion of a constant critique of seemingly natural cultural products, never shying away from controversial topics throughout his long career. He deconstructed slum landlordism in *Widower's Houses* (1893), skewered militarism in *Arms and the Man* (1894), explored prostitution in *Mrs. Warren's Profession* (1898), and predicted the neutron bomb in *Far-Fetched Fables* (1948–1950). Born and raised in Ireland, Shaw brought the outsider's gaze of the colonized subject to expose the foibles of British politics and society.

Unlike many radical writers, Shaw became more daring as he grew older, and the shape of his political career followed a trajectory of increasing and more left-leaning commitment, as he developed from Shelleyan socialist to Fabian socialist to communist to Bolshevik. Taking the poet **Percy Shelley** as his original model, Shaw proclaimed himself at an early age an atheist, a vegetarian, and a communist. Shaw's political activism expressed itself beyond literary production and took the form of early organizational work in the formation of the Fabian Society. He was closely associated with such activist figures as **William Morris** and Beatrice and Sydney Webb. He was a tireless public speaker and ran for and won local political office in London. His mature internationalism and anticolonialism emerged in his preface to *John Bull's Other Island* (1904), in which he recounts and denounces colonial atrocities. His internationalism also made him an opponent of some of the narrow Celticism of early versions of Irish nationalism. He questioned the **Easter Rising**, but he supported Roger Casement and opposed his execution by the British as a traitor.

Although Shaw was not a pacifist, he deplored senseless wars and believed that the two world wars were the result of capitalism's relentless exploitation of mankind for the profit of the few. His opposition to **World War I** as expressed in *Heartbreak House* (1919) and scores of pamphlets lowered his popularity, and it took the Nobel Prize and the production of *Saint Joan* (1923) to restore him to the forefront of British literary life. Characterized by **Lenin** as "a good man fallen among Fabians," Shaw grew to admire and support the **Russian Revolution** and the subsequent attempt to build a socialist society in the Soviet Union. His trip to see the effects of Bolshevism in Russia increased his enthusiasm for the social revolution he saw taking place there, as demonstrated in the second ending he wrote for *The Millionairess* (1935); he mounted scathing critiques of parliamentary democracy in plays like *The Apple Cart* (1929) and portrayed the failure of international cooperation in plays like *Geneva* (1938). Shaw's ideological commitment never wavered in his long writing life, from *Immaturity* (1879) to *Far-Fetched Fables*. A dramatic realist, he opposed all shades of philosophical idealism; he dreaded the sludge of a priori judgments and received opinions. He marshaled his formidable wit and intellect to espouse and demonstrate the advantages of experience and reality over prejudice and illusion.

Selected Bibliography: Holroyd, Michael. *Bernard Shaw.* 4 vols. London: Chatto and Windus, 1988–1992; Laurence, Dan H., ed. *Bernard Shaw: Collected Letters.* London: Reinhardt, 1965–1998; Meisel, Martin. *Shaw and the Nineteenth-Century Theater.* Westport, CT: Greenwood, 1976; Peters, Sally. *Bernard Shaw: The Ascent of the Superman.* New Haven, CT: Yale UP, 1996; Weintraub, Stanley. *Journey to Heartbreak.* London: Routledge and Kegan Paul, 1971.

Norma Jenckes

SHELLEY, PERCY BYSSHE (1792–1822). Shelley was born at Field Place in Sussex, the son of a Whig member of Parliament who become a baronet. Shelley was in line for a baronetcy and his father wanted him to be educated at Eton and then Oxford. At Eton, where Shelley enrolled in 1804, he proved an unpopular pupil because of his excellence as a Latin scholar and anarchic refusal to recognize authority.

To his father's dismay, Shelley's undergraduate career at Oxford lasted only six months. On March 25, 1811, Shelley's refusal to renounce the dissenting contents of *The Necessity of Atheism* (1811) ended in his dismissal from University College. After an unsettled period in his life, Shelley initiated an important relationship with **William Godwin** (1756–1836), author of *Enquiry Concerning Political Justice* (1793). Godwin's political philosophy formed a basis for Shelley's agitation to revoke the *Act of Union* and establish Catholic emancipation. In February 1812, Shelley distributed his *An Address to the Irish People and Proposals for an Association of Philanthropists in Dublin*, asserting the rights of the impoverished Irish. Godwin's disapproval of these political activities secured Shelley's return from Dublin on April 4. Shelley continued his political activism and authored *A Letter to Lord Ellenborough* (1812) and *A Declaration of Rights* (1812). In London, Shelley privately issued *Queen Mab* (1813), which diagnosed social institutions as pernicious. In July 1814, Shelley eloped to Europe with Mary Godwin (1797–1871), daughter of Godwin and **Mary Wollstonecraft** (1759–1797). Shelley started but never finished *The Assassins*, a piece of **utopian fiction**. Shelley's reputation as an immoral, revolutionary atheist was reinforced by his publication of *A Refutation of Deism* earlier in 1814. In May 1816, financial difficulties forced a return to the continent, where Shelley met Lord Byron. On Shelley's return to England, he resided at Albion House in Marlow (March 1817). Shelley published (under the pseudonym "the Hermit of Marlow") *Proposal for Putting Reform to the Vote throughout the Kingdom* and, in November 1817, *An Address to the People on the Death of the Princess Charlotte*. Shelley's major composition at this time was a poetic epic, first published as *Laon and Cythna* (December 1817) and later reissued as *The Revolt of Islam* (January 1818). Pressured by personal and financial matters, Shelley departed England for Italy on March 11, 1818, and never again returned to British shores. Shelley wrote his satirically acidic *The Mask of Anarchy* (printed in 1832, the year of the *Great Reform Bill*); the political treatise *A Philosophical View of Reform* (started in November 1819); and a revolutionary lyric, "Ode to the West Wind" (1819). His last published work, *Hellas* (February 1822), was inspired by the Greek War of Independence. On July 8, 1822, Shelley accidentally drowned on a return voyage from visiting the radical orator Leigh Hunt (1784–1859). Shelley's enduring legacy of political writings and their opposition to tyranny, oppression, and poverty can be gauged from the proletariat **Chartist** movement's adoption, in the 1840s, of *Queen Mab* as their political manifesto.

Selected Bibliography: Duff, David. *Romance and Revolution: Shelley and the Politics of a Genre.* Cambridge: Cambridge UP, 1994; Foot, Paul. *Red Shelley.* London: Bookmarks, 1984; Fuller, Jean Overton. *Shelley: A Biography.* London: Cape, 1968; Guin, John Pollard. *Shelley's Political Thought.* Paris: Mouton, 1969; Holmes, John Clellon. "This Is the Beat Generation." *New York Times Magazine,* 16 November 1952, SM 10–13; O'Neill, Michael. *Percy Bysshe Shelley: A Literary Life.* London: Macmillan, 1989.

Mark Sandy

SHEN CONGWEN (1902–1988), modern Chinese writer and cultural historian. He was born Shen Yuehuan in Fenghuang, a garrison town in the west part of Hunan Province. The family were of Han military elite, though starting from the grandfa-

ther, the Shens intermarried with aboriginal Miao and Tujia. As was the family tradition, Shen Congwen served in the army (1916–1922). In 1923, he left Hunan for
Beijing, determined to pursue a literary career. While in Beijing, Shen Congwen tried
but failed to gain admission to university due to his lack of academic preparation.
He nonetheless started to write and began to publish in 1924. His early writing is
autobiographical in the classical sense of the word, concentrating on experiences, desires, and frustrations of a struggling scholar from the rural interior.

Though a frustrated academic, Shen Congwen maintained close personal and professional connections with what is known as the Peking school of writers—writers,
critics, and academics, most of whom had attended universities abroad or been otherwise exposed to Western culture. Inspired by the cultural criticism and romanticism popularized by some writers of this group, Shen Congwen turned his attention
to rural themes. Lyrical re-creations of rural life and characters in his west Hunan
stories have won him popular as well as critical acclaim since the late 1920s. In the
1930s, he became the most prominent writer of the Peking school and his representation of west Hunan the most alluring landscape in modern Chinese literature. At
the same time, his experiments with new narrative approaches and topic interests
won him the reputation of a literary stylist, a quality accepted even by critics who
disapproved of his criticism of modernization.

Never in favor with the politics of the Chinese **Communist Party** (CCP), Shen
Congwen was deemed not fit to continue writing after the founding of the People's
Republic of China and was not admitted to the **Chinese Writers' Association.** Excluded from the canon of modern Chinese literature, his name disappeared from text-
books. These acts of exclusion compelled him to choose a different career path under
communism. After a period of political reeducation, Shen Congwen was assigned a
job at the Palace Museum to categorize ancient artifacts.

Ironically, Shen Congwen's works were also banned in Taiwan, though for different reasons. He was considered and treated as a communist in Taiwan because he
stayed on in China after the communist takeover. Shen Congwen's resurrection came
in the 1980s when he was reintroduced to China from abroad. Sinologists in the
United States in particular upheld Shen Congwen as a representative of an alternative tradition to the overtly political literature that had reigned in China since the
May Fourth movement of the early twentieth century. In the mid-1980s, many
among a younger generation of writers of regional fiction acknowledged their in-
debtedness to Shen Congwen.

Selected Bibliography: Kinkley, Jeffrey C. *The Odyssey of Shen Congwen.* Stanford, CA: Stanford UP,
1987; Wang Dewei. *Fictional Realism in Twentieth-Century China: Mao Dun, Lao She, Shen Congwen.*
New York: Columbia UP, 1992.

Donghui He

SHOLOKHOV, MIKHAIL (1905–1984), highly acclaimed Soviet writer best
known for his novel *Tikhii Don* (*Quiet Flows the Don,* 1928–1940). Sholokhov was
born in the village of Kruzhilin, in the Don Military Region, to a lower-middle-class
Russian family. His formal education was interrupted by the **Russian Revolution** and
subsequent civil war. His sympathies were with the Bolsheviks, whom he joined to

become a member of a food requisition detachment in the Don region. This dangerous time of fierce fighting against various counterrevolutionary gangs, kulaks opposing food requisitions, and various criminal gangs became the background for Sholokhov's later creative work.

In 1922, Sholokhov went to Moscow and began his literary career, writing short stories about the civil war and the bitter political strife of the 1920s. In 1925, he returned to the Don region, where he remained for the rest of his life. In 1926, his first collection of short stories, *Donskie rasskazy* (*Tales of the Don*), was published to immediate acclaim. In 1928, he began writing *Tikhii Don*, a four-volume epic about Don Cossacks and the revolution, for which he has often been compared to **Leo Tolstoy**. Critics found parallels in the scenes he depicted and characters he portrayed, as well as in the epic style he used to portray the revolution. The novel begins in 1912, introducing the lives of the Cossacks before the revolution, and then goes on to offer a panoramic picture of the society of the Don Cossacks during the civil war and of the birth of a new Soviet society. The novel heavily relies on the use of *skaz,* as well as dialecticisms and Don regionalisms. Its innovations and linguistic freshness were praised despite the occasional difficulties they posed for an average Soviet Russian reader. Sholokhov's vivid descriptions of the lives of the Don Cossacks and his colorful depictions of age-old traditions intertwined with the new made the book very popular among Soviet readers immediately after the publication of the first installment. The critics received it less warmly, charging him for the book's lack of proletarian elements, lack of "objectivity," and lack of proper contextualization of the collectivization and struggle against the kulaks. The debate about the novel and its unproletarian writer went on for several years. However, the publication of each subsequent part of the novel was a major literary event in the Soviet Union, and *Tikhii Don* became one of the most popular works of Soviet fiction.

In 1932, Sholokhov began the publication of *Podniataia Tselina* (*Virgin Soil Upturned,* 1932–1960). The publication of this novel, which depicts class struggle among peasants during the collectivization of agriculture, helped Sholokhov firmly establish his literary standing. That same year, he became a member of the **Communist Party**; in 1937, he became a delegate to the Supreme Soviet; and in 1939, he became a member of the Soviet Academy of Science. Throughout his career, he received the highest Soviet awards, including the Order of Lenin in 1939 and the Stalin Prize in 1941.

During **World War II**, while continuing to write fiction, Sholokhov began writing speeches and journalistic articles about war efforts for *Pravda* and *Krasnaia zvezda.* His unfinished novel *Oni srazhalis za rodinu* (*They Fought for Their Country,* published in chapters: 1943–1944, 1949, 1954, 1969) depicts the Soviet Union during World War II, while the story "Sudba cheloveka" ("The Fate of a Man," 1956–1957, later made into a film) describes the power and resilience of human love under adversity. His collected works were published in 1956–1960. In 1961, Sholokhov became a member of the Central Committee. In 1965, he received the Nobel Prize for Literature.

Selected Bibliography: Ermolaev, Herman. *Mikhail Sholokhov and His Art.* Princeton, NJ: Princeton UP, 1982; Iakimenko, Lev Grigor'evich. *Tvorchestvo M. A. Sholokhova.* Moscow: Sovetskii Pisatel, 1970; Semanov, S. N. *Tikhii Don—literatura i istoria.* Moscow: Sovremennik, 1977; Semanov, S. N. *V mire*

"Tikhogo Dona." Moscow: Sovremennik, 1987; *Sovetskii Entsiklopediiski Slovar.* Moscow: Sovetskaia Entsiklopedia, 1989.

Dubravka Juraga

SILKO, LESLIE MARMON (1948–). Laguna writer Leslie Marmon Silko was raised in Laguna Pueblo, where her community's enduring oral tradition shaped her cultural identity and artistic vision. Silko became a leading Native writer and a premiere indigenous woman's voice during "red power," when American Indians began to assert the viability of Indian history, spirituality, and ecology. Among the first Indian writers to invest her popular narratives with Laguna and Navajo ritual patterns of quest, heroism, healing, and renewal, Silko announced to Indian writers and mainstream readers alike that Native worldviews were adequate to solve our most modern problems, such as alienation, global nuclear warfare, and environmental destruction—issues she confronts in her first novel, *Ceremony* (1977).

In this breathtaking novel, Silko celebrates the power of story to heal the spiritually and socially broken. From childhood, the protagonist Tayo is alienated from his Pueblo community for having a white father and blue eyes. Then, on returning from **World War II**, traumatized and guilt-ridden for his cousin's death in battle and a draught in his homeland, Tayo undergoes a ritual cleansing, recovers in a Laguna mythic world, and returns with rain to wash the land clean and subdue global destructive forces. *Ceremony* concludes with Tayo in the kiva, a storyteller now fully integrated in the Pueblo. Silko becomes a central woman writer in *Storyteller* (1981), an organic collection of poetry, photographs, and stories largely rooted in the oral traditional figures and contemporary lives of Laguna women. Her poetry is collected in *Laguna Woman* (1974), and her essays in *Yellow Woman and a Beauty of Spirit* (1996). Silko is perhaps most politically engaged in her massive *Almanac of the Dead* (1991), a novel to explore the conquest of the Americas as the source of contemporary moral decline, and the indigenous prophecy of the eventual expulsion of Europeans from the Americas. After this exhaustive work, Silko considers the theme of Indian-white friendship in her most recent novel, *Gardens in the Dunes* (2000).

Selected Bibliography: *American Indian Quarterly* 5 (1979). Special Issue on Leslie Marmon Silko's *Ceremony*; Barnett, Louise K., and James L. Thorson, eds. *Leslie Marmon Silko: A Collection of Critical Essays.* Albuquerque: U of New Mexico P, 1999; Krupat, Arnold. *The Voice in the Margin: Native American Literature and the Canon.* Berkeley: U of California P, 1989; Sequoya-Magdaleno, Jana. "Telling the *Différance*: Representations of Identity in the Discourse of Indianness." *The Ethnic Canon: Histories, Institutions, and Interventions.* Ed. David Palumbo-Liu. Minneapolis: U of Minnesota P, 1995. 88–116.

Sean Teuton

SILLITOE, ALAN (1928–). Sillitoe was born in a working-class district of Nottingham to a blacksmith's daughter and a tanner. With his father unemployed in the 1930s, conditions were particularly harsh and, despite a keen interest in education, Sillitoe left school at the age of fourteen to work in the local Raleigh bicycle factory. Sillitoe held several factory jobs over the next few years before signing up for the Air Training Corps at age seventeen. After contracting tuberculosis in Malaya, Sillitoe spent almost a year and a half in a sanatorium recovering before being pensioned out of the military in 1949. It was during this period, with time to read and think, that Sillitoe decided to become a writer.

Encouraged by the poet Robert Graves to write from his own experiences, Sillitoe crafted what was to become his best-known novel, *Saturday Night and Sunday Morning* (1958). A searing tale of working-class realism, the book tells the story of Arthur Seaton, a young and rebellious factory worker who, through a series of events that are both personal and emblematic of class relations at the time, comes to a greater understanding of his milieu and the responsibilities that it entails. More an anarchist than a socialist or communist, Arthur sees little future in the status quo, although the love and marriage that end the book seem like resignation. While Sillitoe was quickly associated with the group of writers known as the angry young men of the late 1950s and early 1960s, he has always resisted such labels, often preferring instead class-inflected but idiosyncratic narratives of aesthetic engagement. Sillitoe's short story "The Loneliness of the Long-Distance Runner" (1959) (which, like his first novel, was made into a successful film) is perhaps even "angrier" than the work of contemporaries like John Osborne, John Braine, and David Storey. The main character, Smith, is sent to a Borstal for boys (a reform school) to mend his stealing ways, but here again Sillitoe displays a practiced eye and ear for working-class ressentiment. Nevertheless, taken together, Sillitoe's early writing (including *The Rats and Other Poems* [1960] and the novels *The General* [1960] and *The Death of William Posters* [1965]) is complex and rewards careful reading as the product of a creatively engaged working-class intellectual. An author of both travel books (*The Road to Volgograd* [1964] is particularly noteworthy) and children's stories, Sillitoe has displayed a remarkable range and perseverance, even while the tradition to which he has been attached is quietly being forgotten. This relative neglect is not unconnected to broader social forces like the deindustrialization of Britain, the recasting of Labour Party politics as something other than the politics of labor, and a significant restructuring of popular culture in which class discourse is negotiated in more complex and perhaps oblique ways. Sillitoe remains, however, a key figure in the history of English working-class expression. His memoir, *Life without Armour*, was published in 1995.

Selected Bibliography: Brooke, Stephen. "Gender and Working Class Identity in Britain during the 1950s." *Journal of Social History* 34.4 (Summer 2001): 773–95; Hawthorn, Jeremy, ed. *The British Working-Class Novel in the Twentieth Century.* London: Edward Arnold, 1984; Hitchcock, Peter. *Working-Class Fiction in Theory and Practice: A Reading of Alan Sillitoe.* Ann Arbor, MI: UMI, 1989; Vaverka, Ronald D. *Commitment as Art: A Marxist Critique of a Selection of Alan Sillitoe's Political Fiction.* Stockholm: Almqvist and Wiksell, 1978.

Peter Hitchcock

SILONE, IGNAZIO (SECONDINO TRANQUILLI) (1900–1978) received a religious education but, after discovering Marxism, became an advocate for the peasantry and a founding member of the Italian **Communist Party** (1921). He was driven into exile by fascism (and may have been blackmailed into becoming for a time a low-level informant), but having met **Lenin**, **Trotsky**, and **Stalin** in Moscow, he was disillusioned with communism and by 1931 had become "a socialist without a party and a Christian without a church." This painful and difficult "uscita di sicurezza" (emergency exit) gives its title to an essay (1949) that appeared in Richard Crossman's *The God That Failed* (1950) and to a volume (1965) describing postwar Italy's conversion to Western consumerism. From the 1930s, Silone practiced his antifascism mainly through literary means. His folk epic *Fontamara* (1933) shows the peasants' collective resistance to exploitation by both traditional landowners and modernizing agribusiness under fascism. The novels *Vino e pane* (*Bread and Wine*, 1936) and its sequel *Il seme sotto la neve* (*The Seed Beneath the Snow*, 1938)—also turned into a play, *Ed egli si nascose* (*And He Hid Himself*, 1944)—focus on a revolutionary who fails to mobilize the peasants politically and eventually gives himself up to save a peasant from a life sentence. *Der fascismus* (1934) is a political history of the triumph of fascism in Italy and *La scuola dei dittatori* (*The School for Dictators*, 1938) is a sardonic dialogue in which a U.S. millionaire eagerly takes lessons in totalitarianism. Silone's postwar literary works include another ebullient peasant epic, *Una manciata di more* (*A Handful of Blackberries*, 1952), in which the Communist Party is now the antagonist, and the **Brecht**ian medieval parable play *L'avventura di un povero cristiano* (*The Adventure of a Poor Christian*, 1968), in which a peasant becomes pope but cannot reform the church. Silone coedited the journal *Tempo Presente* from 1956 to 1968, resigning when he discovered it was funded by the CIA. Silone's works are widely read in the third world.

Selected Bibliography: Lewis, Richard W. B. *The Picaresque Saint.* Philadelphia: Lippincott, 1959; Paynter, Maria Nicolai. *Ignazio Silone: Beyond the Tragic Vision.* Toronto: U of Toronto P, 2000.

John Gatt-Rutter

SINCLAIR, UPTON (1878–1968). The most prolific of U.S. radical authors (along with **Howard Fast**), still more rare as a radical author personally launching a political challenge to the system, Sinclair failed to live up to his early potential but was for generations of readers a liberal-socialistic icon. Born to a decaying middle-class family in Baltimore, the young man began turning out reams of payment-by-word juvenilia, jokes, and short stories by the time he entered college. In 1902, the noted socialist minister George D. Herron allotted him sufficient funds to put aside hack work and embark on his first serious novel, *Manassas*, a civil-war narrative. Under Herron's influence, Sinclair experienced political conversion to a kind of Christian socialism heavily inflected through the American disciples of the wholistic, poetic-minded **William Morris**.

Sinclair's breakthrough came with *The Jungle* (1906), written after two years of investigating conditions in the Chicago stockyards and serialized in the most popular American socialist weekly, *The Appeal to Reason*. **Jack London** dubbed it the "*Uncle Tom's Cabin* of wage-slavery," and the tale of an immigrant proletarian's suffering instantly earned best-seller status. The public outcry, however, earned only a modest reform of meat-packing sanitary standards and no improvement in workers' conditions. *Samuel the Seeker* (1910) reflected an early feeling of despair that the sentimental socialist, prompted by the beauty of a countryside still unspoiled and the moral appeal of Eugene V. Debs, would likely find martyrdom rather than victory in materialistic America.

Yet Sinclair persisted, becoming a founder of the Intercollegiate Socialist Society and of his own socialist weekly tabloid, actually joining a socialist colony in Englewood, New Jersey, for a time. No raving revolutionist, Sinclair abandoned the socialist movement to support U.S. entry into **World War I** and then exited from the war fever in 1919, badly disillusioned. His war novel *Jimmie Higgins* (1917) reflected both sides of war expectations, along with horrifying experiences from the war itself. A series of subsequent novels (especially *The Brass Check*, 1919; *The Goose Step*, 1923; and *Mammonart*, 1925) was devoted to a critique of capitalistic repression and bourgeois hypocrisy. With a talent for turning scandals into literary melodrama, he meanwhile turned out political potboilers like *King Coal* (1917) and *Oil!* (1927), exposing the greed and exploitative practices of the captains of industry and their financial-swindler accomplices of the banking world. By the time the Depression hit, Sinclair had already written his best. Stung by the criticism of communist literary critics—uncharitable when it was not unfair—he had far fewer radical readers in the younger generations. His *Mental Radio* (1931) was a quest into spiritualism and contact between the dead and the living, a ghost of a nineteenth-century movement wholly outside the emerging leftism of the 1930s.

But Sinclair had one more great adventure in his adopted home of Southern California. There, in the vicinity of Los Angeles, producers' cooperatives took on new life with the economic collapse, and the idea of a new civilization within a collapsing old one offered a definite alternative to the Soviet-influenced communist movement, looking to strikes and as much as anticipating class war. In this spirit, Sinclair put himself forward for the 1934 Democratic gubernatorial primary, writing the extraordinary science-fiction-like self-published document *How I, Upton Sinclair, Ended Poverty in California*. EPIC, an acronym derived from "end poverty in California," suddenly became a sweeping regional movement encompassing a cooperative vision and a threat to the powerful. When Sinclair swept the state Democratic primary, the threat became more palpable. Most notably in the motion-picture capital of the world, studio bosses extracted unwilled contributions from employees and made documentaries warning against blood-curdling revolution by foreign-looking agitators, ironically prompting, by the bias and the bullying of these demands, the rise of left-wing and union sentiment within the film industry. Overwhelmed by the antileftist propaganda and the scale of conservative spending, Sinclair narrowly lost a post that would have projected him into national importance.

By 1936, with the coming of the **Popular Front**, the California Communists who had bitterly opposed his campaign, claiming it was not radical enough, moved themselves centerward to occupy the same territory within the liberal wing of the state Democratic party. Sinclair had lost more than his potential electoral base; he had, with the disappointing Norman Thomas campaign of 1936, lost his hopes for a noncommunist American Left. His most notable subsequent work was the eleven-volume Lanny Budd series (1940–1953, also known as the World's End series). These novels together present a sweeping chronicle of American, and indeed Western, history in the first half of the twentieth century. The eleven novels all feature a single protagonist, Lanny Budd, who often seems to have a great deal in common with Sinclair. While the narratives are unified by a focus on Lanny's experiences and perspectives, they are most important for the comprehensive way they present the historical context of Lanny's life. As William Bloodworth puts it, the novels seem to "include about everything presented on the front page of the *New York Times* for nearly forty years" (144). Assessing the cycle through the optic of **Georg Lukács's** important discussions of the historical novel, André Muraire rightly concludes that the cyle shows a fundamentally bourgeois orientation in Sinclair's aesthetic and historical vision (197). Nevertheless, the novels together constitute an important commentary on the tumultuous history of the first half of the twentieth century that is generally sympathetic to leftist causes, even if Sinclair is never fully able to transcend the worldview of the bourgeoisie and ultimately winds up, by the end of the cycle, in the camp of **cold-war anticommunism**. Sinclair continued to write, but seemed after **World War II** like a voice from an increasingly distant American past.

Selected Bibliography: Bloodworth, William A., Jr. *Upton Sinclair*. Boston: Twayne, 1977; Harris, Leon. *Upton Sinclair: American Rebel*. New York: Crowell, 1975; Homberger, Eric. *American Writers and Radical Politics: Equivocal Commitments, 1900–39*. New York: St. Martin's, 1989; Muraire, André. "History and Ideology in the 'World's End' Series." *Upton Sinclair: Literature and Social Reform*. Ed. Dieter Herms. New York: Peter Lang, 1990. 195–205; Scott, Ivan. *Upton Sinclair: The Forgotten Socialist*. Lewis, NY: Edwin Mellen, 1997.

Paul Buhle

SLAVE NARRATIVES. The North American slave narrative as it developed in the nineteenth century testifies to the fact that early American literature was not only born of conflict between diverse peoples but also heavily weighted with religious, political, and didactic significance. The genre that was to be made famous by African American writers such as Olaudah Equiano, **Frederick Douglass**, Harriet Jacobs, William Wells Brown, and Henry Bibb originated in the captivity narratives of the seventeenth and eighteenth centuries. These were the stories of European settlers, such as the British expatriate Mary Rowlandson, who were taken into captivity by Native Americans as a result of raids on Puritan settlements. By the late eighteenth and early nineteenth centuries, the concerns of the European female captivity genre became the domain of the slave narrative. This quintessentially American literary genre registered a *volte-face* in national consciousness, as it was inspired by an Enlightenment belief in man's natural capacity for both rational thought and reform. All slave narratives, of whatever period or place, share a determination to dramatize one individual's journey from slavery to freedom for the benefit of converting their audiences to the abolition of slavery. Key features to be found in most, if not all, such works include a narration of wrongs to prove both "man's inhumanity to man" as well as the martyrdom of the suffering slave; an innocent childhood followed by an awakening into the rigors of the slave system to expose its perversion of the natural order; a religious conversion to displace notions of black bestiality in favor of establishing the slave's humanity; a discussion of the acquisition of literacy and a celebration of literary prowess by a demonstrably complex use of language; and, finally, a moment of epiphany in which the slave becomes independent and free, in thought if not in reality. Famous practitioners of the form were African American men such as Douglass and Brown who used the genre as a public forum within which to establish their independence and their exemplary manhood. This prompted ex-slave women such as Jacobs to write their own narratives, lamenting that "slavery is terrible for men, but it is far more terrible for women." Their attempts to tell their story resulted in a particularly creative experimentation with the genre, as they fused conventions of the sentimental novel, religious conversion narrative, and **gothic** tale with the slave narrative. The significance of the slave narrative for African American literature cannot be overestimated, as it continues to inspire numerous works in the twentieth and twenty-first centuries—not least among them Octavia Butler's *Kindred* (1979), **Toni Morrison's *Beloved*** (1987), and Charles Johnson's *Middle Passage* (1990). Today, the demand for slave narratives remains undiminished, as 2004 saw the publication of the Sudanese born Mende Nazer's *Slave,* which testifies to her importance as living proof of the continuing presence of slavery in the modern world.

Selected Bibliography: Andrews, William L. *To Tell a Free Story: The First Century of Afro-American Autobiography, 1760–1865.* Urbana: Illinois UP, 1986; Davis, Charles T., and Henry Louis Gates Jr. *The Slave's Narrative.* Oxford: Oxford UP, 1985; Rushdy, Ashraf. *Neo-Slave Narratives: Studies in the Social Logic of a Literary Form.* Oxford: Oxford UP, 1999; Sekora, John, and Darwin T. Turner, eds. *The Art of the Slave Narrative: Original Essays in Criticism and Theory.* Macomb: Western Illinois UP, 1982; Taylor, Yuval, ed. *I Was Born a Slave: An Anthology of Classic Slave Narratives.* 2 vols. Edinburgh: Payback, 1999.

Celeste-Marie Bernier

SLESINGER, TESS (1905–1945). A New Yorker from a highly assimilated third-generation Jewish-American family, Slesinger attended Swarthmore College and Columbia University School of Journalism. Between 1930 and 1936, she published twenty-two stories in mainstream and literary magazines. In them, she used stream-of-consciousness to probe personal relationships and explored the ways in which gender, class, race, and politics affect the individual. These stories include "White on Black" (1930), which examines racial discrimination in a progressive private school, and "Missis Flinders" (1932), the first story depicting abortion published in a general-circulation magazine.

Slesinger's 1934 novel, *The Unpossessed,* originated in her marriage to Herbert Solow (1927), which ended in divorce (1932) after he insisted that Slesinger have an abortion for political reasons. Solow was assistant editor of the *Menorah Journal,* which began in 1915 to encourage Jewish humanism in America but moved to the left in the early years of the Depression. Through Solow, Slesinger became part of a group surrounding the editor, Elliott Cohen, the later founder of *Commentary.* The circle has since been identified as the earliest source of the New York literary Left.

The first Depression-era novel to treat radical urban intellectuals, *The Unpossessed* is a modernist satire of the Old Left, written from a feminist perspective that questions the separation between private and political life and the place and purpose of the intellectual. The novel was widely and generally favorably reviewed, but also politically controversial because it both mocked and sympathized with radical intellectuals.

In 1935, after publishing *Time: The Present* (selected stories), Slesinger was brought to Hollywood to coauthor the film script for Pearl Buck's *The Good Earth* (released 1937). Slesinger eventually scripted seven films, often working in collaboration with her second husband, Frank Davis (1936)—a former producer who consciously left management for labor when they formed a screenwriting team. Slesinger's other scripts include *Dance, Girl, Dance* (1940), now considered an important protofeminist film, and *A Tree Grows in Brooklyn* (1945), based on the popular novel by Betty Smith.

In Hollywood, Slesinger, who in New York had picketed to support white-collar unionizing, helped establish the Screen Writers Guild—the first film-industry union—whose founding, though bitterly opposed by the producers, was vindicated in an early decision by the NRLB (1938). She also supported many left-wing causes and served on the executive board of the Motion Picture Guild, which encouraged the production of liberal and progressive films. Though she never joined the **Communist Party**, Slesinger attended several conventions of the Writers League of America and supported the **Popular Front**. Slesinger was returning to the full-time writing of fiction when she died of cancer, leaving behind fragments of a serious Hollywood novel exploring connections between personal life and social action in the context of work and politics in the film industry.

Selected Bibliography: Rabinowitz, Paula. *Labor and Desire: Women's Revolutionary Fiction in Depression America.* Chapel Hill: U of North Carolina P, 1991; Sharistanian, Janet. "Tess Slesinger's Hollywood Sketches." *Michigan Quarterly Review* 18.3 (Summer 1979): 429–54; Teres, Harvey M. *Renewing the Left: Politics, Imagination, and the New York Intellectuals.* New York: Oxford UP, 1996; Wald, Alan M. *The New York Intellectuals: The Rise and Decline of the Anti-Stalinist Left from the 1930s to the 1980s.* Chapel Hill: U of North Carolina P, 1987.

Janet Sharistanian

SMEDLEY, AGNES (1892–1950).

SMEDLEY, AGNES (1892–1950). Born into extreme poverty in rural Missouri, Smedley went on to produce some of the best autobiographical fiction and reportage to come out of American **proletarian literature**. Her dual commitment to anti-imperialist politics and feminism originated in the class exploitation and misogyny that pervaded her childhood in the American West. Though Smedley felt that the fight against Western colonialism was the key to combating sexism and racism worldwide, a persistent theme throughout her work is the explicit misogyny of male-dominated revolutionary movements.

Attracted to socialism because of its commitment to women's rights and its opposition to U.S. involvement in **World War I**, Smedley began her political career writing for the *Call*, the official paper of the American Socialist Party. Simultaneously, inspired by anti-imperialist activist Lajpat Rai, she began studying to be a teacher in India. After being arrested for espionage and jailed for her ties to the Indian nationalist movement, Smedley worked at Margaret Sanger's *Birth Control Review* and then moved to Berlin, where she established birth-control clinics and became a prominent member of the Indian nationalist movement, along with her husband, Vivenranath Chattopadhyaya. When accusations of promiscuity ended both her marriage and her political effectiveness, Smedley went to China, where women played a prominent part in the struggle against Japanese imperialism. She served as a war correspondent, traveling with the Red Army in central China. Her sympathetic portrayals of the Chinese Communists' fight against both the Japanese and Chiang Kai-shek's nationalist forces helped forge international ties in the fight against fascism. Upon her return to the United States, she became a leading expert on policy toward China. As that policy shifted from antifascist **Popular Front**ism to **cold-war anticommunism**, however, she was blackballed. She spent the remainder of her life struggling to make a living and to redeem her reputation.

Smedley's writing is marked by its autobiographical character and by its refusal to romanticize working-class life. Her most influential work is the fictional autobiography *Daughter of Earth* (1929), a central text in both the feminist and the U.S. proletarian canons. The novel is particularly notable for its portrayals of the psychology of sexual oppression and the contradictions arising from women's involvement in radical politics. Her subsequent books, *China Fights Back* (1937) and *Battle Hymn of China* (1943), are both important examples of radical documentary reportage. Some of her best reportage is collected in the anthology *Portraits of Chinese Women in Revolution*.

Selected Bibliography: Guttman, Sondra. "Working Towards 'Unity in Diversity': Rape and the Reconciliation of Color and Comrade in Agnes Smedley's *Daughter of Earth*." *Studies in the Novel* 32.4 (Winter 2000): 488–514; MacKinnon, Janice R., and Stephan R. MacKinnon. *Agnes Smedley: The Life and Times of an American Radical*. Berkeley: U of California P, 1988; Rabinowitz, Paula. "Ending Difference/Different Endings: Class, Closure, and Collectivity in Women's Proletarian Fiction." *Genders* 8 (Summer 1990): 62–77.

Sondra Guttman

SOCIALIST REALISM (SOVIET). Term applied to the official method of Soviet literature and literary criticism, introduced at the first **Soviet Writers' Congress** in 1934. It was defined in the bylaws of the Union of Soviet Writers as follows: "Socialist realism, being the basic method of Soviet imaginative literature and literary criticism, demands from the artist a truthful, historically concrete depiction of reality in its revolutionary development. At the same time this truthfulness and historical concreteness of the artistic depiction of reality must be combined with the task of the ideological molding and education of the working people in the spirit of socialism" (qtd. in Ermolaev 197). The definition remarkably sums up the dialectic that was at work as long as the "method" was alive: socialist realism *was* a propaganda tool of the Soviet state and its **Communist Party**, but one that never ceased to truthfully reflect, depict, and express the contradictions of Soviet reality, caught between utopian impulse and state building. Even if most of it is outdated from today's perspective, socialist-realist literature gives us a remarkable insight into Soviet history, the Soviet socialist project, and the attempt to create a literature from below.

Not written by and for a cultural elite, socialist realism was not addressed to a mass consumer either. Socialist-realist writing was a storytelling of sorts, not unlike the "dreambird that hatches the egg of experience," the disappearance of which was mourned by Walter Benjamin (91). Its nesting place was the Soviet Union in flux, caught between the traditional village, the collective farm, the ruralized city, and the new settlements of blast furnaces, a country struggling to construct modernity and socialism at the same time. From the time of the "classics" of socialist realism of the early 1930s to that of the "varnished" novels of the post–**World War II** era, many authors and readers were looking for something that was called, in the West, the "public sphere," a place where storytelling and listening was still possible (or hoped for), where authors, critics, readers, the larger public, and the state could meet and read the book of progress and socialism aloud.

The Historical Context

The historical context in which the term and concept of socialist realism emerged was **Joseph Stalin**'s "great break"—that is, the collectivization and industrialization drive of 1929–1931, and its accompanying cultural revolution. The slogan "socialist realism" appeared for the first time on May 23, 1932, in the publication—by the newspaper *Literaturnaya gazeta*—of a speech made by the chairman of the organizational committee of the Writers' Congress, I. M. Gronsky, during a conference of various Moscow literary circles. One month before, all existing proletarian organizations in literature and in the other arts had been dissolved by the famous Central Committee directive "On the Restructuring of Literary-Artistic Organizations." Stalin's role in the coining of the term and the often quoted expression that writers should be the "engineers of the human soul" is not fully documented, but there is no doubt that he was personally involved in the reorganization of literature and its institutions. More important, however, is the shift from the term "proletarian" to "socialist," which marks the ideological changes from the late 1920s to the early 1930s. According to the directives of the 27th congress of the party (January 30–February 4, 1932), the positive results of the first Five-Year Plan testified that the foundations of a classless, socialist society were laid. Literature should thus truthfully depict the changed reality by adapting to it. In a speech honoring a comrade fallen victim to the counter-revolution, Gleb Chumalov—the hero of **Fyodor Gladkov**'s *Cement*, a novel generally attributed to the canon of socialist realism—refers to the "tremendous task of building socialism." In a previous—mid-1920s—version of the same text, Chumalov spoke about the "great work of building up the Workers' Republic." After its first serialized publication in the journal *Krasnaya Nov'* in 1925, the novel underwent thirty-six editions until Gladkov's death (1958) and has earned, thanks to the relentless labor of its author, the reputation of Soviet self-censorship incarnate. At the time, **Max Eastman** called these types of writers "artists in uniform." But while many *literati* under Stalin and beyond were undoubtedly framed, humiliated, persecuted, and silenced, to apply to those who published and continued publishing the label of literary hacks and lackeys is too easy and too simple. We know from late- and post-Soviet sources that the immediacy that characterized the first volume of **Mikhail Sholokhov**'s *Virgin Soil Upturned* was related to the dramatic correspondence that the author had with Stalin about the excesses of collectivization in the Don region, to which Sholokhov was, indeed, an eyewitness. We also know that the dry and boring dialogues and descriptions of Vasily Azhaev's production novel *Far from Moscow* (Stalin Prize, first class, 1949) were the traumatic product of the "two lines" of his life that the author desperately attempted to keep alive and separate—the "objective" line and the "subjective." The author's personal gulag experiences and his faith in socialism were inescapably entangled. And we know that the readers of socialist realism—and there were many—were capable of reading and feeling between and beyond the lines (Lahusen 151–78). Perhaps Soviet literature was the "synthesis of the wishes and directives of the state and 'mass graphomania,'" as Evgeny Dobrenko has suggested (*State Writer* 210). Finally, the specificity of Soviet socialist realism lies in the paradox that this literature was simultaneously in a state of petrification and flux due to the particular modes of the Soviet politicization of literature, in which writers, readers, and the state at large participated.

The Principles of Socialist Realism

Flux was not limited to the phenomenon of rewriting. The fundamental principles of socialist realism were themselves prone to change. For example, the second part of the definition of socialist realism—"the task of the ideological molding and education of the working people in the spirit of socialism"—was deleted from the by-laws during the second Soviet Writers' Congress in 1954 because it could serve as a pretext of idealization of Soviet reality. However, the text was restored during the third congress in 1959. As noted by Hans Günther in his pathbreaking and so far unequaled book on the development of the socialist-realist canon in the Soviet literature of the 1930s, "the ideological postulates of socialist realism are not well-defined terms, but labels that are semantically flexible, at times even diffuse. And it is because of their flexibility and capacity for adaptation that they can fulfill their regulatory function" (*Die Verstaatlichung* 18, my translation). The discussion that follows employs Günther's presentation of some of the main postulates of socialist realism, limited to the canonical context of the 1930s: the party spirit or party-mindedness (*partiinost'*), the theory of reflection, the typical (or "typicity"), revolutionary romanticism, the positive hero, and the "national/popular spirit" (*narodnost'*).

The party spirit can be considered as the central ideological postulate of socialist realism. Originating in **Vladimir Lenin**'s 1905 article "Party Organization and Party Literature," it was meant, on the one hand, to implement the monopoly of the party over literary life and its institutions. On the other hand, it had an aesthetic, normative function for the literary discourse itself, offering the writers two choices: to be a "screw" in the party "mechanism" or to be an outsider. It is only during the efforts of decanonization during the late 1950s that the historical context in which Lenin's article was produced (as part of the inner-party discussion of 1905) was reintroduced.

Lenin's theory of reflection, as expressed in his articles on **Leo Tolstoy** (1908, 1910), in *Materialism and Empirio-Criticism* (1909), and in his *Philosophical Notebooks* (1914–1915, published in 1929–1930), was transformed into an ideological-normative postulate during the early 1930s, giving directives about what to consider "correct" and "erroneous" reflections. During the second part of the 1930s, **Georg Lukács** and other collaborators of the journal *Literaturnyi kritik* attempted to uphold the cognitive concept of Lenin's original reflection theory. In his 1935 article "Concerning the Problem of the Objectivity of the Artistic Form," Lukács reached back to Lenin's understanding of the spontaneous materialism of great artists, which could lead to an objective reflection of reality, despite their idealist worldview. Being a way to challenge the idea that reflection was *only* a matter of the "correct ideology," these views fell victim to attacks that reaffirmed the dominant role of ideology in literature.

"Realism, to my mind, implies, besides truth of detail, the truthful reproduction of typical characters under typical circumstances." These lines from Friedrich Engels's often-quoted letter to Margaret Harkness of 1888 became one of the cornerstones of the socialist-realist dogma, with an emphasis on the normative and the prophetic: at stake is not the faithful rendition of what *is*, but of *what ought to be* in its ideological perspective. But the older concept of the typical as an empirical, verifiable category, used to define realism, resurfaced periodically. It was used, for example, after Stalin's death to criticize the "varnishing of reality" and "conflictlessness" of the literature produced during the Zhdanov era.

The following formula of revolutionary romanticism is taken from **Maxim Gorky**'s speech at the Writers' Congress: "[I]f to the idea extracted from the given reality we add—completing the idea, by the logic of hypothesis—the desired, the possible, and thus supplement the image, we obtain that romanticism which is at the basis of myth and is highly beneficial in that it tends to provoke a revolutionary attitude to reality, an attitude that changes the world in a practical way" (Gorky et al. 44). Even if Gorky's views—and persona—entered the canon, the concept of revolutionary romanticism was part of a debate of which Alexander Fadeev's 1929 article "Down with Schiller" is a famous and, at the same time, contradictory manifestation. Espousing the antiromantic arguments of the Russian Association of Proletarian Writers (RAPP), equating realism with materialism and romanticism with idealism, the article argued also that revolutionary romanticism, in contradistinction to the romanticism of "the old professors of literature," expressed the ideological perspective contained in Marxism-Leninism, the unavoidable victory of the new over the old. RAPP's views continued to be represented by critics such as V. M. Kirshon and E. Usievich and, later, Lukács, who argued that the slogan of romanticism could mask tendencies of idealization and subjectivism.

The positive hero of socialist realism originates in a long tradition of "new men" in Russian literature, from **Nikolai Chernyshevsky**'s *What Is to Be Done?* (1863) to Gorky's 1906 novel ***Mother***. But it was Gorky's contribution to the volume *Essay of a Philosophy of Collectivism* (1909), opposing the new man to the "superfluous man" (a nineteenth-century conception), that laid the foundations of the socialist-realist definition of the 1930s. On the one hand, the positive hero was a negation of the superfluous man; on the other hand, Gorky referred to heroic figures of the epic and folkloric tradition. For Gorky, heroes were part of the present Soviet reality, but they simply did not realize it. The task of literature was to give them this heroic reflection. Like other principles of socialist realism, the positive hero is not a constant, fixed category but a flexible model within certain limits, endowed with various characteristics. For the canonical period, the portrayal of the positive hero tended to be monolithic; no significant negative aspects were to disturb the overall positive image.

The Russian word *narod* is one of those "untranslatable" words that reveals trouble with its content. In the Russian nineteenth-century context, it translates as the "nation" as well as the "people," depending on who was using it and for what. *Narodnost'* was the second term of the official triad "Autocracy, National Character (or Spirit), Orthodoxy" under Tsar Nicholas I. During the mid-1930s, the "popular" (and proletarian) content of *narodnost'* was increasingly replaced by the "national," with the emphasis, in public discourse, on the socialist "motherland" (*rodina*), the Russian national tradition, and the needs of the masses for a "simple," "natural," "understandable," "harmonious," and "healthy" literature. The other arts, such as theater, music, and painting, followed suit. The campaigns against "vulgar sociologism," naturalism, and formalism of the years 1935–1936 were conducted in the name of *narodnost'*. Under the banner of socialist-realist *narodnost'*, the Russian nineteenth-century literary and critical tradition was reintroduced and reified, together with the call to create a "Soviet classicism," foreshadowing the chauvinistic tendencies of the postwar years.

Interpretations of Socialist Realism

The critical discourse about socialist realism is an intrinsic aspect of the method itself. Since its elaboration before, during, and after the first Writers' Congress, its fundamental categories and principles were relentlessly debated and reinterpreted not only by literary authorities, critics, party leaders, and state officials, but also by an ocean of readers, who produced a tidal wave of opinions for the writers, who, in turn, responded as best they could by rewriting their works. This explains why previous interpretations of what socialist-realist literature ought to be could disappear or resurface, according to the line of the day.

From after Stalin's death and the "thaw" until the mid-1980s, socialist realism remained the official "method" of Soviet literature. But even if its "classics" continued to be published in enormous print runs, it went into a steady decline. Despite regular and persistent attempts to keep it alive—above all, by "theoretical" and official statements—socialist realism became the object of serious challenges in the literary practice of post-1956 Soviet culture, becoming practically replaced by youth and village prose, urban prose, and dissident literature published in the underground (*samizdat*) or abroad (*tamizdat*). The first direct blow to socialist realism can be considered as an example of the latter. Written in Moscow, Andrei Siniavsky's pamphlet *On Socialist Realism* was published under the pseudonym Abram Tertz in the West in 1959. For this and subsequent publications, the author was arrested, put on trial, and sentenced to six years in a labor camp. In this fiercely ironical attack, socialist realism was characterized as a rupture with the Russian nineteenth-century heritage, its "superfluous man," and "the destructive laughter that was the chronic disease of Russian culture from **Pushkin** to Blok and [which] reached its climax among the decadents" (Tertz 74). Tertz considered socialist realism much closer to eighteenth-century Russian classicism, with which it had in common political purposefulness and the "pompous simplicity of style." Trying to "combine the uncombinable" that is, the high ideal with the truthful representation of life—the socialist realist writer, according to Tertz, ends up by producing a "half-classicist half-art, which is none too socialist and not at all realist" (84, 90–91). From today's perspective, the pamphlet can be considered as a witty and altogether typical dissident document, from which accents of the elitist tradition of the Russian intelligentsia are not entirely absent. No wonder, therefore, that its principal message, questioning the literary value of socialist realism, was embraced by critics in the West in the context of the **cold war** for decades to come.

C. Vaughan James's *Soviet Socialist Realism: Origins and Theory*, published in 1973, can be considered the exact counterpart of that type of interpretation. His book is a "de-Stalinized" attempt at reevaluation from a Western communist perspective. Defining socialist realism as "a world-wide artistic phenomenon" that was the "reflection in the arts of the struggle for the victory of socialism," the author reiterates, for the most part, the well-known principles, such as the party spirit, typicity, revolutionary romanticism, and *narodnost'*. Also valuable are the appendices of the book, containing some fundamental texts, such as Lenin's "Party Organization and Party Literature" and the text of the 1932 Central Committee's decree on the restructuration of literary-artistic organizations.

A decisive step away from (left or right) ideological postulates is Vera S. Dunham's stunning exercise in Soviet literary sociology, *In Stalin's Time: Middleclass Values in Soviet Fiction*, first published in 1976. Dunham focuses on Soviet postwar literature, which she defines as a "middlebrow fiction," reflecting what she calls the "Big Deal" between the state and a new middle class, "born out of Stalin's push for the industrialization, reeducation, and bureaucratization of the country, flesh of the flesh of Stalin's revolutions from above in the thirties, and ready to fill the vacuum created by Stalin's Great Purge and by the liquidation of the Leninist generation of activists" (13). Socialist-realist categories receive in Dunham's book a new, context-bound interpretation. The "positive hero," for example, "comes from a gap between the real and the ideal, his character revealing itself in confrontation not with the ideal but with real problems" (30). Fiction, therefore, became a "safety valve," serving to detect problems and leading to their diagnosis. Dunham was one of the first to understand the social use of socialist-realist fiction and anticipated for about twenty years the scholarship of the 1990s focusing on the production and reception of Soviet literature: "At that tragic time, and in a unique way, literature stood between the regime and the people, and constituted the conversation between the two. . . . Neither before nor after that period did literature, banal, dry and tendentious as it was, mean so much to the reader" (24–25).

In Katerina Clark's influential book *The Soviet Novel: History as Ritual* (1985), socialist-realist fiction is defined by one overarching "master plot," which is itself a parable for the "spontaneity"-"consciousness" dialectic by which, for Marxism-Leninism, history progresses. Consciousness (*soznatel'nost'*) designs actions—political activities that are controlled, disciplined, and guided by politically enlightened leaders. Spontaneity (*stikhiinost'*) stands for elemental, uncontrollable forces (of nature, of the non-educated masses, the "darkness" of the spontaneous peasants). The resolution of the master plot is the working out of the dialectic by the final triumph of consciousness. In this parabolic structure, the "positive hero" undergoes some personal revolution when he passes in stages from a state of spontaneity to a higher degree of consciousness. According to Clark, in Gorky's novel *Mother* (1906), the spontaneity-consciousness dialectic was already at work, but it is only during the 1930s that socialist realism's master plot was worked out, together with one of the fundamental myths of Stalinist political culture—the myth of the "great family," in which Soviet society and history are described in terms of a hierarchy of fathers and sons. The spontaneous "sons" are educated to political consciousness by the "fathers." In this sense, the socialist-realist novel is a politicized **bildungsroman**. What distinguishes earlier revolutionary fiction from the Soviet novel of the 1920s and 1930s is the replacement of the biological family with a symbolic one. In *Mother*, the hero comes to consciousness thanks to her son. In *Cement*, for example, as in many other Soviet novels of the time, the hero cuts off his/her biological ties, while the "fathers" are now political mentors, such as more conscious workers, military commanders, and party activists. Clark's "master plot" applies to the following typology of Soviet novels: the production novel, the historical novel, the novel about the worthy intellectual or inventor, the novel of war and revolution, the villain or the spy novel, the novel about the West. The first three types are the most common and representative. In the postwar period, the master plot is still alive, but loses its inner force and logic because of the cliched rhetoric of what is otherwise known as "varnishing" and "conflictlessness." Clark's analysis of the Soviet socialist-realist novel is heavily influenced by the structuralist model, in particular by Vladimir Propp's *Morphology of the Folk Tale* (1928), from whom she borrows a number of "functions" to show the progression of the prototypical socialist-realist plot. Undeniably seductive and pedagogical, this model also has a major weakness: because the text has been reduced to a mere political ritual, some of what is most interesting *politically* in socialist-realist novels—its aesthetic and plot variations—disappears.

A work that underlines the inadequacy of Clark's Proppian model for allowing no secondary "transversal" narrative programs is Régine Robin's *Socialist Realism: An Impossible Aesthetic*, first published in French in 1986. Following Marc Angenot's "social discourse" project, of which Robin was one of the cofounders, Robin traces "the discursive base" of socialist realism forward from the mid-nineteenth century. Upon arrival, this base is censured; frozen; fixed in preexisting, preconstructed, preasserted significations. The result is an "impossible aesthetics," even if certain works resist the unifying canon by their own "effet de texte." As shown by Leonid Heller in a review-debate of Robin's book, in addition to many errors and omissions, the thesis of *Socialist Realism: An Impossible Aesthetic* remains unclear, caught in between predominantly (and indiscriminately quoted) Soviet source material and Western narrative theory. For example, the Greimasian schemes of the book are not convincing because the search for equivalencies masks more than it clarifies. The socialist-realist novel is not based on symmetries of "actants" but on hierarchies: that of the leader above the subordinate, the industrial landscape above the rural, the literary-normative style above the popular, and so on (Heller, "L'esthétique" 298, my translation). Another problem with Robin's analysis is that it mythologizes the Soviet avant-garde; by emphasizing the distinction between the discursive levels of modernism and (socialist) realism, the political involvement of the Soviet avant-garde and its responsibility in the "Stalinist" transformation of Soviet culture are minimized.

Boris Groys's *The Total Art of Stalinism: Avant-Garde, Aesthetic Dictatorship, and Beyond* (1992), first published in German in 1988 under the much more telling title *Gesamtkunstwerk Stalin*, takes up precisely the issue just mentioned. Contrary to the traditional interpretation that socialist realism is the absolute antithesis of the formalist avant-garde, Groys argues that "the Stalin era satisfied the fundamental avant-garde demand that art cease representing life and begin transforming it by means of a total aesthetico-political project." According to Groys, "Socialist realism represents the party-minded, collective surrealism that flourished under Lenin's famous slogan 'it is necessary to dream.' . . . The popular definition of the method as 'the depiction of life in its revolutionary development,' 'national in form, socialist in content,' is based on this dream realism, in which a national form conceals the new socialist content: the magnificent vision of a world built by the party, the total work of art born of the will of its true creator and artist—Stalin" (38–39). The "typical" of socialist realism is therefore redefined as "Stalin's dream made visible" (39); the "positive hero" and its negative alter ego, the "wrecker," have not much to do with reflection of concrete events and motivations, but they are hagiographic or demonological depictions of transcendental events—a fact that, again, invokes the irrational and "demiurgic" practice of the avant-garde. Whether we agree with Groys's thesis or not is finally unimportant from the perspective of "post-Utopian art," to which the second half of *The Total Art of Stalinism* is devoted, and with which the author obviously identifies. In a lengthy but significant excerpt, Groys explains:

> The meaning of postutopian art is to show that history is nothing other than the history of attempts to escape history, that utopia is inherent in history and cannot be overcome in it, that the postmodernist attempt to consummate history merely continues it, as does the opposite aspiration to prove that historical progress is infinite. Postutopian art incorporates the Stalin myth into world mythology and demonstrates its family likeness with supposedly opposite myths. Beyond the historical, this art discovers not a single myth but an entire mythology, a pagan polymorphy; that is, it reveals the nonhistoricity of history itself. If Stalinist artists and writers functioned as icon painters and hagiographers, the authors of the new Russian literature and art are frivolous mytho*graphs*, chroniclers of utopian myth, but not mytho*logists*, that is, not critical commentators attempting to "reveal the true content" of myth and "enlighten" the public as to its nature by scientifically demythologizing it. (115)

The question of the relation between history and mythology is certainly to be asked about the work of Dobrenko, one of the most prolific scholars of socialist realism. From his first monograph, *Metafora vlasti: Literatura stalinskoi epokhi v istoricheskom osveshchenii* (Metaphor of Power: Literature of the Stalin Era in Historical Context, 1993) to *The Making of the State Reader: Social and Aesthetic Contexts of the Reception of Soviet Literature* (1997) and *The Making of the State Writer: Social and Aesthetic Origins of Soviet Literary Culture* (2002), Dobrenko's central thesis is that socialist realism was a cultural revolution not only from above but from below as well, that between the Soviet writer, reader, and the state, no real gap existed, and that Soviet literature was ultimately the meeting ground between two currents, the masses and state power. The two latter volumes are particularly powerful pieces of scholarship, dealing in great detail with largely unknown or hitherto unprocessed data. Most anthologies mention the same ten to fifteen canonical socialist-realist novels, including Gladkov's *Cement*, **Nikolai Ostrovsky's** ***How the Steel Was Tempered*** (1932–1934), Fadeev's *The Young Guard* (1945), Fedor Panferov's *Brusski* (1928–1937), Sholokhov's *Quiet Flows the Don* (1928–1940) and *Virgin Soil Upturned* (1932–1960), **Alexei Tolstoy's** *Peter the First* (1929–1945), and Boris Polevoy's *A Story about a Real Man* (1946). But *The Making of the State Writer* engages with the extraordinary quantity of writing that was produced during the seventy-five years of

Soviet power, with the flow of words that characterizes not only the "army of poets" but also the average verbosity of the typical Soviet text. Dobrenko's writing reproduces, at times, this "flow of words," testifying to the fact that the intense dialogue of socialist realism with itself is not unidirectional and is unfinished. This open-endedness is perhaps what makes the "method" an unprecedented and perhaps still promising endeavor.

To document just this possibility was the goal of the volume *Socialist Realism without Shores* (1997) and of *How Life Writes the Book: Real Socialism and Socialist Realism in Stalin's Russia* (1997). The first gives the occasion to a number of specialists to assess or reassess their positions about socialist realism, its aesthetics or politics, or both. In his contribution to the volume, Leonid Heller shows that the discussions about socialist-realist aesthetics and art were carried out within a continuum of incessant local turbulences and stormy overturnings of the general line. The cultural system of socialist realism was anything but static. "It operated according to an 'uncertainty principle' of sorts, analogous to what Heisenberg formulated for quantum physics: that is, the spin and the position of a particle cannot be simultaneously determined, nor its trajectory predicted, just as the ups and downs of the Party line, of the whole system, were always unpredictable, despite the codification of all its elements" ("World" 58). Similarly, *How Life Writes the Book*, grounded on the extensive personal archive of a Stalinist writer, is an inquiry into the production of a socialist (realist) text and life that attempts to show that being a Soviet "subject" and writing about it was more complicated, dramatic, rewarding, and, above all, unpredictable, than generally assumed.

Selected Bibliography: Baudin, Antoine. *Le Réalisme socialiste soviétique de la période jdanovienne, 1947–1952. Vol. 1: Les Arts plastiques et leurs institutions.* Bern: Peter Lang, 1997; Baudin, Antoine, and Leonid Heller. *Le Réalisme socialiste soviétique de la période jdanovienne, 1947–1952. Vol. 2: Usages à l'intérieur, image à exporter.* Bern: Peter Lang, 1998; Benjamin, Walter. *Illuminations.* New York: Harcourt, Brace and World, 1968; Clark, Katerina. *The Soviet Novel: History as Ritual.* Chicago: U of Chicago P, 1985; Dobrenko, Evgeny. *The Making of the State Reader: Social and Aesthetic Contexts of the Reception of Soviet Literature.* Trans. Jesse M. Savage. Stanford, CA: Stanford UP, 1997; Dobrenko, Evgeny. *The Making of the State Writer: Social and Aesthetic Origins of Soviet Literary Culture.* Trans. Jesse M. Savage. Stanford, CA: Stanford UP, 2002; Dobrenko, Evgeny. *Metafora vlasti: Literatura stalinskoi epokhi v istoricheskom osveshchenii.* Munich: Otto Sagner, 1993; Dunham, Vera S. *In Stalin's Time: Middleclass Values in Soviet Fiction.* Enlarged and updated ed. Durham, NC: Duke UP, 1990; Eastman, Max. *Artists in Uniform: A Study of Literature and Bureaucratism.* New York: Knopf, 1934; Ermolaev, Herman. *Soviet Literary Theories, 1917–1934: The Genesis of Socialist Realism.* Berkeley: U of California P, 1963; Gorky, Maxim, et al. *Soviet Writers' Congress, 1934: The Debate on Socialist Realism and Modernism in the Soviet Union.* London: Lawrence and Wishart, 1977; Groys, Boris. *The Total Art of Stalinism: Avant-Garde, Aesthetic Dictatorship, and Beyond.* Trans. Charles Rougle. Princeton, NJ: Princeton UP, 1992; Günther, Hans. *Die Verstaatlichung der Literatur. Entstehung und Funktionsweise des sozialistisch-realistischen Kanons in der Sowjetischen Literatur der 30 er Jahre.* Stuttgart: J. B. Metzler, 1984; Günther, Hans, ed. *The Culture of the Stalin Period.* New York: St. Martin's, 1990; Günther, Hans, and Evgeny Dobrenko, eds. *Sotsrealisticheskii kanon.* St. Petersburg: Akademicheskii proekt, 2000; Heller, Leonid. "L'Esthétique réaliste socialiste est-elle possible? A propos de l'ouvrage de Régine Robin, *Le Réalisme socialiste: Une esthétique impossible.*" *Revue des études slaves* 61.3 (1989): 293–305; Heller, Leonid. "A World of Prettiness: Socialist Realism and Its Aesthetic Categories." *Socialist Realism with-*

out Shores. Ed. Thomas Lahusen and Evgeny Dobrenko. Durham, NC: Duke UP, 1997. 687–714; James, C. Vaughan. *Soviet Socialist Realism: Origins and Theory*. New York: St. Martin's, 1973; Lahusen, Thomas. *How Life Writes the Book: Real Socialism and Socialist Realism in Stalin's Russia*. Ithaca, NY: Cornell UP, 1997; Lahusen, Thomas, and Evgeny Dobrenko, eds. *Socialist Realism without Shores*. Durham, NC: Duke UP, 1997; Robin, Régine. *Socialist Realism: An Impossible Aesthetic*. Stanford: Stanford UP, 1992; Tertz, Abram. *On Socialist Realism*. Trans. George Dennis. Intro. Czeslaw Milosz. New York: Pantheon, 1960.

Thomas Lahusen

SOLZHENITSYN, ALEKSANDR ISAEVICH (1918–). Solzhenitsyn became world famous during his lifetime for his extraordinarily dramatic life and his voluminous writings. Born in Kislovodsk and educated at Rostov University, he served as an artillery captain in the Soviet army during **World War II** until he was arrested in 1945 for incautious remarks about **Stalin** made in a private letter. He spent eight years in prison camps and three in internal exile under the punishment system known by its acronym, gulag, which through his subsequent writing has become a familiar common noun. While in prison, Solzhenitsyn turned from the Marxism-Leninism of his university days to the Russian Orthodoxy of his early rearing. Also, he launched his lifelong career of writing in opposition to Soviet communism. Given the climate of the **cold war**, the Western press avidly followed the struggle between dissenting author and government power. In 1970, he received the Nobel Prize in Literature. In 1974, after the KGB discovered a copy of *The Gulag Archipelago*—his massive account of Soviet concentration camps—he was exiled, and he and his family moved to Cavendish, Vermont, in 1976. After the Soviet Union collapsed, Solzhenitsyn returned home in 1994, locating near Moscow.

Solzhenitsyn wrote in many genres: novels, short stories, prose poems, plays, poetry, polemical essays, memoirs, and historical treatises. He became an overnight sensation when *One Day in the Life of Ivan Denisovich* was legally published in 1962. This novella and *The Gulag Archipelago* (1973–1976) are his best-known works. Also widely read are the novels *The First Circle* and *Cancer Ward*, the short story "Matryona's Home," and *The Oak and the Calf*, sketches of his life as an underground writer. His *magnum opus, The Red Wheel*—five-thousand pages of historical fiction with separate installments on August 1914, November 1916, March 1917, and April 1917— is not yet fully available in major languages.

Initially lionized in the West as an anti-totalitarian freedom fighter, Solzhenitsyn became embroiled in controversy soon after his exile. Journalistic reaction to his celebrated Harvard commencement speech in 1978 cemented in place a negative consensus that had begun to harden in 1974, when his *Letter to the Soviet Leaders* was published. Disapproving critics describe him as a Jeremiah figure with anti-Western and antidemocratic tendencies. Sympathetic critics describe him as a religious believer, a Russian patriot, a centrist in politics, and an inveterate optimist whose works typically conclude on the note of hope. In any case, detractors and admirers alike typically acknowledge the power of his work and accord *One Day in the Life of Ivan Denisovich* and *The Gulag Archipelago* some role in bringing the Soviet Union to an end.

Selected Bibliography: Dunlop, John B., Richard Haugh, and Alexis Klimoff, eds. *Aleksandr Solzhenitsyn: Critical Essays and Documentary Materials*. 2nd ed. New York: Collier, 1975; Dunlop, John B.,

Richard Haugh, and Michael Nicholson, eds. *Solzhenitsyn in Exile: Critical Essays and Documentary Materials*. Stanford: Hoover Institution P, 1985; Ericson, Edward E., Jr. *Solzhenitsyn and the Modern World*. Washington: Regnery Gateway, 1993; Mahoney, Daniel J. *Aleksandr Solzhenitsyn: The Ascent from Ideology*. Lanham, MD: Rowman and Littlefield, 2001; Scammell, Michael. *Solzhenitsyn: A Biography*. New York: Norton, 1984.

Edward E. Ericson Jr.

SOUTH AFRICAN LITERATURE. Before the European intrusion, orature—praise poems, folktales, riddles and proverbs—was dominant among the preliterate African societies of South Africa. European intrusion in the region began with the Dutch East India Company in 1652, followed by the British in the early nineteenth century. The Europeans brought written literature to the region, beginning with the colonial adventure romance fiction written by visitors (Rider Haggard, Percy Fitzpatrick) and continuing into the present by local authors such as Wilbur Smith. The 1820 settler Thomas Pringle sounded a new liberal humanist note in his poetry, sympathetic to the indigenous people and critical of colonial practices. Olive Schreiner was the first South African to achieve international status as a "free-thinking" feminist and anticolonial writer with the first critical realist South African novel, *The Story of an African Farm* (1883), beginning a tradition that would reach its height with Alan Paton and **Nadine Gordimer**.

Two popular novelistic genres were initiated by British journalists: Percival Gibbon's novel *Margaret Harding* (1911) was the first to deal with "love across the colourbar" in an antiracist spirit, while Douglas Blackburn's *Leaven: A Black and White Story* (1908) began the "Jim Comes to Joburg" story of black migration from rural tradition to the modern city, condemning the colonial industrializing process centered in the Witwatersrand.

In the early twentieth century, black writing began properly to emerge with such works as Thomas Mofolo's Sotho-language novel *Chaka* (submitted for publication as early as 1910, but first published in 1925) and Sol Plaatje's *Mhudi* (1930), the first black novel in English. Between the world wars, Afrikaans literature came into its own with a cosmopolitan modernist poetry movement—the "Dertigers"—implicitly resistant to nationalist parochialism.

An energetic **modernism** characterized Roy Campbell, who remains South Africa's greatest poet despite controversies over his later support—expressed in his long poem *Flowering Rifle* (1939)—for Franco's fascists in the **Spanish Civil War**. His youthful long poem *The Flaming Terrapin* (1924) was followed by the *Adamastor* (1930), a collection containing some of his best anticolonial poetry. Along with William Plomer and Laurens van der Post, Campbell launched the modernist *Voorslag* (1926) magazine, which was hostile to the avarice and philistinism of colonial culture. Plomer published the avant-garde novel *Turbott Wolfe* (1925), scandalously promoting racial and cultural hybridity. H. C. Bosman explored the rural Afrikaner in satiric short stories (*Mafeking Road* [1947]).

The institutionalization of **apartheid** after 1948 dramatically intensified the cultural hostility to racist oppression; what began as a literature of protest became by the 1980s a culture of active resistance. The ominous atmosphere was captured in

Phyllis Altman's novel *The Law of the Vultures* (1952), pointing to the inevitable rise of black militancy in the face of white intransigence. Two novels—Alan Paton's *Cry, the Beloved Country* (1948) and **Peter Abrahams'** *Mine Boy* (1946)—revealed the adverse effects of urban modernization on Africans, which had been accelerated by the manufacturing needs of **World War II**. The African National Congress and its allies launched in the 1950s a decade of increasingly militant opposition. *Drum* magazine became the outlet for black English writing; in the short stories and articles by writers such as Can Temba, Lewis Nkosi, and Nat Nakasa, a modern urban hybridized African culture was being defined. These postcolonial initiatives were closed down with the massive repression that followed the Sharpeville massacre of 1960. By 1966, scores of black authors were banned or fled into exile, thus effectively destroying an entire generation of South African writers.

Many exiled black writers, such as Eskia Mphahlele (*Down Second Avenue,* 1959) and Bloke Modisane (*Blame Me on History,* 1963), wrote autobiographies. Abrahams also wrote an autobiography (*Tell Freedom,* 1954), as well as a string of left-inclined novels about South Africa and the third-world decolonization process. **Alex La Guma**, an exiled Communist, wrote finely drawn stories such as *A Walk in the Night.* From her Botswana exile, Bessie Head produced a masterpiece in *A Question of Power* (1973). Arthur Nortje wrote desolate poems of isolation from England before killing himself in 1970. Dennis Brutus produced a stream of some of the best poetry from exile, beginning with his *Letters to Martha* (1968), dealing with his prison experiences.

In the 1960s, a new dissident and experimental voice in Afrikaans writing emerged with the Sestigers—Breyten Breytenbach, Andre Brink, and Etienne Roux. In white English poetry, technical skill and sensitivity were rarely matched by political acuteness. Guy Butler began a distinguished career with his poetry collection *Stranger to Europe* (1952). Sydney Clouts's volume *Our Life* (1966) announced a major poetic talent. Douglas Livingstone (1932–1996) emerged as one of South Africa's most profound poets with *Sjambok and Other Poems from Africa* (1964). South Africa's greatest playwright, Athol Fugard, first drew critical attention with *The Blood Knot* (1961), then went on to produce a succession of groundbreaking anti-apartheid plays, often workshopped with African collaborators.

By the late 1960s, the black consciousness movement inspired a new generation of black poets, such as Wally Serote and Sipho Sepamla. This renaissance was launched with the publication of Oswald Mtshali's *Sounds of a Cowhide Drum* (1971), which became the best-selling poetry collection in South African history. Miriam Tlali's novel *Muriel at Metropolitan* (1975) was the first novel by a black woman to be published in South Africa. The Soweto Uprisings of 1976 launched a mass struggle that drove black writers to more militant literary output, seen in Oswald Mtshali's second poetry collection, *Fireflames* (1980), and in Serote's later poetry. Serote would write the best novel dealing with the uprising, *To Every Birth Its Blood* (1981).

Black literature became part of the mass struggle against the state, mobilizing the masses at funerals, political rallies, and strike meetings. This populist turn saw the rise of performance poets such as Mzwakhe Mbuli and also the worker poets. Black theater turned agitprop, many of them staged by workers.

The white novel in English during this period reflected the growing marginalization of white liberals in a struggle dominated by black radicalism. Nobel laureate

Gordimer's early novels focused on the growing crisis and isolation of progressive whites. *The Conservationist* (1974), her masterpiece, portrays the demise of white domination and the emergence of an alternative African reality.

By far the most prominent white male novelist writing in English in South Africa today is J. M. Coetzee, who has combined a self-consciously postmodern and experimental literary style with an intense concern with the evils of apartheid to produce an impressive body of novels marked by both technical sophistication and powerful and disturbing content (showing the impact of South African political and social reality). Coetzee's novels begin with the 1974 *Dusklands*, a parody of colonialist discourse reminiscent of the work of postmodern European writers such as **Samuel Beckett** and **Vladimir Nabokov**, and *In the Heart of the Country* (1977), a stream-of-consciousness exploration of the master-slave mentality of South African society.

Coetzee gained wide attention with the 1980 novel *Waiting for the Barbarians*, which combines starkly realistic descriptions of violence with almost surrealistic scenes of symbolic imagery to brilliantly capture the systemic crisis of the apartheid state as it fails to suppress mass resistance. Meanwhile, he became the second African writer to win the Booker Prize with his 1983 novel *The Life and Times of Michael K*, which marks an increasing turn toward metafictional explorations of the nature of fiction and its role in the world. Novels such as *Foe* (1986), *Age of Iron* (1990), and *The Master of Petersburg* (1994) focus self-consciously on writers and the nature of artistic creation. In novels such as *Disgrace* (1999), Coetzee has turned to a sophisticated exploration of the ongoing psychic legacy of apartheid in contemporary South African society. *Disgrace* also awarded Coetzee his second Booker Prize, while contributing to his winning of the Nobel Prize for Literature in 2003, joining Gordimer as a winner of that prestigious award.

One of the best novelists to have emerged in the post-apartheid period (after 1994) is Zakes Mda, whose *Ways of Dying* (1995) caught the mood of internecine violence that characterized the negotiation process to end apartheid. Antjie Krog produced the best account of the deliberations of the Truth and Reconciliation Commission in her *Country of My Skull* (1998), while Coetzee's *Disgrace* confronted the endemic criminal violence of the 1990s and the need for white atonement as power moved ineluctably away from whites. The demise of apartheid has led to a flurry of autobiographies by former activists, including Nelson Mandela, Joe Slovo, and the gloriously maverick Harold Strachan (*Way Up Way Out,* 1998).

Selected Bibliography: Barnett, Ursula A. *A Vision of Order: A Study of Black South African Literature in English (1914–1980).* Amherst: U of Massachusetts P, 1983; Chapman, Michael. *Southern African Literatures.* London: Longman, 1996; Coetzee, A. J., Tim Couzens, and Stephen Gray. "South African Literatures to World War II." *European-Language Writing in Sub-Saharan Africa.* Vol 1. Ed. Albert Gerard. Budapest: Akadēmiai Kaidō, 1986. 173–213; Coetzee, A. J., and Michael Wade. "White South African Literature after World War II." *European-Language Writing in Sub-Saharan Africa.* Vol 1. Ed. Albert Gerard. Budapest: Akadēmiai Kaidō. 1986. 217–50; Gray, Stephen. *Southern African Literature: An Introduction.* Cape Town: David Philip, 1979; Ntuli, D. B., and C. F. Swanepoel. *South African Literature in African Languages: A Concise Historical Perspective.* Pretoria: Acacia, 1993; Smit, Johannes A., Johan van Wyk, and Jean-Philippe Wade, eds. *Rethinking South African Literary History.* Durban: Y Press, 1996.

Jean-Philippe Wade

SOUTH ASIAN LITERATURE. Home of more than a billion people, the South Asian subcontinent has several vibrant literary traditions and a great linguistic diversity. There are more than a dozen languages spoken in the subcontinent, not counting the innumerable local dialects. Therefore, any commentary on the subcontinent's literature must negotiate the evolution of its many languages.

Writing in the South Asian subcontinent existed as early as 3000 B.C.E.; it was used by the dark-skinned Harappans who lived in two cities in the Indus basin, now located in modern Pakistan. The Harappans, also known as Dravidians, were invaded by the light-skinned Aryans who came from central Asia and gradually assimilated them into the Aryan community, relegating them to inferior ranks and replacing their religion and culture. Sanskrit replaced the Dravidian language, and Hinduism became the dominant religion, both of which, incidentally, absorbed elements from the disappearing Dravidian culture. Derivatives of Dravidian did survive in the south, where the Aryan dominance was weak; Tamil and the other southern languages owe their origin to ancient Dravidian.

The *Vedas*, the earliest known Sanskrit texts, were written during 1500–1000 B.C.E. Poetry in the form of hymns and chants, they treat a number of topics, such as man's place in the universe, fire sacrifice, and humanity's origin. In the next two thousand years or so, Sanskrit authors produced a substantial quantity of important works. The *Upanishads*, or mystic principles, were composed by sages who questioned the Vedic doctrines. Through the setting of a teacher and his students, the *Upanishads* focus primarily on man and deal with issues of morality and personal conduct. Attributed to the author Vyasa, the *Mahabharata* still remains the longest epic in the world. With about 100,000 lines, it is nearly ten times longer than the *Iliad* and the *Odyssey* combined. The *Mahabharata* describes two warring clans of Aryans, contains the *Bhagavad Gita*, and, along with Valmiki's *Ramayana*, is regarded as a sacred text by the Hindus. Valmiki treated the life of Rama, a prince sent to exile by his machinating stepmother, in the *Ramayana*. Both works remain extremely popular among Hindus today. Used as children's literature as well as religious texts, they testify to the endurance of Hinduism for nearly four millennia.

Sanskrit scholars treated their language as sacred and were protective of its purity, forbidding non-Brahmans to deal with it. Though no longer a living language after the fifth century, Sanskrit continued to attract literary endeavors for many centuries. Since literature often needed court support in those days, the fate of Sanskrit depended on the cultural leanings of Indian rulers. During the Gupta period (335–470 C.E.), for instance, a great many Sanskrit works appeared. The Guptas were Hindu kings who actively sponsored Sanskrit writing. On the other hand, in later centuries, sometimes even a Muslim king assumed the role of a patron of Sanskrit. Sanskrit is still recognized as a language of creative endeavors in India; even now, the Indian government awards an annual prize to a Sanskrit work.

With the spread of Buddhism, which grew in resistance to Hinduism in the third century B.C.E., Prakrits, a group of regional dialects derived from Sanskrit but removed from it in colloquial form, were fast becoming the languages of learning in India. The Buddha had insisted on teaching his doctrine in the languages of the common people; many Buddhist texts, hence, were written in Pali, a vernacular form of

Sanskrit. Pali received a great deal of support from the great Mauryan king of India Asoka (269–232 B.C.E.), who had the teachings of the Buddha etched in Pali on copper plates. For a number of centuries, though, Sanskrit continued to coexist with the Prakrits, sometimes both appearing in the same work. A case in point is Kalidasa's *Sakuntala*, a play in which characters low in the social hierarchy speak graduated forms of Prakrits, as denoted by their ranks, whereas those high in the scale speak Sanskrit.

The Prakrits were loosely affiliated with different regions. The different versions retained strong similarities with but ceased to remain mutually intelligible to each other. What followed the Prakrits or, as some scholars think, the later stages of Prakrits came to be known as *Apabhramsas*, or decadent languages, perceived as decadent possibly because of their weak adherence to prescribed rules of traditional grammar and vocabulary. The history of works in these languages is sketchy and inconclusive because they were not regarded as the realm of serious scholarly or literary pursuits, which then were reserved for Sanskrit. Modern Indian languages derive from the *Apabhramsas*, the dialects of Indo-Aryan that gained prominence after 500 C.E. Written texts in them began to appear toward the end of the first millennium.

The rise of these languages occurred in two phases, both at least partially owing to political developments of external origin. Muslim invasions of India began in the eighth century; consequently, Arabic and Persian were introduced to the languages of the subcontinent, which began to absorb new words into their vocabularies. A much greater impact on the realm of culture occurred out of the fact that until the Mughal invasion in the sixteenth century, India, since Gupta rule, was split into small kingdoms and principalities, both Hindu and Muslim, and regional rulers favored regional languages.

Regional tongues earned greater legitimacy when populist religious movements, known as the *bhakti* (devotion) movements, swept across India for several centuries. Originating in Hinduism, these movements emphasized personal contact with God through simple devotion and generated exquisite lyric poetry dealing with mysticism. Though growing out of Hinduism, the devotional movements, probably under the ever-increasing influence of Islam, eschewed the polytheism of Hinduism and advocated monotheism. Rejecting caste, class, and gender discrimination, bhakti literature preached absolute equality and created communities of devotees, thus bringing about a social change. Noted figures in the school of bhakti poets include Mahadeviyakka (twelfth century), who wrote in Kannada; Vidyapati (fourteenth–fifteenth century), who belonged to the Vaisnava sect in Bangla and wrote on the love of Krishna and Radha; Kabir (fifteenth–seventeenth century), the weaver poet who authored Hindi poems deeply critical of social discrimination; and Mirabai (sixteenth century), a Rajput woman who wrote poetry on Krishna in Brajbhasa.

The second phase in the growth of local languages started with the arrival of Europeans in the subcontinent. Initially, colonial settlements were located in the coastal regions and were outposts of Portuguese, Dutch, French, and English traders, who vied with each other for trade rights from local rulers, often displacing them with brute force. The English emerged as the ultimate conquerors in the struggle for power and grew keen on developing infrastructure when their grip on the new colony became secure. Education was a major component in this administrative policy. Its thrust—as seen in the baboos, or office clerks, of Bangla—was to create a class of Indians who would serve as functionaries and intermediaries in colonial bureaucracy. British colonial education lessened the roles of Sanskrit and Persian in the curricula, placing greater stress on local languages and also on English, a process that gradually ushered in South Asia's literary modernity. Print culture played a major role in this transformation. Originally introduced in south India by the Portuguese in 1556, print technology promoted the growth of all vernacular languages, leading to a measure of codification in their grammar and mechanics and ultimately paving the way for their standardization into modern Indian languages.

British rule in India began with a stronghold in Bangla. Until 1931, Kolkata (formerly Calcutta) was its center of administration, and hence, among Indians, the Bangalis had the first contact with Enlightenment knowledge and cultural modernity. With a tradition dating back seven centuries, Bangla (also Bengali) flourished and proved adept in handling all literary genres. While poetry, fiction, and nonfiction prose developed as readership increased with the dissemination of education, drama thrived with the founding of theaters in Kolkata. Described as a "renaissance," this phase in Bangla literature spanned the entire nineteenth century and included such luminaries as the social reformer Rammohan Roy, the educator Iswarchandra Vidyasagar, the poet Michael Madhusudan Dutt, the novelist Bankimchandra Chatterjee, and the dramatist D. L. Ray. When **Rabindranath Tagore** began to write and publish his early poems in the 1870s, Bangla literature had attained remarkable sophistication, to which Tagore was to add in the next six decades.

A significant aspect of Bangla literature of this time was its interest in nationalism. Chatterjee was keen on the topic and wrote voluminously on India's history, thus seeking to create the appropriate narrative. Tagore, who was less enthusiastic than Chatterjee about India's nationalist future, also wrote on nationalist issues, delving deep into their complexities in the Indian context. The fiery poetry of Kazi Nazrul Islam, on the other hand, inspired many nationalists and added a new dimension to Bangla poetry. Nationalist works, often influenced by Marxist anticolonialism, continued to appear well into the mid-twentieth century.

India's independence and partition into India and Pakistan in 1947 signaled a remapping of the Bangla cultural scene. The prominence of Bangla in undivided India had already been on the wane in the twentieth century for a number of reasons, one of which was the change of the capital of colonial India from Kolkata to Delhi. The partition hastened the decline because a huge portion of the Bangla populace, in particular those who were Muslim, were domiciled in East Pakistan. These Bangalis, on the other hand, resisted the move made by Pakistan's founder Muhammad Ali Jinnah to make Urdu the national language of Pakistan, which resulted in violent agitations and fueled a political movement that led to the creation of Bangladesh from East Pakistan in 1971. Obviously, the status of Bangla as the national language of an independent country has ensured strong prospects for Bangla literature.

Comparable in some ways to the growth of modern Bangla is Tamil in the south. Like Bangla, Tamil culture experienced a renaissance in the nineteenth century. The situation in the south, however, was slightly different than that of Bangla in that European missionaries, who were more effective in converting Indians to Christianity in south India than elsewhere, produced many religious tracts in Tamil, simplifying its prose. While creative works flourished in Tamil, many Tamil authors exerted their efforts in producing anthologies of ancient Tamil texts and literary histories, sometimes with the intent to carve a Tamil culture independent of the north and its Sanskritic influence. The issue of identity, often depicting the Sanskrit north as a hegemonic cultural power, still creates heated debates in Tamil politics. Contemporary Tamil literature shows a robust production of fiction, poetry, drama, children's literature, detective fiction, essays, and journalistic writing.

Spoken in Sri Lanka (formerly Ceylon), Sinhala has a history comparable to Tamil or Bangla. Since Sri Lankan culture is centered on Buddhism, the influence of Pali can be seen in the language. Modern Sinhala literature began in the nineteenth century and has remained strong in fiction; the most notable novelist has been Martin Wickremasinghe, who enjoyed tremendous popularity in Sri Lanka; several of his novels have been made into films. The Sri Lankan government's decision to make Sinhala the national language, on the other hand, met with stiff resistance from the country's ethnic Tamil population and has contributed to a separatist movement.

In contrast to Sinhala, which is spoken by approximately 1.3 million Sri Lankans, Hindi has about 180 million native speakers in South Asia. It is the national language of India and has the curious history of being a language whose modern identity originates in the "divide and rule" politics of British colonialism, a process at least in part aided by Hindu nationalism. Hindi and Urdu—the official language of Pakistan, also somewhat erroneously known as the language exclusively used by Muslims—began as one language. However, British policies encouraged the perception that Urdu was the language of Indian Muslims and Hindi, that of Hindus. Subsequently, both Hindu and Muslim scholars encouraged this separation, leading to dialectical differences between the two languages.

Hindi received a major boost when the Congress party adopted it as the national language of India. Many authors who used to write in Urdu adopted Hindi, an easy transition for them since only the script needed to be changed. A major growth of Hindi was its development in prose, which Urdu, oriented more toward poetry, had neglected. Perhaps the most accomplished Hindi author was Premchand, the novelist, though he wrote in both Urdu and Hindi—sometimes the same work in the two languages, with two separate titles. His *Godan* earned immense recognition and has been translated into English.

Urdu became the national language of Pakistan, triggering detrimental political consequences. The forceful imposition of Urdu on Bangla speakers—who were in the majority in then Pakistan—set in motion a chain of events that led to the emergence of Bangladesh in 1971, causing Pakistan to lose more than half its people. Subsequently, the Sindhis embarked on a political movement to free themselves of the domination of Urdu—some even arguing for an independent Sindhi state. With memory of East Pakistan/Bangladesh fresh in their minds, Pakistan's rulers showed some acumen in dealing with the crisis. They allowed Sindhi to remain an official language in the province of Sindh.

Though Urdu has been ridden with controversy in Pakistan since its birth, its Urdu literature has fared well. The most celebrated Urdu poet was Faiz Ahmed Faiz. A leftist in political belief, Faiz had an interesting career. He participated in the Indian labor movement, fought in the British Indian army, became the editor of the *Pakistani Times,* and won the Lenin Peace Prize. His brand of politics did not sit well with the authorities in Pakistan, and he was jailed several times for his activism. Faiz was phenomenally popular; thousands gathered when he appeared at *mushairas* (meetings of poets competing against each other to prove mastery of the craft)—a unique tradition of Urdu poetry. Faiz's *ghazals* are often set to music by *ghazal* singers. The *ghazal,* which is a rhymed love lyric rich in metaphors, is Urdu's singular contribution to Indian literature. Originally from eleventh-century Persian literature, the *ghazal* has remained the most popular avenue of Urdu literature since the sixteenth century. Among *ghazal* poets, particularly accomplished was Mirza Asadullah Khan Ghalib in the nineteenth century; he enjoyed the patronage of Bahadur Shah, the last Mughal king. Ghalib has been translated into many South Asian languages and also into English by well-known American poets.

All modern South Asian literatures have experienced impressive growth in the last two centuries or so. For the last five decades in particular, since the departure of British colonial power, these literatures have acquired distinctive nationalist identities and are capable of addressing complex cultural issues. Parallel to the rise of indigenous South Asian literatures, a new genre of English writing, variously known as commonwealth or postcolonial or Indian English or Indo Anglian, has emerged. It is possible to explain the phenomenon as a product of South Asia's intranational politics. English remains a widely spoken language in the subcontinent. When Hindi was made the official language, India avoided a wave of regional nationalisms based on linguistic identities by allowing English to function as another official language. Because of their aggressive promotion of Urdu and Sinhala, Pakistan and Sri Lanka were not as fortunate. However, the use of English by the educated elite in Pakistan, in Bangladesh, or in Sri Lanka is considerable. This status of English causes mixed reactions from critics. Some view it as a positive trend, while some think the growing prominence of English presages the eventual loss of national literary cultures.

Those who are concerned may have reason. Recently **Salman Rushdie**, the best-known South Asian author writing in English, made a derisive comment about literatures written in Indian languages. In the introduction to *The Vintage Book of Indian Writing: 1947–1997,* which Rushdie co-edited with Elizabeth West, he wrote that in the five decades after independence, prose writing "by Indian writers *working in English,* is proving to be a stronger and more important body of work than most of what has been produced in the '16 official languages of India,' the so-called 'vernacular languages'" (Rushdie's emphases). The importance Rushdie attaches to English in a country where it is not the language of the majority is curious. In her review of *The Vintage* in *Ariel* (January 1998), Shyamala Narayan summarizes the angry responses from many Indian authors to Rushdie's bloated contention. Narayan mentions how one author was so incensed that he commented, "No Indian writer in any of the languages can assume to know what is happening in the other Indian languages. Rushdie does not even live in India. How can he make such an enormous assumption?" Another irate author dubbed Rushdie "a late Lord Macaulay," referring to the nineteenth-century imperial policy maker who recommended English to be the only medium of instruction in Indian education. Convinced of Europe's cultural superiority over Asian countries, he famously claimed that a "single shelf of a good European library" could match in value "the whole native literature of India and Arabia." Such hostility to his evaluation of homegrown Indian literature has provoked Rushdie to be undisguisedly contemptuous toward those who have come to its defense. He argued in an interview that his remark aroused such resentment because it was "politically incorrect" and that he was a victim of his critics' "envy aimed at writers in English because they make more money, they get published around the world."

Other possibilities escape Rushdie, but his stating of the obvious, that those who write in English make more money and earn greater recognition, deserves attention. The prominence of English works by South Asian authors in the last quarter of the twentieth century clearly represents an imbrication of **postcolonial literature** and **postmodernism**, which has occurred during a certain phase in the expansion of global capitalism. Rushdie's value judgment notwithstanding, it would be a mistake to imagine that one (minority) branch of South Asian literatures would render the rest extinct.

Selected Bibliography: Arunachalam, M. *An Introduction to the History of Tamil Literature.* Tanjavur, India: Gandhi Vidyalayam, 1974; Dimock, Edward, et al., eds. *The Literatures of India: An Introduction.* Chicago: U of Chicago P, 1974; Pollock, Sheldon, ed. *Literary Cultures in History: Reconstructions from South Asia.* Berkeley: U of California P, 2003; Sadiq, Muhammad. *A History of Urdu Literature.* Delhi: Oxford UP, 1984; Sen, Sukumar. *History of Bengali Literature.* New Delhi: Sahitya Akademi, 1960.

Farhad B. Idris

SOVIET WRITERS' CONGRESS (1934). Following the **Russian Revolution**, the government in the Soviet Union attempted to use every resource at its disposal in the attempt to build a new socialist society. One of the most important of these was culture: postrevolutionary Soviet film, for example, was among the most exciting in the world, led by such directors as Sergei Eisenstein, Dziga Vertov, and Jakov Protazonov. Literature was a somewhat more complex matter, given the low rate of literacy in Russia at the time of the revolution. However, the postrevolutionary Soviet government made unprecedented strides in spreading literacy among the general population. Therefore, by the early 1930s, literature was more and more becoming a crucial part of the effort to promote socialist ideas among the general population. To this end, Soviet writers, with government support, conducted numerous collective efforts to ensure that their work achieved the maximum impact in this direction.

One of the most important turning points in this project was the first Congress of the Union of Soviet Writers, which took place in August 1934 in Moscow. Generally referred to as the first Soviet Writers' Congress, this meeting lasted two weeks and included over two hundred speeches and reports. It was crucial to the development of Soviet literature as its attendees came together to discuss the various alternative strategies available to socialist writers and to make recommendations concerning the strategies that were likely to be most effective. In particular, the congress rejected **modernism** (which had been prominent in Soviet literature of the 1920s) as a decadent bourgeois mode and accepted **socialist realism** as the recommended strategy for Soviet writers, endorsing an earlier recommendation of an official **Communist Party** commission that had included **Joseph Stalin** among its members.

The congress is conventionally cited in the West as a dark moment when Stalin's complete control of Soviet literature became clear, though the writers in attendance showed remarkable unanimity and remarkably little sign that they felt they were being controlled by government repression. There was, however, debate over the endorsement of socialist realism, with writers such as Ilya Ehrenburg and **André Malraux**, who came from France to attend the congress, expressing doubts about the method. Perhaps the most notorious (at least in the West) of the speeches delivered at the congress was Karl Radek's lengthy denunciation of Western modernist writers such as **James Joyce**, a denunciation that has often been cited by Western critics as an example of Soviet shortsightedness in literary matters but one that in fact made numerous salient points. Andrei Zhdanov, Stalin's chief cultural spokesman, also delivered an address at the congress, citing Stalin's now famous declaration that writers should be "engineers of human souls." However, the key figure at the congress was **Maxim Gorky**, who chaired the conference and whose writings emerged as the most important model for future Soviet writers.

Almost all important Soviet writers attended the congress, and there was a large international contingent as well, including **Martin Andersen Nexø** as well as Malraux. A second Soviet Writers' Congress was held in 1954, and altogether a total of eight such congresses were held, the last in 1986.

Selected Bibliography: Booker, M. Keith. Ulysses, *Capitalism, and Colonialism: Reading Joyce after the Cold War.* Westport, CT: Greenwood, 2000; Garrard, John Gordon, and Carol Garrard. *Inside the Soviet Writers' Union.* New York: Free P, 1990; Gorky, Maxim, et al. *Soviet Writers' Congress, 1934: The Debate on Socialist Realism and Modernism in the Soviet Union.* London: Lawrence and Wishart, 1977; Scott, H.G., ed. *Problems of Soviet Literature: Reports and Speeches at the First Soviet Writers' Congress.* 1935. Westport, CT: Greenwood, 1979.

M. Keith Booker

SOYINKA, WOLE (1934–). Nobel Prize–winning Nigerian playwright, novelist, essayist, campaigner for human rights, and outspoken critic of corruption and repression. Soyinka emerged after the nationalist struggle against British imperialism had secured nominal independence. He has confronted the Nigerian politicians and military leaders who have operated in the neocolonial world order with coruscating criticism when they have fallen short of the humane, progressive attitudes proclaimed by the founding fathers of the country.

Born into the educated elite in the Yoruba-speaking administrative and commercial center of Abeokuta, Soyinka grew up close to some of those who contributed to the nationalist movement. In 1960, he returned home from more than five years in the United Kingdom with a university degree and valuable experience in the London theater. While a student and fledgling writer, he had embraced a broadly socialist position; had become aware of the limitations of "vulgar Marxism"; and had taken part in campaigns against apartheid, colonial repression, and nuclear armaments. He distanced himself from nostalgic, essentialist elements in **negritude** while championing the reengagement with African, especially Yoruba, values.

From the early 1960s, Soyinka's literary output embraced radio plays, tragic dramas, intense poetry, revue sketches, journalism, and popular lyrics. His cultivated theatrical sense was sometimes used to mount vigorous political protests. As Nigeria moved from the euphoria of independence to a state of emergency in the western region in 1962 and experienced the first of a series of coups in January 1966, there was much to protest.

Except for brief periods, Soyinka has maintained a commentary on national developments. He was eloquently silent for most of the twenty-seven months he was detained during the **Nigerian civil war**, but subsequently wrote at length and in characteristically personal and vigorous terms about the political situation in *The Man Died* (1975). Though a member of several short-lived protest groups and briefly a "self-suspended member of the People's Redemption Party," Soyinka typically acts alone or with a small group. This was the case when, in October 1965, he quixotically held up the radio station in Ibadan and broadcast an unheeded rallying call to those, like himself, outraged by electoral malpractices.

Ventures involving a larger group of supporters have included his campaigns for road safety and for democratic processes. During the 1990s, Soyinka took on the brutal military dictator Sani Abacha and was declared a traitor. When that happened, Soyinka was operating from a base outside Nigeria, and he remained abroad until after Abacha's death, returning to make forthright contributions to debates about the future of the country. He indicated that he had no ambition to hold an elected or in any sense political office. Some see his reputation for being incorruptible as recommending him for the highest leadership position; others regard his interventions as signifying little.

During the 1970s, Soyinka was attacked by those of the radical Left, **Femi Osofisan** among them. They deplored his lack of a class perspective, complained that he peopled his stage with elitist heroes or undifferentiated workers, and condemned him for writing plays that mystified and depressed. At the same period, feminist and womanist critics pointed to the limited range of his female characters, and nativists, such as Chinweizu, condemned him for being alienated from his community and pandering to Western preferences.

In addition to replying to these criticisms in fiercely worded essays, Soyinka responded through directly political sketches (*Priority Projects*, 1981) and accessible plays (*Opera Wonyosi*, 1977; *The Beatification of Area Boy*, 1995), some of which included songs that won a popular following when released on record (*Unlimited Liability Company*, 1983). His play *King Baabu* (2001) pillories Abacha with the intention of encouraging his fellow countrymen and others to be horrified by and to laugh at dictators.

Selected Bibliography: Gibbs, James. *Wole Soyinka*. New York: Grove, 1986; Gibbs, James, and Bernth Lindfors, eds. *Research on Wole Soyinka*. Trenton: Africa World P, 1993; Jones, Eldred Durosimi. *The Writing of Wole Soyinka*. London: Heinemann, 1973; Wright, Derek. *Wole Soyinka Revisited*. New York: Twayne, 1993.

James Gibbs

THE SPACE MERCHANTS (1952). A premier satirical **science fiction** novel by Frederik Pohl (b. 1919) and C. M. Kornbluth (1923–1958). Published at the height of the **cold war**, *Space Merchants* was widely considered at its appearance, and for decades afterward, as an essential critique of the corporate interplanetary future, anything but utopian. It presents a vivid picture of a future world dominated by huge, corrupt multinational corporations, the most powerful and influential of which are media and advertising firms. *The Space Merchants* shows a profound understanding of the direction in which consumer capitalism was already headed in 1952 and suggests interesting forms of complicity between the corporate manipulation of consumers for profit and the official promotion of anticommunist hysteria during the cold war.

The more important of the coauthors by far was Pohl, a prolific novelist and influential figure within the science-fiction division of the publishing industry. Growing up in New York in the 1920s and 1930s, Pohl joined the Young Communist League and, with liberal-minded friends, formed the Futurian Society of New York (usually remembered by the single word, Futurians). It would be difficult to overestimate the importance of this collection of teenage amateurs. Discussing both craft and politics, they began careers at the moment when science fiction (SF) had barely begun to emerge from the "BEM" (bug-eyed monster) phase of space cadets conquering creatures (and winning fair maidens, but much less often actually kissing them), like so many cowboys with a new and more exotic West.

Isaac Asimov, destined to be the most prominent of the little group, would exemplify the effort during the 1940s–1970s to humanize the field of SF and make it accessible to serious adult readers. His Foundation trilogy (1942–1945) would remain a classic of the field. Other sometime Marxists from the 1930s–1940s generations such as Guy Endore, Thomas McGrath, Rolfe Humphries, Ben Barzman, Henry Myers, Mack Reynolds, Bernard Wolfe, Judith Merril, and leftist pulp master **Howard Fast** contributed an extensive library of mostly satirical works about wounded futures, including issues of atomic war and ecological devastation. But Futurians Damon Knight, James Blish, Kornbluth, and Art Landis constituted a sort of subgroup, playing prominent roles as writers, editors, and publishers (Donald A. Wollheim in particular had his own "DAW" imprint) and urging the whole field forward. Pohl, more writer than commercial editor, has remained a force for socialistic impulses, from the demi-Marxism of the Committee for the Political Advancement of Science Fiction during the 1930s until the present day.

The Space Merchants remains heads above—not for its sometimes stylized dialogue, curiously bound to the manners, morals, and slang of the day, but because it successfully captured the common expectation of the galaxy as the newest and final arena for successful salesmanship rather than the "heavens" of previous centuries' expectations. Only war making, along with specific details, needed to be added to further modernize the picture of the future. More skilled writers like **Philip K. Dick**, **Ursula Le Guin**, and **Kim Stanley Robinson** would therefore understandably look on *Space Merchants* as the marking of a new phase of the science-fiction writers' art.

Selected Bibliography: Knight, Damon. *The Futurians.* New York: John Day, 1977; Moskowitz, Sam. "How Science Fiction Got Its Name." *The Prentice Hall Anthology of Science Fiction and Fantasy.* Ed. Garyn G. Roberts. Upper Saddle River, NJ: Prentice Hall, 2003. 1127–35; Pohl, Frederik. *The Way the Future Was.* New York: Ballantine, 1978; Seed, David. "Take-over Bids: The Power Fantasies of Frederik Pohl and Cyril Kornbluth." *Foundation* 59 (Fall 1993): 42–58; Wald, Alan M. "Science Fiction and Fantasy." *Encyclopedia of the American Left*. Ed. Mari Jo Buhle et al. New York: Oxford UP, 1997. 724–26.

Paul Buhle

SPANISH CIVIL WAR (1936–1939). In the late 1930s, Spain was torn apart by a massive and bloody conflict that eventually drew in Nazi Germany, fascist Italy, and the Soviet Union, while tearing at the conscience of the liberal democracies—Great Britain, France, and the United States. Over one million soldiers and civilians of many different nationalities died in the Spanish Civil War and its immediate aftermath.

After the parliamentary elections of 1933, the Cortes—the Spanish parliament—fell under the control of the CEDA (Confederation of the Autonomous Right). Then, in February 1936, a **Popular Front** coalition of socialists, moderates, communists, and a sprinkling of anarchists won a majority in the Cortes. The platform of the new government contrasted dramatically with that of the Right. The Popular Front, or Frente Popular, called for the separation of church and state (education was removed from control of the Roman Catholic Church, civil marriages were required, divorce was permitted), women were given the vote, church and aristocratic land holdings were expropriated and redistributed, industry was collectivized, and regional autonomy was granted to the traditionally separatist provinces of Catalonia and the Basque Country. In response, Spain's top army officers, in collusion with the church and aristocracy, planned a military uprising to seize control of the government. General Emilio Mola and General Francisco Franco began the rebellion on July 17, 1936, in Spanish Morocco. The next day, July 18, the rebellion spread to the mainland, and the Spanish Civil War had begun.

Officially, the United States never actively took sides in the conflict. Instead, the policy of the Roosevelt administration was one of nonintervention. Congress also approved an embargo on the sale of arms and supplies to both the Spanish Republic and Franco with the Neutrality Act of January 1937. Despite the arms embargo, Secretary of State Cordell Hull did allow Texaco, Ford, and Studebaker to sell oil and trucks to Franco. Unofficially, the American public increasingly sided with the Spanish Republic as foreign intervention by Nazi Germany and fascist Italy on the side of Franco increased, and reports of atrocities against civilians made their way back home.

France's Popular Front government under Prime Minister Léon Blum at first appeared ready to defend the Spanish Republic. However, partisan politics and the increasing dominance of the right on the home front made such intervention impossible. Eventually, France signed the Non-Intervention Agreement in August 1936. Great Britain's policy under Neville Chamberlain aimed at appeasement of Nazi Germany, so it is not surprising that they, too, signed this agreement. The Soviet Union naturally sided with the Spanish Republic, becoming the only major world power to openly provide arms, personnel, and materiel to the government in Madrid. Nazi Germany was an early ally to the Nationalist cause, despite also signing the Non-Intervention Agreement. Hitler supplied elements of his Luftwaffe, military advisors, naval support, and weapons to Franco's forces. Like its Axis partner, Mussolini's Italy actively supported the Nationalists with planes and troops.

Like a magnet, the Spanish Civil War attracted many politically conscious writers. The majority of them sided with the democratically elected republic, believing that it would defend freedom of expression. They went to Spain either to write as authors or journalists about the conflict (**Hemingway**, *For Whom the Bell Tolls*; **Koestler**, *Dialogue with Death*) or to risk their lives (**Malraux**, *Man's Hope* [*L'Espoir*]; **Orwell**, *Homage to Catalonia*) in fighting fascism.

During the conflict, 2,800 American volunteers took up arms to defend the Spanish Republic. To the Abraham Lincoln Brigade, which fought from 1937 through 1938, the defense of the republic represented the last hope of stopping the spread of international fascism. The Lincolns fought alongside approximately 35,000 antifascists from fifty-two countries—the International Brigades—who, like themselves, were organized under the aegis of the Comintern. In keeping with Popular Front culture, the Americans named their units the Abraham Lincoln Battalion, the George Washington Battalion, and the John Brown Battery. One hundred twenty-five American men and women also served with the American Medical Bureau as nurses, doctors, technicians, and ambulance drivers.

As the war progressed, the situation played into the hands of the Communists, who at the outset had been of negligible importance. The Loyalist ranks were split by factional strife, which intensified as their military position worsened; among its manifestations was the Communists' suppression of the anarchists and the Trotskyite Partido Obrero de Unificación Marxista (POUM). On the nationalist side, internal conflict also existed, especially between the military and the fascists, but Franco was able to surmount it and consolidate his position. Gradually the Nationalists wore down Loyalist strength. Bilbao, the last Republican center in the north, fell in June 1937, and in a series of attacks from March to June 1938, the Nationalists drove to the Mediterranean and cut the Republican territory in two. Late in 1938, Franco mounted a major offensive against Catalonia, and Barcelona was taken in January 1939. With the loss of Catalonia, the Loyalist cause became hopeless. Republican efforts for a negotiated peace failed, and on April 1, 1939, the victorious Nationalists entered Madrid. Italy and Germany had recognized the Franco regime in 1936, and Great Britain and France did so in February 1939. International recognition of Franco's government quickly followed, including that of the United States on April 1, 1939. The major political leaders of the Republican government, especially the Communists, fled to France, and some, eventually, to the Soviet Union when **World War II** broke out less than six months later.

Selected Bibliography: Anderson, James M. *The Spanish Civil War: A History and Reference Guide.* Westport, CT: Greenwood, 2003; Bolloten, Burnett. *The Spanish Civil War.* Chapel Hill: U of North Carolina P, 1991; Buckner, Noel, Mary Dore, and Sam Sills. *The Good Fight: The Abraham Lincoln Brigade in the Spanish Civil War.* New York: 1984. Film distributed by First Run Features and Kino International, New York; Jackson, Gabriel. *The Spanish Republic and the Civil War, 1931–1939.* Princeton, NJ: Princeton UP, 1965; Preston, Paul. *The Coming of the Spanish Civil War.* London: Macmillan, 1978; Rosenstone, Robert A. *Crusade of the Left: The Lincoln Battalion in the Spanish Civil War.* New York: Pegasus, 1969.

John B. Romeiser

SPANISH LITERATURE (TWENTIETH CENTURY). While Spain has a long and rich literary and cultural heritage, the loss of Spain's last colonies, Cuba and the Philippines, in 1898 marked the coming of a new era in Spanish history and, consequently, Spanish literature and culture. The "colonial disaster" brought to the fore the ineffectiveness of an archaic ruling system artificially maintained by a façade of parliamentarism, and served to give momentum to a small but highly educated middle bourgeoisie—to its republican, laic, liberal, and capitalist program and its postulates for reform and progress (articulated earlier in the nineteenth century by a number of social and political movements, among them regenerationism and republicanism). The foremost literary representatives of this bourgeoisie were the members of the "Generation of 1898" (Pío Baroja, Azorín, Antonio Machado, Ramón M. del Valle Inclán, Miguel de Unamuno), whose common ground was a deep engagement with "Spain as a problem"—a meditation on the social, cultural, and political origins of the crisis the country was experiencing, and the search for solutions.

A few years into the twentieth century, the reformist program of the educated bourgeoisie was made anachronistic by the rise of the working class, the founding of communist parties and workers' organizations, and the coming to the fore of a revolutionary petit bourgeois intelligentsia inspired by the latest European revolutionary currents and the early apparent successes of the Soviet revolution. While the so-called "Generation of 1927" (**Federico García Lorca**, Rafael Alberti), perhaps the strongest incursion of Spanish literature into the avant-garde (notwithstanding the previous but less-known movements of ultraism and futurism), moved toward surrealist aesthetics (unlike in the rest of Europe, devoid of a political component), a more politicized group of writers (José Díaz Fernández, Joaquín Arderíus) offered a critique not only of the monarchical status quo but also of the reformist, bourgeois program for change and avant-garde aesthetics. These writers, often referred to as "the other Generation of 1927" (a term coined by Víctor Fuentes), started the search for a proletarian literature more in line with the social and political needs of the time, and to debate the social and political engagement of writers.

In 1931, the reformist bourgeoisie came to power in a relatively peaceful manner with the proclamation of the Second Republic, and a national parliament dominated by intellectuals, academics, and writers started a complicated process of social, cultural, political, educational, agricultural, judicial, and military reform, too revolutionary for those who had defended the previous status quo and too backward for those who aimed to lead the country toward a Soviet-style proletarian revolution. The new, more permissive climate of freedom allowed for the proliferation of leftist publishing houses (Cenit, Ediciones Oriente), which popularized Marxist and other communist texts as well as Soviet and European literature written by committed writers; they also contributed to the boom of Spain's own social literature. Debates on proletarian literature, the political engagement of writers, and Spain's own social and political evolution sprang up in an array of literary journals (*Nuevo Cinema*, *Octubre*), contributing to a climate of euphoric hope for both literature and society.

Upon the outbreak of the **Spanish Civil War** in July 1936, the great majority of Spanish writers aligned themselves with the reformist, liberal republic, with a minority defending the rebel nationalist army and a return to the previous status quo, represented by General Franco, and an even smaller minority still defending the proletarian revolution against the reformist bourgeoisie. Although the literary debates continued, they were mostly taken over by the discussion of the need to defend Spain's young and fragile parliamentary democracy against the rise of fascism.

The war was a defining event for a group of young writers (Arturo Serrano Plaja, **Miguel Hernández**)—often referred to as the "Generation of 1936"—deeply committed to the war effort and to the survival of social justice and democracy, and eager to find a model of literary creation that could be revolutionary in both form and content. Their unofficial manifesto was Serrano Plaja's address to the Second International Congress for the Defense of Culture in 1937, held in Spain in the midst of war as proof of the symbolic value that the country had gained in the international fight against fascism. Notwithstanding the literary relevance of this group, one of the most important literary creations of the Spanish Civil War was a body of poetry—the "Romancero de Guerra"—written collectively by soldiers and workers (many of whom had just acquired basic literacy) together with professional writers, and distributed in informal ways, from public recitations to leaflets.

After the nationalist victory in the civil war, many influential Spanish writers, including most of the writers of the "generations" of 1927 and 1936 and many other leading novelists—Max Aub, Francisco Ayala, Ramón J. Sender—joined a mass exodus from the country. Those writers who stayed in Spain ranged from firm supporters of the dictatorship to those whom Paul Ilie has called "inner exiles," whose work was subjected to often draconian censorship. In the first years after the war, some poets, including Dionisio Ridruejo, openly sang the praises of the fascist Falange, but many others—such as José García Nieto, collaborator on the journal *Garcilaso*—cultivated instead a poetry rooted in the themes and styles of the Renaissance, while Leopoldo Panero, soon dubbed the unofficial poet laureate of the régime, created delicate lyrics on the themes of religion, homeland, and family. For Dámaso Alonso, one of the few 1927 poets to stay in Spain, Panero's was a "rooted" poetry while his own was radically "unrooted." Alonso's *Children of Wrath* (*Hijos de la ira*) and fellow 1927 poet Vicente Aleixandre's *Shadow of Paradise* (*Sombra del paraíso*), both published in 1944, introduced a note of metaphysical anguish into Spanish poetry, anguish that not only pointed to the existence of cosmic injustice but also subtly implied, often through the use of analogy and even allegory, the existence of more earthly and social forms of injustice. Their influence—together with that of Victoriano Crémer and Eugenio de Nora, founders of the journal *Espadaña*—helped to usher in a period of social poetry, which saw poets such as Gabriel Celaya and Blas de Otero create a new, direct language of denunciation and solidarity that was to dominate poetry during the 1950s. Toward the middle of that decade and throughout the 1960s, new poets appeared—first the generation of Jaime Gil de Biedma and Claudio Rodríguez, then the so-called *novísimos*, such as Pere Gimferrer and Manuel Vázquez Montalbán—who, without rejecting the oppositional ethos of social poetry, made use of more artistic, more personal, and—increasingly—more contemporary themes, references, and images. Meanwhile, prose fiction—believed by the authorities to reach a wider reading public than poetry—was always more controlled by the censors. It is therefore remarkable that Camilo José Cela (who eventually won the Nobel Prize for Literature in 1989) was able to publish *The Family* of *Pascual Duarte* (*La familia de Pascual Duarte*, 1942)—a disturbing tale of incest and matricide set in rural Spain—and less remarkable that he had to publish his next novel, *The Hive* (*La colmena*, 1951)—a structurally innovative and darkly sordid portrayal of early 1940s Madrid—in Argentina. More commonly, the Spanish novel, from Carmen Laforet's *Nada* (1945) to Rafael Sánchez Ferlosio's *El Jarama* (1956), was dominated by a stark and gritty realism that acted as a form of both testimony and denunciation. Only in the 1960s, with works such as Luis Martín-Santos's *Time of Silence* (*Tiempo de silencio*, 1962), Miguel Delibes's *Five Hours with Mario* (*Cinco horas con Mario*, 1966), **Juan Goytisolo**'s *Marks of Identity* (*Señas de identidad*, 1966), and Juan Benet's *Return to Región* (*Volverás a Región*, 1967), did the Spanish novel start to use complex narrative and structural devices in its exploration of the origins and nature of the national trauma and its effects on the individual psyche. Finally, drama—the most public of the literary genres—was slow in challenging the escapist fare that continued to fill theaters throughout the dictatorship. However, Antonio Buero Vallejo, with works such as *Story of a Stairway* (*Historia de una escalera*, 1949) and *Las meninas* (1960), used techniques as diverse as realism, allegory, and even fantasy to suggest alternative ways of reading Spain's past and present history, while Alfonso Sastre's more explicitly political theater always landed him in trouble with the censors. Perhaps unsurprisingly, the most innovative dramatist of the period, Fernando Arrabal, had to write most of his works in France and produce them in French translation.

Transition to democracy, after the death of General Franco in November 1975, is the major event framing contemporary Spanish society. The political account of such an event has itself become an elaborate discourse modeled on the rhetorical conventions of a fictional story. Presented as a fairy tale—crowned head and happy ending included—the Spanish transition is generally presented as the triumph of democracy over the forces of dictatorship. Although Spain is, nowadays, a state conventionally functioning as any western European democracy, ambiguities and contradictions resulting from the transition are left to be read, and activated when convenient, in the major texts providing the legislative framework (above all the Spanish Constitution, 1978) and in the political compromises from which these have emanated: not a constituent process proper but an internationally intervened self-transformation of the state structures (which began well before the dictator's death), directed by Francoist politicians with the collaboration—from 1974 to 1975—of oppositional parties' hierarchies, which either had progressively abandoned important components of anti-Francoist politics, including Republican aspirations, or had been reinvented as forces to guarantee the "smoothness" of the process.

The shadow of this (unfinished) transition is still projecting its effects on contemporary Spanish society, being a crucial factor behind current political issues (from institutional corruption and state terrorism to the various nationalist conflicts). Those effects and others related to the economic and cultural transformations as well as the identity crisis resulting from political struggles since the late sixties (such as the consequences of the defeat of revolutionary hopes to radically transform society, which in the Spanish case were articulated as the only actively engaged way to fight the dictatorship by the minority and mainly communist-organized antifascist forces) together with the manipulation, or absence, of memory (the very condition under which the transition could acquire some sort of spurious democratic legitimacy) have been the precious though extremely sensible and fragile material of fiction (José Jiménez Lozano, Manuel Vázquez Montalbán, Juan Marsé, Rafael Chirbes, Antonio Muñoz Molina, Rosa Montero, Miguel Espinosa, Fanny Rubio, José Luis Rodríguez García, **Gabriel Albiac**), drama (Alfonso Sastre), poetry (Agustín García Calvo, Montalbán, Leopoldo María Panero, Eduardo Haro Ibars, Ramón Buenaventura, Jon Juaristi, Jenaro Talens, Ana Rosetti, Rodríguez García), and song lyrics (Joan Manuel Serrat, Luis Eduardo Aute, Joaquín Sabina).

Two groups of authors active after 1975 can be distinguished according to their age at the moment of the dictator's death because their respective literary engagements with politics usually differ. All those in the preceding lists were adults by that time, some of them already established authors, while the younger writers began to publish only in the 1980s and 1990s. There is a heavier presence of explicitly macropolitical issues in the writing of this first group than in that of the younger group of authors (Juan Bonilla, Ray Loriga, Lucía Etxebarria, José Ángel Mañas, Luisa Castro, and Javier Álvarez, with Juana Salabert constituting, perhaps, the significant exception), born at the end of the 1960s.

Fighting against an intellectual environment of general impoverishment, an important renovation in nonfiction writing began in the 1970s, especially in philosophy and critical theory but also in political essays by authors of the two age groups (Gustavo Bueno, Agustín García Calvo, Jesús Ibáñez, Rafael Sánchez Ferlosio, Lidia Falcón, Antonio Escohotado, Fernando Savater, Albiac, Rodríguez García, Víctor Gómez Pin, José Jiménez, Miguel Morey, Celia Amorós, José Luis Pardo, Javier Echeverría, Eugenio Trías, Carlos Fernández Liria, Santiago Alba Rico, Raúl Fernández Vítores), most of them continuing the Hispanic tradition of intellectuals intervening regularly in the public debate through the writing of columns and articles for the newly created newspapers and political magazines.

Selected Bibliography: Amell, Samuel, ed. *Literature, the Arts, and Democracy: Spain in the Eighties.* London: Associated UP, 1990; Gies, David T., ed. *The Cambridge Companion to Modern Spanish Culture.* Cambridge: Cambridge UP, 1999; Ilie, Paul. *Literature and Inner Exile: Authoritarian Spain, 1939–1975.* Baltimore: Johns Hopkins UP, 1980; Jordan, Barry, and Rikki Morgan-Tamosunas. *Contemporary Spanish Cultural Studies.* London: Arnold, 2000; Labanyi, Jo. *National Identity in Modern Spain.* London: U of London, 1994; Labanyi, Jo, and Helen Graham, eds. *Spanish Cultural Studies.* New York: Oxford UP, 1995; Pérez, Janet, and Wendell Aycock, eds. *The Spanish Civil War in Literature.* Lubbock: Texas Tech UP, 1990; Perriam, Chris, et al. *A New History of Spanish Writing, 1939 to the 1990s.* Oxford: Oxford UP, 2000.

Mayte Gómez, Stephen G. H. Roberts, and Álvaro J. Vidal-Bouzon

SPENSER, EDMUND (ca. 1552–1599). In England, Spenser developed the idea of using a poetic career primarily to construct one's public image as a professional poet. This was a class-driven move, given that Spenser was the son of a London weaver and had received his education at Cambridge on a working scholarship. His first major publication was *The Shepheardes Calender* (1579), which announced by its very form that its author was on the road to fame. Brashly, the *Calender* came ready-supplied with the trappings of an expensive scholarly edition of a classical text:

an introduction, summaries, illustrations, and footnotes supposedly written by "E. K."—perhaps Spenser himself.

In 1580, Spenser became secretary to Lord Grey de Wilton, Queen Elizabeth's lord deputy in Ireland. After Lord Grey was recalled—either because of fiscal mismanagement or because of a massacre committed by his troops—Spenser held minor governmental positions, acquiring an estate at Kilcolman in 1589. On a visit to England from 1589 to 1591, he read to the queen from the first installment of his epic *The Faerie Queene* (published in two parts in 1590 and 1596). Elizabeth never gave him a position at court, although she awarded him a generous £50 per annum before he returned to Ireland. Back at Kilcolman, Spenser wrote *Amoretti* and *Epithalamion* (1595) to celebrate his second marriage in the context of celebrating Ireland—though not the Irish. In another distancing move, Spenser published *Colin Clouts Come Home Againe*, ambiguously satirizing the English court.

Spenser's construction of a self was inextricable from his use of Elizabeth as both audience and subject—*his* queen in more than one sense. Layered allegory, interlaced plots, and evaporating conclusions allowed him to treat political issues with a high degree of deniability, and Elizabeth favored him enough to ignore the Scottish King James's demands that the poet be punished for allegorizing Mary, Queen of Scots, as a witch with a fox's tail. Spenser's major prose work was less successful; *A View of the Present State of Ireland* was denied publication. This dialogue criticizes Elizabeth's Irish policies, with its interlocutors recommending more consistent rule, better funding, and a program of massacre and starvation. The book is an extraordinarily complex representation of the incipient British Empire. Irish rebels burned Kilcolman in 1598; Spenser died the following year in Westminster.

Spenser's work strongly influenced his friend Sir Philip Sidney, as well as Shakespeare, Milton, and the romantics. Spenser lost critical favor during the era of the New Criticism, then surged back into view with the diversification of literary criticism.

Selected Bibliography: Gregerson, Linda K. *Powers of Desire: Specularity and the Subject of the Tudor State.* Ann Arbor: U of Michigan P, 1992; Hadfield, Andrew. *Shakespeare, Spenser, and the Matter of Britain.* New York: Macmillan, 2004; McCabe, Richard A. *Spenser's Monstrous Regiment: Elizabethan Ireland and the Poetics of Difference.* Oxford: Oxford UP, 2002; Montrose, Louis Adrian. "The Elizabethan Subject and the Spenserian Text." *Literary Theory/Renaissance Texts.* Ed. Patricia Parker and David Quint. Baltimore: Johns Hopkins UP, 1986. 303–40.

Dorothy Stephens

SPIVAK, GAYATRI CHAKRAVORTY (1942–). Born in Calcutta on February 24, 1942, Spivak went on to become one of the leading cultural theorists of the contemporary era. The daughter of a middle-class Hindu family, Spivak attended a missionary school in Calcutta before graduating from the University of Calcutta in 1959. After taking a master's degree in English at Cornell University in the United States, Spivak took up an instructor's position at the University of Iowa while completing her doctoral dissertation on the work of **William Butler Yeats**, which was directed by Paul de Man at Cornell. This dissertation was subsequently developed into a book entitled *Myself I Must Remake* (1974). Spivak went on to translate **Jacques Derrida's**

De la Grammatologie (1976) and short fiction by the Bengali writer Mahasweta Devi, as well as publishing numerous books and articles on Marxism, feminist theory, deconstruction, and postcolonial criticism.

Although Spivak is best known for her groundbreaking contribution to **postcolonial theory** in essays such as "Can the Subaltern Speak?" (1987) and "Three Women's Texts and a Critique of Imperialism" (1985), she has subsequently rejected the postcolonial label in *A Critique of Postcolonial Reason* (1999). This shift in position represents a critical vigilance against complicity with forms of knowledge that support rather than question global capitalism and the international division of labor. For this reason, Spivak has advocated a persistent critical interruption of Marxism, feminism, and deconstruction that refuses the explanatory power of any single theoretical discourse. While Spivak has been accused of perpetuating the silencing of subaltern groups in her writing, her ongoing activist work with schoolteachers in rural India and Bangladesh to improve children's literacy demonstrates how her engagement with critical theory has always been informed by an ethical and political commitment to social and political change.

Selected Bibliography: Landry, Donna, and Gerald McLean, eds. *The Spivak Reader.* London: Routledge, 1995; Morton, Stephen. *Gayatri Chakravorty Spivak.* London: Routledge, 2002; Spivak, Gayatri Chakravorty. *A Critique of Postcolonial Reason: Toward a History of the Vanishing Present.* Cambridge, MA: Harvard UP, 1999; Spivak, Gayatri Chakravorty. *Death of a Discipline.* New York: Columbia UP, 2003; Spivak, Gayatri Chakravorty. *In Other Worlds: Essays in Cultural Politics.* London: Methuen, 1987; Spivak, Gayatri Chakravorty. *Outside in the Teaching Machine.* London: Routledge, 1993; Spivak, Gayatri Chakravorty. *The Postcolonial Critic.* London: Routledge, 1990.

Stephen Morton

STALIN, JOSEPH VISSARIONOVICH (1879–1953).

Born Joseph Dzugashvili in Gori, Georgia, the son of a shoemaker. In his teen years, he studied for the priesthood but converted to Marxism and was expelled from the seminary. In 1903, he became a follower of **Vladimir Lenin**, joining the Bolshevik faction of the Social Democratic Labor Party. Stalin remained an active member of the party for the next several years, joining the central committee in 1912. Soon afterward, he adopted the name Stalin (Man of Steel). Because of his political activities, he was constantly harassed by the authorities and arrested several times, eventually being exiled in 1913 to northern Siberia. He remained in exile until the general amnesty that followed the February Revolution of 1917 allowed him to return to Petrograd, where he became an editor of *Pravda.*

After the October Revolution, Stalin assumed the post of commissar of nationalities in the new Soviet government, gradually gaining power until his election as general secretary of the central committee of the **Communist Party** in 1922. After Lenin's death in 1924, Stalin worked to solidify his position as Lenin's ultimate successor, and by 1929, he stood unchallenged at the head of the Soviet government, instituting a program of Five-Year Plans for industrialization and collectivization of agriculture that reversed the more moderate policies of Lenin's New Economic Program. Stalin's actions in subsequent years have won him a reputation as a totalitarian despot, though it is also clear that many of his more extreme policies of the 1930s grew out of a perceived sense of urgency to develop an industrial and military structure that could withstand the looming threat of fascism. In that sense, he was successful, building a Red Army that was able to repel the German invasion in **World War II**. Stalin ruled until his death in 1953, an event that was generally greeted with great sorrow and mourning among the Soviet population.

Like many of the initial leaders of the Soviet Union, Stalin recognized the importance of literature and culture as tools in the attempt to build socialism in the Soviet Union. One of the greatest achievements of his years in power was a dramatic rise in literacy among the Soviet population, a phenomenon that went hand in hand with party-supported attempts to produce literature that would convey the value of socialist ideas. This literature, especially after the **Soviet Writers' Congress of 1934**, was generally produced in the mode of **socialist realism**, largely following a path set down by the writing of **Maxim Gorky**.

During his rule, Stalin was frequently represented in Soviet literature as a hero of the people, though generally only in an indirect mode of allegory. After his death and his subsequent denunciation by Nikita Khrushchev in 1956, Stalin began to be represented in less positive terms in Soviet literature. The best-known literary critique of Stalinism was that conducted by **Aleksandr Solzhenitsyn**, who won a Nobel Prize for Literature for his efforts in 1970. By the 1970s, satirists such as **Vladimir Voinovich**, Yuz Aleshkovsky, and Sasha Sokolov were treating Stalin and his policies as objects of farcical derision, greatly furthering the reception of such writers in the West.

Selected Bibliography: Booker, M. Keith, and Dubravka Juraga. *Bakhtin, Stalin, and Modern Russian Fiction: Carnival, Dialogism, and History.* Westport, CT: Greenwood, 1995; Groys, Boris. *The Total Art of Stalinism: Avant-Garde, Aesthetic Dictatorship, and Beyond.* Trans. Charles Rougle. Princeton, NJ: Princeton UP, 1992; Lahusen, Thomas. *How Life Writes the Book: Real Socialism and Socialist Realism in Stalin's Russia.* Ithaca, NY: Cornell UP, 1997; Suny, Ronald Grigor. *The Soviet Experiment: Russia, the USSR, and the Successor States.* New York: Oxford UP, 1998; Thurston, Robert W. *Life and Terror in Stalin's Russia, 1934–1941.* New Haven, CT: Yale UP, 1996; Tucker, Robert C. *Stalin in Power: The Revolution from Above, 1928–1941.* New York: Norton, 1990.

M. Keith Booker

STEAD, CHRISTINA (1902–1983). A Sydney-born writer who lived for forty years in England, Europe, and the United States, Christina Stead was the daughter of David Stead—a Fabian socialist, conservationist, and public servant influential in establishing state regulation of fisheries in New South Wales. Passionate about natural history and evolutionary theory, David inspired his daughter's portrait of the loquaciously dominating father in her novel *The Man Who Loved Children* (1940). At age twenty-six, Stead departed for England and there met her lifelong partner, a Jewish American economist and Marxist, William Blake (formerly Wilhelm Blech). Blake drew Stead into productively diverse circles, where she met international stockbrokers and radical writers like **Ralph Fox** and **Mike Gold**. In Paris in 1935, Stead encountered **Popular Front** politics, attending the First International Congress of Writers for the Defence of Culture as the English delegation's secretary. Her congress report appeared in the British communist organ *Left Review*. Stead's early fictional works—*The Salzburg Tales* (1934), *Seven Poor Men of Sydney* (1934), and *The Beauties and Furies* (1936)—display extraordinary verbal precocity as well as a materialist grasp of characters in social struggle. *House of All Nations* (1938), an epic satire of international finance and corruption, experiments with documentary form and cinematic technique.

Stead and Blake mostly managed to elude, through fortuitous migration, the perils of shifting political climates and world events. The couple left Europe in 1937 for the United States, where they stayed during the war, working for a time in Hollywood as scriptwriters. As Terry Sturm argues, Stead's fiction experiments with a version of critical realism resistant to prescriptive **socialist realism** but politically radical nevertheless. Such novels as *The Man Who Loved Children* and *For Love Alone* (1944) bend mythic, autobiographical energies toward political ends, their focus on the emerging artist empowered by Stead's narrative critique of liberal patriarchy. In *Letty Fox, Her Luck* (1947), *A Little Tea, a Little Chat* (1948), and *The People with the Dogs* (1952), Stead conducts an extended satire of everyday American manners and society. Though a Marxist sympathizer, Stead never joined the American **Communist Party**, privately expressing strong distaste for its petty bureaucracy. Yet Stead, like Blake, remained loyal to the ideal they saw represented in **Stalin**'s Soviet regime. The couple's involvement, peripheral though it was, attracted FBI surveillance during the era of McCarthyism, and Stead's subsequent fiction dissects these **cold-war** brutalities.

In postwar Europe and England, Stead and Blake endured penury and obscurity. Although then producing some of her most powerful works—including *Cotters' England* (1967), *The Puzzleheaded Girl* (1967), *The Little Hotel* (1973), *Miss Herbert (The Suburban Wife)* (1976), and much of her posthumously published masterpiece *I'm Dying Laughing* (1987)—Stead was unable to secure publication. However, a change in cultural climate as the cold war eased along with the 1965 reissue of *The Man Who Loved Children* renewed Stead's readership, and spurred critical recognition of her achievement. Belated publication of her postwar novels ensued. After Blake's death in 1968, Stead returned to Australia for the last decade of her life.

Selected Bibliography: Arac, Jonathan. "The Struggle for the Cultural Heritage: Christina Stead Refunctions Charles Dickens and Mark Twain." *Cultural Critique 2* (1985–1986): 171–89; Harris, Margaret, ed. *The Magic Phrase: Critical Essays on Christina Stead.* St. Lucia, Queensland: U of Queensland P, 2000; Rowley, Hazel. *Christina Stead: A Biography.* Port Melbourne, Victoria: William Heinemann Australia, 1993; Sheridan, Susan. *Christina Stead.* Great Britain: Harvester Wheatsheaf, 1988; Stead, Christina. "The Writers Take Sides." *Left Review* 1.11 (August 1935): 453–63, 469–75; Sturm, Terry. "Christina Stead's New Realism: *The Man Who Loved Children* and *Cotters' England*." *Cunning Exiles.* Ed. Don Anderson and Stephen Knight. Sydney: Angus and Robertson, 1974. 9–35.

Brigid Rooney

STEINBECK, JOHN (1902–1968).

Born into precarious middle-class respectability in Salinas, California, Steinbeck would in the 1930s write some of the most famous novels about poor working-class people in all of American literature. Always intending to become a writer, he attended Stanford University in the early 1920s without graduating, and then garnered experiences for his fiction in a series of working-class jobs. His first success was the novel *Tortilla Flat* (1935), a somewhat condescending portrayal of unemployed Mexican Americans in Monterrey, California, that, nonetheless, contains a critique of bourgeois values common to most of his writing, and displays what would be Steinbeck's enduring sympathy for underdogs and his interest in communal human relationships unmediated by materialism. Similar sentiments inform his popular novella *Of Mice and Men* (1937), which describes the vulnerable lives of itinerant ranch workers, or "bindle stiffs." As is evidenced by his two most overtly political novels, Steinbeck grew increasingly interested in the exploitation of migrant crop pickers in the rich agricultural valleys of California, particularly the so-called Dust Bowl refugees. The subject of *In Dubious Battle* (1936) is a strike pitting migrant workers against the powerful growing companies and their quasi-fascist supporters. While the novel reserves its harshest criticism for the growers, it is decidedly suspicious of the labor organizers, who are portrayed as ruthlessly calculating Communists concerned only with abstract results. The narrative is informed by Steinbeck's notion of the "phalanx," a theory of group behavior superior to "great man" individualism that is, however, narrowly deterministic. The novel also implies that all the migrant workers were Anglo-Saxon whites by excluding the Mexican American and Filipino workers who had actually been the backbone of militant labor actions in the period. The exclusive focus on white workers continued in Steinbeck's 1936 series of newspaper articles, later collected as *The Harvest Gypsies*. The series was sympathetic in tone and effective as an exposé, but it displayed an unconscious middle-class condescension. Steinbeck's masterpiece **The Grapes of Wrath** (1939) transcended most of these shortcomings, although it also effectively excluded nonwhites. While his biographers repeatedly note that Steinbeck was a New Deal liberal, not a Socialist or Communist, *The Grapes of Wrath* offers some of the most elegant and impassioned descriptions of the ravages of capital accumulation in the English language. Moreover, the Joad family and their fellow "Okie" migrants in California are not merely caught up in the phalanx; they are, as is consistent with Marxist thought, subjects and agents of history. While Steinbeck wrote interesting novels later, including *Cannery Row* (1945), *East of Eden* (1952), and *The Winter of Our Discontent* (1961), the success of *The Grapes of Wrath* brought burdensome fame and unrealistic expectations, which contributed, along with the general postwar prosperity, to a diminishing of his radical impulse. Nevertheless, he was awarded the Nobel Prize in 1962, and his novels were still selling nearly two million copies a year in the early years of the twenty-first century.

Selected Bibliography: Benson, Jackson. *The True Adventures of John Steinbeck, Writer*. New York: Viking, 1984; Daniel, Cletus E. *Bitter Harvest: A History of California Farmworkers, 1870–1941*. Ithaca: Cornell UP, 1981; Parini, Jay. *John Steinbeck: A Biography*. New York: Henry Holt, 1995; Steinbeck, John. *A Life in Letters*. Ed. Elaine Steinbeck and Robert Wallsten. New York: Viking, 1975.

Charles Cunningham

STEVENSON, PHILIP EDWARD (1896–1965). A devoted U.S. communist cultural worker for over three decades, Stevenson was the son of an affluent New York attorney and grandson of a professor of physiology at Columbia University. Educated in an English-style boarding school that featured the Latin, Greek, French, and German classics, and holding a degree in literature from Harvard University (1920), Stevenson embodied many characteristics of established writers who affiliated with U.S. communism due to moral and ethical concerns in the early 1930s. His second wife, Janet Stevenson (b. 1913), was also a Communist in the 1940s and 1950s, and later a prolific author of fiction and nonfiction works.

For most of the 1920s and early 1930s, Stevenson resided in the Southwest, recovering from the tuberculosis he contracted while he served as a commissioned officer in the navy during **World War I**. By the advent of the Great Depression, Stevenson had published two conventional autobiographical novels, *The Edge of the Nest* (1929) and *The Gospel According to St. Luke's* (1931), as well as short stories in *Midland* and *Southwest Review*. As he radicalized and participated in social struggles, Stevenson launched a successful career as the author of one-act plays for the radical theater in New Mexico, as well as in New York City, where he relocated in 1936. These include *The Gentleman from Hooverville* (1934), *Road Closed* (1936), and *Transit* (1938). He also contributed reportage and criticism to the *Nation* and **New Masses**. In the 1940s, Stevenson turned to full-length plays, such as *Counterattack* (1943, with Janet Stevenson), and then moved to Hollywood in 1944, where he became a screenwriter, working on *The Story of G. I. Joe* (1945). Following his blacklisting by the House Un-American Activities Committee, he edited the left-wing *California Quarterly* from 1951 to 1957.

Stevenson was deeply affected by his thirteen years in New Mexico. There he observed the life, work, and religious practices of the native peoples, living among the Zuni and Navajo. He also came to know the poverty-stricken small ranchers, and the Mexican American workers employed in basic industries such as coal and hard-rock (zinc, silver) mining. After inaugurating a chapter of the **John Reed Club** in Sante Fe, Stevenson witnessed a successful strike of Mexican, Mexican American, Indian, and Anglo workers launched by the Communist-led National Miners Union (NMU) in 1933 in nearby Gallup. In 1935, while the NMU was in the process of fusing with John Lewis's United Mine Workers (UMW), a gun battle erupted in the midst of an attempt by police to evict a largely Mexican and Mexican American community of mine workers from their homes near Gallup. When the news broke that the sheriff and two deputies had been killed, a wave of repression was launched against the NMU and all suspected Communists. Over a hundred individuals were arrested, and fourteen were eventually charged with murder. International Labor Defense (ILD) officials who came to the aid of the miners were kidnapped and beaten. After several trials, the last two defendants received pardons in 1939, on the condition that they leave the state. In 1948, Stevenson commenced a three-volume epic in novel form that was inspired by these events, under the general rubric *The Seed*. At the time of his death, during a trip to the Soviet Union, the first two-thirds had been completed and published in two volumes each: *Morning, Noon, and Night* (1954), *Out of the Dust* (1956), *Old Father Antic* (1961), and *The Hoax* (1961).

Selected Bibliography: Booker, M. Keith. *The Modern American Novel of the Left: A Research Guide.* Westport, CT: Greenwood, 1999; Rubinstein, Harry R. "Political Regression in New Mexico: The Destruction of the National Miners' Union in Gallup." *Labor in New Mexico: Union, Strikes, and Social History since 1881*. Ed. Robert Kern. Albuquerque: U of New Mexico P, 1983. 91–140; Thorson, Connie Capers, and James L. Thorson. "Gomorrah on the Puerco: A Critical Study of Philip Stevenson's Proletarian Epic *The Seed.*" *Labor in New Mexico: Union, Strikes, and Social History since 1881*. Ed. Robert Kern. Albuquerque: U of New Mexico P, 1983. 183–270.

Alan M.Wald

STOWE, HARRIET BEECHER (1811–1896). Harriet Beecher Stowe's political reputation rests on her two great antebellum abolitionist novels. *Uncle Tom's Cabin* (1852) immortalized her as, in Abraham Lincoln's famous description, "the little lady who made this big war." The first American novel to sell more than a million copies, it was quickly translated into thirty-seven languages and briskly adapted for the stage, becoming the most popular nineteenth-century American play, with five hundred troupes performing it on the road in 1900. **James Baldwin**'s ringing 1949 condemnation of Stowe as portraying whites in blackface and creating in Uncle Tom a fleshless figure, robbed of his humanity and divested of his sex, relies as much on the stereotypes of the "Tom shows" as on the novel. Stowe's second antislavery novel, *Dred: A Tale of the Great Dismal Swamp* (1856), challenges any ideological dismissal of Stowe as favoring passivity, undermining the black male, and extoling the domestic angel, with its violent black insurrectionist (based on Nat Turner), its thinly disguised portrait of Sojourner Truth, its evocation of white mobocracy, and its forthright rejection of any reparatory fantasy of North-South reconciliation. It is often forgotten that *Uncle Tom's Cabin,* for all its success, did not mark an immediate downturn in the fortunes of slavery. If anything, the South had consolidated its powers. Apologists for slavery often pointed to the example of the poor in Europe. In response, in *Dred,* Stowe directed attention to the condition of poor American whites, constructing an economic case against slavery.

Neglected in America after the turn of the century, Stowe's political works remained enormously popular in the Soviet Union. Originally smuggled into Russia (in Yiddish) to evade the tsarist censor, they speedily found an audience that responded to the indictment of slavery as a facet of the capitalist marketplace. In America, the rise of **feminist criticism** in the 1970s led to a comprehensive reevaluation of both Stowe and the sentimental novel, understood as involving a massive attempt to reorganize culture from the woman's point of view. The bodily nature of sentimental fiction's effects was also recognized as effective in combating the sleight of hand by which apologists for slavery erased the black body from American culture. In a nation divided according to the body, physicality thus became fundamental to resistance against oppression.

Selected Bibliography: Ammons, Elizabeth, ed. *Critical Essays on Harriet Beecher Stowe*. Boston: G. K. Hall, 1980; Hedrick, Joan D. *Harriet Beecher Stowe: A Life*. Oxford: Oxford UP, 1994; Hovet, Theodore R. *The Master Narrative: Harriet Beecher Stowe's Subversive Story of Master and Slave in "Uncle Tom's Cabin" and "Dred."* New York: UP of America, 1989; Newman, Judie. Introduction to *Dred: A Tale of the Great Dismal Swamp* by Harriet Beecher Stowe. Edinburgh: Edinburgh UP, 1998; Sánchez-Eppler, Karen. *Touching Liberty: Abolition, Feminism and the Politics of the Body*. Berkeley: U of California P,

1993; Weinstein, Cindy, ed. *The Cambridge Companion to Harriet Beecher Stowe.* Cambridge: Cambridge UP, 2005.

Judith Newman

SURREALISM. Influenced by the theories of Sigmund Freud and Carl Jung, the early twentieth-century surrealists (Breton, Magritte, Ernst, Duchamp, Miro, Man Ray, Artaud, Bunuel) argued that unhappiness, alienation, and brutality originate in the contradiction between internal desires and external reality. They said that the Enlightenment's emphasis on rational thinking, while repressing the irrational elements of human nature, made **World War I** possible. They believed that through the play of thought, exploitation of chance effects and unexpected juxtapositions, combinations of high and low culture, and insertions of "fragments of reality" (usually in collage or montage), they would be able to collapse all rationalized categories and unite subject with object, the pleasure principle with the reality principle, not only in art but in life. They wanted to relate art to sensuous-material experience and make art an integrated part of reality.

After World War I, Tristan Tzara (1896–1963), leader of the Dada movement in Zurich, said that a society that creates the monstrosity of war does not deserve art, so he decided to give it anti-art, not beauty but anti-beauty. With phrases like "Dada destroys everything!" Tzara tried to offend the bourgeoisie who had institutionalized art, separating it from praxis, neutralizing possible political impacts. Surrealism grew out of Dada. However, under the leadership of André Breton (1896–1966), a French doctor and writer who fought in the trenches of World War I, surrealists sought productive rather than anarchic responses to the group's convictions. By collapsing the separation between art and life that they saw as central to bourgeois aesthetics, surrealists expected to transform human nature and bring about a social revolution that would radically transform the world. Thus, the surrealists made transgression against bourgeois values central to their art and their lives.

However, the bourgeoisie soon embraced surrealist art, appropriating its anti-establishment stance (ignoring the fact that they were the establishment). The avant-garde aesthetics of shocking transgression against taboo became merely a source of bourgeois pleasure, avant-garde anti-art became institutionalized as art, and the surrealist strategy of creating intoxicating-immediate life experiences became simply another commodity. Thus, capitalism's incorporation of the surreal suggests, as **Georg Lukács** argued, that modernist and avant-garde art were a decadent diversion from real counter-forces seeking to overcome capitalism. Indeed, with the rise of fascism and the outbreak of **World War II**, many surrealists decided political engagement and self-survival were more important than experimenting with art and language.

Surrealism's historical desire to abolish capitalism largely forgotten, writers, artists, filmmakers, and (perhaps most importantly) advertisers continue to use surrealist techniques in the early twenty-first century, particularly the technique of fragmentation, which has become a principal commodified and commodifying force of postmodern consumer culture. Art remains an institution separate from praxis (despite, or perhaps because of, the absorption of dreams and fantasy into postmodern reality), and any art with political content has been thus far rendered ineffective against the alienating psychic effects of capitalism.

Selected Bibliography: Breton, André. *Manifestoes of Surrealism.* Trans. Richard Seaver and Helen R. Lane. Ann Arbor: U of Michigan P, 1969; Bürger, Peter. *Theory of the Avant-Garde.* Trans. Michael Shaw. Minneapolis: U of Minnesota P, 1984; Calinescu, Matei. *Five Faces of Modernity.* Durham, NC: Duke UP, 1987; Lukács, Georg. *Realism in Our Time: Literature and the Class Struggle.* Trans. John Mander and Necke Mander. New York: Harper and Row, 1964.

Sandy Rankin

SWIFT, JONATHAN (1667–1745). Poet, pamphleteer, and satirist, Swift was born in Dublin to English parents and educated at Trinity College Dublin. He became a priest in the (Anglican) Church of Ireland and was installed as dean of St. Patrick's Cathedral, Dublin, in 1713. Swift identified himself as a High Churchman, and an intransigent defense of the established Anglican Church informed his political writing and allegiance throughout his life. His pamphleteering in defense of Irish interests in the 1720s earned him an enduring reputation as an Irish patriot.

Swift's first writings date from soon after the Glorious Revolution of 1688–1689. He wrote odes praising William III (looking to the new king to restore Anglican hegemony) and Dr. William Sancroft, the archbishop of Canterbury, who had been deprived for refusing to recognize William III and the revolution settlement. His first major prose satires *A Tale of a Tub, The Battle of the Books,* and *The Mechanical Operation of the Spirit* (published together anonymously in 1704) attack Roman Catholicism and Protestant dissent as abuses in religion and take an antimodernist cultural stance. Although Swift was aligned with the Whig party in the first decade of the eighteenth century, publishing *A Discourse of the Contests and Dissentions between the Nobles and the Commons in Athens and Rome* (1701) in their interest and moving among Whig writers and politicians, he rejected Whig ecclesiastical policy that was sympathetic to Protestant dissent. Swift's particularly destructive satire on dissent in *A Tale of a Tub* and *The Mechanical Operation of the Spirit* is symptomatic of his High Church Tory conformism. His public conversion to the Tories (or "Church Party" as Swift called them) occurred in 1710. He became a powerful propagandist for the Tory ministry of 1710–1714, writing *The Examiner* in 1710–1711 and producing pamphlets and poems attacking the previous pro-war Whig ministry and the Duke of Marlborough. His *The Conduct of the Allies* (1711), written in consultation with the Tory leaders, was an influential statement of Tory foreign policy and prejudices aimed at securing support for peace with France, achieved in the Treaty of Utrecht in 1713.

With the collapse of the Tory government after the Hanoverian accession in 1714, Ireland became Swift's principal political theater. His incendiary pamphleteering in the area of political economy, particularly in *The Drapier's Letters* (1724–1725), powerfully fueled Irish resistance to the English Whig government. The fourth *Drapier's Letter* claimed Irish legislative independence from the parliament of England. In *A Modest Proposal* (1729), a masterpiece of black humor and cold-blooded satiric irony, the solution proposed for the problem of Irish poverty is for the Irish to eat their babies. Swift's most famous prose work, *Gulliver's Travels* (1726), is a radical satiric anatomy of corruption in the contemporary body politic and urges the need for public conformity in the state. A passage in part 3 of *Gulliver's Travels*, unprinted in Swift's lifetime, contains an allegory of Irish resistance to the Hanoverian Whig government in which Gulliver learns that the oppressed people were determined to kill their king and entirely change the government. Swift was ideologically conservative, but a signature of his satire is its imaginative extremism.

> *Selected Bibliography:* Ehrenpreis, Irvin. *Swift: The Man, His Works, and the Age.* 3 vols. London: Methuen, 1962–1983; Lock, F. P. *Swift's Tory Politics.* London: Duckworth, 1983; Rawson, Claude, ed. *Jonathan Swift: A Collection of Critical Essays.* Englewood Cliffs, NJ: Prentice Hall, 1995; Said, Edward. "Swift's Tory Anarchy." *The World, the Text, and the Critic.* Cambridge, MA: Harvard UP, 1983. 54–71.

Ian Higgins

SWINGLER, RANDALL (1909–1967), British playwright, novelist, librettist, critic, editor, and poet. Swingler was born in Aldershot, Hampshire, where his father was the assistant curate of the parish church. One grandfather was an ironmaster, railway builder, coal owner, and deputy lieutenant of Derbyshire. The other was a colonel in the Seaforth Highlanders and the Madras Artillery. His uncle and godfather was the archbishop of Canterbury, Randall Davidson.

Swingler was educated at home until he was ten, when he went to prep school, followed by Winchester and New College, Oxford, where he earned a reputation as a runner, flautist, and poet. In 1931, he met the concert pianist Geraldine Peppin, for whom he wrote *Poems* (1932). They married in 1933. Two more books of poems followed, *Reconstruction* (1933) and *Difficult Morning* (1933).

In 1934, Swingler joined the **Communist Party**, and was the best-known young writer then active in the party. He edited *Left Review* and published **Nancy Cunard**'s *Authors Take Sides on the Spanish War.* He wrote a new version of *Peer Gynt* for the Group Theatre and several plays for Unity Theatre, including the mass declamation *Spain* (1936) and the antifascist play *Crisis* (1938). He wrote *Peace and Prosperity* (1937) for the London Choral Union, a new version of Handel's *Belshazzar* (1938) for the London Co-op Choirs, and the chorale finale of Alan Bush's *Piano Concerto* (1938). In 1938, he launched his own radical paperback-publishing company, Fore Publications, selling half a million books in twelve months. He was active in the Workers Music Association and in the Left Book Club, for whom he and Bush edited the *Left Song Book* (1938). They also organized the 1939 Festival of Music and the People, which included an Albert Hall pageant written by Swingler and starring Paul Robeson, as well as the premier of Benjamin Britten's *Ballad of Heroes*, for which Swingler and **W. H. Auden** wrote the libretto. He published two novels, *No Escape* (1937) and *To Town* (1939). In 1939, he became literary editor of the *Daily Worker*; in 1941, he founded the radical cultural magazine *Our Time.*

Called up at the end of 1941, Swingler took part in the Salerno landings, was made a corporal at Anzio, and was awarded the Military Medal for bravery for his part in the battle of Lake Commachio. In **cold-war** London, Swingler was blacklisted at the BBC and his adult-education classes investigated; inside the Communist Party, he was attacked as a "bohemian" and forced to resign from *Our Time.* His last collections of poetry were *The Years of Anger* (1946) and *The God in the Cave* (1950). He resigned from the Communist Party in early 1956. The following year, he helped found the *New Reasoner*.

Swingler spent the last decade of his life in the village of Pebmarsh in Essex. He wrote several libretti for his friends Bernard Stevens and Alan Rawsthorne. By 1965, writer's block, political despair, financial worries, heavy drinking, and medication for a serious heart condition combined to cause a breakdown. He died of a heart attack in 1967.

Selected Bibliography: Croft, Andy. *Comrade Heart: A Life of Randall Swingler*. Manchester: Manchester UP, 2003; Croft, Andy, ed. *A Weapon in the Struggle: The Cultural History of the Communist Party in Britain*. London: Pluto, 1998; Rattenbury, Arnold. "Poems by Randall Swingler." *The 1930s: A Challenge to Orthodoxy*. Ed. John Lucas. Hassocks, UK: Harvester, 1978.

Andy Croft

T

TAGGARD, GENEVIEVE (1894–1948). Born in Waitsburg, Washington, and raised in Hawaii, where her missionary parents ran a school, Taggard graduated from the University of California and moved to New York City in the early 1920s. A socialist since her Berkeley days, Taggard moved in the Greenwich Village bohemian circle of Floyd Dell, **Max Eastman**, John Sloan, and Edna St. Vincent Millay, among others. She worked for the experimental publisher B. W. Huebsch and helped edit the modernist journal the *Measure*. Taggard's early verse is situated in the feminist love-lyric tradition of the 1920s, but her interest in the convergence of literary practice and social commitment would consume her until the end of her life. In 1925 she edited *May Days*, an anthology of the socially inspired lyrics originally published in the radical journals the *Masses* and the *Liberator*. Taggard's poetic vision began to change in the 1930s. The Great Depression, perhaps coupled with the approach of middle age, found her throwing off her love-poet mantle for the title of social poet. Nothing is more evident than the class critique Taggard makes in her 1936 collection *Calling Western Union*. Poems such as "Feeding the Children," "A Middle-Aged, Middle-Class Woman at Midnight," "Mill Town," and "Up State—Depression Summer" explore themes of social inequality and deprivation and their significant impact on America culture at that time.

In addition to her literary endeavors, Taggard was involved in a variety of progressive organizations and causes. She was a member of the New York Teacher's Union and served on the executive council of the League of American Writers. As a contributing editor for the **New Masses**, she wrote articles about literature and politics.

Taggard published thirteen books of verse, including a selection of her early work, *Traveling Standing Still* (1928), and *Collected Poems, 1918–1938* (1938). She also edited several poetry anthologies and published a biography of Emily Dickinson. Taggard explores her development as a radical in two autobiographical pieces, "Hawaii, Washington, Vermont"—her preface to *Calling Western Union*—and *Poet out of Pioneer,* which appeared as part of the These Modern Women series that was published in the *Nation* in 1926.

Selected Bibliography: Berke, Nancy. *Women Poets on the Left: Lola Ridge, Genevieve Taggard, Margaret Walker.* Gainesville: UP of Florida, 2001; Drake, William. *The First Wave: Women Poets in Amer-

ica, 1915–1945. New York: Macmillan, 1987; Lisella, Julia, et al. "Readings: Genevieve Taggard." *How2* 2.1 (Spring 2003), http://www.scc.rutgers.edu/however/print_archive/1184.html; Miller, Nina. *Making Love Modern: The Intimate Public Worlds of New York's Literary Women.* New York: Oxford UP, 1998.

Nancy Berke

TAGORE, RABINDRANATH (1861–1941). Tagore was born in Bengal, the eastern region of colonial India, to a family of wealthy landed aristocrats. He was the fourteenth child in a large extended family including uncles, aunts, and grandparents. Tagore grew up in affluence but not in pomp. While the Tagores believed in economic prudence, they were generous in supporting poets and musicians and wrote and composed themselves. Tagore was educated by private tutors and began to write at an early age, earning fame home and abroad. He received the Nobel Prize for Literature upon the publication of his own English translation of a selection of his poetry, *Gitanjali,* in 1913.

Lionized by poets such as **W. B. Yeats** and **Ezra Pound**, Tagore grew immensely popular in the West. Much of this high esteem derived from the perception that he was a product of eastern spiritualism and that his poetry expressed a unique mysticism. Within two decades or so, however, his reputation began to decline; both Yeats and Pound turned against him. Tagore's failure to deliver to Western audiences was because his poetry on mysticism—which never translates well into English—comprised only a part of his work. His other interests didn't attract much following.

Tagore was a prolific author; in his six-decade-long writing career, he produced nearly two hundred books. He tried his hand at a variety of genres and wrote on countless topics. A major concern of his writing was India's transition into modernity. His writing, in fact, represents both sides of this transition, and in a curious way, he remains traditional as well as modern. For example, he appreciated the modernizing power of nationalism but, like Mahatma Gandhi, was apprehensive of the way nationalism had the potential to promote a Hindu identity in a country with a Hindu majority but also with other significant minorities, thus provoking violence. Tagore treated the complexities of competing national identities in India in the novel *The Home and the World* (1915, English translation 1919), a work that often draws major attention in postcolonial studies and of which a film was made by Satyajit Ray, the Oscar-winning Indian filmmaker. Unlike Gandhi, however, Tagore was not opposed to modernity, nor was he an enthusiast of "holy poverty." Aware of the abject illiteracy and destitution of many Indians, he believed that mass education could set in the mechanism of improving their lot.

Among poets of the world, Tagore enjoys a unique distinction: two of his songs have become national anthems of India and Bangladesh, two sovereign nations. Not only is his poetry the staple of the literary diet among the Bengalis in both Bangladesh and India, but his fiction, nonfiction prose, drama, music, and painting continue to delight and inspire them to this day, sixty years after his death. Tagore is a key figure in Indian studies, and his reputation, far from being on the wane, remains strong in the world.

Selected Bibliography: Chatterjee, Bhabatosh. *Rabindranath Tagore and Modern Sensibility.* Delhi: Oxford UP, 1996; Dutt, Krishna, and Andrew Robinson. *Rabindranath Tagore: The Myriad-Minded Man.*

New York: St. Martin's, 1996; Henn, Katherine. *Rabindranath Tagore: A Bibliography*. Metuchen, NJ: Scarecrow, 1985; Hogan, Patrick, and Lalita Pandit, eds. *Rabindranath Tagore: Universality and Tradition*. Cranbury, NJ: Fairleigh Dickinson UP, 2003.

Farhad B. Idris

TESTIMONIO, a nonfiction narrative genre depicting the lives and struggles of subaltern groups. Generally associated with the civil rights and social movements of the 1960s in Latin America, *testimonio* literature sought to give voice to the voiceless: the poor, Indians, workers, and peasants.

Historically, Latin American literature was produced and consumed mostly by an urban, educated elite in countries with large illiterate populations. *Testimonio,* in contrast, sought to tell, in its own words, the story of the vast, excluded majority. For example, the experience of slavery and the precarious existence of Afro-Cubans is described by Esteban Montejo, a former slave whose life story is transcribed by Miguel Barnet in *Autobiography of a Runaway Slave* (*Biografía de un cimarrón,* 1966). The life story of Jesusa Palancares, an Indian woman from Oaxaca, Mexico, who participated in the Mexican Revolution, is told in Elena Poniatowska's *Here's to You, Jesusa!* (*Hasta no verte, Jesús Mío,* 1969). *Child of the Dark* (*Quarto de despejo,* 1960) tells the story of Carolina Maria de Jesus, an Afro-Brazilian woman from one of Rio de Janeiro's *favelas* (shanty towns) who collects scrap paper for a living. The story of Bolivian mine workers lives is narrated by Domitila Barrios de Chungara in *Let Me Speak!* (*Si me permiten hablar,* 1977). One of the most widely read and controversial *testimonios* is **Rigoberta Menchú**'s *I, Rigoberta Menchú, an Indian Woman from Guatemala* (*Me llamo Rigoberta Menchú y así me nació la conciencia,* 1983).

As a narrative genre, *testimonio* has affinities with autobiography, ethnography, confessions, memoirs, and journalism. *Testimonio* narratives, however, are often not centered on the life of one particular individual, as in the case of autobiography. In *testimonio,* the main narrator often represents a whole group. Unlike the claimed objectivity and disinterested nature of ethnographic narratives, *testimonios* are openly politically motivated and often seek solidarity from their readership by calling attention to present conditions of oppression.

The validity, reliability, and political effectiveness of *testimonio* as the voice of the voiceless has been widely debated. From its production to its reception, a range of epistemological, political, and ethical questions arise. Is the native informant reliable and representative of a whole group? Can we assume that subaltern groups are fully knowable, transparent subjects and that they are always willing to tell us their story? *Testimonios* are often transcribed and edited by mainstream intellectuals. In *I, Rigoberta Menchú,* for example, Venezuelan anthropologist Elizabeth Burgos interviewed Menchú and edited the recorded information into separate, chronologically organized chapters. In all the *testimonios* cited, the relationship of the interviewer and transcriber with the subaltern groups is clearly asymmetrical. In terms of readership and the now globalized cultural market, a relevant concern is which narratives reach this market. From an ethical perspective, a critical concern is whether *testimonio* calls for a new pact between metropolitan readers and subaltern groups. Also, does *testimonio* change the traditional, aesthetically oriented definition of literature? Notwithstanding all these issues, *testimonio* has become a valid tool for marginal groups to address the state and the international community with their demands for social justice.

Suggested Bibliography: Beverley, John. *Against Literature.* Minneapolis: U of Minnesota P, 1993; Carey-Webb, Allen, and Stephen Benz, eds. *Teaching and Testimony: Rigoberta Menchú and the North American Classroom.* Albany: SUNY P, 1996; Gugelberger, Georg M., ed. *The Real Thing: Testimonial Discourse in Latin America.* Durham: Duke UP, 1996; Gugelberger, Georg M., and Michael Kearney, eds. "Voices of the Voiceless: Testimonial Literature in Latin America." Two-part special issue of *Latin American Perspectives* 18.3–4 (1991); Harlow, Barbara. *Resistance Literature.* New York: Methuen, 1987; Sklodowska, Elzbieta. *Testimonio hispanoamericano.* New York: Peter Lang, 1992; Sommer, Doris. *Proceed with Caution When Engaged by Minority Writing in the Americas.* Cambridge: Harvard UP, 1999.

Luis Fernando Restrepo

THEATER, POLITICAL. Since the late nineteenth century, political theater has been widely understood as comprising theatrical performances that demand that an audience reflect on contested social, historical, political, economic, and cultural "realities" beyond the stage. The category "political theater" must take into account not only the politics of a given "text" but also the way those politics necessarily manifest themselves in performance. This discussion centers on five fundamental, though by no means mutually exclusive, kinds of political theater: satire, social **realism**, **epic theater**, absurdism, and performance art.

Satire, as a kind of performance, finds its earliest extant examples in the works of the Greek playwright Aristophanes, whose plays exaggerate and deride widespread social foibles. Seventeenth-century satirists, including Molière in France and Aphra Behn in England, reclaimed the form to produce highly topical social comedy. In the eighteenth century, Irishmen Oliver Goldsmith and Richard Brinsley Sheridan became widely admired for their mastery of the form. More recent examples of satire on stage include the works of Oscar Wilde, Noel Coward, Joe Orton (1933–1967), and Tom Stoppard.

Satire typically presents stock characters in potentially serious situations, the tensions of which arise from the conflict between an individual's desires and the social mores and customs according to which she or he is expected to behave. The comic element emerges in satire most notably from the exaggeration of those customs and expectations to the point of ridicule. Though the personal quirks of each character and the relative unimportance of the crisis contribute to the humorous effect, the politics of satire emerge primarily from its lampoon of ideological and political systems.

Social realism found one of its earliest and staunchest supporters in Ireland's **George Bernard Shaw.** In his reviews and essays, Shaw, sympathetic to continental naturalism, valorizes the realistic representation and consideration of serious social questions. **Henrik Ibsen**'s plays—performed by small touring companies and produced at the subscription theaters and societies that emerged in late Victorian England as a means of sidestepping the Lord Chamberlain's imprimatur—represented the pinnacle of socially responsible drama for Shaw. He repeatedly praises Ibsen's willingness to address the problems of women's subordination, venereal disease, poverty, and social prejudice centrally in his work. Characters such as Nora Helmer and Hedda Gabler became the model for what Shaw would call "the new woman": independent, intelligent, assertive, and fierce in defending her equality with the (usually) small-minded, cowardly, repressive, and socially conservative men and institutions that regulate her life.

In his own plays, Shaw sought to address similar topics—particularly in his thesis plays, which deliver not only a diagnosis of social problems but also a solution to them. Most of Shaw's plays, particularly from the first half of his long career, deploy a combination of broad comedy, witty repartee, earnest philosophizing, and personal tragedy—or at least peripety—to make their points. However, the overwhelming sense of Shavian social realism is that of a serious and well-reasoned debate.

Shaw emphasized the necessity of realistic production. In print, he repeatedly berated actors for exaggerated gesture, manifestly false diction, poor vocal technique, and a tendency to lapse into the stock characterizations of melodrama and high tragedy. This aesthetic, for Shaw, carried with it political nuances; taking its cue from naturalism's mandates, he often reproduced lifelike domestic scenes, employing naturalistic lighting and functional furnishings and accessories built on a human—rather than a tragic or melodramatic—scale to engage the spectator fully in the world of the play.

Shaw and Ibsen served as models for later dramatists as well, particularly in Great Britain, where the founding of London's English Stage Company at the Royal Court Theatre (1955) encouraged the generation of social realists known as "the Angry Young Men," including Arnold Wesker, John Arden and Margaretta D'Arcy, and—most famously—John Osborne. In the United States, social realism thrived primarily in two early theater collectives: the Provincetown Players and the Group Theater. Founded by Susan Glaspell and Eugene O'Neill, the Provincetown Players (1916–1929) produced a wide variety of social drama, though rarely plays expounding an explicit thesis. However, they soon began producing more expressionistic, experimental, and less manifestly socially-relevant pieces.

The Group Theater (1931–1941), founded by Harold Clurman, Lee Strasberg, and Cheryl Crawford, produced a combination of social realism and agitation-propaganda (agit-prop) drama largely devoted to contemporary questions of labor and class. Borrowing heavily from Russian director Constantin Stanislavsky's naturalistic views on staging and character building, almost all Group Theater productions emphasized realistic performance. As a result, the Group Theater served as the early testing ground for theories of production and acting that have almost single-handedly shaped American dramaturgy, both on stage and in film.

Social realism in political theater has waned in recent decades, as most politically motivated dramaturgy has turned toward more experimental, alienating forms. With the exceptions of such playwrights as David Mamet and Arthur Miller in the United States and David Hare in Great Britain, political theater today relies more heavily on the absurdist and epic dramaturgies discussed below.

Since its inception in the theatrical experiments of German producer-director Erwin Piscator in the 1910s and 1920s, epic dramaturgy has been linked with leftist—and usually Marxist—political theater. Combining the resources and capabilities of professional theater with the textures, motifs, and techniques of impromptu, amateur agit-prop performance—or "street theater"—Piscator and his later collaborator **Bertolt Brecht** saw epic drama as an antidote to popular escapist theater predominating in Western Europe between the wars. According to Brecht, whose many essays and reflections on theater and politics have provided the basic vocabulary of epic drama, political theater should attempt to awaken the audience's powers of analysis and observation by forestalling their impulse to identify emotionally with the action and characters on stage. Once awakened—or "estranged," to use Brecht's term—the spectators should be ready to consider carefully the social argument presented on stage. To achieve this estrangement, Brecht and later epic theorists employed crude set designs, dissonant musical interludes, sung poetry, projected images, placards, and a tongue-in-cheek gestic style of acting to disrupt the realistic surface and the Aristotelian unities of the performed drama.

Because of Brecht's prolific output, because his Berliner Ensemble became the most important state-sanctioned theatrical company in communist East Germany after **World War II**, and because of their tour through England in 1957, these techniques of estrangement became, by the 1960s, almost synonymous with leftist political theater. Brecht's inheritors, including German playwrights **Peter Weiss** and **Heiner Müller** and English writers **Edward Bond**, Howard Brenton, and **Caryl Churchill**, continued to refine his approach after his death. Bond, Brenton, Weiss, and Müller, for instance, have deployed Artaudian depictions of cruelty and violence on stage as another kind of estranging technique in their works in order to investigate historical and potential abuses of power. Churchill's plays synthesize epic production choices, collaborative and improvisational rehearsal processes, and a radical **Marxist-feminist** agenda.

Brechtian epic has also proved effective as a means for allowing underrepresented ethnic and national voices to make themselves heard on stage. Chinese American David Henry Hwang's *M. Butterfly*, South African Athol Fugard's *The Island*, Anglo-Chicana Cherrie Moraga's *Shadow of a Man*, and African American **Amiri Baraka**'s *Dutchman*, among other plays, critique the dominance of white, Western ideology by rewriting or reimagining colonial and imperial histories. While twentieth-century Irish drama—with its tendency toward the comic, mythopoetic, and realistic—by and large provides an exception to the apparent complementarity between postcolonial politics and Brechtian staging, the impulse to find new ways of speaking on stage inform the works of **W. B. Yeats**, J. M. Synge, and Marina Carr. In addition, occasional epic devices help link the plays of Brian Friel and Brendan Behan to the larger global traditions of postcolonial drama.

In the United States, epic drama has developed somewhat differently. Also originating in leftist agit-prop drama of depression, starkly deployed in **Clifford Odets**'s *Waiting for Lefty* (1935), and developed further in Luis Valdez's brief plays, or "actos," written for his El Teatro Campesino in support of Cesar Chavez's United Farm Workers of America, epic as a dramatic form seems to have found a less hospitable reception in mainstream, or even prominent fringe, drama in the last two decades of the twentieth century. With the notable exceptions of Hwang, Tony Kushner, and Baraka, few contemporary American playwrights have relied on epic thematics and production techniques in North American drama.

Growing out of the avant-garde experiments of Dada performance—such as Alfred Jarry's *Ubu Roi* (1896)—and inflected with the increasingly resonant existentialist philosophy of identity and responsibility emergent in the works of Franz Kafka and **Jean-Paul Sartre**, absurdism comprises a wide range of dramatic experiments by such playwrights as Germany's **Günter Grass**, Ireland's (and France's) **Samuel Beckett**, Romania's Eugene Ionesco, Czechoslovakia's **Vaclav Havel**, France's Jean Genet, and England's **Harold Pinter** and **Sarah Kane**. Martin Esslin, whose study *The Theatre of the Absurd* created the very term "aburdism," argues that absurdism is primarily marked by a worldview—either explicitly espoused by the characters or implied in their latent anxieties and tensions—that sees meaning, significance, and purpose as highly contingent values, always under negotiation and always inflected by apparently objective considerations on them.

In Esslin's view, absurdism does not concern itself with material reality beyond the stage, and therefore is an apolitical form in relation to other modes discussed above. Rather, absurdism seems, for Esslin, to explore the stakes of personal identity on the level of the individual, providing models for and warnings about various modes of self-fashioning. However, more recent scholarship sees absurdism as profoundly political, inasmuch as the various plays often included under this heading seem to deconstruct the individual as a legible political unit. Thus, the enlightenment humanist notions of will, responsibility, rights, and action on which most Western juridical, political, and economic theory rests begins to give way to a concept of the human whose relation to other humans and to his or her society more broadly is always under revision, always open to renegotiation, and always more than mainstream notions of the individual are able to account for.

Within absurdism, two broad impulses emerge. Many plays set their deconstruction of the individual within an explicitly politicized context on stage. Ionesco's *Rhinoceros* (1959), Havel's *Garden Party* (1963), Genet's *Blacks: A Clown Show* (1958), Grass's *Plebeians Rehearse the Uprising* (1966), and Pinter's *Mountain Language* (1988) are among the plays whose commentary on social, economic, and institutional power and the injustice it gives rise to is most explicit. However, other works only implicitly politicize the power dynamics they present. Most of Beckett's plays, the early works of Pinter, Kane's *4.48 Psychosis* (1999), and Ionesco's *Chairs* (1959) typify this latter mode of absurdism.

Performance art is perhaps the broadest, most varied category of political performance. Serving as a kind of catch-all category for performance pieces that do not adhere to traditional notions of characterization and plot structure, performance art includes dance, monologues, happenings, staged montage, mime, and concerts. The salient features of most (though not all) political performance art are experimental form; improvisation; marked heteroglossia; emphasis on the disjunction among voice, body, and identity; the transgression of socially sanctioned boundaries and categories; highly stylized representation; and episodic, rather than unified, narratives. In deploying these strategies, it attempts to question contemporary boundaries of good taste, political orthodoxy, and conceptions of right and wrong by willfully and flagrantly transgressing them.

Performance art has, during the twentieth century, been a particularly attractive mode for discussing and commenting on gendered and sexualized identities. Laurie Anderson, Holly Hughes, Karen Finley, Hélène Cixous, and Eddie Izzard have all used non-narrative staged presentation to question widely held notions concerning heterosexuality, the sexualized body, intersexual violence, gender coding, and gender and sex as ideological (rather than biological) categories. Often borrowing from popular-cultural mediums, such as television, rock and pop music, and film, performance art often integrates artifacts from the very culture it attempts to analyze and critique, as evidenced in the staged and filmed productions of John Cameron Mitchell's musical *Hedwig and the Angry Inch* (1998).

Though scholarly interest in the history and theory of performance art has grown significantly during the 1990s and early twenty-first century, it has as yet not garnered widespread public interest, certainly in large part because of its inherent resistance to co-optation into mainstream cultural tastes and institutions. Moreover, the American **culture wars** of the 1980s and 1990s did much to separate popular conceptions of performance art from a deeper understanding of its forms and positions. Also, because performance art tends to respond immediately to pressing social concerns and because it often relies on improvisational self-presentation by the artist herself, performance art is rarely reproduced after an initial run or tour.

Selected Bibliography: Esslin, Martin. *The Theatre of the Absurd.* 3rd ed. New York: Vintage-Random House, 2004; Gainor, J. Ellen. *Imperialism and Theatre: Essays on World Theatre, Drama, and Performance.* London: Routledge, 1995; Martin, Carol, ed. *A Sourcebook of Feminist Theatre and Performance: On and Beyond the Stage.* London: Routledge, 1996; Piscator, Erwin. *The Political Theatre: A History, 1914–1929.* Trans. Hugh Rorrison. New York: Avon, 1978; Reinelt, Janelle. *After Brecht: British Epic Theater.* Ann Arbor: U of Michigan P, 1994; Roberts, Philip. *The Royal Court Theatre and the Modern Stage.* Cambridge: Cambridge UP, 1999; Watt, Stephen, Eileen Morgan, and Shakir Mustafa, eds. *A Century of Irish Drama: Widening the Stage.* Bloomington: Indiana UP, 2000; Worthen, W. B. *Modern Drama and the Rhetoric of Theater.* Berkeley: U of California P, 1992.

Craig N. Owens

THIRD INTERNATIONAL. In March 1919, the Third International, also called the Communist International (Comintern), was founded in Moscow by an association of nineteen socialist parties and affiliated groups. Like its predecessors, the Third International was established to provide a communist theoretical orientation and political leadership to its affiliated working-class parties and organizations in their struggles for both capitalist reform and socialist revolution.

The Third International was formed in response to two major political events of the postwar period. First, it took over the leadership of the world communist movement after the political and organizational collapse of the Second International (1889–1918), whose capitulation to nationalism and imperialism delegitimated it for millions of workers and elicited scathing critiques, notably from **Vladimir Lenin**. Second, the increasingly revolutionary situation in postwar Europe and America— from the revolutionary wave in Germany, Hungary, Italy, and the Balkans to the strike waves in England, France, and the United States—precipitated the need for renewed international political coordination and solidarity based on Marxian principles. Moreover, the Soviet Union was in the throes of counter-revolution and under attack by the imperialist powers. The time was ripe for the formation of a new communist international.

The policies of the Third International were formally decided on at its first and founding congress in March 1919. The founding members reaffirmed the Marxist program for a revolutionary seizure of power and the establishment of a dictatorship of the proletariat in a socialist society. Aside from returning to the work of **Marx** and Engels, the founders of the Third International were guided by Lenin's critique of the revisionism of the leadership of the Second International and especially by his *Imperialism, the Highest Stage of Capitalism* (1917) and *State and Revolution* (1917).

Over its twenty-four-year life span, the Third International held a total of seven congresses—the last held in 1935, during which it elaborated and revised both strategy and tactics for the world communist movement. The first six congresses remained true in large part to the theories of Marx, Engels, and Lenin. Indeed, at the Sixth World Congress of the Comintern (1928), the Communists made important strides in their understanding of racism as one of the chief obstacles to fostering class consciousness and the proletariat's seizure of political power. They also consistently emphasized the limits of reformism for the working class under a bourgeois dictatorship and the need for a communist revolution. At the Seventh World Congress (1935), however, the Third International took a significant ideological turn by ushering in the **Popular Front** policy to defeat the spread of fascism. The Popular Front policy downplayed the "class against class" analysis (formally adopted at the Sixth Congress) in favor of creating a broad "democratic" front of people, irrespective of their class.

The rightward trend of the Third International culminated in June 1943 when the Executive Committee of the Comintern (ECCI) dissolved the Third International. The ECCI claimed the Comintern could no longer be useful in directing the increasingly complicated internal and external situations of its member countries or in strengthening national working-class parties. Moreover, **Joseph Stalin** asserted that the dissolution of the Third International was consistent with the Popular Front and proved that, contrary to Hitler and other anticommunists, Moscow did not intervene in the labor movements of other nations.

Selected Bibliography: Dutt, R. Palme. *The Internationale.* London: Lawrence and Wishart, 1964; Foster, William Z. *History of the Three Internationals: The World Socialist and Communist Movements from 1848 to the Present.* New York: International Publishers, 1955; Lenin, Vladimir Ilyich. "The Collapse of the Second International." *Collected Works.* Vol. 21. Moscow: Progress Publishers, 1980. 207–59; Lenin, Vladimir Ilyich. "Opportunism, and the Collapse of the Second International." *Collected Works.* Vol. 21. Moscow: Progress Publishers, 1980. 438–53.

Anthony Dawahare

THOMPSON, JIM (1906–1977). James Meyers Thompson was a pulp crime novelist of the 1950s and 1960s who used his life experiences to create a nightmare vision of American desires and dreams. Thompson's life reads like fiction. Although he was born in Oklahoma, Thompson's formative years were spent in Texas. Due to his father's squandering of all the money he had made in the oil business, the high-school-aged Thompson was forced to support the family by working as a bellboy at the Hotel Texas in Fort Worth, where he procured drugs and alcohol for the guests and had a nervous breakdown by the time he was nineteen. Thompson then traveled to West Texas, where he lived in hobo jungles and worked in the oil fields. After a brief stint at the University of Nebraska, Thompson joined the **Communist Party** in 1935 and, through party contacts, gained employment with the Oklahoma **Federal Writers' Project**. Thompson left the party in 1938, though his former connections with the party prompted an investigation by the FBI during his work at an industrial plant during **World War II**.

Robert Polito, in his biography of Thompson, notes that reading the works of **Karl Marx** was one of the crucial formative experiences of Thompson's life as a writer. Polito quotes Thompson as having told a colleague at the Writers' Project, Gordon Friesen, that reading Marx was "the turning point in his life . . . his first real education." Marx, Thompson reportedly proclaimed, had "given him the words to understand his life." Importantly, Polito concludes that much of this basic Marxist outlook survived the 1930s and Thompson's membership in the party. He quotes the testimony of another Thompson friend, Pierre Rissient, that Thompson continued to see all of literature—and the world—through a fundamentally Marxist lens as late as the 1960s (128–29).

Thompson's best-known work, *The Killer Inside Me* (1952), is a nihilist novel narrated by Lou Ford, a psychotic (and murderous) small-town sheriff. The novel explores the hypocrisies and violence that underlie a supposedly peaceful American small town. As is typical of noir writers, Thompson's writing continually exposes the shortcomings of the American Dream. A typical Thompson protagonist, such as Dolly Dillon in *A Hell of a Woman* (1954), strives for success through hard work but ends up turning to crime in order to get the material things he or she wants. Thompson conveys these themes in a mode of gritty realism supplemented by bizarre turns reminiscent of **surrealism**, suggesting the influence of the European avant-garde and marking Thompson as a forerunner of American **postmodernism**.

Other major Thompson novels include *Savage Night* (1953), *The Getaway* (1958), *The Grifters* (1963), and *Pop. 1280* (1964). Altogether, he was the author of twenty-nine published novels. His work experienced a brief period of moderate commercial success in the 1950s, and he gained some critical recognition during his lifetime as well, as when R. V. Cassill, writing in 1968, praised Thompson's writing as that of a modern-day Sophocles. However, Thompson's greatest success, both commercially and critically, came posthumously, during the so-called Thompson revival of the 1980s and 1990s—a revival partly spurred by the crucial role given Thompson in Geoffrey O'Brien's rousing survey of pulp crime fiction, *Hardboiled America: Lurid Paperbacks and the Masters of Noir* (1981). This revival included the reappearance of most of Thompson's books under the Black Lizard imprint and the production of a number of film versions of his novels, such as *The Grifters* (1990) and *The Getaway* (1993), though the latter had originally been adapted to film in 1972.

Selected Bibliography: Booker, M. Keith. *The Post-Utopian Imagination: American Culture in the Long 1950s*. Westport, CT: Greenwood, 2002; Brewer, Gay. *Laughing Like Hell: The Harrowing Satires of Jim Thompson*. San Bernardino: Brownstone, 1996; Cassill, R. V. "The Killer Inside Me: Fear, Purgation, and the Sophoclean Light." *Tough Guy Writers of the Thirties*. Ed. David Madden. Carbondale: Southern Illinois UP, 1968. 230–38; Hendershot, Cyndy. "Rolling Toward the Horizon on Empty: Jim Thompson's West Texas Crime Fiction." *Bad Boys and Bad Girls in the Badlands*. Ed. Steve Glassman and Maurice J. O'Sullivan. Bowling Green: Popular P, 2001. 177–89; McCauley, Michael J. *Jim Thompson: Sleep with the Devil*. New York: Mysterious P, 1991; O'Brien, Geoffrey. *Hardboiled America: Lurid*

Paperbacks and the Masters of Noir. 1981. Expanded ed. New York: Da Capo, 1997; Polito, Robert. *Savage Art: A Biography of Jim Thompson.* New York: Knopf, 1995.

Cyndy Hendershot

THOREAU, HENRY DAVID (1817–1862). Born in Concord, Massachusetts, where he lived most of his life, Thoreau has become a cultural icon because of his nature writing, his influence on **environmentalism**, and his life as a nonconformist and social critic. A philosopher, essayist, poet, and lecturer, Thoreau was disenchanted with the excessive materialism and **routinization** of nineteenth-century American society, leading him to conclude that "the mass of men lead lives of quiet desperation." His influence on society has been profound throughout the twentieth and twenty-first centuries.

Thoreau graduated from Harvard University in 1837. Soon afterward, a budding relationship with his mentor, Ralph Waldo Emerson, encouraged him to pursue a life of letters. By 1840, Thoreau wrote poetry and helped edit Emerson's magazine the *Dial,* in which Thoreau published his first nature essay in 1842, "Natural History of Massachusetts." Under the influence of Emerson, he also became a force in the transcendentalist movement. Putting transcendentalism into practice, Thoreau embarked on his famous experiment of living simply and deliberately at Walden Pond, just a few miles outside Concord.

Symbolically, Thoreau moved into the cabin he built at Walden Pond on July 4, 1845 (Independence Day), where he would live for two years, two months, and two days. During this period of study, meditation, and farming, Thoreau drafted his first book, *A Week on the Concord and Merrimack Rivers* (1849), and also gathered the material for his masterpiece, *Walden; or, A Life in the Woods* (1854). At turns philosophical, poetic, and didactic, the latter has become a guidebook for self-reliant, economical, and antimaterialistic living. In the book, Thoreau says that "I went to the woods because I wished to live deliberately, to front only the essential facts of life, and see if I could not learn what it had to teach, and not, when I came to die, discover that I had not lived." In addition to its spiritual rather than materialistic striving, *Walden*'s proto-ecological themes challenged the political and economic status quo of the period, as they still do today.

The Walden Pond experiment led Thoreau to a series of lectures and essays known as his "reform papers." The most famous of these, "Resistance to Civil Government" (1849, posthumously retitled "Civil Disobedience") describes another symbolic event that occurred during Thoreau's stay at Walden Pond. While visiting Concord, Thoreau was jailed for refusing to pay a poll tax. In his typically principled fashion, Thoreau chose to spend a night in jail rather than pay a tax that he believed supported the slave system and an imperial war against Mexico. This "civil disobedience" by Thoreau has had a profound impact on the twentieth century, directly influencing Gandhi and the nonviolent activism of Martin Luther King Jr., among others. Thoreau also argues against the injustices of slavery in essays like "Slavery in Massachusetts" (1854) and "A Plea for Captain John Brown" (1860), and he was active in helping runaway slaves along the Underground Railroad.

Selected Bibliography: Buell, Lawrence. *The Environmental Imagination: Thoreau, Nature Writing, and the Formation of American Culture.* Cambridge: Harvard UP, 1995; Harding, Walter. *The Days of Henry Thoreau.* Princeton, NJ: Princeton UP, 1982; Harding, Walter, and Michael Meyer. *The New Thoreau Handbook.* New York: New York UP, 1980; Meyer, Michael. *Several More Lives to Live: Thoreau's Political Reputation in America.* Westport, CT: Greenwood, 1977; Thoreau, Henry David. *The Writings of Henry David Thoreau.* Boston: Houghton Mifflin, 1906.

Brian Hardman

THE THREEPENNY OPERA (*DIE DREIGROSCHENOPER,* 1928/1931) is **Bertolt Brecht**'s most popular work and the best-known product of his collaboration with the avant-garde composer Kurt Weill. *Threepenny* premiered with enormous popular success in Berlin on August 31, 1928; although designated an opera, it is actually a play with songs and musical interludes. The libretto used for the premiere was an adaptation of Elisabeth Hauptmann's translation of John Gay's eighteenth-century parody of opera in the style of Handel, *The Beggar's Opera,* so that the initial version of *Threepenny* was a collaborative product involving at least three contributors. In 1931, however, Brecht fundamentally revised the 1928 libretto, and the 1931 text forms the basis for all subsequent translations and editions. Between 1928 and 1931, Brecht's views on politics and society had become more explicitly Marxist, and he had made significant advances in the theory and practice of **epic theater.** While both these developments are reflected in the 1931 text, it also emphasizes the power of sexuality as a motivating force in human behavior, and the work's continuing interest depends very much on this later version's complex negotiations between the socioeconomic and the sexual, which are embedded in its highly self-conscious play with discourse and theatricality.

Set in a comical Victorian underworld populated by beggars, whores, and thieves, *Threepenny* grotesquely demonstrates capitalist exploitation through the nature of Jonathan Jeremiah Peachum's small enterprise the Beggars' Friend, whose employees exchange their labor power for begging licenses. *Threepenny* highlights the commercialization of all interpersonal relationships under capitalism, notably bourgeois marriage and prostitution. However, its simultaneous emphasis on sexual appetite—exemplified in the myriad sexual encounters of the robber baron Captain Macheath, aka Mac the Knife, and his implicitly homoerotic association with Tiger Brown, the Chief of Police—also indicates that social relationships in capitalist society cannot be defined in purely socioeconomic terms. *Threepenny* shows that in bourgeois society, all forms of sexuality are organized with reference to the norm of masculinity, and also suggests that biologically based human needs underpin economic exploitation.

Although *Threepenny*'s account of capitalist society is compelling and suggestive, its implied political stance is less convincing. The instances of resistance to capitalism that we encounter in the course of the work tend to involve recourse to physical violence generated by resentment or frustration of material needs, rather than a politically articulated opposition. In its devastating review of the 1928 premiere, the **Communist Party** daily the *Red Flag* criticized the weakness of *Threepenny*'s political satire and its inadequate depiction of the revolutionary working class, and even the revised 1931 version does not overcome the criticisms. Nevertheless, the 1931 version is a brilliant example of early epic theater. It repeatedly plays with the theatrical conventions of mimetic illusionism, defamiliarizes and deconstructs dramatic discourse, hilariously demystifies the rhetorical gestures of romantic love, and demolishes the convention that opera should be the authentic voice of human emotion. Crucially, the songs differ from conventional operatic arias in that they are not direct expressions of the feelings of the characters but highly self-conscious and ironic performances that invite the audience to adopt a critical perspective on music, theater, and society.

Selected Bibliography: Giles, Steve. "From Althusser to Brecht: Formalism, Materialism and *The Threepenny Opera.*" *New Ways in Germanistik.* Ed. Richard Sheppard. Oxford: Berg, 1990; Giles, Steve. "Rewriting Brecht: *Die Dreigroschenoper,* 1928–1931." *Literaturwissenschaftliches Jahrbuch* 30 (1989): 249–79; Hinton, Stephen, ed. *Kurt Weill: "The Threepenny Opera."* Cambridge: Cambridge UP, 1990; Willett, John, ed. *Brecht on Theatre.* London: Methuen, 1964.

Steve Giles

TOLSTOY, ALEXEI (1882–1945) is one of the most important Russian Soviet authors—a prolific novelist, short-story writer, playwright, and historian. He was born in Nikolaevsk (Samara Province) into a wealthy Russian landowning family related to both **Leo Tolstoy** and **Ivan Turgenev**. He was educated at home until the age of thirteen. After secondary school in Samara, he attended St. Petersburg Technological Institute.

Tolstoy published a number of poems and stories before **World War I**, during which he was a war correspondent for *Russke Vedomosti,* writing from the front, and later from France and England. His wartime experiences are the theme of the collection of short stories *Na voine.* The **Russian Revolution** brought a period of great turbulence for Tolstoy. Originally rejecting the revolution, he worked for Denikin's propaganda section in 1917 and immigrated to Paris and Berlin. In Berlin, however, he became a supporter of the revolution and began to work as the editor of the Bolshevik newspaper *Nakanune.* He returned to the Soviet Union in 1923, remaining a staunch supporter of the Soviet Republic for the rest of his life. Nicknamed the "Red Count," he became a leading Soviet author, honored and respected, and received three Stalin Prizes—the highest Soviet literary award—for his work.

Tolstoy's opus is large and varied, but his focus from 1922 onward remained the Soviet revolution and its goals. Working in a variety of genres, he published important works of science fiction, including the novels *Aelita* (1922–1923)—on Soviets visiting Mars, which was adapted to film by Jakov Protazanov in 1924—and *Giperboloid inzhenera Garina* (1926–1927); his play *Bunt mashin* was based on **Karel Čapek**'s science-fiction play *R.U.R.*

In 1922, Tolstoy began writing *Khozhdenie po mukam* (*Road to Calvary,* 1922–1942), a trilogy about Russian intelligentsia during the revolution, and the autobiographical novel *Detstvo Nikiti.* In 1924, Tolstoy wrote a satirical novel entitled *Pokhozhdenie Nevzorova ili Ibikus.* One of his major works is the unfinished historical novel *Petr I* (*Peter the First,* books 1–2, 1929–1945). Centering on the figure of the Russian tsar Peter the Great, the novel is an epic portrayal of the Russian society of that period and its arduous move from its feudal backwardness toward a society based on Western concepts of state and society. It represents one of the finest examples of **socialist realism**. Tolstoy's political novels include *Chornoe zoloto* (*Black Gold,* 1932), which centered on Russian émigrés, and *Khleb* (*Bread,* 1937).

Tolstoy was politically active throughout his life. He participated in antifascist congresses in Paris and London in 1935 and 1936; he was elected chairman of the Writers' Union and a deputy to the Supreme Soviet in 1937. In 1939, he was elected a member of the Soviet Academy of Sciences. During **World War II**, Tolstoy worked as a journalist and propagandist. During this period, he published a number of plays, including *Oryol and orlitsa* (*The Eagle and Its Mate,* 1942) and *Trudnye gody* (*The Difficult Years,* 1943), which drew a parallel between **Stalin** and Ivan the Terrible, an idea later explored by Sergei Eisenstein in his film *Ivan the Terrible*. Altogether, Tolstoy wrote over twenty plays, and also wrote a number of popular children's stories.

Selected Bibliography: Alpatov, A. V. *Aleksei Tolstoi—master istoricheskogo romana.* Moscow: Sovetskii pisatel, 1958; Petelin, Viktor. *Zhizn Alekseia Tolstago: Krasnyi Graf.* Moscow: Tsentropoligraf, 2001; Poliak, L. M. *Aleksei Tolstoi—khudozhnik.* Moscow: Nauka, 1964.

Dubravka Juraga

TOLSTOY, LEO (LEV) NIKOLAEVICH (1828–1910).

Among Russian writers, only **Aleksandr Pushkin** and **Fyodor Dostoevsky** can claim a reputation as extensive as Tolstoy's. Born in 1828 on his aristocratic family's estate at Yasnaya Polyana, Tolstoy's personal life was nearly as tumultuous as his country's politics. Though Tolstoy has often been categorized as a moralist, his work both implicitly and explicitly addresses political themes throughout his career. His beliefs were sometimes contradicted by his actions, but Tolstoy's body of work validates his youthful assertion that he was destined "to have great influence over the happiness and well-being of others."

Tolstoy's first extensive involvement with politics came during his military service as a junior artillery officer in the Crimean War, which he fictionalized in three "sketches" published in 1855 and 1856. He was dismayed by the corruption, incompetence, and indifference he witnessed among his fellow officers in the defense of Sevastopol. He came to believe that the aristocracy's obsession with politics detached them from the ordinary Russian, whom he believed to be innately moral and virtuous. In the wake of his direct experience with the hardheaded bureaucracy of the army, Tolstoy turned away from direct efforts at political reform, believing instead that a reconnection with the moral values he ascribed to the peasantry was the means to improving Russian society. He embodied this attitude in some of his most memorable characters, such as Andrey Bolkonsky and Pierre Bezukhov in *War and Peace* (1865–1869) and Konstantin Levin in *Anna Karenina* (1875–1877).

Though Tolstoy frequently condemned explicitly political literature—especially radical works by writers like **Nikolai Chernyshevsky**—his writings and his actions both challenged the norms of Russian society in a way that had clear political implications. His support—both philosophical and financial—of education for the peasantry put him at odds with the ruling class, of which he was hereditarily a part. Although a number of revolutionary and reformist groups attempted to co-opt Tolstoy's name and ideas to their ends (as a number of Soviet critics would later do), he steadfastly disavowed such attempts, preferring his own idiosyncratic methods of improving the lot of the Russian people.

By the early 1880s, Tolstoy's literary reputation was cemented by a string of remarkable novels, of which *War and Peace*—a massive historical novel detailing the Napoleonic War in Russia—is the most widely known and respected. At the same time, his antiauthoritarian politics became more pronounced, especially after the reactionary crackdown that followed in the wake of Tsar Alexander II's assassination in 1881. Tolstoy increasingly abandoned fiction in favor of ethical and moral tracts, such as *What Then Must We Do?* (1886), in which he advocated an end to the Russian state in favor of small, self-sufficient religious communities. Tolstoy's version of Christianity was distinct from Russian Orthodoxy, which he saw as having been distorted by its lengthy political association with the tsars. Over the last three decades of his life, Tolstoy developed an international reputation thanks as much to his polemics on pacifism, charity, and moral responsibility as to his artistic works. Until his death in 1910, Tolstoy's politics remained iconoclastic. His religious fervor (and his class origins) made him unpalatable to revolutionaries like **Lenin**, and his opposition to the state and to Orthodoxy set him apart from the Slavophiles who supported the Romanov dynasty.

Selected Bibliography: Berlin, Isaiah. *The Hedgehog and the Fox: An Essay on Tolstoy's View of History.* New York: Simon and Schuster, 1970; Orwin, Donna Tussig. "Tolstoy as Artist and Public Figure." Introduction to *The Cambridge Companion to Tolstoy.* Ed. Donna Tussig Orwin. Cambridge: Cambridge UP, 2002. 49–62; Tolstoy, Leo. *I Cannot Be Silent: Writings on Politics, Art and Religion by Leo Tolstoy.* Bristol, UK: Bristol P, 1989; Wasiolek, Edward, ed. *Critical Essays on Tolstoy.* Boston: G. K. Hall, 1986; Wilson, A. N. *Tolstoy.* New York: Norton, 1988.

Derek C. Maus

TOOMER, JEAN (1894–1967). Author of *Cane* (1923), the first major text of the **Harlem Renaissance**, Jean Toomer is not ordinarily viewed in the context of left politics. His origins among the District of Columbia's light-skinned "Negro Four Hundred" and his complicated views on racial identity have led some critics to situate him among early twentieth-century discourses on race. His close ties with Waldo Frank and other young Americans, as well as his experimental style, have led other critics to view him as a practitioner of **modernism**. Yet as a young man, Toomer proclaimed himself a Socialist, and his first published writings—defending 1919 socialist revolutions in Europe and applauding African American militancy during the 1919 race riots—appeared in the left press. Moreover, *Cane*—when placed in the historical contexts to which it obliquely alludes—is more politically engaged than it first appears. A semi-autobiographical gathering of short stories, poems, and drama, *Cane* chronicles Toomer's 1921 journey to Sparta, Georgia; alternating between nostalgia and realism, irony and frontal self-questioning, the text foregrounds the sophisticated, urbanized author's encounter with a premodern peasant way of life "before an epoch's sun declines." Through its references to a number of recent lynchings widely publicized in the left and African American press, however, as well as its satirical treatment of prominent local Georgia figures, black and white, *Cane* undertakes a critique of U.S. racism continuous with that voiced in such radical New Negro journals as the *Messenger* and the *Crusader*.

Soon after publishing *Cane*, Toomer changed orientation and became a passionate advocate of the Bulgarian mystic Georges Gurdjieff; he continued to write but published little of lasting value (with the possible exception of his Whitmanesque 1936 poem about American multiracialism, "The Blue Meridian"). He married white women two times, became a Quaker, and passed over the color line. But his unpublished 1935–1936 autobiography—written during a temporary hiatus in his various spiritualist quests—looks back on his radicalism of the postwar period and reinforces the importance of reading *Cane* in the context of the crucible of 1919.

Selected Bibliography: Fabre, Genevieve, and Michel Feith. *Jean Toomer and the Harlem Renaissance.* New Brunswick, NJ: Rutgers UP, 2001; Foley, Barbara. "'In the Land of Cotton': Economics and Violence in Jean Toomer's *Cane*." *African American Review* 32 (Summer 1998): 181–98; Foley, Barbara. "Jean Toomer's Sparta." *American Literature* 67 (December 1995): 747–75; Scruggs, Charles. "'My Chosen World': Jean Toomer's Articles in *The New York Call*." *Arizona Quarterly* 51 (Summer 1995): 103–26; Scruggs, Charles, and Lee Van DeMarr. *Jean Toomer and the Terrors of American History.* Philadelphia: U of Pennsylvania P, 1998.

Barbara Foley

TRAVEN, B. (1890–1969), pen name of the author best known for the novel *The Treasure of the Sierra Madre* (1927), which was turned into a movie in 1948, directed by John Huston and starring Humphrey Bogart. His true identity remains a mystery, though theories abound. His novels were originally published in Germany, and Traven was initially thought to be German; however, in letters to publishers, he always maintained that he was American. It is generally accepted that Traven was Ret Marut, a minor actor (1907–1915) and revolutionary writer in Germany who edited an anarchist magazine *Der Ziegelbrenner* (the *Brickburner*) from 1917 to 1921. Stories from the *Brickburner* have been published in *To the Honorable Miss S: And Other Stories from the Brick Burner* (1982). Official German documents listed Marut first as a British national but were later changed to American. In 1922, Marut disappeared from Germany, and B. Traven emerged in Mexico, where he spent the remainer of his life. He is believed to have adopted the name Hal Croves, who claimed to be Traven's agent during and subsequent to the filming of *Treasure*. Theories on his true identity range from Marut being the illegitimate son of Kaiser Wilhelm II to Traven being two different people, Marut and a man he met while in Mexico.

Traven was heavily influenced by the German anarchist Max Stirner (pseudonym for Johann Kaspar Schmidt, 1806–1856). Stirner's book *The Ego and His Own* (1845) condemned the state and all institutions outside one's own ego that lay claim to a person's loyalty. Traven's novels show an antipathy to those external forces that impose themselves on the individual, attacking communism in his first novel, *The Death Ship* (1926), as well as capitalism and unions in novels such as *The White Rose* (1929). After his move to Mexico, a major theme in his work is the clash of cultures between the Indians of Mexico, a culture based on land and tradition, and the industrial might of American companies investing in Mexico, a culture based on money and capitalist might. In this period, Traven often writes about the Mexican individual struggling, usually in vain, against the monolithic system of American capitalism. Traven develops this theme in many of his subsequent novels, including the Caoba (mahogany) cycle of novels, comprising *The Carreta* (1931), *Government* (1931–1932), *March to Monteria* (1933), *Trozas* (1936), *The Rebellion of the Hanged* (1936), and *General from the Jungle* (1940). Traven also dealt with personal responsibility, as people in Traven's novels are often as much victims of their own fears and desires as they are victims of social forces beyond their control. In *The Treasure of the Sierra Madre*, for example, it is personal greed that drives the characters and their actions, though this greed may have been partly a product of the capitalist system.

Selected Bibliography: Baumann, Michael L. *B. Traven: An Introduction.* Albuquerque: U of New Mexico P, 1976; Guthke, Karl. *B. Traven: The Life behind the Legends.* Chicago: Lawrence Hill, 1991; Mezo, Richard E. *A Study of B. Traven's Fiction: The Journey to Solipaz.* Lewiston, NY: E. Mellen, 1993; Raskin, Jonah. *My Search for B. Traven.* New York: Methuen, 1980; Zogbaum, Heidi. *B. Traven: A Vision of Mexico.* Wilmington, DE: SR Books, 1997.

Steve Cloutier

TROTSKY, LEON (1879–1940). Born Lev Davidovich Bronstein in the Ukraine, Trotsky joined the revolutionary Narodniks (Populists) as a teenager but soon became a Marxist. Trotsky was arrested in 1898 and was deported to Siberia in 1900. Under the name Antid-Oto, he gained a reputation as a commentator and literary critic. He fled Siberia in 1902 and joined **Vladimir Lenin** in London. He returned to Russia in 1905 during the failed revolution. He was arrested again in 1907 and sentenced to life deportation to Siberia, but he fled to Europe. In 1917, he traveled to the United States before returning to Russia to participate in the October **Russian Revolution**. He was briefly detained by British authorities in Halifax, Canada, on his return trip in 1917. In 1918, Trotsky was appointed the commissar of war of the revolutionary government and created the Red Army. He held this post until 1925 when, after Lenin's death, **Stalin** removed Trotsky from power.

Stalin and Trotsky were sharply divided over the issue of Stalin's policy of "socialism in one country." Trotsky argued his idea of "permanent revolution," which stated that the revolution could not sustain itself unless it spread to other industrialized nations. Trotsky was also critical of the growing bureaucracy within the Stalinist Soviet Union, which he attacked in *The Revolution Betrayed* (1936). Trotsky was finally exiled in 1929 and deprived of Soviet nationality in 1932. The Moscow Trials of 1936 found Trotsky and his son guilty in absentia of directing terrorist attacks in Soviet Russia. He took up residence in Mexico in 1937, living there until he was assassinated in 1940. In addition to publishing an autobiography—*My Life* (1930)—he wrote *The History of the Russian Revolution* (1930) as well as a book about Lenin, simply titled *Lenin* (1925). Trotsky published a number of essays on literature and culture, including "The Social Function of Literature and Art" (1923) and "Art and Politics in Our Epoch" (1938). Trotsky's major contribution to literary criticism, however, is *Literature and Revolution* (1924), suppressed by Stalin in 1928. In it, Trotsky analyzes contemporary literary movements such as futurism. Futurism, Trotsky believed, was merely an intellectual revolution that could not bring about social change. When faced with a true social revolution, futurists abandoned futurism and absorbed themselves in the new revolutionary force, such as fascism in Italy or communism in Russia. Futurism was a necessary, if brief, link in the evolution of a new literature. Trotsky dismissed Russian formalism, which he saw as being opposed to Marxism. Formalism's focus on form meant that, for Trotsky, the movement was superficial and ultimately reactionary. Trotsky was very broad-minded about art, arguing that themes should not be proscribed, that it was natural for writers to have a wide range of literary views, and that art "must plow the entire field in all directions."

Selected Bibliography: Brotherstone, Terry, and Paul Dukes. *The Trotsky Reappraisal.* Edinburgh: Edinburgh UP, 1992; Deutscher, Isaac. *The Prophet Armed: Trotsky, 1879–1921.* New York: Oxford UP, 1954; Deutscher, Isaac. *The Prophet Disarmed: Trotsky, 1921–1929.* New York: Oxford UP, 1959; Deutscher, Isaac. *The Prophet Exiled: Trotsky, 1929–1940.* New York: Oxford UP, 1963; Thatcher, Ian D. *Trotsky.* London: Routledge, 2003; Volkogonov, Dmitri. *Trotsky: The Eternal Revolutionary.* London: HarperCollins, 1996.

Steve Cloutier

TSVETAYEVA, MARINA (1892–1941). Born in Russia into a generation of great poets, Tsvetayeva produced some of the most highly regarded and innovative poetry of the period. Her life spanned the cultural renaissance and revolutions of early-twentieth-century Russia, the subsequent large-scale emigration of Russian intellectuals, the **Stalin** period, and **World War II.** No other individual life seems to encapsulate the turmoil of that era more fully than does Tsvetayeva's. Raised in a privileged environment, she lived in poverty all her adult life. During the Russian civil war, she struggled to support two daughters, losing one to starvation. She left the Soviet Union to rejoin her husband, who had been fighting against the revolution as an officer in the White Army. Ironically, she later followed him back to the Soviet Union, after seventeen years in European exile. (Despite his previous anti-bolshevism, her husband had become a Soviet sympathizer and had participated in assassinations on behalf of the Soviet secret police.) This return proved disastrous. Her husband was eventually arrested and executed, and Tsvetayeva's daughter would spend seventeen years in the gulag and in Siberian exile. Tsvetayeva herself committed suicide in 1941.

Tsvetayeva wrote plays, essays, and autobiographical sketches, but she is best known for her poetry—especially the collections *Milestones* (*Versty*), *Craft* (*Remeslo*), and *After Russia* (*Posle Rossii*), and the narrative poem *The Ratcatcher* (*Krysolov*). Much of her subject matter extends from personal biography, but she also reimagines characters from Russian folklore and ancient classical literature, as well as legendary figures and types as disparate as Casanova, the gypsy, and the Pied Piper of Hameln. In such retellings, in her idiosyncratic imagery and emphatic voice, Tsvetayeva frequently revised traditional gender roles. In life and in writing, Tsvetayeva was a fearless nonconformist. Émigré writers criticized her formal experiments as too futurist, while the elliptical and allusive qualities of her style seemed to place her on the right. She scandalously championed the Soviet poet **Vladimir Mayakovsky** when he came to Paris. Addressing a communist audience years earlier, she had boldly read poems ostensibly celebrating the White Army (from the collection *Swans' Encampment* [*Lebedinyj stan*]). While she espoused no political ideology (even *Swans' Encampment* is ambiguous as a political statement), her work is an uncompromising pronounce-ment on behalf of individual freedom, a condemnation of hypocrisy (e.g., that of the comfortable middle class), and a vehement refusal of social norms. It is also, as she herself said poetry ought to be, a way of speaking "on the side of the victims and not the executioners." During World War II she wrote, "To your mad world there is one answer: to refuse!" ("Poems to Czechoslovakia"). Tsvetayeva's poetry was among the most popular of all Russian *samizdat* literature during the 1960s and 1970s. No-toriously difficult to translate, her work nevertheless exists in a number of worth-while English translations.

Selected Bibliography: Feiler, Lily. *Marina Tsvetaeva: The Double Beat of Heaven and Hell.* Durham: Duke UP, 1994; Karlinsky, Simon. *Marina Tsvetaeva: The Woman, Her World, and Her Poetry.* Cam-bridge: Cambridge UP, 1985; Makin, Michael. *Marina Tsvetaeva: Poetics of Appropriation.* Oxford: Clarendon, 1993; Schweitzer, Viktoria. *Tsvetaeva.* Ed. Angela Livingstone. Trans. Robert Chandler and H. T. Willetts. London: HarperCollins, 1992.

Joy Dworkin

TURGENEV, IVAN SERGEEVICH (1818–1883). Russia's first internationally renowned author of prose fiction and drama, Turgenev exhibited a cosmopolitan, humane liberalism that eventually set him at odds with both radical Russian "West-ernizers" and archconservative "Slavophiles." Born on his mother's estate south of Moscow and educated in St. Petersburg and Berlin, Turgenev was "internally exiled" in 1852 for publishing a banned tribute to **Nikolai Gogol** upon Gogol's death. Tur-genev also attributed this punishment to twenty-two short stories he collected in 1852 under the title *A Sportsman's Sketches* (*Zapiski okhotnika*). These restrained yet vivid narratives treated peasants for the first time as serious literary subjects and allegedly helped persuade Tsar Nikolai I to abolish serfdom in 1861. The *Sketches* both pleased Russian critics on the left for exposing many of serfdom's ills and appealed to critics on the right for lyrically evoking Russia's natural beauty and peasant wisdom.

By contrast to the *Sketches*, the six novels Turgenev wrote (mostly in Europe) pro-voked dissatisfaction among Slavophiles for being too politically radical and among Westernizers for not being radical enough. The first three novels—*Rudin* (1856), *A Nest of Gentry* (*Dvorianskoe gnezdo*, 1859), and *On the Eve* (*Nakanune*, 1860)—focus on individual characters and their relationships against a background of fervent de-bates over Russia's current conditions and future prospects—debates that, true to his temperate liberalism, Turgenev declined to resolve. In his most famous novel, *Fathers and Sons* (*Otsy i deti*, 1862), these debates come to the fore, as the defiant views and boorish behavior of a self-styled nihilist and member of the Russian intelligentsia, Bazarov, so strongly offend a conservative defender of aristocratic tradition that the two finally fight a duel. Neither antagonist triumphs in the duel or in life—although both are rendered sympathetically—and only the politically moderate, socially pro-gressive brother of Bazarov's opponent prospers at the novel's end. Ignoring this vic-tory of moderation, radicals faulted Turgenev for portraying Bazarov as ineffectual and lovelorn, whereas conservatives denounced Turgenev for depicting Bazarov as an admirable protorevolutionary rather than condemning him as a dangerous anarchist.

Embittered by these attacks, Turgenev represented political ideologues of all stripes with far less sympathy in his last two novels, lampooning both radicals and conservatives in *Smoke* (*Dym*, 1867) and consigning the populist protagonist in *Virgin Soil* (*Nov'*, 1877) to suicide. In later, shorter works, Turgenev turned away from politics altogether, and even made some forays into the supernatural, emphasizing the ambiguities of human experience and affirming the need for enduring liberal open-mindedness.

Selected Bibliography: Berlin, Isaiah. "Fathers and Children: Turgenev and the Liberal Predicament." *Russian Thinkers*. Ed. Henry Hardy and Aileen Kelly. New York: Viking, 1978. 261–305; Howe, Irving. "Turgenev: The Politics of Hesitation." *Politics and the Novel*. Ed. Irving Howe. New York: Horizon, 1957. 129–33; Ripp, Victor. *Turgenev's Russia: From "Notes of a Hunter" to "Fathers and Sons."* Ithaca, NY: Cornell UP, 1982; Schapiro, Leonard. *Turgenev: His Life and Times*. New York: Random House, 1978; Turgenev, Ivan. *The Essential Turgenev*. Ed. Elizabeth Cheresh Allen. Evanston, IL: Northwestern UP, 1994.

Elizabeth Cheresh Allen

◦ U ◦

UNAMUNO, MIGUEL DE (1864–1936). As well as being one of the leading philosophers, novelists, poets, and dramatists of Spain's so-called silver age of literature and art (1890s–1936), Miguel de Unamuno was also the writer who played the most consistently prominent place in Spanish politics over this period. In order to do this, he constructed a new role for himself as Spain's first modern intellectual. In the 1880s and 1890s, Unamuno wrote first as an incipient Basque nationalist and then as a committed socialist, opposing Spain's colonial war in Cuba and proposing a dual program of collective self-examination and openness to new ideas from abroad as an antidote to national decline. Although he soon moved away from his youthful socialism toward concerns of a more intimate and spiritual nature, Unamuno continued to apply the skills of political persuasion to the task of ensuring the intellectual and cultural regeneration of his nation. Taking full advantage of the rapidly expanding Spanish press's need for a new type of writer who could explore and explain the complexities of the modern world, Unamuno fashioned himself as both an interpreter of the most recent political and philosophical developments at home and abroad, and an *agitador de espíritus*—an awakener of the minds and spirits of his compatriots. By creating a new sort of essay—part autobiography, part criticism, and part commentary—Unamuno projected an image of himself in the daily press and in such works as *Our Lord Don Quixote: The Life of Don Quixote and Sancho* (*Vida de Don Quijote y Sancho*, 1905) as a modern-day Don Quixote, committed to the creation of a new community of readers and, by extension, a new nation. From 1900 onward, he fought a series of quixotic political battles in favor of a strong liberal state that would be capable of challenging the cultural hegemony of the Catholic Church and, later, against the authoritarian traditionalism of the king, Alfonso XIII, and of General Primo de Rivera, Dictator of Spain between 1923 and 1930. This latter struggle led to Unamuno spending six years in exile (1924–1930), where he wrote *How to Make a Novel* (*Cómo se hace una novela*, 1924–1927), a work that provided both a justification of the intellectual's role and an exploration of the negative effects that playing such a role can have on the intellectual's sense of selfhood. Although Unamuno returned to Spain in 1930 as a herald of the future republic (1931–1936), he soon became disillusioned with the new regime and initially gave his support to the nationalist insurrection in July 1936. By October, however, he had turned against Franco and his followers, and he died under house arrest on the final day of that year. His friend and sometime disciple José Ortega y Gasset paid the most eloquent tribute to this groundbreaking intellectual by claiming that his death had caused an awful silence to descend on Spain.

Selected Bibliography: Roberts, Stephen G. H. "Unamuno and the Restoration Political Project: A Reevaluation." *Spain's 1898 Crisis: Regenerationism, Modernism, Post-Colonialism.* Ed. J. Harrison and A. Hoyle. Manchester: Manchester UP, 2000. 68–80; Roberts, Stephen G. H. "Unamuno, Spanishness and the Ideal Patria: An Intellectual's View." *Journal of the Institute of Romance Studies* 8 (2000): 125–36; Sinclair, Alison. *Uncovering the Mind: Unamuno, the Unknown and the Vicissitudes of the Self.* Manchester: Manchester UP, 2002.

Stephen G. H. Roberts

U.S.A. **TRILOGY (1930–1936).** On the night in August 1927 when the Italian-born anarchists Nicolo Sacco and Bartolomeo Vanzetti were executed, **John Dos Passos** was inspired to begin the three-volume chronicle of the first three decades of the twentieth century that would become *U.S.A.* Drawing on an ecumenical political leftism and written in a kaleidoscopic experimental style based on futurism, cubism, and cinematic montage, the trilogy represents the most fully realized example of what proletarian writers and critics of the 1930s were calling the collective novel. *The Forty-second Parallel* (1930) covers approximately 1900–1916; *Nineteen-Nineteen* (1932) focuses on the war years, 1917–1919; *The Big Money* (1936) covers 1920–1928, with provocative nods toward the 1929 stock-market crash and the Depression. Overlaid onto the different political movements occurring in these periods are significant shifts within Dos Passos's own political outlook. *The Forty-second Parallel* portrays the nation's emergence as a global capitalist power and the prewar activities of the Socialist Party and the **IWW** from the standpoint of a freewheeling, somewhat bohemian radicalism. *Nineteen-Nineteen* depicts the carnage of the Great War, the imperialist power grab of the Versailles Peace Conference, and the revolutionary upsurge of 1919 from the closest approach to a Marxist perspective in the author's dramatic political orbit. *The Big Money* narrates its history of labor repression and growing consumerism from a stance more technocratic than Marxist, invoking the sardonic spirit of Thorstein Veblen.

Each novel consists of four types of interspersed materials: fictional narratives, biographies, "newsreels," and "camera eyes." The fictional narratives treat a range of characters—from blue-collar workers to media moguls, from left-wing organizers to Hollywood starlets—whose lives embody in microcosm the effects of ideological obfuscation, sexual commodification, the lure of the "big money," and radical politics on a range of representative Americans. Some characters appear in only one volume, others in all three; some lives intersect frequently, while others remain solitary and marginalized. Although Dos Passos's distanced and ironic approach to his characters has been criticized as mechanical and behaviorist, his array of imagined types is intended to convey a searing critique of capitalism's dulling of human capacities for both understanding and love.

The biographies are prose poem jeremiads, alternately ironic and eloquent, depicting men (and one woman, Isadora Duncan) who, for better or worse, shaped culture, technology, and politics in the early twentieth century. Dos Passos's heroes—while rarely portrayed without a trace of irony—include Eugene Debs, Luther Burbank, Wesley Everest, Joe Hill, Big Bill Haywood, **John Reed**, Randolph Bourne, "Fighting Bob" La Follette, the Wright Brothers, Frank Lloyd Wright, Duncan, and Veblen. His villains—or at least objects of contempt—include Theodore Roosevelt, Minor C. Keith, the house of Morgan, Woodrow Wilson, William Randolph Hearst, Samuel Insull, Henry Ford, and Rudolph Valentino. Two of the most moving biographies are of anonymous figures: the "Body of an American" buried in the Tomb of the Unknown Soldier (to whom the hypocritical top-hatted Wilson "brought a bouquet of poppies") and "Vag," the unemployed Depression-era hitchhiker, failed by the American Dream, whose anti-Whitmanian portrait closes *The Big Money*. At once challenging the mythology of the "great man" view of history and exploring the role of the individual in history from a class-conscious standpoint, the biographies link the lives of the fictional characters to larger historical forces of which they are largely unaware.

The newsreels consist of one- to three-page clumps of newspaper headlines, advertising slogans, fragments of speeches, and snatches of popular songs. Principally they satirize the capitalist mass media's promulgation of jingoism, anti-working-class propaganda ("Jobless riot at agency"), voyeuristic identification with the lives of the rich and famous, consumerist values, and plain old lies ("Lenin Dead"). Occasionally, however, they include snatches from the left press ("Workers March on Reichstag"; "Ex-Servicemen Demand Jobs"). The effect of this ideological montage is at once to reveal the dominant discourses by which consent is manufactured and to highlight the importance of forging—and publicizing—an alternative language through which to comprehend the class struggle.

The camera-eye passages, written in a stream-of-consciousness style reminiscent of **James Joyce**, are musings, often verging on incoherence, representing Dos Passos's own gradual growth into the author of the text. The passages in *The Forty-second Parallel* cover the author's childhood—privileged, but sad and sequestered. *Nineteen-Nineteen* reveals the authorial self coming of age as a wartime ambulance driver, would-be soldier, and witness to the fizzling of the 1919 upsurge. In *The Big Money*, the camera eye explores his mission as a writer of wavering leftist partisanship who reaches clarity as he participates in the movement to save Sacco and Vanzetti. In the famous climactic words of the trilogy, he declares, "all right we are two nations."

Dos Passos's politics in *U.S.A.* invite leftist critique. His "representative" range of characters contains not one nonwhite, and those African American, Asian, and Hispanic characters making brief appearances conform to denigrating racial stereotypes. Most of Dos Passos's female characters evince even less agency or capacity for joy than the males. Dos Passos's portraits of Communists are largely caricatured. Most important, even at his most impassioned, Dos Passos voices disappointment that the nation has been taken over and betrayed rather than a revolutionary commitment to abolishing the class system he has so brilliantly anatomized. Nonetheless, in its dialectical and totalizing grasp of U.S. history, as well as its acute awareness of the hegemonic and counterhegemonic roles language necessarily plays in narrating history, the *U.S.A.* trilogy represents one of the high marks of U.S. literary radicalism and supplies the basis for **Jean-Paul Sartre**'s 1940 judgment, "Dos Passos is the finest writer of our time."

Selected Bibliography: Casey, Janet Galligani. *Dos Passos and the Ideology of the Feminine.* Cambridge: Cambridge UP, 1998; Foley, Barbara. *Radical Representations: Politics and Form in U.S. Proletarian Fiction, 1929–1941.* Durham, NC: Duke UP, 1993; Landsberg, Melvin. *Dos Passos' Path to "U.S.A.": A Critical Biography, 1912–1936.* Boulder, CO: Associated UP, 1972; Pizer, Donald. *Dos Passos' "U.S.A.": A Critical Study.* Charlottesville: UP of Virginia, 1988; Smith, Jon. "John Dos Passos, Anglo-Saxon." *Modern Fiction Studies* 44 (Summer 1998): 282–305.

Barbara Foley

***UTOPIA* (1516).** In modern usage, "utopian" may have become a byword for unachievable ideals, but the founding work of **utopian fiction** from which the word is coined did not strike its own author as being so safely sequestered from the real world. Thomas More's *Utopia* was first published in Latin, and it was not translated into English until 1551—sixteen years after More's own execution marked the progress of the Protestant Reformation in England. Attacking the Protestant "heresy" in the 1530s, however, More wrote that he would rather burn some works of his own than see them translated into English. If *Utopia* was one of those works (as it is likely to have been), More must have seen that it had the potential to resonate with the tumultuous times in ways that he might not approve of or be able to control.

On the surface, *Utopia* is written in the manner of a traveler's tall tale, full of Greek names that are erudite jokes. The last name of Raphael Hythlodaeus, the Portugese traveler who returns from Utopia to regale Peter Giles and More (a character in his own book) with an account of its government and way of life, means "well-versed in nonsense." The main river that runs past Utopia's capital city is Anydrus, or "without water," and the name "Utopia" would seem to locate its waterless course "nowhere."

But such playfulness should not obscure the almost evangelical fervor of Hythlodaeus. European societies, Raphael reminds the character More, are plagued with deep-rooted problems and injustices: kings with an insatiable appetite for conquest, vast inequities between the rich and the poor, and judicial systems whose very harshness encourages crime. Raphael presents Utopia as a blueprint for radically reforming these injustices, whose existence the character More does not dispute. In particular, the basis of Utopian society, the absence of private property, offers the most striking challenge to the hording and materialism of Europe. But there are other challenges, too. Raphael brings Christianity to Utopia, yet the Utopians adapt it to their own religious institutions rather than conform to those of sixteenth-century Europe. Paradoxically, Utopian Christianity may be truer to the origins of the church than its sixteenth-century European counterpart.

By 1532, it must have seemed to More that history had caught up with his book, as reformers everywhere were using the printing press to disseminate their messages. Though not all of these messages addressed the issues raised in *Utopia*, there was enough overlap to warrant More's wish to keep *Utopia* out of the vernacular. One sect, the Anabaptists, even advocated communism. Playful ironic devices may frame Hythlodaeus's tale in *Utopia*, but in the end, More feared they might not be able to guarantee the separation of "nowhere" from the real world.

Selected Bibliography: Ames, Russell. *Citizen Thomas More and His Utopia.* Princeton, NJ: Princeton UP, 1949; Baker, David Weil. *Divulging Utopia: Radical Humanism in Sixteenth-Century England.* Amherst: U of Massachusetts P, 1999; Logan, George. *The Meaning of More's Utopia.* Princeton, NJ: Princeton UP, 1983; Manuel, Frank E., and Fritzie P. Manuel. *Utopian Thought in the Western World.* Cambridge, MA: Harvard UP, 1979; Skinner, Quentin. "Sir Thomas More's *Utopia* and the Language of Renaissance Humanism." *The Languages of Political Theory in Early-Modern Europe.* Ed. Anthony Pagden. Cambridge: Cambridge UP, 1987.

David Weil Baker

UTOPIAN FICTION. In one sense, all fiction is utopian fiction. If, following the lead of **Ernst Bloch** and **Fredric Jameson**, we take utopia to refer to a universal human desire for a radically other existence, then utopia is ubiquitous, making itself evident in all products of human labor, including literature and fiction. The fundamental task for literary and cultural criticism is to develop a hermeneutic sensitive to even its most fleeting manifestations.

However, there is also a specific literary genre of utopia. Two of the more significant attempts to define the genre are offered by Darko Suvin and Lyman Tower Sargent. Suvin describes the literary utopia as "the verbal construction of a particular quasi-human community where sociopolitical institutions, norms, and individual relationships are organized according to a more perfect principle than in the author's community, this construction based on estrangement arising out of an alternative historical hypothesis" (49). Suvin emphasizes the "quasi-human" aspect of the utopia to mark the difference between this genre and related forms, such as golden-age myths or millenarian visions; utopian communities are presented as part of our world and the products of human rather than divine or mystical labors. Second, Suvin stresses the ways works making up this genre focus on the collective social and cultural machinery rather than on individual characters. Finally, Suvin's definition emphasizes the link between any utopia and the historical context out of which it emerges. Every utopia appears as "more perfect" only in comparison to the society of its moment. Moreover, the utopian narrative offers a double estrangement of that context, highlighting problems in the reigning social order and showing that what is taken as natural and eternally fixed is in fact the product of historical development and open to change.

Sargent defines utopia as "a non-existent society described in considerable detail and located in time and space," and then elaborates a typology of the form. In the "eutopia or positive utopia," the author offers us a detailed description of a nonexistent society that she or he intends "a contemporaneous reader to view as considerably better than the society in which that reader lived." In the "dystopia or negative utopia," the author intends a contemporaneous reader to see the fictional society "as considerably worse." In the "utopian satire," the vision is meant "as a criticism of that contemporary society," while in the "anti-utopia," it serves "as a criticism of utopianism [defined as 'social dreaming'] or of some particular eutopia." Finally, in the most recent of these subgenres—the "critical utopia"—the imagined world is to be understood as "better than contemporary society but with difficult problems that the described society may or may not be able to solve and which takes a critical view of the utopian genre" (9).

Less evident in either definition is the relatively recent emergence of the form, be-ginning in 1516 with the publication of Thomas More's *Utopia*. There were mani-festations of social dreaming preceding More's work—among others, the ideal societies, earthly paradises, and golden-age visions represented in Plato's *Republic* and *Laws*, the book of Genesis, the works of Pindar and Hesiod, Augustine's *City of God*, and the popular medieval tales of the Land of Cockaigne and Prester John's king-dom. Nor are such imaginings the exclusive property of the Western world, utopian strands being evident, for example, in Confucianism and classical Chinese poetry. However, the specific formal strategies deployed by More differentiate the genre from these similar practices and, in turn, set the template for subsequent productions.

Utopia influenced generations of subsequent authors. One of the first of these was More's French contemporary François Rabelais, who not only refers to the Utopian people in the second book (1534) of his *Gargantua and Pantagruel,* but also includes his own utopian fiction, "The Abbey of Thélème," in its first book (1532). Rabelais thus not only helps establish the genre but offers one of the first critiques of More, as he replaces the strict regulation of daily life in Utopia with a society whose fun-damental maxim is "Do as Thou Wouldst." The pairing of More and Rabelais es-tablishes another pattern that recurs throughout the genre's history. For example, William Morris offers his *News from Nowhere* (1890), with its sensual and pastoral vision of an "epoch of rest," as a "reply" to the structured urban existence portrayed in Edward Bellamy's *Looking Backward, 2000–1887* (1888); and Samuel Delany writes *Triton* (1976) in part as a critique of **Ursula K. Le Guin**'s *The Dispossessed: An Ambiguous Utopia* (1974).

The years following the publication of More's work saw a proliferation of utopias. Some of the more prominent include Johann Valentin Andreae's *Christianopolis* (1619), Tommaso Campenella's *City of the Sun* (1623), Francis Bacon's *The New At-lantis* (1627), Gabriel Platt's *A Description of the Famous Kingdom of Macaria* (1641), Gerrard Winstanley's *The Law of Freedom in a Platform* (1651), James Harrington's *The Commonwealth of Oceana* (1656), and Margaret Cavendish's "The Inventory of Judgements Commonwealth" (1655) and *The Description of a New World, Call'd The Blazing-World* (1666). The titles of Harrington's and Cavendish's first utopia also point toward another crucial contribution made by the genre. Utopia is not only the one place that could lay the claim to being ordered in the interest of the "public good"—the older definition of the Latin term *respublica* or its English translation "a common weale"—but also the only place that was already a "commonwealth" as the term would subsequently be defined—as a synonym for the modern nation-state. The utopia's imaginary community set the stage for the "imagined community," as More's work, and the genre to which it gave birth, helped fix the nation-state as the "natural" scale for imagining modern collective life.

Two of the most important utopias of the eighteenth century mark further devel-opments in the form. **Jonathan Swift**'s *Gulliver's Travels* (1726) is one of the mas-terpieces of utopian satire. Swift uses the four sea journeys of Lemuel Gulliver to parody the values of the Enlightenment middle class and the more general utopian desires of his moment. Swift's work would not only serve as the model for later utopian satires, such as Samuel Butler's *Erewhon* (1872), but be an important re-source for the development of the dystopia and anti-utopia. The French writer

Sébastien Mercier's influential *The Year 2440: A Dream If There Ever Was One* (1771) marks the definitive transformation of the utopia into a "uchronia," the voyage occurring in time rather than in space and the utopian community heretofore a vision of a transformed present.

The late eighteenth and early nineteenth centuries saw a period of change and revolutionary ferment. Not surprisingly, this moment saw both an outpouring of utopian writings and the establishment in North America of experimental "intentional communities." Some of these—such as the Shakers, the Amana community, and the Oneida settlement—were religiously based, while others were founded on the ideas presented in the work of the "utopian Socialists." Among the most prominent of the latter were the Scottish industrialist and reformer Robert Owen; the French thinker Henri de Saint-Simon, who argued for the formation of an industrial European union led by an enlightened elite; and Saint-Simon's brilliant and eccentric countryman Charles Fourier, who in his voluminous writings proposed the dismantling of restraints imposed on the natural passions, and the reorganization of society into a series of "phalansteries," with all labor being divided according to people's natural tendencies. Another figure from this moment who bridged the gap between utopian fiction and social experimentation was the French radical Etienne Cabet. Inspired by Owen and More, Cabet produced the utopian fiction *Voyage in Icaria* (1840), which was a tremendous success, and led to both the birth of a vibrant political movement in France and an attempt to establish an Icarian community in the United States.

The single most influential utopian fiction of the century would come from the United States as well, in the form of Bellamy's *Looking Backward*, which tells the story of an upper middle-class man who is cast into a hypnotic slumber, only to awaken in Boston in the year 2000. He discovers a world in which the political chaos and social divisions of his moment have been replaced by a rational and equitable system, with the labor force organized into a pyramidical "Industrial Army" and the distribution of goods occurring through a centralized system of warehouses. Few books in the history of American letters rival the success of *Looking Backward*; it was a world-wide best-seller, it sparked an outpouring in the next decade of more than one hundred new utopias, and it even gave rise to a political movement, which, though short-lived, influenced the platform of the Populist Party and led to progressive calls for, among other reforms, the nationalization of public utilities.

A range of literary utopias appeared in the early years of the twentieth century. Perhaps the most significant English utopian author was **H. G. Wells**. Beginning with *A Modern Utopia* (1905)—a work that draws inspiration from Bacon's *New Atlantis* and presents a vision of an orderly and efficient society directed by a voluntary scientific elite—and continuing in later works such as *Men Like Gods* (1923) and *The Shape of Things to Come* (1933), Wells produced a wealth of utopias to complement his now better-known **science fiction**. The new century also saw the reemergence of a rich tradition of utopian speculation in Russia. Alexander Bogdanov, **Lenin**'s colleague and an important figure in the 1905 **Russian Revolution**, wrote the most significant of these Russian utopias. Bogdanov's *Red Star* (1908) tells the story of a revolutionary's journey to the planet Mars, a world where competitive capitalism has been supplanted by egalitarian socialism, and money and compulsory work have vanished. Finally, the U.S. writer Charlotte Perkins Gilman put the issue of women's rights at center stage in "A Woman's Utopia" (1907), *Herland* (1915), and *With Her in Ourland* (1916).

Three developments in the early twentieth century shaped the genre in some important ways. First, the older vision of a utopia as a location "somewhere else" in the world continued to wane, and utopia was increasingly identified with speculations concerning the future. (There are notable exceptions to this trend, such as James Hilton's *Lost Horizon* [1933], B. F. Skinner's *Walden Two* [1948], and Aldous Huxley's *Island* [1962].) Second, there was a growing sense within the genre of the insufficiency of the nation-state as a container for utopian speculation. Wells made this shift explicit in the opening of *A Modern Utopia*: "No less than a planet will serve the purpose of a modern Utopia" (11). Finally, and most significantly, these years witnessed the growing influence of **dystopian literature**. First emerging in the latter part of the nineteenth century by way of a fusion of the utopia and the naturalist novel, locating in the future the latter's desperate portrait of the present and of human nature more generally, the dystopia was often elided with the anti-utopia, and thus became a crucial ideological weapon in the assault on all forms of utopian thinking.

The success of dystopia and anti-utopia did not, however, mean the end of utopian fiction. Indeed, a "re-birth" occurs in the late 1960s, its first inklings found in works like R. A. Lafferty's *Past Master* (1968) and Monique Wittig's *Les Guérillères* (1969). At its height in the mid-1970s, this outpouring produced Christiane Rochefort's *Archaos, or the Sparkling Garden* (1972), Mack Reynolds's *Looking Backward, from the Year 2000* (1973), Le Guin's *The Dispossessed* (and her later *Always Coming Home* [1985]), **Joanna Russ**'s *The Female Man* (1975), Ernest Callenbach's *Ecotopia* (1975), Marge Piercy's *Woman on the Edge of Time* (1976), Delany's *Triton*, E. M. Broner's *A Weave of Women* (1978), Louky Bersianik's *The Eugélionne* (1978), and Sally Miller Gearheart's *The Wanderground: Stories of the Hill Women* (1978). These works are products of the political and cultural ferment of their moment; they address a whole series of new concerns and adopt a skeptical stance toward their predecessors, becoming what Tom Moylan first called "critical utopias."

This upsurge of utopian fiction would dwindle once again with the neoconservative retrenchment of the 1980s. However, the unexpected fall of the Soviet Union in 1991 and the end of the **cold war** created a situation favorable once again to the production of utopias. The most important of these is **Kim Stanley Robinson**'s Mars trilogy—*Red Mars* (1993), *Green Mars* (1994), and *Blue Mars* (1996)—a monumental narration of the terraforming of the red planet, its first colonists, and their ultimate break with Earth. (Robinson has also written a Southern California utopia, *Pacific Edge* [1990].) Also significant is the Scottish writer Ken MacLeod's Fall Revolution quartet—*The Star Fraction* (1995), *The Stone Canal* (1996), *The Cassini Division* (1998), and *The Sky Road* (1999). Both narratives differ from their predecessors in that they focus primarily on the process by which these new communities are established. In this respect, they reveal a kinship with the most important contemporary "nonliterary" utopia, Michael Hardt and **Antonio Negri**'s *Empire* (1999). The 1990s also witnessed the publication of utopian fictions that deployed new resources in imagining other worlds. These include the Scottish writer Alasdair Gray's *A History Maker* (1994); Mike Resnick's *Kirinyaga: A Fable of Utopia* (1998), based on traditional Kikuyu practices; and Nalo Hopkinson's *Midnight Robber* (2000), which draws on Caribbean culture.

Selected Bibliography: Bartkowski, Frances. *Feminist Utopias.* Lincoln: U of Nebraska P, 1989; Bloch, Ernst. *The Principle of Hope.* 3 vols. Trans. Neville Plaice, Stephen Plaice, and Paul Knight. Cambridge, MA: MIT P, 1995; Claeys, Gregory, and Lyman Tower Sargent, eds. *The Utopia Reader.* New York: New York UP, 1999; Jameson, Fredric. *The Political Unconscious: Narrative as a Socially Symbolic Act.* Ithaca, NY: Cornell UP, 1981; Jameson, Fredric. "The Politics of Utopia." *New Left Review* 25 (2004): 35–54; Jameson, Fredric. "Progress versus Utopia; or, Can We Imagine the Future?" *Science Fiction Studies* 9.2 (1982): 147–58; Kumar, Krishan. *Utopia and Anti-Utopia in Modern Times.* Oxford: Basil Blackwell, 1987; Manuel, Frank E., and Fritzie P. Manuel. *Utopian Thought in the Western World.* Cambridge, MA: Harvard UP, 1979; Moylan, Tom. *Demand the Impossible: Science Fiction and the Utopian Imagination.* New York: Methuen, 1986; Moylan, Tom. *Scraps of the Untainted Sky: Science Fiction, Utopia, Dystopia.* Boulder, CO: Westview P, 2001; Parrinder, Patrick, ed. *Learning from Other Worlds: Estrangement, Cognition, and the Politics of Science Fiction and Utopia.* Durham, NC: Duke UP, 2001; Roemer, Kenneth M. *The Obsolete Necessity: America in Utopian Writings, 1888–1900.* Kent, OH: Kent State UP, 1976; Roemer, Kenneth M. *Utopian Audiences: How Readers Locate Nowhere.* Amherst: U of Massachusetts P, 2003; Ruppert, Peter. *Reader in a Strange Land: The Activity of Reading Literary Utopias.* Athens: U of Georgia P, 1986; Sargent, Lyman Tower. "The Three Faces of Utopianism Revisited." *Utopian Studies* 5.1 (1994): 1–37; Schaer, Roland, Gregory Claeys, and Lyman Tower Sargent, eds. *Utopia: The Search for the Ideal Society in the Western World.* New York: Oxford UP, 2000; Suvin, Darko. *Metamorphoses of Science Fiction: On the Poetics and History of a Literary Genre.* New Haven: Yale UP, 1979; Wegner, Phillip E. *Imaginary Communities: Utopia, the Nation, and the Spatial Histories of Modernity.* Berkeley: U of California P, 2002.

Phillip E. Wegner

◦ V ◦

VALENZUELA, LUISA (1938–). Luisa Valenzuela was already a published journalist and novelist when the military regime took control of her native Argentina in 1976. The early works of her career, such as the novel *Clara* (*Hay que sonreír*, 1966), focused on the social fabric of Argentina and particularly on the position of women in Argentine culture, but as the political situation grew increasingly repressive in the 1970s, she began to critique the political realities of her country more openly. Valenzuela's 1974 collection of stories, *Strange Things Happen Here* (*Aquí pasan cosas raras*) reveals the "strange" and disturbing things that can happen in a society where political discourse is patently false, and language is manipulated to subvert rather than express the truth. Valenzuela went into exile in New York in 1979, and returned to Argentina only after the restoration of democracy in 1983. Her 1982 collection of stories, *Other Weapons* (*Cambio de armas*), synthesizes the personal and political natures of violence and oppression as it reflects the systemic character of brutality and the inevitable manifestation of that brutality in the sexual and romantic lives of individuals. In 1983, Valenzuela published the technically innovative novel *The Lizard's Tail* (*Cola de lagartija*), a thinly veiled caricature of Isabel Perón's minister of social welfare—José López Rega—and his delusional quest for power. Throughout her career, Valenzuela focused on domination through the abuse of discourse and the influence of censorship, both explicit and internal, in shaping our psyches. For her, there can be no true political or social change without a transformation of the language that simultaneously shapes and reflects the systems of control and oppression. While Valenzuela never diminishes the impact of political repression on men, she concentrates on the unique relationship that women have with both language and power. Works published after her return to Argentina, such as *Black Novel with Argentines* (*Novela negra con argentinos*, 1990) and *Bedside Manners* (*Realidad nacional desde la cama,* 1991), reflect on the legacies of violence in the postdictatorship society and the impossibility of ever returning to normalcy after such atrocities.

Selected Bibliography: Castillo, Debra. "Appropriating the Master's Weapons: Luisa Valenzuela." *Talking Back: Toward a Latin American Feminist Literary Criticism*. Ithaca: Cornell UP, 1992; Cordones-Cook, Juana María, ed. Special issue of *Letras Femeninas* 27.1 (Spring 2001); Cordones-Cook, Juana María, ed. *Poética de la transgression en la novelística de Luisa Valenzuela*. New York: Peter Lang, 1991;

Díaz, Gwendolyn, ed. *Luisa Valenzuela sin máscara*. Buenos Aires: Feminista, 2002; Magnarelli, Sharon. *Reflections/Refractions: Reading Luisa Valenzuela*. New York: Peter Lang, 1988; Medeiros-Lichem, María Teresa, and Gladys M. Varona-Lacey, eds. *Reading the Feminine Voice in Latin American Women's Fiction: From Teresa de la Parra to Elena Poniatowska and Luisa Valenzuela*. Latin America Series, vol. 2. New York: Peter Lang, 2003.

Alexandra Fitts

VALLEJO, CÉSAR (1883–1938). Born into a poor family in the isolated northern Peruvian sierra town of Santiago de Chuco, Vallejo is renowned in Hispanic letters for his vanguardist verse. Less known is the political content of his work. Central in the poet's political development was his 1919 generation of Peruvian mestizo intellectuals, including Víctor Raúl Haya de la Torre—organizer of the American Popular Revolutionary Alliance (APRA)—and **José Carlos Mariátegui**—translator of the general strike myth into that of socialist indigenist revolution. Vallejo's poetry is the cultural front of his generation's ideas.

Vallejo's trajectory began in 1915 when he joined the Trujillo Bohemians, a literary political group that was articulating a nationalist, anti-imperialist, and anarchist response to the effects of modernization in the region. Vallejo moved to Lima in 1917 and, as collaborator on Mariátegui's journal *Reason (La razón)*, witnessed the internecine battles between Socialists and anarcho-syndicalists for political control of growing worker unrest. In *The Black Heralds (Los heraldos negros)* (1918) and *Trilce* (1922), the poetic works published in Lima, Proudhon's idea that property is theft and Kropotkin's idea that property belongs to all, along with the call for redistribution, are present in Vallejo's thematic use of bread. His cover poem for *Trilce* is an allegorical account of the Peruvian guano trade, which constituted the pillage and mortgaging of raw materials by European and North American interests.

Concerned about his legal status and literary opportunities, Vallejo moved to Paris in 1923. In 1925, he became a founding member of the Parisian APRA cell; his chronicles from 1926 contain a Leninist analysis of imperialism. During this time, he underwent a period of moral introspection. Vallejo rejected bourgeois possessive individualism and became a disciplined practitioner and divulger of socialist morality—in particular of the ethics of the producers as personified by the Bolshevik, the peasant, and the militiaman. Vallejo chartered his transition to the new man in both *Human Poems (Poemas humanos)* and *Spain, Take This Cup from Me (España, aparta de mí este cáliz)* (1939), where as poet and intellectual he positioned himself at the rear guard in his glorification of common men and women, the warring redeemers and crafters of the new society. The influence of Mariátegui's socialist party and the **Third International**'s newly adopted perspective of imminent revolutionary conflagration (1928) were crucial in the poet's transition to communism.

Critics claim that Vallejo was apolitical until 1926, when he discovered Marxism via **Trotsky**, whose doctrine he rejected in favor of **Stalin**'s in 1929, but that by 1932, Vallejo was disillusioned with communism. However, **cold-war** scholarship misrepresented Vallejo's politics by failing to examine the political content of his early work and by misinterpreting his communism. His travelogue *Rusia en 1931* (1931) and his book of articles *Art and Revolution (El arte y la revolución)* (1932) express a heterodox Marxist, not Stalinist, doctrine. As a Left Oppositionist, Vallejo became disillusioned with Stalin's **Popular Front** strategy but not with communism.

Selected Bibliography: Franco, Jean. *César Vallejo: The Dialectics of Poetry and Silence.* Cambridge: Cambridge UP, 1976; Kishimoto, Jorge Luis. "Vallejo y la Bohemia de Trujillo." *Intensidad y altura de César Vallejo.* Ed. Ricardo Gónzalez Vigil. Lima: Editorial Pontificia Universidad Católica del Perú, 1993. 33–58; Mejía, Marisol. "Politics in the Poetry and Prose of César Vallejo." Diss. Florida State University, 1998; Paoli, Roberto. *Mapas anatómicos de César Vallejo.* Florence: D'Anna, 1981.

Marisol Mejía

VARGAS LLOSA, MARIO (1936–). Born in Arequipa, Peru, Vargas Llosa was educated in Bolivia and Peru before entering a military academy in Lima in 1950. He had already published a play and several stories when he moved to Paris in 1959. He lived there until 1966, then later lived in the United States, England, and Spain before returning to Peru in 1974. His first novel, *The Time of the Hero* (*La ciudad y los perros*, 1963), is set in a military school but already shows some of the political engagement that was typical of his early work and of many novels of the boom in **Latin American literature**, partly because of the successful revolution against American domination in Cuba in 1959. *The Green House* (*La casa verde*, 1966) is a complex modernist work that shows Vargas Llosa already at the height of his powers.

The novel *Conversation in a Cathedral* (*Conversación en la Cathedral*, 1969), a critique of military repression, is one of Vargas Llosa's most overtly political works. It was followed by *Captain Pantoja and the Special Service* (*Pantaleón y las visitadoras*, 1973), which also focuses on the military but marks a turn toward postmodern comedy. Vargas Llosa continued in this mode in *Aunt Julia and the Scriptwriter* (*La tía Julia y el escribidor*, 1977), a semiautobiographical, metafictional romp that intermingles literary fiction with soap opera. *The War of the End of the World* (*La guerra del fin del mundo*, 1981) was a more serious historical novel (based on an actual rebellion spurred by a nineteenth-century apocalyptic sect in Brazil) but maintained a postmodern skepticism about the knowability of the past. A similar epistemological uncertainty underlay such subsequent novels as *The Real Life of Alejandro Mayta* (*Historía de Mayta*, 1984), *The Storyteller* (*El hablador*, 1987), and *Who Killed Palomino Molero?* (*Quién mató a Palomino Molero?* 1986). Such postmodern doubts also seemed to mark a decline in Vargas Llosa's earlier political idealism and belief that literature could contribute to positive political change.

By the late 1980s, the turn away from progressive politics in Vargas Llosa's writing was joined by a similar turn in his own activities, as he became involved in Peruvian politics as an outspoken opponent of the leftist *Sendero Luminoso* guerrillas. In 1990, he stood as an unsuccessful candidate for the presidency of Peru in a campaign that drew significant international attention. After his defeat, he remained an extremely productive writer. *Death in the Andes* (*Lituma en los Andes*, 1993) continued Vargas Llosa's engagement with Peruvian politics in a work that is highly critical of the *Sendero Luminoso* and that, for some, cemented Vargas Llosa's new reputation as a right-wing convert. *The Feast of the Goat* (*La fiesta del chivo*, 2000) expanded the scope of Vargas Llosa's political writing to cover the last days of the brutal right-wing Trujillo regime in the Dominican Republic. In *The Way to Paradise*

(*El paraíso en la otra esquina*, 2003), Vargas Llosa turns to European culture, interweaving a narrative of the life of painter Paul Gauguin with the story (told rather sympathetically) of Gauguin's grandmother, Flora Tristán, a half-French, half-Peruvian radical feminist-socialist of the early nineteenth century. These latter two novels suggested that Vargas Llosa, though clearly no longer a leftist, had not moved entirely to the right.

Selected Bibliography: Booker, M. Keith. *Vargas Llosa among the Postmodernists*. Gainesville: UP of Florida, 1994; Kristal, Efrain. *Temptation of the Word: The Novels of Mario Vargas Llosa*. Nashville: Vanderbilt UP, 1999; Williams, Raymond Leslie. *Mario Vargas Llosa*. New York: Ungar, 1986.

M. Keith Booker

VIETNAM WAR LITERATURE. While the American war in Vietnam can trace its literary roots back to Graham Greene's *The Quiet American* (1955), most of what is now considered important within this unique subset of war literature did not begin to appear until the latter half of the 1970s. Indeed, very few novels or memoirs published while the war was going on were able to attract an appreciative readership. Typical in this regard is James Crumley's *One to Count Cadence* (1969), Tim O'Brien's memoir *If I Should Die in a Combat Zone* (1969), William Eastlake's *The Bamboo Bed* (1969), John A. Williams's *Captain Blackman* (1972, probably the first novel to cover the African American experience in Vietnam), and William Turner Huggett's *Body Count* (1973). Although all of these works would be reissued in very different political circumstances a decade or more later, their initial failure to find an audience is one measure of just how deeply unpopular the war in Vietnam had become by the late 1960s. Nevertheless, it is already possible in the 1960s to discern the outlines of the major ideological tropes that would come to dominate the political discourse of the Vietnam War by the 1980s—in particular, David Halberstam's *The Making of a Quagmire* (1964), which introduced one of the most powerful metaphors for understanding the American experience in Vietnam, and Arthur Schlesinger's *The Bitter Heritage: Vietnam and American Democracy* (1966), which introduced the notion that "no one was to blame" for the Vietnam War because it was a "tragedy without villains" that resulted from "a politics of inadvertence." These notions would be extended further in the 1980s by some historians, such as Stanley Karnow in his highly popular *Vietnam: A History* (1983), which claimed that "Vietnam was a war that nobody won" because it was "a struggle between victims" who shared the effects and the pain of the war in equal measure. The end result of this kind of thinking has added greatly to the mystification of the war and to recent claims that Vietnam was, at base, a postmodern event that produced America's first truly postmodern literature. Thus, on the one hand, Vietnam has had an ambiguous political legacy that is open to interpretation by politicians, publicists, and advertisers alike, and, on the other, the war has been appropriated as a suitably ambivalent event that is available for the latest cultural and literary theory.

As the first trickle of popular Vietnam War novels and memoirs began to appear in the late 1970s, however, they were received as an extension of the political debates of the 1960s. In a sense, these works provided the missing element from that debate because they gave voice to the individual experiences and consequences of the war in Vietnam. Among these were Ron Kovic's *Born on the Fourth of July* (1976), Philip Caputo's *A Rumor of War* (1977), Michael Herr's *Dispatches* (1978), and Tim O'Brien's *Going After Cacciato* (1978). Although offering quite different formal and stylistic approaches to the war experience, these authors all share in common a searing critique of the formative cultural and political forces that had set them up for Vietnam. *A Rumor of War*, for instance, while clearly drawing on the recognizable naturalist traditions of past American war writings, forwards a bitter condemnation of the formative cultural and political forces that had packed Caputo off and abandoned him in what he terms the ethical wilderness of the Vietnam War. Kovic's memoir takes this critique a step further and turns attention to the home culture. As a severely wounded veteran (he was shot and paralyzed from the chest down), much of Kovic's story deals with his experiences in an indifferent medical system, which was clearly not up to the demands put upon it by the war, and to the painful readjustment to family and home. But Kovic is also concerned with tracing the seminal cultural influences on his life, particularly the militarized mass culture of the **cold war**, which had eventually turned him into "a thing to put a uniform on and train to kill, a young thing to run through the meat grinder, a cheap small nothing to make mincemeat out of." Michael Herr is also convinced that the Vietnam War, and the American conduct of and in the war, had deep roots in American history and culture. He writes in *Dispatches* that nothing happened in Vietnam "that hadn't already existed here [the United States] coiled up and waiting"—thus making Vietnam "a fatal environment" where "all the mythic tracks intersected, from the lowest John Wayne wet dream to the most aggravated soldier-poet fantasy." Journalists like Herr were caught between two worlds: the "psychotic vaudeville" of the military's "mission flunkies" in Saigon, who offered the press core an "Orwellian grope through the day's events," all of which would be dutifully reported, and "the grungy men in the jungle who talked bloody murder and killed people all the time." Like Caputo and Kovic, Herr is bitter about the small-minded war planners whose ideas got young soldiers killed wholesale. But he is also insightful about the effects of mass culture on "all the kids who got wiped out by seventeen years of war movies before coming to Vietnam to get wiped out for good."

By the time *Dispatches* appeared in 1978, the works of witness and experience were entering the cultural terrain in competition with Hollywood's film versions of the war: *The Boys in Company C, Go Tell the Spartans, Coming Home,* and *The Deer Hunter* were all released in 1978. *Apocalypse Now* would follow in 1979. Under these conditions, the proliferation of texts either representing or about the war were beginning to naturalize and make popular what earlier seemed an almost taboo topic. Increasingly, throughout the 1980s, the war became a fit subject for TV serialization and Oscar-winning films, while the much maligned veterans of Vietnam became the heroes of a whole range of popular cultural texts. And it is this expansion of the war into mass culture that has convinced some theorists that Vietnam was at base a postmodern event and that, therefore, the literature of the war illuminates the postmodern condition. Central to this approach is the work of O'Brien, whose *Going After Cacciato* is a surreal mediation on the possibility of escaping the horrors of the present through fantasy. Thus, the novel's central character, Paul Berlin, constructs an elaborate fabulation in which his squad attempts to track down a young soldier, the enigmatic Cacciato, who has deserted in order to walk from Vietnam to Paris. Having given up on finding any meaning or structure in Vietnam, Berlin investigates the subversive and subjective possibilities of an imagined escape, which at least has a stated goal if only a quite impossible one. In this process, O'Brien is said to have created a postmodern parody of war that undercuts the great mythic metanarratives that make wars possible, and even desirable, in the first place. Moreover, O'Brien has continued to investigate the ambivalent nature of his war in Vietnam, especially in *The Things They Carried* (1990) in which he self-reflexively questions the possibility of expressing experience in anything remotely approaching the truth. And, in many ways, that is where we are in regard to the American war in Vietnam, where even the veteran writers who attempt to write about their experiences cannot escape the need to explore and to question the conventions and limitations of writing itself.

Selected Bibliography: Beidler, Philip D. *Rewriting America: Vietnam Authors in Their Generation.* Athens: U of Georgia P, 1991; Bibby, Michael, ed. *The Vietnam War and Postmodernity.* Amherst: U of Massachusetts P, 1999; Hellman, John. *American Myth and the Legacy of Vietnam.* New York: Columbia UP, 1986; Jeffords, Susan. *The Remasculinization of America: Gender and the Vietnam War.* Bloomington: Indiana UP, 1989; Melling, Philip L. *Vietnam in American Literature.* Boston: Twayne, 1990.

Andrew Martin

***A VINDICATION OF THE RIGHTS OF WOMAN* (1792),** a work by **Mary Wollstonecraft** that was arguably the greatest feminist treatise of the eighteenth century. A controversial polemic, it relates closely to Wollstonecraft's earlier work, *A Vindication of the Rights of Men* (1790), in which she replied to Edmund Burke regarding the nature of the **French Revolution.** Contending that inequality caused both rulers and subjects to become degraded, Wollstonecraft had argued that intellectual and moral independence, in contrast, benefited society. In the second *Vindication*, this argument is applied to the condition of women.

Signaling its revolutionary nature, *A Vindication* is dedicated to the political activist M. Talleyrand-Périgord. His pamphlet *Rapport sur l'instruction publique, fait nom du Comité* (1791) argued in favor of physical, moral, and intellectual education for all, yet his ideas on female education reflected Rousseau's belief that women should be educated primarily to please men.

Attacking this as immoral, Wollstonecraft argues that reason is given to humans to allow them to inquire into the nature of social behavior. She then examines how women's current position hinders society's progress—in particular, because females are viewed as sexualized, weak, and irrational. *A Vindication* critiques systems of education that encourage this situation, notably Rousseau's *Émile; ou, l'éducation* (1762), Dr. Fordyce's *Sermons* (1765), and Dr. Gregory's *Legacy to His Daughters* (1774). The resultant trivialization of women is, for Wollstonecraft, a state of slavery that degrades both master and dependent, such tyranny undermining morality and the state itself. Correspondingly, she suggests that it benefits the nation to have virtuous women, which would be facilitated through the development of their reason. In particular, to avoid a degrading state of slavery, Wollstonecraft argues that women should be educated to have a sense of political responsibility.

Given the volatile climate in Britain after the French Revolution, *A Vindication* is interestingly positioned. Throughout the work, Wollstonecraft insists on her plain speaking, distinguishing herself from the rhetoric she associates with aristocratic sophistry. Hence, she allies herself with proponents of male suffrage, such as Paine. However, the work addresses itself to women in the middle ranks more than those of the upper or lower classes.

Selected Bibliography: Butler, Marilyn. *Jane Austen and the War of Ideas.* 1975. Oxford: Clarendon P, 1987; Kelly, Gary. *Revolutionary Feminism: The Mind and Career of Mary Wollstonecraft.* 2nd ed. Basingstoke: Macmillan, 1996; Wollstonecraft, Mary, and William Godwin. *A Short Residence in Sweden: Memoirs of the Author of* "The Rights of Woman." 1796. 1798. Ed. Richard Holmes. London: Penguin, 1987.

Fiona Price

VIZENOR, GERALD ROBERT (1934–). Mixed-blood, Anishinaabe high school dropout, soldier, social worker, college professor, newspaper reporter, poet, and novelist, Gerald Vizenor embodies and writes about *change* to a greater degree than any other writer of **Native American literature**. Cultural instability defined Vizenor's childhood. His French-Anishinaabe father was murdered just twenty months after he was born; his white mother was often absent and eventually abandoned him during adolescence, leaving him to his last stepfather, who died soon after. After military service in the early 1950s, Vizenor earned an undergraduate degree from the University of Minnesota. During the 1960s, while working toward a graduate degree, Vizenor began to get involved in the native politics of Minnesota and the northern plains by organizing protests against the politics of the Bureau of Indian Affairs (BIA), especially that organization's refusal to help tribal people who had moved to urban areas. He won BIA support for Minneapolis's American Indian Employment Center (AIEC) and was subsequently named director of an AIEC office. Vizenor then reported for several Minneapolis newspapers, covering the activities of the American Indian movement (AIM) at Wounded Knee in a series of honest and unflattering reports that earned him threats of violence from AIM members. His grassroots work at the AIEC and the reporting work that followed gave Vizenor a perspective rarely found in, and often at odds with, the Native American cultural studies programs that were to become his eventual working environment.

After being deeply involved with the welfare of both city and reservation tribal peoples, Vizenor began to shape his experience into short stories and novels. He published his first novel, *Darkness in Saint Louis Bearheart* (later retitled *Bearheart: The Heirship Chronicles*), in 1978 and has since produced dozens of works—novels, short fiction and nonfiction collections, biography, and poetry, including his collections of haiku. His storytelling explores the violent space created by the encounter between European and Native American cultures. For Vizenor, the simple story of a clash of two cultures does not describe reality, especially for hundreds of thousands of mixed-bloods. His project has been to assimilate contemporary reality into the living framework of Anishinaabe culture by writing the stories of real mixed-blood experience both on the reservation (*Wordarrows* [1978] and *Earthdivers* [1983]) and in the city

(*Dead Voices* [1992]). He often turns the old savage versus civilized dichotomy on its head, exposing the destructive "terminal creeds" and savagery of mainstream North American culture and the "postindian" culture that has emerged. A culture of the victim might be expected, yet this is not the case. Playing the victim is a terminal creed for Vizenor, and he is effective at pointing out that, for white culture, "Indian" is synonymous with "victim." Instead, Vizenor's cross-blood characters learn how to adapt themselves and their living culture to the bizarre landscape of **postmodernism** with equally bizarre and unexpected—yet liberating—results. Vizenor continues to share his stories through teaching at the University of California–Berkeley, writing, and lecturing.

Selected Bibliography: Blaeser, Kimberly. *Gerald Vizenor: Writing in the Oral Tradition.* Norman: U of Oklahoma P, 1996; Lee, Robert A., ed. *Loosening the Seams: Interpretations of Gerald Vizenor.* Bowling Green, KY: Popular P, 2000; Vizenor, Gerald. *Shadow Distance.* Hanover, NH: Wesleyan UP, 1994; Vizenor, Gerald, and Robert A. Lee. *Postindian Conversations.* Lincoln: U of Nebraska P, 1999.

David Leaton

VOINOVICH, VLADIMIR NIKOLAEVICH (1932–). Often compared with **Nikolai Gogol**, Voinovich is one of the most popular and prolific of contemporary Russian satirists. Born in Dushanbe (Tadzhikistan), he completed only seven years of formal education, instead toiling at a variety of menial jobs that gave him familiarity with the everyday lives of Soviet workers. A formative event of his early youth was the arrest and five-year imprisonment of his father, a journalist. Voinovich served four years in the Red Army in the early 1950s and began to write and publish verse in military newspapers. He first achieved success writing song lyrics, composing about fifty songs in all. His composition "Fourteen Minutes to Go" became the unofficial anthem of the Soviet cosmonauts.

In the 1960s, five of Voinovich's stories were published in *Novyi mir*, the most prestigious liberal literary journal in the Soviet Union. Voinovich's only other significant work to appear in his homeland prior to Glasnost is a historical novel about Vera Figner called *A Degree of Trust* (1972). In 1974, Voinovich was expelled from the Soviet Writers' Union in reprisal for his activities in support of dissident intellectuals, including Andrei Sinyavsky, Yuli Daniel, and **Aleksandr Solzhenitsyn**. The publication of his works abroad, which began with the appearance of the first part of *The Life and Extraordinary Adventures of Private Ivan Chonkin* (1969), exacerbated the situation. A marvelous satirical tour de force, this novel lampoons collectivized agriculture, the Red Army, the NKVD, **Stalin**, communist ideology, and other Soviet sacred cows. As Voinovich's foothold in Soviet literature eroded in the 1970s, he turned openly toward the West and published several more works in the émigré press: "By Way of Mutual Correspondence" appeared in 1973; *The Ivankiad*, in 1976, and *Pretender to the Throne* (which comprises the third and fourth parts of *Ivan Chonkin*), in 1979. After several years of systematic harassment by the Soviet authorities, Voinovich emigrated in 1981 and settled in Munich.

Voinovich's first major work to appear in emigration was a collection of essays and feuilletons, *The Anti-Soviet Soviet Union* (1985). *Moscow 2042*, a futuristic satire of Soviet politics and culture and an *ad hominem* exposé of Solzhenitsyn, followed in

1987. With glasnost, the publication of Voinovich's works in his homeland became possible. In 1989, when "The Fur Hat" appeared in the West, the story came out almost simultaneously in the Soviet Union. Voinovich's citizenship was restored in 1990 and he reestablished a residence in Moscow. *Ivan Chonkin,* "The Fur Hat," and *Moscow 2042* were adapted to the stage, and film versions of both *Ivan Chonkin* and "The Fur Hat" were made.

In addition to the works mentioned above, Voinovich has written two plays, sketches, fairy tales, and many poems. He is also a visual artist and has produced several series of oil paintings. Occasional pieces by him have appeared in the popular press (both in Russia and in the West), and he has continued to make frequent public appearances.

Selected Bibliography: Brown, Deming. *The Last Years of Soviet Russian Literature: Prose Fiction, 1975–1991.* Cambridge: Cambridge UP, 1993; Matich, Olga, and Michael Heim, eds. *The Third Wave: Russian Literature in Emigration.* Ann Arbor, MI: Ardis, 1984; Perryman Sally Anne. "Vladimir Voinovich: The Evolution of a Satirical Writer." Ph.D. diss., Vanderbilt U, 1981; Ryan-Hayes, Karen. *Contemporary Russian Satire: A Genre Study.* Cambridge: Cambridge UP, 1995.

Karen Ryan

∘ W ∘

WALKER, MARGARET (1915–1998). Born in Birmingham, Alabama, and raised in New Orleans, Walker grew up in an atmosphere of intellectual and artistic stimulation, all the while remaining deeply conscious of the racial politics that surrounded her. At the urging of **Langston Hughes**, whom the Walker family met when Hughes visited New Orleans, Walker went north to take her B.A. degree at Northwestern University, which she completed in 1935. During the remainder of the 1930s, Walker stayed in Chicago and worked for the **Federal Writers' Project**, where she came into contact with other noted black artists such as **Richard Wright**, Katherine Dunham, Frank Yerby, and Margaret Burroughs. Walker's friendship with Wright, which ended after a misunderstanding, ultimately resulted in her writing a biography of him, which she published in 1988.

During her tenure with the Federal Writers' Project, Walker began a collection of poetry, which she would publish as *For My People* and which would win the Yale Younger Poets Award in 1941. Walker became the first African American to win this prestigious award. Divided into three sections (free-verse narratives, folk ballads, and sonnets), *For My People* explores and celebrates African American life from its beginnings to Walker's contemporary moment in a nation at the brink of global crisis. While in Chicago, Walker worked in a mentoring program for "delinquent" females. This experience inspired her to write *Goose Island,* an unpublished novel about a talented young musician who ends up a Division Street prostitute. In 1940, Walker completed an M.A. at the University of Iowa's writing program. In 1943, she married Firnist James (Alex) Alexander. The couple moved to Jackson, Mississippi, in 1949, where they raised four children and where Walker taught at Jackson State College (now University) until her retirement in 1979. It was at Jackson State that Walker founded one of the nation's first institutes for African American studies, which now bears her name.

In 1966, Walker published *Jubilee,* a novel based on her maternal grandmother's recollections of slave life during the civil war. Walker published two other books, *Prophets for a New Day* (1970) and *October Journey* (1973), both with the black arts movement publishing house Broadside Press. Walker's influence on younger black artists can be seen in her published dialogue with poet Nikki Giovanni, *A Poetic*

Equation. Walker received numerous awards throughout her lengthy career, and in 1989, the University of Georgia Press published *This Is My Century: New and Collected Poems.*

Selected Bibliography: Berke, Nancy. *Women Poets on the Left: Lola Ridge, Genevieve Taggard, Margaret Walker.* Gainesville: UP of Florida, 2001; Graham, Maryemma. *Conversations with Margaret Walker.* Jackson, MS: UP of Mississippi, 2002; Graham, Maryemma, ed. *Fields Watered with Blood: Critical Essays on Margaret Walker.* Athens, GA: U of Georgia P, 2001; Walker, Margaret. *How I Wrote "Jubilee" and Other Essays on Life and Literature.* Ed. Maryemma Graham. New York: Feminist P, CUNY, 1990; Walker, Margaret. *On Being Female, Black and Free: Essays 1932–1992.* Ed. Maryemma Graham. Knoxville: U of Tennessee P, 1997.

Nancy Berke

WANG SHUO (1958–). *Get High, Then Die!* is the title of one of Wang Shuo's two-dozen novels and is also the catchphrase of a personal philosophy. Born in Nanjing, Wang experienced the Cultural Revolution (1966–1976) as an unsupervised, thrill-seeking youth. He then spent four years in the navy and held a variety of odd and shady jobs before beginning to write in the 1980s. Quickly rising to the status of pop icon, he launched a style with its own terminology—*pizi,* or "hooligan" literature. Wang is viewed variously as the person most responsible for the commercialization—or even commodification—of Chinese culture in the 1990s; the first writer to openly mock the government and the political system; and a cultural, if not political, dissident. Unlike writers who focused on linguistic and formal experimentation and were keen to deconstruct the realism that dominated Chinese literature in previous decades, Wang became the spokesman for a new era. Claiming to be anti-intellectual, he railed against literary bureaucrats and the hypocrisy of official culture, and invented a new form of mass popular literature that eschewed moralizing. Writing in the language of Beijing youth and capturing its sustained and lively rhythms, Wang's forte was his use of dialogue, shot through with bold and heavily ironic comments on politics, the family, and society.

Wang was one of the first to create central characters that rebel against the established order and to treat taboo subjects head on. The characters of his short novel *The Operators* (*Wan zhu,* 1987), for instance, are unprincipled young men who sell their services as proxies—for lovers, people in trouble, henpecked husbands—thus thumbing their nose at social norms; anything for a buck. In *Playing for Thrills* (*Warde jiushi xintiao,* 1989), a mystery with a twist, Wang creates a cadre of young urban slackers—at least one of whom may be a murderer—who are the antithesis of the "model citizens" favored by the official establishment. In *Please Don't Call Me Human* (*Qianwan bie ba wo dang ren,* 1992), a satirical farce that mocks an increasingly prevalent ultranationalism, a cabby is chosen by Beijing hooligans to defend the nation's honor by getting castrated in order to participate in an international sporting event as a woman.

To be sure, the subversive nature of Wang's fiction exists not in the flaunting of societal norms per se but in the degree to which he celebrates (or disparages) his characters' spirit in their struggle to survive in an increasingly materialistic and cut-throat urban environment. In the eyes of Chinese officials, Wang, who stopped writing fiction for several years after his four-volume collected works were published in 1996 (and quickly pulled from bookstore shelves on orders from the government), is something far more dangerous than a dissident; he is, at least most of the time, a poison-pen satirist. To be considered a dissident, of course, one ought to embrace political ideals; not Wang, however, who once told an interviewer that he held no political beliefs whatsoever. In a society that advocates, at least gives lip-service to, political participation and social conformity, that in itself is a political statement.

Selected Bibliography: Barmé, Geremie. *In the Red: On Contemporary Chinese Culture.* New York: Columbia UP, 1999; Huot, Claire. *China's New Cultural Scene: A Handbook of Changes.* Durham, NC: Duke UP, 2000; Zha Jianying. *China Pop: How Soap Operas, Tabloids, and Bestsellers Are Transforming a Culture.* New York: New P, 1995.

Howard Goldblatt

WARNER, SYLVIA TOWNSEND (1893–1978). Already a noted poet, novelist, and musicologist, Warner's political commitment became public in 1935 when she joined the **Communist Party** and began her involvement with *Left Review.* Her earlier works show an already established interest in gender, class, and colonialism; her book-length pastoral poem *Opus 7* (1931) may not call for collective action but shows an unromanticized rural society firmly grounded in material and economic conditions. Some of her concern with the politics of class may derive from her brief experience as a "lady worker" in a munitions factory in 1915.

By Warner's later account, her overt political engagement was sparked by reading of the conduct of Georgi Dimitrov at the Reichstag fire trials, and she has linked her party membership with opposition to fascism and the national government. With her partner Valentine Ackland, Warner twice visited Spain during the **Spanish Civil War**, doing administrative work for the Red Cross in 1936 and attending the Writers' Congress in 1937. Poems written in this period often address the topic of the Spanish war, occasionally with a direct call for support but more often indirectly. Her novel *After the Death of Don Juan* (1938), which begins at the point where Mozart's *Don Giovanni* ends, also alludes to the Spanish Civil War despite its earlier historical setting.

The degree of Warner's commitment to communism has been questioned. Late in life she indicated a sympathy for anarchism (although she supported the Communist Party's treatment of POUM—the Workers Party of Marxist Unification—in Spain). Warner's journals indicate continued admiration for **Stalin** at the time of his death, even though her Party membership had lapsed.

Much of Warner's writing is distinguished by a slightly unsettling level of detachment from her subjects, which encourages a thoughtful response from her readers. *Summer Will Show* (begun in 1932, published in 1936)—a radical historical novel—tells the story of an aristocratic British lady whose journey to Paris in 1848 leads her to a love affair with her husband's Jewish mistress and a commitment to revolutionary change. Warner herself described *The Corner That Held Them* (1948)—the story of a medieval Benedictine convent through several generations, with no central character—as her most Marxian novel; it is certainly strongly aware of economic and material circumstances as motivating forces. This awareness of the importance of the material world—often combined with an interest in rural life and always marked by a concern for precision in form and diction—is a key characteristic of Warner's writing.

Selected Bibliography: Harman, Barbara Leah. *The Feminine Political Novel in Victorian England.* Charlottesville: UP of Virginia, 1998; *The Journal of the Sylvia Townsend Warner Society*, 2000– ; Mulford, Wendy. *This Narrow Place: Sylvia Townsend Warner and Valentine Ackland: Life, Letters and Politics.* London: Pandora P, 1998.

Kathleen Bell

WE (1924). One of the first and most important works of modern **dystopian literature**, this novel by Russian writer **Evgeny Zamyatin** was written in 1919–1920 and published in English in 1924. The original Russian version was not authorized for publication in the Soviet Union until 1988, when Gorbachev's policy of cultural openness (*glasnost*) allowed readers access to twentieth-century Russian literature inimical to the communist project. The novel *We* is set in the twenty-ninth century. It posits that almost all of remaining humanity (most of which had earlier been wiped out in a world war of apocalyptic proportions) lives in the One State: a perfectly organized, rational, and harmonious city of glass buildings and happy citizens. Citizens of the One State have been raised to see themselves as part of a collective, and their seeming lack of individual desire or will might indicate that the state's methods have been effective—both the "carrot" of predictable, material happiness (even the weather is always perfect) and the "stick" of execution if deviation from the norm is caught by one of the ubiquitous Guardians. Every aspect of this society is regimented, ostensibly for the good of all. Citizens are designated by numbers rather than personal names, and both their meals and their sex lives are organized to maximize health benefits and minimize the potential for irrational indulgence and passion. The entire novel is a record of the diary of D-503, an engineer who is building a rocket that will carry the One State's message of collective bliss to other planets. As the novel proceeds, D-503's narrative voice registers his slowly dawning consciousness of the hazards of imposed mass happiness. His irrational dream world comes out in startling symbolic imagery, whereas in his conscious life, he tries to express his emotions with mathematical metaphors. When he falls hopelessly in love with a female revolutionary, I-330, he is lured into her conspiracy to escape the One State's regime of happiness. For I-330, freedom is not compatible with ideas of fixed, eternal order, since "There is no such thing as a 'last' revolution. The number of revolutions is infinite." **Huxley's Brave New World** (1932) and **Orwell's Nineteen Eighty-Four** (1949) both pursue Zamyatin's dystopian theme of enforced conformity in modern industrialized societies, but Zamyatin's novel is funnier and more ironic. It has been read as a prophecy of twentieth-century fascism and as a prescient anticommunist parable, and it can certainly prompt post-Soviet readings as a satire aimed at any ideological establishment (bourgeois or socialist, secular or religious) that claims to have the final answer to the problem of human happiness.

Selected Bibliography: Booker, M. Keith. *The Dystopian Impulse in Modern Literature: Fiction as Social Criticism.* Westport, CT: Greenwood, 1994; Brown, Edward J. *"Brave New World," "1984" and "We": An Essay on Anti-Utopia (Zamyatin and English Literature).* Ann Arbor, MI: Ardis, 1976; Burns,

Tony. "Zamyatin's *We* and Postmodernism." *Utopian Studies* 11.1 (2000): 66–90; Cooke, Brett. *Human Nature in Dystopia: Zamyatin's "We."* Evanston, IL: Northwestern UP, 2002; Kern, Gary, ed. *Zamyatin's "We": A Collection of Critical Essays.* Ann Arbor, MI: Ardis, 1988.

Yvonne Howell

WEATHERWAX, CLARA (1905–1958). The descendant of an early, prominent Aberdeen family, Clara Weatherwax was the author of *Marching! Marching!* one of the most ironically positioned novels of American **proletarian fiction**. While the novel was awarded a prize as the best American novel on a proletarian theme in a contest sponsored by the John Day Publishing Company and *New Masses*, it also came to be, over time, the most widely abused of its genre, characterized as inept and programmatic. Nevertheless, *Marching! Marching!* was one of the most formally innovative of American proletarian novels and deserves a closer critical scrutiny.

At the time she decided to write the novel, Weatherwax and her husband, composer Gerald Strang, lived in the hills above Berkeley and associated themselves with the cultural and political left. Strang was a friend of several musician/composers associated with the New Music community, a loose association of avant-garde figures who mixed social and aesthetic innovations into their compositions and performances. Weatherwax's brother, John, was closely connected to the **Communist Party** in California and wrote music and cultural journalism. He also translated the Mayan epic myth *Popol Vuh* and convinced his friend, Diego Rivera, to produce twenty-three watercolor illustrations for it. During Rivera's sojourn in northern California, he and Frida Kahlo became friends of and frequent visitors to the Weatherwax/Strang household.

Weatherwax observed the San Francisco general strike of 1934–1935 while writing her novel, and drew from it and from stories of the labor unrest that had plagued her hometown earlier in the century. With the $750 prize money, Clara and Gerald moved to Los Angeles, where she attempted to continue to write. The onset of rheumatoid arthritis hindered her, and she gradually declined in health. By the mid-1950s, she was virtually blind. She died without having completed another novel or work of any considerable length.

In *Marching! Marching!* Weatherwax sought and found a collective persona for the center of her story and represented its voice via the use of stream-of-consciousness techniques and experiments in the use of fonts, layout, and punctuation. In effect, hers was the first real attempt to apply modernist stylistic innovations to the American propagandistic novel of the left. Nevertheless, *Marching! Marching!* drew few reviews and fewer good reviews. Neither Weatherwax nor her book were mentioned in the landmark collection of 1935, *Proletarian Literature in the United States*, nor was the book mentioned in most later histories of the proletarian "moment" except as an object lesson in what not to do. These judgments were both premature and unfortunate. Weatherwax's role as an innovator in political narrative and her connections to the cultural left of the early 1930s go uninvestigated and unappreciated to this day.

Selected Bibliography: Cantwell, Robert. "A Town and Its Novels." *New Republic* 86 (February 1936): 51–52; Suggs, Jon-Christian. Introduction to *Marching! Marching!* by Clara Weatherwax. Detroit: Omnigraphics, 1990. iii–xliv; Suggs, Jon-Christian. "*Marching! Marching!* and the Idea of the Proletarian Novel." *The Novel and the American Left: Critical Essays on Depression-Era Fiction.* Ed. Janet Galligani Casey. Iowa City: U of Iowa P, 2004. 151–71.

Jon-Christian Suggs

WEBER, MAX (1864–1920) was the son of a prominent politician whose family had made its fortune in the Bielefeld (Germany) linen trade and a mother from a Huguenot family with academic connections. Weber was trained in the law and appeared destined for a career as a legal historian, but accepted a position teaching national economics in 1892 in Freiburg. He later moved to Heidelberg, where he spent much of the rest of his life. In 1903, he resigned his professorship due to a nervous condition and thereafter pursued the life of a private scholar. His wife hosted a salon in which the leading literary and intellectual figures of Heidelberg as well as promising students—such as **Georg Lukács**—participated, thus extending his personal influence across many disciplines.

Between 1903 and 1907, Weber produced a series of methodological essays advancing a relativistic conception of the *Geisteswissenschaften*, which nevertheless allowed for causal analysis. During the same period, he published his best-known work, *The Protestant Ethic and the Spirit of Capitalism* (1904–1905), which introduced the thesis that the modern rational and autonomous individual was the product of the combination of Calvinist doctrines of predestination and election and the notion of "callings," which he argued had been taken out of the monasteries and applied to the world as a whole by Protestantism. This movement, for Weber, results in the sacralization of work as well as capitalist accumulation, while at the same time contributing to the phenomenon of rationalization, or **routinization**, in which human life is stripped of magic, becoming dominated by rationality and a drive toward productivity and profit.

Subsequently, Weber worked on a handbook eventually published as *Economy and Society* (1968), which traced the internal histories of various forms of political authority, elaborating a distinction between traditional, rational legal, and charismatic authority. In a series of political writings, Weber encouraged a strong president independent of parliament who could use his charisma to control the bureaucratized state. Among the models for Weber's concept of charisma was the poet Stefan George, whose circle both overlapped and competed with Weber's circle in Heidelberg.

After **World War I**, Weber made two famous speeches, widely discussed among German intellectuals, on the vocation of science and the vocation of politics. The speech on science provoked a huge response, particularly from literary intellectuals who were hostile to his dismissal of **Johann Wolfgang Goethe**'s conception of the unity of thought. Weber died in Munich in 1920, attended by both his wife, Marianna Weber—an early feminist writer on the common German language feminist theme of *Mutterrecht*—and his mistress, Elsa Jaffe—the sister of Frieda Lawrence. Weber went on to become one of the most influential figures in the subsequent development of the social sciences in both Europe and the United States. He has also exercised considerable influence in the realm of literary studies, as in **Fredric Jame-**

son's use of the concept of rationalization to explain the ongoing popularity of romance genres in the twentieth century.

Selected Bibliography: Jameson, Fredric. *The Political Unconscious: Narrative as a Socially Symbolic Act.* Ithaca, NY: Cornell UP, 1981; Turner, Stephen P., ed. *The Cambridge Companion to Weber.* New York: Cambridge UP, 2000; Weber, Max. *Economy and Society: An Outline of Interpretive Sociology.* 1968. 3 vols. Ed. and trans. Guenther Roth and Claus Wittich. Berkeley: U of California P, 1978; Weber, Max. *From Max Weber: Essays in Sociology.* Trans. H. H. Gerth and C. W. Mills. Oxford: Oxford UP, 1946; Weber, Max. *General Economic History.* New Brunswick, NJ: Transaction, 1961; New York: Collier Books, 1981; Weber, Max. *The Methodology of the Social Sciences.* Ed. and trans. E. A. Shils and H. A. Finch. New York: Free P, 1949; Weber, Max. *Political Writings.* Ed. Peter Lassman and Ronald Speirs. Cambridge: Cambridge UP, 1994; Weber, Max. *The Protestant Ethic and the Spirit of Capitalism.* 1904–1905. Trans. Talcott Parsons. New York: Scribner's, 1958.

Stephen P. Turner

WEISS, PETER (1916–1982). Author of *Marat/Sade* (1964), a drama about the French revolution and one of the most spectacular stage events of the twentieth century, and of *The Investigation* (*Die Ermittlung*, 1965), an unbearably detailed inventory of the destruction of human life at Auschwitz and a play whose perceived political bent continues to provoke bitter polemics. Weiss was born in Berlin, the son of a Hungarian Jewish father who after the First World War acquired Czech citizenship and converted to Protestantism, and a Swiss German mother. Weiss was raised a protestant with Czech citizenship, leaving Germany after the Nazis came to power and living for the rest of his life in Sweden, first as a painter, then as a filmmaker, and eventually as a writer, writing his early works in Swedish before returning to his German mother tongue. Weiss's works are located at the intersection of historical events, ideological discourses, and avant-garde movements of the twentieth century, including two world wars, the **Holocaust**, Marxism, Freudian psychology, the student movement of 1968, colonial and postcolonial debates, surrealism, and documentary literature. Weiss was already in his forties when he turned to literature, producing a series of solipsistic and hermetic texts before moving from a focus on individual revolt to one on political revolution with *Marat/Sade*. His effort at understanding the Holocaust during work on *The Investigation* brought him to socialism and Marxism, and in 1968 he joined the Swedish **Communist Party**.

In the play *Song of the Lusitanian Bogey* (*Gesang vom lusitanischen Popanz,* 1967), Weiss explores the structure of colonial exploitation in Portugal's African territories. Weiss was openly critical of the American policy in the **Vietnam War**, and in 1967 he participated in the second Vietnam War crimes tribunal, the so-called Russell tribunal, during which leading European intellectuals, writers, and artists condemned the war of the United States against Vietnam. In the play *Viet Nam Discourse* (*Viet Nam Diskurs*, 1968), Weiss staged a compressed version of the two-thousand-year history of oppression of the Vietnamese people, which culminated in the Vietnam War. With such works, as well as with his political activism, Weiss became an important thinker, both admired and reviled, for the German student movement of 1968. Weiss followed with a play about **Leon Trotsky**, *Trotsky in Exile* (*Trotzky im*

Exil, 1969). He spent most of the 1970s on his monumental novel *Die Ästhetik des Widerstands* (The Aesthetics of Resistance, 3 vols., 1975, 1978, 1981), a historical vision of the European Left and its struggle against fascism, as well as a heroic effort to reinterpret some of the great works of world art and culture and thereby wrest them from bourgeois tradition and integrate them into a culture of the masses.

Weiss was a writer of enormous artistic complexity. While he wrote "engaged literature," in the sense in which **Jean-Paul Sartre** defined the term, his most openly political works—such as *Marat/Sade*, the play about Trotsky, *Die Ästhetik des Widerstands*, and *The Investigation*—are also among his most aesthetically powerful, owing as much to surrealist preoccupations with visions, dreams, hallucinations, and madness and to what might be called an aesthetic of excess as to any political theory.

Selected Bibliography: Cohen, Robert. "The Political Aesthetics of Holocaust Literature: Peter Weiss's 'The Investigation' and Its Critics." *History and Memory* 10.2 (1998): 43–67. Cohen, Robert. *Understanding Peter Weiss.* Trans. Martha Humphreys. Columbia, SC: U of South Carolina P, 1993; Garner, Stanton B. "Post-Brechtian Anatomies: Weiss, Bond and the Politics of Embodiment." *Theater Journal* 42.2 (1990): 145–64; Hermand, Jost, and Marc Silberman, eds. *Rethinking Peter Weiss.* New York: Peter Lang, 2000; Roberts, David. " 'Marat/Sade' or the Birth of Post-Modernism from the Spirit of the Avant-garde." *New German Critique* 38 (1986): 112–30.

Robert Cohen

WELLS, H. G. (1866–1946). Born into middle-class genteel poverty in Bromley, a small town outside of London, Herbert George Wells struggled hard to become educated and establish himself as a writer. A prolific writer of novels, short stories, and works of nonfiction, he praised the wonders of science and technology, mostly in his nonfiction. In the manner of Fabian socialism, Wells imagined how industrial-technological society could be organized to benefit the masses. Yet he also sketched out its potential horrors in his **science-fiction** writings, which stand as great achievements in the history of **dystopian literature**, providing cautionary warnings about science and technology out of control. Moreover, in Wells's dystopic vision, human beings were potentially a transitory phenomenon that could vanish like dinosaurs or Neanderthals.

Wells possessed wide-ranging philosophical and historical vision, imagining that the coevolution of science, technology, and human beings could alter the forms of space and time and the patterns of human life, producing both marvels and monsters. Deeply influenced by theories of evolution, he imagined that the human species could mutate in surprising and discontinuous ways, anticipating positive leaps and negative regressions in the human adventure. Combining congenital pessimism with hope for a socialist humanism, Wells articulated both positive visions of the future and dystopic fears of the demise of the human race and the earth itself.

Wells pursued the "what if" logic of modern science fiction (SF) to new dimensions, conceiving radically other universes and beings, and anticipating developments in which humans are forced to discern that they are no longer the dominant species. In *War of the Worlds* (1898), Wells imagined that superior alien races could travel to earth and defeat and destroy humans, thereby decentering and dethroning humanity as the highest form of evolution. In the first major tale of interplanetary warfare,

Wells instilled in the popular psyche a fear of aliens that remains a major SF tradition. A pointed satire of imperialist invasion that elicited similarities to destructive forms of colonization in modernity, Wells's story provided a cautionary warning that imperialist forces themselves could be made subject to unknown and calamitous counterforces. Similarly, in his story "Empire of the Ants" (1996), he showed intelligent, giant killer ants naturally evolving in a Brazilian rain forest and threatening humanity with extinction, suggesting again that humans could be displaced as masters of earth by other life forms.

In *The Time Machine* (1895) and *The Invisible Man* (1897), Wells portrayed humans transcending the boundaries of space and time, and mutating into new forms. *The Time Machine* depicts a terrifying future for humanity. It imagines an entropic collapse not only of civilization but of the earth itself, ultimately devoured in the red hot fireball of an exploding sun. *The Time Machine* also articulates a critique of the Enlightenment notion of progress, warning that human species might fall prey to catastrophe rather than build ever new and better engines of progress. In his division of humanity into two transhuman species—the Eloi and the Morlocks, who are descendants of contemporary humanity—Wells warns that an irrational organization of society can produce monstrous results. The Eloi are hyperrefined and decadent, while the Morlocks are crude and degenerate, providing a parable of the deleterious effects of class division in which one group suffers the effects of excessive leisure while the other group is condemned to constant labor. The brutalization of the Morlocks allegorizes the outcome of a life of alienated labor, while the Eloi represent the results of excessively passive consumption and leisure. There is thus a Marxist subtext to the story: unless exploitation stops and the division of a class society is overcome, the human species faces disastrous dichotomization, discord, and decline.

The Invisible Man presents human beings shattering the limits of scientific possibility and creating a new type of freakish being. An alien among his own kind, Dr. Griffin is a Faust-like scientist whose "strange and evil experiment succeeds on a technical level, rendering him invisible, but the discovery dooms him in the social context he cannot escape. Ruthlessly selfish, "powerful, angry, and malignant," driven toward immoral acts and insane visions, Griffin symbolizes all that can go wrong with science, as the communities he terrorizes unite against him. Griffin's knowledge remains secret, but the slumbering power of science to create miracles and/or monstrosities could be recovered and used at any time, suggesting the need for citizens to be ever vigilant about the development of science and technology.

In two key novels, Wells anticipated biotechnology and the ways that humans could radically alter nature and their own species. In *Food of the Gods* (1904), Wells vividly portrays the possibly destructive consequences of genetically modified food and, more generally, a culture based on unrestrained growth imperatives. *The Island of Dr. Moreau* (1896) projects a frightening vision of an emerging condition in which human and animal life implode. In its multileveled complexity, the novel is a powerful protest against the self-proclaimed right of science to experiment on animals and to engineer new life forms. It provides a profound meditation on the conflicts within human beings endowed with reason but unable to escape the violent legacy of their animal past.

Like *The Invisible Man, The Island of Dr. Moreau* crystallizes Wells's antipathy toward scientific arrogance and its lack of social conscience. As Shelley and Wells anticipated, science and technology can indeed create monstrosities. Yet a new century and increased literary fame helped generate a more optimistic vision, and in *Anticipation of the Reaction of Mechanical and Scientific Progress upon Human Life and Thought* (1901), Wells envisaged a "new class of capable men," largely scientists and engineers, who would put aside petty party politics and harness science and industry to create a new era of progress.

Wells spent the rest of his life engaged in the battles for the future of Fabian socialists, Marxists, and various political and literary groups. While he published many political treatises and novels and a popular *History of the World* while becoming one of the most best-selling writers in the world, it is probably his 1890s science fiction and fantasy stories and novels that have most shaped the contemporary imagination and that constitute Wells's most significant legacy.

Selected Bibliography: Bergonzi, Bernard. *The Early H. G. Wells.* Manchester: Manchester UP, 1961; Best, Steven, and Douglas Kellner. *The Postmodern Adventure.* London: Routledge, 2001; Hillegas, Mark. *The Future as Nightmare: H. G. Wells and the Anti-Utopians.* Carbondale: Southern Illinois UP, 1974; McConnell, Frank. *The Science Fiction of H. G. Wells.* Oxford: Oxford UP, 1981.

Douglas Kellner

WEST, NATHANAEL (1903–1940). The son of well-to-do Jewish immigrants living on Manhattan's Upper West Side, West became one of America's most unorthodox leftist writers. Born Nathan Weinstein, West dropped out of high school but used a false transcript to enter Brown University. In the late 1920s, he changed his name legally to Nathanael West and spent three months in Paris. After returning, he worked as a night manager at two hotels in New York and got to know several progressive writers, including **Mike Gold**, **Dashiell Hammett**, and **John Dos Passos**. In 1935, West moved to Hollywood to work as a screenwriter. He died in an automobile accident at the age of thirty-seven.

Unlike many leftist writers of the 1930s, West was interested less in the problems of working-class labor than in mass consumer culture, which he called "the business of dreams." West's fiction blends biting satire and grotesque depictions of suffering in a unique brand of American **surrealism** that conveys both sympathy for social outcasts and a precocious critique of the culture industry's capacity to mold and commodify human desires. West's first novel, *The Dream Life of Balso Snell* (1931)—a boldly experimental text—is a bizarre, scatological vision of Western civilization gone mad. In the early 1930s, West joined poet **William Carlos Williams** in editing the experimental magazine *Contact* and published *Miss Lonelyhearts* (1933). Inspired by actual letters West had seen in 1929, *Miss Lonelyhearts* chronicles the professional and personal crisis of a newspaper advice columnist. A savagely funny book that West described as "a novel in the form of a comic strip," it both protests the culture industry's capacity to turn pain into profit and, paradoxically, takes mass cultural forms as inspiration for literary aesthetics. *A Cool Million* (1934), a brutal parody of Horatio Alger stories, recounts the comic-tragic adventures of Lemuel Pitkin, a poor farm boy who sets off to seek his fortune when the bank forecloses on his family's mortgage. Pitkin's efforts lead to disaster, and he is eventually maimed and killed.

In Hollywood, West became politically active. He signed the anticapitalist American Writers Congress statement in 1935, participated in the Screenwriters Guild's drive for union recognition, and joined the communist-led Hollywood Anti-Nazi League. His novels, however, did not express much hope for political change. His final novel, *The Day of the Locust* (1939), is written from the perspective of Tod Hackett, a Yale-educated painter living in Los Angeles, where he encounters a motley group of exiled Hollywood extras and social dropouts. The novel ends apocalyptically at a riot outside a movie premier, as the restless crowd becomes a violent mob. The book depicts Hollywood, and mass culture in general, as what West called a "dream dump"—a cluttered field of discarded and disregarded hopes that signals American culture's desperate need for redemption.

Selected Bibliography: Barnard, Rita. *The Great Depression and the Culture of Abundance: Kenneth Fearing, Nathanael West, and Mass Culture in the 1930s.* Cambridge: Cambridge UP, 1995; Madden, David, ed. *Nathanael West: The Cheaters and the Cheated: A Collection of Critical Essays.* De Land, FL: Everett Edwards, 1973; Martin, Jay. *Nathanael West: The Art of His Life.* New York: Farrar, Straus and Giroux, 1970; Siegel, Ben, ed. *Critical Essays on Nathanael West.* New York: G. K. Hall, 1994; Veitch, Jonathan. *American Superrealism: Nathanael West and the Politics of Representation in the 1930s.* Madison: U of Wisconsin P, 1997.

Joseph Entin

WEST, REBECCA (1892–1983). Born Cicely Fairfield, Rebecca West changed her name to that of the heroine of **Henrik Ibsen**'s *Rosmersholm* when she began writing for the feminist journal the *Freewoman* in 1911, launching a seventy-year career as novelist, journalist, critic, political essayist, and feminist thinker. A formidable moral presence with a voice at once sweepingly judgmental, acerbic, and wickedly precise, she was one of the most respected public intellectuals of her time.

The sheer range and diversity of West's output have, paradoxically, detracted from her critical reputation, as individual commentators have tended to embrace only certain aspects or periods of her voluminous oeuvre. In particular, West's transition from socialist feminist to fervent anticommunist (and, as her biographer Carl Rollyson discovered, informant for the FBI) has made her difficult for political progressives to embrace wholeheartedly. Yet certain basic concerns remained constant throughout her career and across her oeuvre: rejection of orthodoxies, championing of the oppressed, exploration of the bases of affiliation, and what she called in a 1952 essay the "balancing of competitive freedom."

West's early commitment to the women's suffrage movement prompted her first forays into journalism, and provided the basis for both *The Judge* (1922) and the unfinished novel *The Sentinel* (recently discovered and published in 2002, though written when West was still a teenager). In her early articles, West inveighs against not only patriarchy, inequity, and the insidious notion of female self-sacrifice, but also the bourgeois phenomenon of the "parasite woman" complicit in the operations of empire, a phenomenon she explored in the antiwar novel *The Return of the Soldier*

(1918). The unflinching moral honesty that allowed her to spare no group or class from scrutiny and excoriation in her political journalism and fiction informed her literary criticism as well; she was repelled by what she saw as the self-aggrandizing prescriptions of **T. S. Eliot** and the "new humanists," whom she termed the "call to order" critics.

West is perhaps best known today for *Black Lamb and Grey Falcon* (1941), a groundbreakingly genre-bending memoir of her late-1930s travels through Yugoslavia that plumbed the region's history and culture to show "the past side by side with the present it created." West's exploration of the past "catastrophic aspects of Empire" reveals ominous resonances with the growing fascist threat and the coming war she sees as inevitable, allowing her, she says in her epilogue, "to follow the dark waters of that event back to its source." West's embrace, in *Black Lamb*, of an idealized nationalism as the symbolic counterforce to fascist aggression led to a continued fascination with modes of loyalty and affiliation, explored in *The Meaning of Treason* (1949) in her *New Yorker* essays on the Nuremberg trials, in her collection *A Train of Powder* (1955), and in her late novel *The Birds Fall Down* (1966).

Selected Bibliography: Norton, Ann. *Paradoxical Feminism: The Novels of Rebecca West.* Lanham, MD: International Scholars Publications, 2000; Rollyson, Carl. *Rebecca West: A Life.* New York: Scribner, 1996; Scott, Bonnie Kime. *Refiguring Modernism.* 2 vols. Bloomington: Indiana UP, 1995; Stetz, Margaret. "Rebecca West's Criticism: Alliance, Tradition, and Modernism." *Rereading Modernism: New Directions in Feminist Criticism.* Ed. Lisa Rado. New York: Garland, 1994. 41–66; West, Rebecca. *The Young Rebecca: Writings of Rebecca West, 1911–1917.* Ed. Jane Marcus. New York: Viking, 1982.

Debra Rae Cohen

WHITMAN, WALT (1819–1892). After growing up on Long Island and in Brooklyn, the descendant of working-class farmers and raised in a family with liberal Hicksite Quaker beliefs, Whitman worked variously as typesetter, journalist, teacher, editor, political hack, carpenter, small businessman, federal clerk, and minor bureaucrat. As a poet, especially in the many editions of his "Song of Myself," he celebrated America in all its diversity and energy, and he developed the prosody and poetic techniques that were to define American poetic modernism. Although later, in his very popular "O Captain! My Captain!" and in his great poem "When Lilacs Last in the Dooryard Bloomed," Whitman became the chief elegist for Abraham Lincoln, Whitman, in his days as an active political partisan, defined himself as a radical "free soil" Democrat of the Barnburner type, opposed to the "Old Hunker" conservatives. In that role, he wrote for and edited many New York Democratic papers in the 1840s and 1850s. In 1848, he was discharged as editor of the *Brooklyn Eagle* for his support of the Wilmot Proviso, which would have banned slavery in the territories. Later that year, Whitman was a delegate to the breakaway convention in Buffalo of the Free-Soil Party that nominated Van Buren, and he founded the briefly lived *Brooklyn Weekly Freeman*. However, Whitman was a "strict constructionist" in his views of the Constitution and, far from advocating abolition, supported the moderate position of Senator Stephen Douglas until the 1860 election. His long alienation from disciple William Douglas O'Connor stemmed from his disagreement with O'Connor's more radical ideas concerning Reconstruction; Whitman favored a gradualist approach to the rights of blacks. He also championed imperial ambitions of the United States and grew in his later "Good Gray Poet" years to admire American capitalists and the business-inspired technological innovations of the late nineteenth century.

Especially in his earlier poetry, Whitman presented a somewhat different emphasis, positively portraying African Americans, Native Americans, and working-class people in an important articulation of American democracy and multiculturalism. The Soviet critic Maurice Mendelson asserts that Whitman condemned not only slavery but "also other forms of the enslavement of man" (53), and notes that Gorky emphasized Whitman's "unconscious" preference for socialism (11). Newton Arvin similarly noted socialist themes, while Whitman has been admired by later radical American writers as different as **Michael Gold** and **Allen Ginsberg**. Later biographers and critics trace the political changes in Whitman from his early individualistic democratic themes to his retreat from liberalism in the 1870s and 1880s, when he expressed his admiration for Rutherford B. Hayes, Andrew Carnegie, and Grover Cleveland. By the mid-1880s, Whitman had become largely apolitical.

Selected Bibliography: Arvin, Newton. *Whitman.* New York: Macmillan, 1938; Beach, Christopher. *The Politics of Distinction: Whitman and the Discourses of Nineteenth-Century America.* Athens: U of Georgia P, 1996; Cmiel, Kenneth. "Whitman the Democrat." *A Historical Guide to Walt Whitman.* Ed. David S. Reynolds. New York: Oxford UP, 2000. 205–33; Loving, Jerome. *Walt Whitman: The Song of Himself.* Berkeley: U of California P, 1999; Maurice Mendelson. *Life and Work of Walt Whitman: A Soviet View.* Trans. Andrew Broomfield. Moscow: Progress Publishers, 1976; Reynolds, David S. *Walt Whitman's America: A Cultural Biography.* New York: Knopf, 1995.

Keith W. Schlegel

WIESEL, ELIE (1928–). Of the hundreds of authors whose stories and words have shaped our understanding of the **Holocaust**, none has been more influential than Elie Wiesel. In terms of name recognition and worldwide readership, of course, Anne Frank trumps them all, but because Wiesel survived the event that claimed Anne and has devoted his long career to writing, teaching, and service in conveying his message, his writings have become the touchstone for those who seek a fuller picture of the horror than Anne's slender *Diary* can provide.

Born in 1928 and raised in an orthodox community in what was then rural Hungary, Wiesel was swept into the camps when Hungary turned on its Jews in 1944. Although Wiesel and two of his sisters survived, their parents and a third sister perished. Bearing witness to their deaths, contending with a God who would demand such a sacrifice, and struggling against hatred and indifference constitute the hallmarks of Wiesel's message.

By far the best known of his more than forty books is *Night* (*La Nuit*). A radical condensation of the more spontaneous *Un di Velt hot geshvign* (And the World Remained Silent, 1956), *Night* is often categorized as memoir, although in terms of the attention paid to language—especially metaphor—and in the liberties taken with details recorded differently in the two volumes of memoirs published decades later, it is better understood as a novel (of the interesting class of creative nonfiction constituting much of the witness literature of the Holocaust, including Anne's "diary").

The passage in which the boy, Elie, describes his arrival in Auschwitz has become one of the most often quoted in Holocaust literature:

> Never shall I forget that night, the first night in camp, which has turned my life into one long night, seven times cursed and seven times sealed. Never shall I forget that smoke. Never shall I forget the little faces of the children, whose bodies I saw turned into wreaths of smoke beneath a silent blue sky. Never shall I forget those flames which consumed my faith forever.

Writing originally in Yiddish, then in French, which he mastered in the years spent in Paris after his liberation from Buchenwald, Wiesel also publishes and lectures in English, learned after immigrating to the United States in 1956. While Andrew Mellon Professor of Humanities at Boston University, Wiesel was named chair of the President's Commission on the Holocaust, which was instrumental in creating the U.S. Holocaust Memorial Museum in Washington, D.C. Awarded the Nobel Peace Prize in 1986 for his activism in the cause of tolerance and human rights, Wiesel remained active into the twenty-first century as a commentator on incidents of human suffering and a much sought-after, charismatic lecturer. His proprietary view of the Holocaust—expressed in the oft-quoted "Not all the victims of the Holocaust were Jews, but all the Jews were victims" (*And the Sea Is Never Full* 129)—and the paradoxical, cabalistic quality of much of his writing have limited the success of his later novels, but *Night* and the companion stories *Dawn* and *The Accident* from the early trilogy are obligatory reading for those confronting the Holocaust through literature.

Selected Bibliography: Bloom, Harold, ed. *Elie Wiesel's "Night."* Philadelphia: Chelsea House, 2001; Cargas, Harry James, ed. *Responses to Elie Wiesel.* New York: Persea, 1978; Rosenfeld, Alvin H., and Irving Greenberg, eds. *Confronting the Holocaust: The Impact of Elie Wiesel.* Bloomington: Indiana UP, 1978.

Mark E. Cory

WILLIAMS, RAYMOND (1921–1988). Among the most influential cultural theorists, critics, and literary scholars of the second half of the twentieth century, Williams critically examined dramatic forms, the novel, the popular press, television, and the cinema in their historical context. He is also the author of several novels, short stories, and plays, as well as a public intellectual and one of the founders of the British New Left. Yet Williams is perhaps best remembered as one of the creators of **cultural studies**: the interdisciplinary and critical study of culture that has profoundly reshaped the humanities.

Williams grew up on the border between England and Wales. Coming from a Welsh working-class background, he attended Cambridge University on a scholarship. He spent the majority of his academic career at Cambridge but always considered himself an outsider. Williams's perception of himself as traversing multiple borders had important ramifications for his intellectual work. In his first major book, *Culture and Society* (1958), he argues that the logical outcome of the largely conservative tradition of English romantic social criticism are the democratic and socialist values of the working-class community. In arguably his finest work of cultural history and criticism, *The Country and the City* (1973), he deconstructs the binary opposition suggested by the book's title, viewing "country" and "city" as interrelated components of a unified cultural and social whole.

Williams's cultural theory developed in a dialogue with the two intellectual forces that dominated Cambridge literary discussions in the 1930s. On the basis of his critical interrogation of Marxist economic determinism and of the literary scholar F. R. Leavis's practical criticism, he produced a new theoretical space: "cultural materialism." Williams rejects the conventional distinction between "high" and "popular" culture in favor of the idea that culture is "ordinary," that is, it gives meaning to everyday life. It is on this basis that Williams—in conjunction with cultural theorist **Stuart Hall** and historian E. P. Thompson—helped shape British cultural Marxism: an unorthodox theoretical tradition that acknowledged the semiautonomy of the cultural realm within the context of material social relations, while providing a theoretical space for human agency. Particularly important here is Williams's reworking of **Antonio Gramsci**'s idea of **hegemony** in *Marxism and Literature* (1977). He defines hegemony as a lived system of meanings and values—constitutive and constituting—which, as they are experienced as practices, appear as reciprocally confirming. Yet it is never static or total; it is continually defended and reformulated by the power bloc as well as being challenged by the "residual" and "emergent" practices of subservient groups.

Williams is not without his critics. For some, his work is so dependent on the authenticity of his own experience that it borders on being parochial. His preoccupation with the idea of community implies the homogeneous experience of a particular group bound to a particular place, a problematic idea in an era of globalization and hybridity. Yet if cultural studies has developed in directions that Williams never imagined, the remarkable growth of this new field is unthinkable without his pioneering work.

Selected Bibliography: Dworkin, Dennis. *Cultural Marxism in Postwar Britain: History, the New Left and the Origins of Cultural Studies.* Durham, NC: Duke UP, 1997; Dworkin, Dennis, and Leslie G. Roman, eds. *Views Beyond the Border Country: Raymond Williams and Cultural Politics.* London: Routledge, 1993; Eagleton, Terry, ed. *Raymond Williams: Critical Perspectives.* Boston: Northeastern UP, 1989; Higgins, John. *Raymond Williams: Literature, Marxism and Cultural Materialism.* London: Routledge, 1999; Inglis, Fred. *Raymond Williams.* London: Routledge, 1995; O'Connor, Alan. *Raymond Williams: Writing, Culture, Politics.* Oxford: Basil Blackwell, 1989.

Dennis Dworkin

WILLIAMS, WILLIAM CARLOS (1883–1963). One of the most influential American poets of the twentieth century, Williams was born, lived, worked, and died in Rutherford, New Jersey. A busy medical doctor serving the largely poor communities of the area, Williams was also a lifelong friend of **Ezra Pound**, whom he had met in college, and a central figure among the New York artistic and literary avant-garde.

Hostile to **T. S. Eliot**'s Eurocentric cultural conservatism, Williams was an instinctive American Democrat more interested in Jeffersonian perpetual revolution than Marxist class struggle, which he felt did not travel well. Throughout his long career, Williams argued for "contact" with the local and a celebration of the improvised, mongrel condition of the American people as the preconditions for a successful indigenous culture. A restless drive for new beginnings informed both his writing—alongside the poetry, Williams wrote novels, short stories, and plays, as well as numerous essays, prose pieces, and reviews—and his politics, which refused to be constrained by party line or ideological agenda. While from his early collection *Al Que Quiere!* (1917) through to his epic *Paterson* (1946–1961) Williams explored the social circumstances of America's working classes, he never considered himself a political writer. Even as he contributed to radical publications like ***New Masses*** during the 1930s and promoted the work of proletarian poets like H. H. Lewis, he remained suspicious of any instrumental function for art and insisted on the imagination as the true agent of liberty.

Offered the appointment of consultant in poetry for the Library of Congress in 1952, Williams found himself publicly attacked both for his alleged communist sympathies during the 1930s and for his friendship with the fascist Pound. Thus had Williams's liberalism got him caught in a **cold-war** pincer movement, and while the first of a series of strokes probably ruled out his taking up the Washington job anyway, the controversy exposed the extent to which his fears for the integrity of American democracy had come to pass. Williams's cultural pluralism demanded a more liberal polity, and his status grew during the 1960s and 1970s as a new generation of poets adopted his optimistic celebration of American creative revolution. His presence remains so extensive that Williams could plausibly be said to be the most important figure in the history of American avant-garde poetry.

Selected Bibliography: Beck, John. *Writing the Radical Center: William Carlos Williams, John Dewey, and American Cultural Politics.* Albany: State U of New York P, 2001; Frail, David. *The Early Politics and Poetics of William Carlos Williams.* Ann Arbor, MI: UMI P, 1987; Mariani, Paul. *William Carlos Williams: A New World Naked.* New York: McGraw-Hill, 1981.

John Beck

WOLF, CHRISTA (1929–). Politics, specifically her relationship with the German Democratic Republic, has always played an important role in the life and works of Christa Wolf. In *Divided Heaven (Der Geteilte Himmel,* 1963), her first major work, the heroine opts to remain in the East rather than follow her lover to West Germany. In the 1960s, Wolf was a candidate for the Central Committee of the Socialist Unity Party, yet her criticism of the 1965 clampdown in cultural policy led to her removal from that position in 1967. She also joined the protests against the expulsion from the GDR of the singer Wolf Biermann in 1976.

This difficult relationship with the GDR authorities is reflected in her fiction, whose main characters often have difficulty adapting to the requirements of society. This is true of *The Quest for Christa T. (Nachdenken über Christa T.,* 1968), which is set in the GDR, and of *Cassandra (Kassandra,* 1983), in which the portrayal of Troy can be seen in part as an allegory of the second German state. None of this was enough to save her from opprobrium at the time of German unification. The casus belli was the publication of her autobiographical story *What Remains (Was bleibt)* in early 1990, which chronicles her surveillance by the Stasi secret police. That this work, largely written in the late 1970s, wasn't published until after the fall of communism was seen as a sign of weakness and opportunism. Instead of being viewed as a critical sympathizer of the GDR, she was lambasted as the "state poet" of a flawed system, not least because she had signed the anti-unification petition "for our country" in late 1989. It also transpired a little later that she had herself provided information, albeit of a trivial nature, to the Stasi between 1959 and 1961. As was recognized at the time by, for example, **Günter Grass**, Wolf undoubtedly fell afoul of vicious attempts in newly united Germany to vilify the GDR and all its works.

Following unification, *Medea: A Modern Retelling* (*Medea: Stimmen,* 1996)—another historical fiction, this time set in ancient Greece—was generally badly received because it appeared to uphold GDR values against Western materialism. However, most recently, with the publication of *One Day in the Year* (*Ein Tag im Jahr,* 2003)— a diary spanning forty years but with only one annual entry—the extent of her doubts about her chosen country and her own actions have become more apparent.

While it would be impossible to deny the importance of politics in Wolf's work, other aspects should not be overlooked, including the portrayal of the situation of women and its undoubted aesthetic qualities. In particular, she has sought for a "subjective authenticity," which combines the personal and the historical, an ideal that set her apart from conventional GDR **socialist realism** and that she sees as distinct from the traditions of male discourse.

Selected Bibliography: Drees, Hajo. *A Comprehensive Interpretation of the Life and Work of Christa Wolf, Twentieth-Century German Writer.* Lewiston, Queenston: Lampeter, 2002; Resch, Margit. *Understanding Christa Wolf: Coming Home to a Foreign Land.* Columbia: U of South Carolina P, 1997; Wallace, Ian, ed. *Christa Wolf in Perspective.* Amsterdam: Rodopi, 1994.

Stuart Parkes

WOLLSTONECRAFT, MARY (1759–1797). The daughter of a handkerchief weaver born in Spitalfields, London, Mary Wollstonecraft went on to become a central figure in the post–**French Revolution** literary debate in Britain. Establishing a school in 1784 in Newington Green, Wollstonecraft made the acquaintance of Joseph Priestley and Richard Price (principal preacher there from 1758 to 1783). In his work *Observations on the Importance of the American Revolution* (1785), Price, a radical dissenter, argued in favor of equality in a way that was to prove profoundly influential for Wollstonecraft.

At Price's home, Wollstonecraft met leading dissenters, including the radical publisher Joseph Johnson, who encouraged her to write *Thoughts on the Education of Daughters* (1786). The first of a number of her works emphasizing the importance of rationality, this guide acknowledged traditional female social roles yet stressed the need for girls to learn to think. Wollstonecraft's dissatisfaction with the female condition was also evident in her semi-autobiographical novel *Mary: A Fiction* (1788).

As reviewer for the *Analytical Review* from 1787, Wollstonecraft met radical thinkers including Thomas Paine, William Blake, and **William Godwin**. In 1790, following Edmund Burke's monarchist *Reflections on the Revolution in France* (1789), Wollstonecraft became directly involved in politics. Defending Richard Price, whom Burke had attacked for supporting the revolution, in her *Vindication of the Rights of Men* Wollstonecraft argued that the pursuit of property and power caused rulers and subjects to become degraded; moral independence, in contrast, would promote human liberty. This emphasis on human perfectibility was expanded in *A Vindication of the Rights of Woman* (1792), which suggested that both sexes would benefit if women developed intellectual autonomy. Later, in *An Historical and Moral View of the Origin and Progress of the French Revolution* (1794), Wollstonecraft, who witnessed the violence of events under Robespierre, struggled with these ideas of human perfectibility. Yet her sensitivity to the political-economic causes of suffering is evident in *Letters Written during a Short Residence in Sweden, Norway, and Denmark* (1796) and her second novel, published posthumously, *Maria, or The Wrongs of Woman* (1798).

Vilified by contemporaries and nineteenth-century critics, Wollstonecraft's reputation revived in the twentieth century, and she is now regarded as a key feminist figure and acute political commentator.

Selected Bibliography: Butler, Marilyn. *Jane Austen and the War of Ideas.* 1975. Oxford: Clarendon P, 1987; Kelly, Gary. *Revolutionary Feminism: The Mind and Career of Mary Wollstonecraft.* 2nd ed. Basingstoke: Macmillan, 1996; Wollstonecraft, Mary, and William Godwin. *A Short Residence in Sweden; Memoirs of the Author of "The Rights of Woman."* 1796. 1798. Ed. Richard Holmes. London: Penguin, 1987.

Fiona Price

WOOLF, VIRGINIA (1882–1941). Daughter of Leslie Stephen and sister of Vanessa Bell, Woolf grew up in a prominent British intellectual family. She and Vanessa moved to the Bloomsbury section of London in 1904 after their father's death, and they subsequently became central figures in the influential Bloomsbury group of British cultural intellectuals. In 1912, Virginia married Leonard Woolf, forming an intellectual partnership that led to the founding of Hogarth Press and helped to keep the two of them at the center of some of the most dynamic activity in British intellectual and cultural life until her death by suicide following a life troubled by mental illness. Virginia Woolf published widely as a critic and cultural commentator in places such as the *Times Literary Supplement*. She is also now recognized as an important diarist, but her most important legacy is as the author of some of the most important and influential novels of British **modernism**.

Woolf's well-developed feminist consciousness (informed by her own lesbianism) has made her one of the central figures in the emergence of **feminist criticism** as a central force in literary studies of the past few decades. *A Room of One's Own* (1929), a treatise on the special difficulties faced by women writers in a literary tradition dominated by males, has become a leading manifesto for feminist critics, while the followup, *Three Guineas* (1938), has also been influential. Important published collections of critical essays include *The Common Reader* (1925), *The Second Common Reader* (1932), and *The Death of the Moth* (1942).

Woolf began her career as a novelist with *The Voyage Out* (1915), a relatively realistic account of the tragic experiences of a young Englishwoman on a journey to South America. *Night and Day* (1919), whose protagonist is loosely based on Vanessa Bell, takes a more political turn in its account of phenomena such as the women's suffrage movement. It is in *Jacob's Room* (1922), however, that Woolf's work begins to show the experimental modernist form and lyric intensity for which she is now best known. The novel's focus on the death of its protagonist in **World War I** (based partly on Woolf's painful memories of the premature death of her brother Toby in 1906) indicates a horror of war that would become crucial to Woolf's political consciousness.

World War I is also central to *Mrs. Dalloway* (1925) and *To the Lighthouse* (1927), perhaps the two novels for which Woolf is best known and the ones in which she reached the height of her powers as a modernist stylist and as a chronicler of the sometimes crippling psychic experience of upper-class British women. Her next work, *Orlando* (1928), received little serious attention when published but has become an important text for feminist critics in recent years. In a work that, among other things, parodies the masculine dominated genre of biography and can be considered a forerunner of **magical realism**, Woolf recounts the life of her eponymous protagonist over several centuries as first a man, then a woman. *The Waves* (1931) is perhaps Woolf's most intensely lyrical, poetic, and experimental novel as it details, through a series of interior monologues, the efforts of six different characters to establish viable subjective identities within the constraints placed on them by modern British society. *Flush* (1933) is a whimsical fictionalized biography of E. B. Browning's spaniel, while *The Years* (1937) a relatively conventional realistic novel, traces the history of the Pargiter family from 1880 to 1936. Woolf's last novel, left nearly finished at her death, shows a return to experimental form; *Between the Acts* (1941) is built around a village pageant that seeks to present a sweeping panorama of English history.

Woolf's essay "Modern Fiction" (written in 1919) serves as a sort of manifesto of literary modernism in general, as well as a statement of Woolf's own aesthetics. Criticizing realists such as **H. G. Wells**, Arnold Bennett, and John Galsworthy (then dominant in British fiction), Woolf argues that, with their concern for the material, such writers have failed adequately to represent the emotional and spiritual side of life. For Woolf, they "write of unimportant things; that they spend immense skill and immense industry making the trivial and transitory appear the true and the enduring" (210). Modernist writers like **James Joyce**, on the other hand, write of deeper levels of experience that actually make their works more realistic representations of the human condition. In a famous passage, she argues that "life is not a series of gig lamps symmetrically arranged; but a luminous halo, a semi-transparent envelope surrounding us from the beginning of consciousness to the end. Is it not the task of the novelist to convey this varying, this unknown and uncircumscribed spirit, whatever aberration or complexity it may display, with as little mixture of the alien and external as possible?" (212–13).

Nevertheless, Woolf, like other modernists, has sometimes been accused of being an elitist aestheticist, divorced from the problems of real people, especially those in the lower economic classes. It is certainly true that her central characters come from the British upper classes. One might also note that her brother-in-law Clive Bell's 1928 book *Civilization*, which probably did as much as any single work to create the image of modernism—and especially Bloomsbury—as snobbishly elitist, begins with a letter of dedication to Woolf. As Alex Zwerdling puts it, Bell's book "tries to justify the continued existence of an elite whose primary function is to preserve high art by cultivating taste among its members" (102).

On the other hand, Zwerdling, who particularly emphasizes Woolf's ongoing concern with World War I, has argued that Woolf's work is strongly engaged with the real world. He notes in detail the importance of Woolf's biography to her writing and of how Woolf went beyond her personal family history to explore the "domestic politics" of Victorian marriage and family life. Jane Marcus has attempted to combine feminist and socialist points of view on Woolf's work. She notes that, under the circumstances, "writing, for Virginia Woolf, was a revolutionary act," then goes on to call Woolf "a guerrilla fighter in a Victorian skirt" (*Art and Anger* 73). Meanwhile, Marxist-feminist Michèle Barrett emphasizes the materialist aspect of Woolf's politics, but only by ignoring the novels and focusing on Woolf as an essayist and a critic. For Barrett, "Woolf's critical essays offer us an unparalleled account of the development of women's writing, perceptive discussion of her predecessors and contemporaries, and a pertinent insistence on the material conditions which have structured women's consciousness" (36).

Selected Bibliography: Barrett, Michèle, ed. *Virginia Woolf: Women and Writing*. London: Women's P, 1979; Goldman, Jane. *The Feminist Aesthetics of Virginia Woolf*. Cambridge: Cambridge UP, 1998; Marcus, Jane. *Art and Anger: Reading Like a Woman*. Columbus: Ohio State UP, 1988; Marcus, Jane. *Virginia Woolf and the Languages of Patriarchy*. Bloomington: Indiana UP, 1987; Minow-Pinkney, Makiko. *Virginia Woolf and the Problem of the Subject*. New Brunswick, NJ: Rutgers UP, 1987; Roe, Sue, ed. *The Cambridge Companion to Virginia Woolf*. Cambridge: Cambridge UP, 2000; Zwerdling, Alex. *Virginia Woolf and the Real World*. Berkeley: U of California P, 1986.

M. Keith Booker

WORLD WAR I. Since the publication in 1975 of Paul Fussell's *The Great War and Modern Memory*, it has been difficult to dislodge analysis of the literature of the war from the compelling master narrative Fussell promulgated: that the pressures of the western front prompted a nostalgic return to traditional forms but that those forms finally proved insufficient to describe the war itself, meaning that the war, in effect, "caused" **modernism**. The narrative of disillusion that Fussell traced through the writings of soldier-poets, soldier-novelists, and soldier-memoirists is often conflated with the narrative of modernism itself, with fragmentary literary form becoming the analogue for the fragmentation of liberal ideals under the onslaught of wartime horror.

Within the limited range of texts examined by Fussell, such a political-literary trajectory is compelling. Between early poems—such as those by Rupert Brooke—that saw the war as an opportunity to purge, "as swimmers into cleanness leaping," the perceived sordidness and effeminacy of modern life, and those of later writers—such as **Siegfried Sassoon**, **Wilfred Owen**, Isaac Rosenberg, and David Jones—lay a no-man's land of shattered bodies, shattered certainties (such as those bitterly invoked in Owen's "Dulce et Decorum Est"), and, often, shattered syntax. Trench-centered prose like Henri Barbusse's *Under Fire* (*Le Feu*, 1916), Sassoon's George Sherston books (*Memoirs of a Fox-Hunting Man*, 1928; *Memoirs of an Infantry Officer*, 1930; and *Sherston's Progress*, 1936), Frederic Manning's *The Middle Parts of Fortune* (1929), and Erich Maria Remarque's *All Quiet on the Western Front* (*Im Westen nichts Neues*, 1929) categorized the reality of the trenches as "a frightful curtain which divides us from the world, which divides us from the past and from the future" (Barbusse 253).

Like Sassoon's poetry, such works underscored with bitterness the distance between behind-the-lines decision makers and the victims of their decisions, dwelling on military disasters such as the first day on the Somme, when the British suffered sixty thousand casualties due to outmoded and inefficient military planning; they mocked, too, civilian patriots (especially women, who were often configured, despite their lack of political voice, as "sending" men to battle), caricaturing them as unthinking in their support for vague and often contradictory war aims.

The emphasis here on the incommensurability and incommunicability of the soldier's experience helped codify what Samuel Hynes calls the "myth" of the war, the sense that it represented "a gap in history," creating a world in which "*now* does not follow from *then*" (xiii, 425). In the postwar years, and down through the decades, British literature in particular nostalgically transformed the prewar past into a land of lost content: "never such innocence again," Philip Larkin put it in his 1960 poem "MCMXIV," locating in his title the fault line of change. *Good-bye to All That* (1929), Robert Graves's memoir, bade farewell not only to the England from which he was self-exiled but to an entire "English" way of life. Ford Madox Ford's magisterial *Parade's End* sequence (1924–1928), by contrast, locates the lost golden age not in the immediate prewar years but in an idealized eighteenth century. In it, in other words, the war exacerbates rather than sets in motion the disintegration of society, though it too renders the modern world as separated from its past by an unbridgeable abyss.

The related notion of the "lost generation"—configured differently in British culture, where it referred to the heroicized dead who left the nation "leaderless," than in American culture, where it evoked such "rootless" survivors as **Ernest Hemingway** and F. Scott Fitzgerald, who chose artistic exile in Paris—was often subsumed into this conservative response to modernity. But the trope of disintegration could also be invoked with progressive intent; for example, **John Dos Passos**, in *Three Soldiers* (1921) and the *U.S.A.* trilogy (1930–1936), figured the war as the apotheosis of a vulgar and destructive materialism.

To concentrate exclusively on the narrative of disillusion, however—to buy into the myth—is to oversimplify greatly the literary politics of the war, ignoring, for example, the extent to which literary heavyweights (not only imperial apologists like **Rudyard Kipling** but also Arnold Bennett, Edith Wharton, and many others) were drawn into the operation of the allied propaganda machine. The myth occludes, too, the significance, complexity, and heterogeneity of home-front writing—an ironic omission in relation to the first "total" war. While home-front works such as Vera Brittain's *Testament of Youth* (1933) and **H. G. Wells**'s *Mr. Britling Sees It Through* (1916) enact the familiar passage to disillusion (Wells himself started out the war avidly producing propaganda), they necessarily complicate the notion of ignorant and jingoistic civilians ranged against the citizen-soldier. Female writers in particular examined and troped on the idea of the incommunicability of battlefield experience to examine women's own role in the conflict and the vexed place of the female as (non)citizen. Rose Macaulay's *Non-Combatants and Others* (1916), for example, enacts the drama of psychological "conscription" as experienced by a young female artist, while **Rebecca West**'s *The Return of the Soldier* (1918) uses shell shock as a metaphor against which she plays various models of female complicity and denial.

Home-front narratives, too, often both exposed and suffered from the increasing bureaucratization that the nature of total war entailed, with several of them—such as
Macaulay's satirical *What Not* (1919) and Rose Allatini's *Despised and Rejected*
(1918)—either suppressed or delayed under the terms of Britain's Defense of the
Realm acts.

Recent scholarship on World War I has used such home-front works—and the
protomodernist battlefield writings of nurses and female observers such as Mary Borden and Ellen La Motte—to flesh out and expand the "myth" of the war, not "adding"
gender by simply laying a unitary women's narrative alongside men's narratives but
understanding that gender as a category complicates and multiplies our understanding of the cultural and political history of the period. Fussell's own work has been a
primary target in this reconception. Indeed, while the durability of the myth of World
War I as the origination point of the modern is reinforced by its centrality as a site
for contemporary reinvention by such writers as Sebastian Faulks (*Birdsong*, 1994),
many of these contemporary works, notably Pat Barker's *Regeneration* trilogy (1991–
1995), focus on the war as a locus for the renegotiation of ideas about gender and
sexuality.

Selected Bibliography: Booth, Allyson. *Postcards from the Trenches: Negotiating the Space between Modernism and the First World War.* New York: Oxford UP, 1996; Buitenhuis, Peter. *The Great War of Words:
Literature as Propaganda, 1914–18 and After.* 1987. London: Batsford, 1989; Ecksteins, Modris. *Rites
of Spring: The Great War and the Birth of the Modern Age.* Boston: Houghton Mifflin, 1989; Fussell,
Paul. *The Great War and Modern Memory.* New York: Oxford UP, 1975; Hynes, Samuel. *A War Imag-
ined: The First World War and English Culture.* New York: Collier, 1990; Ouditt, Sharon. *Fighting Forces,
Writing Women: Identity and Ideology in the First World War.* New York: Routledge, 1994; Sherry, Vin-
cent. *The Great War and the Language of Modernism.* New York: Oxford UP, 2003; Tate, Trudi.
Modernism, History and the First World War. Manchester: Manchester UP, 1998; Tylee, Claire. *The Great
War and Women's Consciousness: Images of Militarism and Womanhood in Women's Writings, 1914–64.*
Iowa City: Iowa UP, 1990.

Debra Rae Cohen

WORLD WAR II. Although World War II produced the greatest man-made devas-
tations of modern history, its literary representations do not cohere into an epic story
of mythic battles and tragic heroes. If this war challenged the meanings of "human"
and "humanism," it was not, as modernist heirs of **World War I** argued, because ab-
stractions such as honor and duty were demolished by incoherent war aims and hor-
rifically wasteful battles. Despite the mess of combat, writers who emerged from the
wastelands of World War II were moved by the all too coherent and material evidence of fascist malevolence. Unlike World War I, World War II did not make its
political statement through radical changes in literary form. Where the modernists
felt it necessary to demythicize warfare, World War II writers found no myths in ancient or modern history that provided any language or form to represent a war that
produced the **Holocaust**. Instead, for British poet Alun Lewis and American Muriel
Rukeyser, World War II inspired an urgency to provide witness to both battleground
and home-front devastation. As refugees reported the new front of death camps and
mass extermination, Scottish poet Edwin Muir depicted their "rejection bred by re-

jection" ("The Refugees"). The incomparable scope of the war produced literary effects designed to convey the psychological disorientation of the besieged, but instead of finding analogues in fragmented literary forms, writers' experiments humanized those who were demonized by fascism and dramatized a radical shift in political attitudes. Where the trenches of World War I produced an international peace movement, the Axis slaughterhouses drove writers like **Rebecca West** and Storm Jameson to reject pacifism, as it bore no value for Hitler's victims.

If World War II was an urgent enterprise to defend the remaining free nations and people, it also produced frustration for British and American writers. The reportage of Martha Gellhorn's *Face of War* (1959) and **George Orwell**'s *My Country Right or Left* and *As I Please: 1940–45* (1968) recorded their sense that neither disillusionment nor "doing their bit" offered sufficient justice to fascism's victims. As witnesses, many World War II writers found that their own politics were relevant only if they could speak on behalf of those who would never have the chance, and so the ambiguities that enrich fiction meshed with polemical forms to register the anguish of history's most urgent war effort. Phyllis Bottome, who lived in Austria and Germany between the wars, rallied for the defeat of Hitler in novels such as *The Mortal Storm* (1937) and chronicled Nazi conquest in such novels as *Within the Cup* (1943). Similarly, Kay Boyle's novel *Primer for Combat* (1942) and Storm Jameson's *Europe to Let* (1940), *And Then We Shall Hear Singing* (1942), and *Cloudless May* (1944) depict the fall of Europe and its dire consequences. Edna St. Vincent Millay dramatizes these concerns in her compelling play about the German decimation of a Czech village, *Lidice* (1942). Like her 1938 antiwar polemic, *Three Guineas*, **Virginia Woolf**'s posthumous 1941 novel, *Between the Acts*, expresses anger at patriarchal myths that uphold all wars, but as war planes invade the novel's ending, the defensive battle on the horizon deconstructs the possibility of a universalized condemnation of warfare. By contrast, Vera Brittain's novel *Born 1925* (1948) resists the justness of this war, even as the dimensions of the Holocaust became common knowledge.

Once the Battle of Britain began, conventional depictions of reality were challenged daily. Elizabeth Bowen's stories in *The Demon Lover* (1945) and her masterpiece novel *The Heat of the Day* (1949) deploy gothic forms, while Betty Miller's novel *On the Side of the Angels* (1945) revises domestic realism to capture the disorienting dispossession of this war on civilians. American poet H. D. (Hilda Doolittle), who spent the war years in Britain, wrote poetic eulogies for the men and women working to defend civilian London. The "new bare alert senses with their own savage warnings" (Preface, *The Demon Lover*) could also be depicted as social panorama in novels such as Marguerite Steen's *Shelter* (1942), which reflected the new kinds of community building across social classes that we find in Fitzrovia—London's wartime literary café society, where poets Dylan Thomas, **Cecil Day Lewis**, and Louis MacNeice shared cheap beer and creative support. Persistent conflict between immediate concerns with personal safety and politics are recounted in wartime memoirs like Margery Allingham's *The Oaken Heart* (1941) and Storm Jameson's collection, *London Calling* (1942). While paper shortages and bombings curtailed publication in Britain, the imperative to bear witness and prevail culturally also led to periodicals such as John Lehmann's *Penguin New Writing* and Cyril Connolly's *Horizon*, which published poetry, short stories, and cultural reviews throughout the war by such writers as V. S. Pritchett, Stephen Spender, Julia Strachey, William Sansom, and Rosamond Lehmann. *Convoy*, edited by Robin Maugham, used writing to fill the "gulf...between civilian life and the fighting Services," while *Poetry in Wartime* (1942), edited by M. J. Tambimuttu, expressed "the strain of sadness" that extended from reflections on the global nature of the war, from Norway to Carpatho-Russia. Important critiques of the U.S. home front are narrated by Monica Sone in *Nisei Daughter* (1953) and Yoshiko Uchida in *Desert Exile: The Uprooting of a Japanese-American Family* (1982), about the internment of Japanese Americans.

Battle experience was generally represented as brutal and urgent and rarely as a tragic waste. Americans **Norman Mailer**, in *The Naked and the Dead* (1948), and James Jones, in *The Thin Red Line* (1962), created powerful fictional breakthroughs by representing the battles of the Pacific and Europe through the brutal and terse language of combatants, which also conveyed the social cross-currents of their enlisted and conscripted positions. Combat was also sometimes depicted with an occasional touch of the absurd, as we might expect from Evelyn Waugh, even in his magisterial *Sword of Honor* trilogy (1952–1962). This absurdist vein would become especially prominent in later representations of the war and its aftermath, especially in the work of American writers such as Joseph Heller in *Catch-22* (1961), Kurt Vonnegut in *Slaughterhouse-Five* (1969), and Thomas Pynchon in *Gravity's Rainbow* (1973).

Suggested Bibliography: Aldritt, Keith. *Modernism in the Second World War*. New York: Peter Lang, 1989; Blum, John Morton. *V Was for Victory: Politics and American Culture during World War II*. New York: Harcourt Brace Jovanovich, 1976; Briggs, Susan. *The Home Front: War Years in Britain, 1939–45*. London: Weidenfeld and Nicolson, 1975; Calder, Angus. *The People's War*. London: Cape, 1969; Featherstone, Simon. *War Poetry*. London: Routledge, 1995; Harrisson, Tom. *Living Through the Blitz*. London: Penguin, 1990; Hewison, Robert. *Under Siege: Literary Life in London, 1939–45*. New York: Oxford UP, 1977; Honey, Maureen. *Creating Rosie the Riveter: Class, Gender and Propaganda during World War II*. Amherst: U of Massachusetts P, 1984; Irons, Peter. *Justice at War: The Story of the Japanese American Internment Cases*. New York: Oxford UP, 1983; Lassner, Phyllis. *British Women Writers of World War II: Battlegrounds of Their Own*. New York: St. Martin's, 1998; Lewis, Jane. *Women in England, 1870–1950*. Bloomington: Indiana UP, 1984; Plain, Gill. *Women's Fiction of the Second World War*. Edinburgh: Edinburgh UP, 1996; Schneider, Karen. *Loving Arms: Women's Writing of World War II*. Lexington: UP of Kentucky, 1996; Schweik, Susan. *A Gulf So Deeply Cut: American Women Poets and the Second World War*. Madison: U of Wisconsin P, 1991; Smith, Harold. *War and Social Change: British Society in the Second World War*. Manchester: Manchester UP, 1986; Sternhell, Zeev, Mario Sznajder, and Maia Asheri. *The Birth of Fascist Ideology*. Princeton: Princeton UP, 1994; Summerfield, Penny. *Women Workers in the Second World War*. London: Routledge, 1984; Wasserstein, Bernard. *Britain and the Jews of Europe, 1930–1945*. Oxford: Clarendon P, 1996.

Phyllis Lassner

THE WRETCHED OF THE EARTH (1961), a theoretical work that studies the plights of many African nations upon decolonization, and one of the founding texts of **postcolonial theory and criticism**. The author, **Frantz Fanon**, deconstructs many Western stereotypes about the nations of the third world. It is customary for Western media and cultural establishments to blame the victims of colonialism for the woes of the postcolonial world. Fanon's trenchant analyses of decolonized societies prove that their problems arise from deeply rooted causes, many of which are inherent in colonization itself.

Decolonization often brings to mind the image of a violent world, and the violence, Fanon contends, happens for a variety of reasons. Decolonization is violent because the phenomenon replaces "a certain 'species' of men by another 'species' of men." The violence, in fact, balances the violence with which colonization began in the first place. Much of this violence Fanon attributes to anger, the anger the subdued native harbors against the settler who forced him to "stay in his place." The settler builds a world of his own at the expense of the native; not surprisingly, it is a world from which the native is excluded. Consequently, resentment builds up. Fanon characterizes this resentment as one of "Manichean" opposition in which the settler views the native "as a sort of quintessence of evil." The native's desire to usurp the settler's privilege through violent means, thus, is understandable. Fanon adds that movements leading to decolonization often resemble other movements, such as that of the working class.

A major thrust in *The Wretched* is to explain the roles of the national elite and the bourgeoisie, which are detrimental to the national interest. Native intellectuals often conspire with their colonial counterparts to avoid a violent confrontation. During colonial rule, the native is given constant reminders of the supremacy of Western values, mostly disseminated through institutions of higher learning. In no time do colonized intellectuals learn to accept that "essential qualities remain eternal in spite of all the blunders men may make," but Fanon astutely observes that these are "the essential qualities of the West" and that colonized intellectuals are quite keen "to defend the Greco-Latin pedestal." Similarly, the national bourgeoisie share the class interests of the colonialist bourgeoisie, but this group is merely a caricature of the one it imitates. "The national middle class which takes over power at the end of the colonial regime," according to Fanon, "is an underdeveloped middle class" with "no economic power." Nation building is not its forte because it is composed of people of "intermediary type," uninterested in production or invention.

It is clear that Fanon sees no possibility that the nation's elite or the bourgeoisie would spearhead a movement to serve true national interests. He sees potential in other segments of the population instead, including peasants and the lumpen proletariat, both of which Marx regarded as useless in any revolutionary project. These two groups are natural allies, as the lumpen proletariat is formed by landless peasants living in "tin-shack settlements" in the urban areas. They are "the pimps, the hooligans, the unemployed," people who are "the hopeless dregs of humanity, all who turn in circles between suicide and madness."

Many would disagree that a revolution through the lumpen proletariat is a viable option of change in the third world. However, Fanon's critique of the decolonized nation, especially his study of violence and the nature of the bourgeoisie, has proven to be exceedingly valuable in postcolonial studies, and many major African novelists draw on *The Wretched* in their delineation of contemporary African societies.

Selected Bibliography: Allesandrini, Anthony, ed. *Frantz Fanon: Critical Perspectives.* New York: Routledge, 1999; Gibson, Nigel. *Fanon: The Postcolonial Imagination.* Malden, MA: Blackwell, 2003; Gibson, Nigel, ed. *Rethinking Fanon: The Continuing Dialogue.* Amherst, NY: Humanity Books, 1999;

Gordon, Lewis. *Frantz Fanon and the Crisis of European Man*. Cambridge, MA: Blackwell, 1995; Gordon, Lewis, ed. *Fanon: A Critical Reader*. Cambridge, MA: Blackwell, 1996; Sekyi-Otu, Ato. *Fanon's Dialectic of Experience*. Cambridge, MA: Harvard UP, 1996.

Farhad B. Idris

WRIGHT, RICHARD (1908–1960). Wright was born into Jim Crow poverty in 1908 near Natchez, Mississippi. His father, a porter and manual laborer, left the Wright family when Wright was five; his mother, a cook, sometimes took Wright and his brother with her to work in white families' homes. Wright entered school late for his age but excelled, becoming class valedictorian in high school. His desire to write was kindled by early publication of a short story, support from his mother, and a precocious self-education that included readings of **Theodore Dreiser**, **Fyodor Dostoevsky**, and H. L. Mencken.

In 1927, Wright moved to Chicago with his mother and brother. They settled on the South Side, where Wright worked in numerous low-paying jobs and the post office. In 1932, Wright joined the **John Reed Club**, a writers' group formed by the Chicago branch of the **Communist Party**. Wright's best-known writing was produced while he was a Communist. His first book, *Uncle Tom's Children* (1938), was a collection of stories set in the Jim Crow south in which communism offers an alternative to systemic racist brutality. The climactic tale in the collection, "Bright and Morning Star," depicts a woman, Aunt Sue, who avenges the killing of communists trying to organize against racists in a small southern town. Wright's essay "The Ethics of Living Jim Crow—an Autobiographical Sketch," included in the second edition of the book, described southern racism as a monstrously deforming experience for blacks, necessitating resistance that could often be fatal.

With *Native Son* (1940), Wright transplanted this theme to Chicago's South Side. In the book, Bigger Thomas is sentenced to death for raping and murdering a white woman named Mary Dalton, the daughter of a real estate baron from whom Thomas's family rents a squalid tenement apartment. The first crime Thomas does not commit, symbolic of America's enduring miscegenation and lynch hysteria; the second he does (though perhaps inadvertently), Wright suggests, because of fear produced by racism, capitalism, and a savage environment of violence and racial terror. The book was an instant landmark of American literature; it quickly sold 250,000 copies, was a Book of the Month Club selection, and was praised in *Time* magazine. The communist press praised the book—Samuel Sillen in *New Masses* hailed its "revolutionary vision of life" (49). Yet Wright had written the book during a period of ambivalence about communist commitment, perhaps symbolized in *Native Son* by the failed defense of Bigger by communist lawyer Boris Max. Wright had left Chicago and the Communist Party before he wrote *Native Son*, he later claimed in *Black Boy* (1945), to preserve his artistic freedom, though when he arrived in New York to write the novel, he continued as a correspondent for the *Daily Worker*. In 1944, he publicly broke with the party in "I Tried to Be a Communist," an essay published in the *Atlantic Monthly*. The essay became the ending to the second portion of *Black Boy*.

McCarthyism, enduring racism, and a desire to become part of an emerging international cadre of African and Caribbean writers moved Wright to leave the United States for Paris in 1947. The last piece of fiction he authored on U.S. soil, "The Man Who Lived Underground," predicted both Wright's movement into exile and the preoccupations of his work written abroad, namely the rootlessness and deterritorialization of diasporic black intellectuals like himself. *The Outsider* (1953), his first novel written in exile, hitched these themes to existential philosophy (Wright had read and met **Sartre** and Camus, who in turn admired his work). In Paris, Wright met **Léopold Senghor**, **George Padmore**, and **Kwame Nkrumah**, the rising leaders of a new international Pan-Africanist anticolonial movement. In 1953, he began a correspondence with **Frantz Fanon** and traveled to Africa's Gold Coast to write a book on Africa. *Black Power* (1954) described the efforts of Nkrumah to develop independent Ghana. In 1955, Wright traveled to Indonesia to report on the Bandung Conference of Afro-Asian decolonizing states. The book, *The Color Curtain*, was a complex **cold-war** text—sympathetic to decolonization, anticommunist in orientation, and funded, in part, by the Congress for Cultural Freedom, later discovered to be an arm of the CIA. Wright's third and last excursionary book, *Pagan Spain* (1957), was a muddled account of his travels in that country. Cumulatively, Wright's three nonfiction books in exile thematize what Ngwarsungu Chiwengo has called Wright's status as a "border citizen." The books also identify Wright's role in cold-war literary **anticommunism** and the inception of postcolonial and transnational studies. These themes are most explicit in *White Man, Listen!* (1957), a collection of essays Wright delivered as lectures across Europe.

The last Wright book published during his lifetime, *The Long Dream* (1958), was a commercial and critical failure. *Eight Men* (1961), a story collection, appeared the year after his death in Paris from a heart attack. Wright's legacy is profound, his open commitment to communist politics and aesthetics, brilliantly articulated in the South Side Writers' Group's 1937 *New Challenge* essay "Blueprint for Negro Writing," helped to influence a generation of black writers to social protest writing. Wright's negative recounting of his break with communism helped inspire the Brotherhood section of **Ralph Ellison**'s *Invisible Man*. During the 1950s and 1960s, **James Baldwin**, Eldridge Cleaver, and a score of black nationalist critics recuperated and debated Wright's example in defining both the civil rights and the black power and **black arts movements**. Wright's frequent representation of male violence against women led a generation of feminist critics to reconsider his reputation and questions of gender in African American literature. Wright's exile books, out of print for some time, have recently earned reconsideration as part of diasporic scholarship on African American literature. *Native Son*, meanwhile, remains for many critics and readers both the best novel of urban racial terror in American literature and a classic proletarian text. The book still best bespeaks the importance of Wright, Chicago, and African American literature to African American radical culture and politics of the mid-twentieth century.

Selected Bibliography: Chiwengo, Ngwarsungu. "Gazing Through the Screen: Richard Wright's Africa." *Richard Wright's Travel Writings: New Reflections*. Ed. Virginia Whatley Smith. Jackson: UP of Mississippi, 2001; Fabre, Michel. *The Unfinished Quest of Richard Wright*. Urbana: U of Illinois P, 1993;

Kinnamon, Keneth. *The Emergence of Richard Wright: A Study in Literature and Society*. Urbana: U of Illinois P, 1972; Mootry, Maria K. "Bitches, Whores, and Woman Haters: Archetypes and Typologies in the Art of Richard Wright." *Richard Wright: A Collection of Critical Essays*. Ed. Richard Macksey and Frank E. Moorer. Englewood Cliffs: Prentice Hall, 1984. 117–28; Rampersad, Arnold. ed. *Richard Wright: A Collection of Critical Essays*. Englewood Cliffs: Prentice Hall, 1995; Sillens, Samuel. Review of *Native Son. Richard Wright's "Native Son": A Critical Handbook*. Ed. Richard Abcarian. Belmont: Wadsworth, 1970. 49–52; Webb, Constance. *Richard Wright: A Biography*. New York: G. P. Putnam's Sons, 1968; Wright, Richard. *The Color Curtain*. Jackson: UP of Mississippi, 1994.

Bill V. Mullen

Y

YEATS, WILLIAM BUTLER (1865–1939). The eldest child of John Butler Yeats, a lawyer-turned-artist, and Susan Pollexfen Yeats, daughter of a well-to-do merchant family in Sligo, Ireland, Yeats became one of the most important English-language poets of the twentieth century, winning the Nobel Prize for Literature in 1923. In his youth, Yeats belonged to the Irish Republican Brotherhood and admired the exiled nationalist John O'Leary. While opposing the use of violence, he admired courage, especially that of actress and activist Maud Gonne (1866–1950), who inspired his lifelong passion. Even though he adopted very unpopular stands on some issues, he influenced the movement toward the independence of Ireland from Great Britain through his poetry and drama, particularly with the early nationalist play *Cathleen Ni Houlihan* (1902). Believing that culture was central to nationalism, Yeats argued that Irish mythology and folklore could help forge the nation's political identity. Hoping to raise the intellectual level of the people, he founded, with Lady Augusta Gregory and Edward Martyn, the Irish Literary Theatre and Irish National Theatre, producing some plays that met with intense hostility, such as his own *The Countess Cathleen* (1892) and J. M. Synge's *The Playboy of the Western World* (1907). Claiming that passive suffering was not a subject for poetry, he scandalously omitted **Wilfred Owen**, **Siegfried Sassoon**, and others from *The Oxford Book of Modern Verse* (1936), which he edited. Always stating his disdain for politics, he nevertheless accepted the position of senator for education and the arts (1922) in William Cosgrave's Irish Free State. Later in his life he articulated more fully his unpopular conviction that countries are best served by an aristocracy of the intellect that alone could raise the cultural level of the people. His advocation of aristocratic rule, identification with the Protestant ascendancy, friendship with **Ezra Pound**, and interest in Irish fascism and eugenics (examined in the controversial play *Purgatory* and essay *On the Boiler*) in the 1930s led to intense criticism of his social philosophy.

Critics and scholars who comment on Yeats's politics focus on his elitist brand of cultural nationalism. Convinced that negotiation was a better path to nationalism than violence, he praises the heroism of the rebels in "Easter, 1916" even as he questions the necessity of their sacrifice. His aristocratic notions stemmed from his being the product of two influential Anglo-Irish (Protestant) families and close friend of

Lady Gregory, whose estate in County Galway formed the landscape for many of his most powerful works, including "Upon a House Shaken by the Land Agitation" and "Coole and Ballylee, 1931." The former of these laments the forced breakup of some of the larger estates due to land reform, arguing that the landowners must be allowed to keep their wealth because only they possess the ability to govern well; the latter mourns the passing of the age that valued intellect, culture, and art. While believing in privilege, however, Yeats also held that it carried responsibilities. In the poem "To a Wealthy Man who promised a second Subscription to the Dublin Municipal Gallery if it were proved the People wanted Pictures," he puts forward his opinion that rich and cultured people in Ireland should give freely to the people in order to raise the cultural level, as he believed the nobles of Renaissance Italy had done. Furthermore, he defended Jim Larkins's workers against their employers during the Dublin Lockout of 1913. The poem "Fragments" and passages from his famous essay "A General Introduction for My Work" illustrate Yeats's dislike of materialism, utilitarianism, and capitalism; wealth must be inherited and shared, not earned through competition. Poems like "The Second Coming," "Meru," and "Lapis Lazuli" articulate Yeats's theory of recurring historical cycles (influenced by the philosophy of Friedrich Nietzsche) and his belief that the growing violence of the century was evidence that the millennium would bring forth a new era of chaos and upheaval. The late poem "The Black Tower" advises Irish neutrality in **World War II**.

George Orwell believed Yeats's aristocratic notions naive ("W. B. Yeats"); Conor Cruise O'Brien states that had the Nazis occupied Ireland, they would have found a willing collaborator in Yeats. Elizabeth Butler Cullingford counters O'Brien's charges, concluding that Yeats was a cultural nationalist in the tradition of John O'Leary. Roy Foster's definitive biography claims that "WBY's affinity with Fascism (not National Socialism) was a matter of rhetorical style; and the achievement of style, as he himself had decreed long before, was closely connected to shock tactics" (483). His last published poem, "Politics," makes clear that he was to the end more interested in lyric beauty than in any political movement. The primary political issue involving Yeats's work is his nationalism, with some critics and poets (notably Seamus Deane) arguing that his Anglo-Irishness and his unequivocal allegiance to the English language ("A General Introduction for My Work") make him a colonialist, and others (particularly **Edward Said**) claiming that he is one of the foremost poets of decolonization ("Yeats and Decolonization"). Postcolonial writers such as Seamus Heaney, Derek Walcott, Eavan Boland, **Chinua Achebe**, and **Salman Rushdie** have testified to his profound influence on **postcolonial literature**.

Selected Bibliography: Allison, Jonathan, ed. *Yeats's Political Identities.* Ann Arbor: U of Michigan P, 1995; Cullingford, Elizabeth Butler. *Yeats, Ireland and Fascism.* London: Macmillan, 1981; Deane, Seamus. "Yeats and the Idea of Revolution." *Yeats's Political Identities.* Ed. Jonathan Allison. Ann Arbor: U of Michigan P, 1995. 133–44; Foster, R. F. *W. B. Yeats: A Life. Vol. 2: The Arch-Poet.* London: Oxford UP, 2003; Heaney, Seamus. "Yeats as an Example?" *Preoccupations: Selected Prose, 1968–1978.* London: Faber and Faber, 1980. 98–114; Howes, Marjorie. *Yeats's Nations: Gender, Class, and Irishness.* Cambridge UP, 1996; O'Brien, Conor Cruise. "Passion and Cunning: An Essay on the Politics of W. B. Yeats." *Passion and Cunning and Other Essays.* London: Weidenfeld and Nicolson, 1988. 8–61; Orr, Leonard. *W. B. Yeats and Postmodernism.* Syracuse, NY: Syracuse UP, 1991; Said, Edward. "Yeats and Decolonization." *Culture and Imperialism.* New York: Knopf, 1993. 220–38; Yeats, William Butler.

Essays and Introductions. New York: Collier Books, 1961; Yeats, William Butler. *Explorations.* New York: Collier Books, 1962.

Deborah Fleming

YEZIERSKA, ANZIA (1885?–1970). Born Hattie Meyer in the *shtetl* Plinsk, near Warsaw, Yezierska would become known in the 1920s as the "Sweatshop Cinderella," with her popular stories about New York's colorful Lower East Side ghetto. A once neglected and belittled author, Yezierska is now seen by critics, feminists, and sociologists as an exciting and innovative writer, critically commenting on naive myths of American immigration and their readily implied social and economic mobility, linguistic assimilation, and erasure of ethnicity in a standardized WASP culture. For feminists, Yezierska is a key figure in documenting women's experience of ethnic groups and the important role of women in America's mass-consumer society.

Yezierska first received national attention when her story "The Fat of the Land," won the prestigious Edward O'Brien Best Short Story award in 1919, which led to the publication of her first collection of short stories, *Hungry Hearts* (1920). That work drew the attention of the Hollywood studio Goldwyn, which paid Yezierska generously for the film rights and also hired her as a scriptwriter. Goldwyn's tremendous publicity campaign promoted Yezierska's story as an American fairy tale, describing how a poor immigrant who had at various times been a scrubwoman, servant, and factory worker had been instantly transformed into a great writer and Hollywood success.

She quickly gained a reputation as a Jewish local-color writer, who used the distinctive immigrant idiom to protest the poor social conditions of the ghetto and to express the immigrant's desire to live the American Dream. Yezierska's second work, the novel *Salome of the Tenements* (1923), was also made into a film, but she left Hollywood disgruntled, turning down a lucrative contract with William Fox. She returned to New York to be near her muse, the Lower East Side ghetto, and continued writing. Yezierska subsequently published another collection of short stories, *Children of Loneliness* (1923), and *Bread Givers* (1925), which, decades later, became her most famous novel. The novels *Arrogant Beggar* (1927) and *All I Could Never Be* (1932) would delve even deeper into philanthropic concerns as well as her intimate affair with the philosopher John Dewey. With the onset of the Depression, her stories and novels depicting immigrant life were no longer in demand, and Yezierska and her work were soon forgotten. In 1950, she published *Red Ribbon on a White Horse,* an autobiography that many consider fiction, recounting the story of her Cinderella success and subsequent failure, and was once again briefly rescued from obscurity. She died in 1970 in California, a reviewer for the *New York Times Book Review* and a forgotten author. Since the 1980s, critics have been reassessing her work and have revised the prevailing view that her works uphold an assimilationist stance. Yezierska is now seen as a complex writer, commenting on the hybrid nature of immigrant culture.

Selected Bibliography: Dearborn, Mary V. *Love in the Promised Land: The Story of Anzia Yezierska and John Dewey.* New York: Free P, 1988; Ferraro, Thomas. *Ethnic Passages: Literary Immigrants in Twentieth Century America.* Chicago: U of Chicago P, 1993; Henrikson, Louise Levitas. *Anzia Yezierska: A*

Writer's Life. Brunswick, NJ: Rutgers UP, 1988; Konzett, Delia C. *Ethnic Modernisms: Anzia Yezierska, Zora Neale Hurston, Jean Rhys, and the Aesthetics of Dislocation.* New York: Palgrave Macmillan, 2002; Zaborowska, Magdalena. *How We Found America: Reading Gender through East European Immigrant Narratives.* Chapel Hill: U of North Carolina P, 1995.

Delia C. Konzett

YUGOSLAV LITERATURE. Ever since the concept of the South Slavic nationhood emerged in the nineteenth century, South Balkan intellectuals and writers actively supported the goal of unifying South Slavic people through their literary works. Nineteenth-century Serbian writers, such as Vuk Karadzić, Jovan Jovanovic Zmaj, Branko Radičević, Slovenian Jernej Kopitar, members of the Illyrian movement in Croatia, and many others worked vigorously to create literatures in people's spoken languages (as opposed to then official Church Slavonic and German languages).

When Yugoslavia became a political entity in 1918, literature in its many national languages flourished in a variety of forms, mirroring different backgrounds as well as diverse intellectual developments ongoing elsewhere in Europe. One group of writers, which included Nobel Prize winner Ivo Andrić and Jovan Dučić, as well as the poet Desanka Maksimović, consisted of authors writing in a realist mode. Andrić and Dučić were also active in the political life of the country (serving as diplomats at some points of their career). Another group of writers was strongly influenced by modernism, surrealism, the avant-garde, and Dadaism. The group included Miloš Crnjanski, Oskar Davico, members of the Zenitizam group (Dragan Aleksić, Ljubomir Micić, Branko Ve Poljanski), Rastko Petrović, Stanislav Vinaver, Marko Ristić, Vane Bor (Stevan Živadinović), Aleksandar Vučo, Oskar Davičo, Milan Dedinac, Mladen Dimitrijević, Đorđe Jovanović, Đorđe Kostić, Dušan Matić, Branko Milovanović, Koča Popović, Petar Popović, and others.

These authors rebelled against the bourgeois values of this nascent class and its rigid social rules, both in art and in life; they vigorously sought new ways of understanding and expressing reality. Their focus was on creative freedom, experimentation, and free forms. They organized many (short-lived) journals in which they propagated their ideas: *Svetokret, Zenit, Dada Tank, Dada Jazz, Dada-Jok, Ut, Večnost, 50 u Evropi, Almanah Nemoguće/L'impossible, Nadrealizam danas i ovde,* and others.

During the 1920s and 1930s, another active group consisted of writers who were politically on the left—Communists and Socialists such as August Cesarec, Radovan Zogović, Milovan Djilas, Ognjen Prica, Veselin Masleša, Jovan Popović, Otokar Keršovani, and others (many of whom perished during **World War II**, thus significantly tilting the scale of intellectual and creative potential to the modernist side). The ongoing debate between the writers espousing **socialist realism** and the modernists paralleled the contemporary so-called **Brecht-Lukács** debate in Europe. These debates could be roughly delineated as the debates about the conflict between aesthetic value and political commitment, between the singular nature of artistic creation and the need for art of the revolution, which will contribute to the struggle for the liberation of the oppressed proletariat. The socialist-realist group was struggling to create a new art, more appropriate to their socialist goals, and to define new aesthetic criteria better equipped to understand this new art. Modernist writers, despite their proclaimed animosity toward the bourgeoisie and the established order, nevertheless unquestioningly accepted bourgeois criteria for evaluating art.

Publishing his polemics in his own journals *Danas* (1934) and *Pečat* (1939), **Miroslav Krleža** was one of the main participants in the debate and one of the major Yugoslav writers of the twentieth century. Throughout the debates and in his own essayist writing, Krleža, although a Communist, maintained the fundamentally bourgeois notions of artistic autonomy, and of the idea of a universal standard of beauty by which all art is judged. Neither he nor other participants in this debate attempted to try to define aesthetic principles that would be more adequate for the art created in a socialist Yugoslav society. Instead, they continued to follow inherited bourgeois aesthetic models.

This debate between modernism and socialist realism continued in the new Yugoslavia, after the end of World War II and throughout the 1940s and 1950s. Immediately after the war, most published works adhered to socialist-realist aesthetic criteria. Writers such as Mira Alečković, Oskar Davičo, Esad Mekuli, and Branko Copić, whose commitment to socialism was evident in their earlier work, wrote about contemporary historical events and their positive impact on the new society and culture. However, the split between Yugoslavia and the Soviet Union in 1947 prompted the withdrawal of the official support for socialist realism as well. However, the process (at least in literature) was not abrupt; it lasted throughout the 1950s with many accompanying debates and polemics. Writers emphasizing separation of literature from political life were rapidly gaining prominence. Engaged writers abandoned their themes and retreated into esoteric and philosophical subjects—into poetry or fiction whose focus was removed from the political, often focused on introversive individual subjectivity. Davičo's novel, *Beton i svici*, which won a major literary award in 1957, was perhaps one of the finest and one of the last products of socialist-realist writing. The distancing from the social and political reality was evident: from this point on, the work of nonpolitical writers—especially poets like Vasko Popa, Stevan Raičković, and Miodrag Pavlović—dominated the Yugoslav literary scene.

Political writing reemerged in the 1970s, when a new generation of writers—including **Danilo Kiš**, Borislav Pekić, Mihajlo Lalić, Dobrica Ćosić, and Miodrag Bulatović—came to prominence. These writers explored various moments of Yugoslav history and politics, often coming into conflict with the official power. The play *Golubnjača* by Jovan Radulović (and especially its performance at the influential *Sterijino pozorje* Theater Festival in 1980) and Kiš's novel *A Tomb for Boris Davidovič* (1976) are probably the most prominent examples of contraversial and political works that challenged the official historical narratives and social reality of Yugoslavia during this period. They were the inspiration of many subsequent polemics and new works of fiction among the Yugoslavs. During the next two decades, the engagement of Yugoslav writers with history and politics became even more intensive and influential in everyday political and cultural life, producing sometimes vituperative debates that only exacerbated the tensions that led to the disintegration of Yugolsavia in the 1990s.

Selected Bibliography: Hawkesworth, Celia. "Yugoslav Literature of the Second World War." *Journal* *of European Studies* 16 (1986): 217–26; Lalić, Ivan V. "Some Notes on Yugoslav Literature: A Historical Approach." *North Dakota Quarterly* 61.1 (1993): 12–17; Lasić, Stanko. *Sukob na književnoj ljevici, 1928–1952.* Zagreb: Liber, 1970; Palavestra, Predrag. *Posleratna srpska knjizevnost, 1945–1970.* Belgrade: Prosveta, 1972; Zogović, Radovan. *Na poprištu.* Belgrade: Kultura, 1947.

Dubravka Juraga

∘Z∘

ZAMYATIN, EVGENY IVANOVICH (1884–1937), Russian engineer, fiction writer, critic-essayist, and editor. Zamyatin was born in the provincial town of Lebedyan in central Russia. He joined the Bolshevik Party in opposition to the tsar's regime while still a student of naval engineering in the imperial capital of St. Petersburg. He was imprisoned and exiled from St. Petersburg, an experience that provided material for his first short novels and stories. Zamyatin's early works are distinguished by stylistic experimentation with ornamental prose, grotesque imagery, and (in some stories) neoprimitivist aesthetics. During **World War I**, Zamyatin was sent to England to oversee the construction of Russian icebreakers. His encounter with middle-class conformity in the West provided material for two satirical novels on the cultural inertia of bourgeois values, *Ostrovityane* (The Islanders, 1918) and *Lovets chelovekov* (The Fisher of Men, 1922). He returned to Russia when the **Russian Revolution** broke out in 1917, and for the next decade he was one of the most important figures in the explosion of innovative intellectual and aesthetic movements that characterized culture in the first years of the new Soviet state. He edited influential literary journals, led writing workshops that trained a generation of writers in modernist formal experimentation, and supervised translations into Russian of **H. G. Wells**, O. Henry, Anatole France, and others. Zamyatin's own mature style is an elliptical prose featuring a unique synthesis of modernist color symbolism, striking imagery, and an expert, highly effective incorporation of mathematical symbolism and scientific allusion. He is best known for his brilliant novel *We* (*My,* English publication in 1924, first Russian publication in 1987), which in many ways still surpasses its progeny in **dystopian literature** (such as **Orwell**'s *Nineteen Eighty-Four*, **Huxley**'s *Brave New World*, and **Atwood**'s *The Handmaid's Tale*) in the psychological and political acumen of its depiction of the modern totalitarian society. Likewise, Zamyatin's 1924 essay "On Literature, Revolution, Entropy, and other Matters" still stands as a startlingly brilliant philosophical and aesthetic manifesto proclaiming the importance of heretics in art, science, and social life. Zamyatin's commitment to the idea of "infinite revolution" was increasingly out of step with the hardening dogma of Soviet communism, and from 1929 on, Zamyatin was vilified in the official Soviet press. In 1931, he wrote a letter directly to **Stalin** asking for permission to leave his homeland, in which it was no longer possible for him to write. He spent the rest of his life in France, working on an unfinished novel depicting the conflict between Rome and Attila as a parallel to the conflict between the West and Russia.

Selected Bibliography: Brown, Edward J. *"Brave New World," "1984" and "We": An Essay on Anti-Utopia (Zamyatin and English Literature).* Ann Arbor, MI: Ardis, 1976; Cooke, Brett. *Human Nature in Dystopia: Zamyatin's "We."* Evanston, IL: Northwestern UP, 2002; Shane, A. M. *The Life and Works of Evgenij Zamjatin.* U of California P, 1968.

Yvonne Howell

ZIZEK, SLAVOJ (1949–). Born in Ljubljana, Slovenia, Zizek went on to become one of the leading Lacanian philosophers of the contemporary era. He obtained degrees in sociology and philosophy, a doctorate in philosophy, and another doctorate in psychoanalysis, the latter supervised by the Lacanian psychoanalyst Jacques Alain Miller. Influenced by the Slovene Lacanian school, Zizek has consistently demonstrated the importance of Jacques Lacan's concept of the Real to an understanding of contemporary culture and the possibilities of political action. A committed Marxist, Zizek stood as a presidential candidate for the Liberal-Democratic Party during the 1989 elections in postcommunist Slovenia as a strictly tactical move to prevent the seizure of power by rightist nationalists. Well known for a style that combines obscenity, jokes, and references to popular culture with theoretical readings of German philosophy and Lacanian psychoanalysis, Zizek frequently adopts the rhetorical strategies of both analyst and analysand in order to expose his readers to the Real.

For Zizek, the process of exposure to the Lacanian Real is torturous, but it is also always motivated by a materialist commitment to bring about political change. In *The Sublime Object of Ideology* and *Tarrying with the Negative* he offers a Hegelian reading of Lacan, demonstrating the importance of Lacan's thought for contemporary ideology criticism. Other books, such as *Looking Awry* and *The Metastases of Enjoyment*, examine Lacan's account of sexual difference. Zizek's provocative writing on themes such as political correctness and totalitarian politics have led him into a debate with **Judith Butler** and Ernesto Laclau about the possibilities of a universal political imaginary in *Contingency, Hegemony, Universality* (2000). More recently, Zizek has made a plea for Leninist intolerance to neoliberalism in *Revolution at the Gates* (2002) and characterized the attacks of September 11, 2001, as America's encounter with the desert of the Real.

Selected Bibliography: Butler, Judith, Slavoj Zizek, and Ernesto Laclau. *Contingency, Hegemony, Universality: Contemporary Dialogues on the Left.* London: Verso, 2000; Kay, Sarah. *Zizek: A Critical Introduction.* Cambridge: Polity, 2003; Myers, Tony. *Slavoj Zizek.* London: Routledge, 2003; Wright, Elizabeth, and Edmund Wright, eds. *The Zizek Reader.* Oxford: Blackwell, 1999; Zizek, Slavoj. *The Indivisible Remainder: An Essay on Schelling and Related Matters.* London: Verso, 1996; Zizek, Slavoj. *Looking Awry: An Introduction to Jacques Lacan through Popular Culture.* Cambridge, MA: MIT P, 1991; Zizek, Slavoj. *The Metastases of Enjoyment.* London: Verso, 1994; Zizek, Slavoj. *The Sublime Object of Ideology.* London: Verso, 1991; Zizek, Slavoj. *Tarrying with the Negative: Kant, Hegel, and the Critique of Ideology.* Durham, NC: Duke UP, 1993; Zizek, Slavoj. *Welcome to the Desert of the Real.* London: Verso, 2001; Zizek, Slavoj, ed. *Revolution at the Gates.* London: Verso, 2002.

Stephen Morton

ZOLA, ÉMILE (1840–1902). Born in Paris to an Italian father and a French mother and raised in Aix-en-Provence, Zola was the principle proponent of French **naturalism**. Claude Bernard's seminal work, *Introduction to Experimental Medicine* (1865), convinced him that the novel could contribute to the advancement of science and prompted him to consult treatises in the domains of genetics and physiology. In his *Experimental Novel* (1880), Zola advocated a literary adaptation of the scientific method. The novelist, he reasoned, ought to mimic the scientist by engaging in objective observation, the formation of hypotheses, experimentation, and the establishment of laws. Convinced that the information gleaned from this literary experiment would help bring about social change, Zola put his theories to the test in the novels of the *Rougon-Macquart* cycle (1871–1893), which traced the natural and social history of a fictional family under the Second Empire. Written at a time of medical, scientific, and political revolutions, the epic twenty-volume series chronicles the difficult existence of the members of a family haunted by a hereditary defect originating in its matriarch, Adélaïde Rougon. Adélaïde's descendants, who include criminals, social climbers, and artists, all struggle, with varying degrees of success, to overcome a destiny determined by their genetic inheritance and by societal constraints. Dismissed by his contemporary Jules Lemaitre as a "pessimistic epic of human animality," Zola's opus was celebrated by other critics for its compassionate, if graphic, narratives. *L'Assommoir* (1877), the seventh novel in the series and the author's first literary triumph, is the cautionary tale of a laundress who is brought down by the fatal combination of alcoholism and her poor choice in men. One of Zola's best-known works, **Germinal** (1885), exemplifies his interest in socialism and trade unionism, which he saw as an integral part of establishing a just society. After the *Rougon-Macquart* novels, Zola composed the *Trois Villes* (*Three Cities*) series (1894–1898), in which he focused on the political and sociological implications of the Catholic revival in fin de siècle France. He envisioned *Les Quatre Evangiles* (*The Four Gospels*) as the forum for his utopian solutions to the problems plaguing society, but he never completed the project.

In Zola's final years, he shifted from idealism into political engagement. He mobilized the intelligentsia with his famous letter to the newspaper *L'Aurore* in which he condemned the treason conviction of a Jewish army captain, Alfred Dreyfus. That letter, *J'accuse!* (*I accuse!*), published on January 13, 1898, was an outraged cry for justice that triggered one of the most divisive civic and political crises of the Third Republic. The inflammatory epistle made Zola the target of virulent personal attacks and forced him into a year's exile in England. Four years later, on September 30, 1902, Zola was found dead of asphyxia in his home in Paris. Ruled an accident at the time, many today believe his death might have been the result of retaliation for his unrelenting crusade to vindicate Dreyfus.

Selected Bibliography: Brown, Frederick. *Zola: A Life.* New York: Farrar, Straus and Giroux, 1995; Hemmings, F.W.J. (Frederick William John). *The Life and Times of Émile Zola.* New York: Scribner, 1977; Schom, Alan. *Émile Zola: A Biography.* New York: Holt, 1988.

Kathy Comfort

○○○ *Bibliography* ○○○

Aaron, Daniel. *Writers on the Left: Episodes in American Literary Communism*. New York: Harcourt, Brace and World, 1961.

Abelove, Henry, Michele Aina Barale, and David M. Halperin, eds. *The Lesbian and Gay Studies Reader*. New York: Routledge, 1993.

Abrahams, Cecil A. *Alex La Guma*. Boston: Twayne, 1985.

Abrams, M. H. *The Mirror and the Lamp: Romantic Theory and the Critical Tradition*. New York: Norton, 1953.

_____. *Natural Supernaturalism: Tradition and Revolution in Romantic Literature*. New York: Norton, 1971.

Achebe, Chinua. *Home and Exile*. New York: Oxford UP, 2000.

_____. *Hopes and Impediments: Selected Essays*. New York: Doubleday, 1989.

_____. "An Image of Africa." *Research in African Literatures* 9.1 (1978): 1–15.

_____. *Morning Yet on Creation Day: Essays*. New York: Doubleday, 1975.

_____. *The Trouble with Nigeria*. Oxford: Heinemann, 1984.

Achinstein, Sharon. *Milton and the Revolutionary Reader*. Princeton, NJ: Princeton UP, 1994.

Achugar, Hugo. "Local/Global Latin Americanisms: 'Theoretical Babbling,' a propos of Roberto Fernández Retamar." *Interventions* 5.1 (2003): 125–41.

Ackroyd, Peter. *Dickens*. London: Sinclair Stevenson, 1990.

Acocella, Joan Ross. *Willa Cather and the Politics of Criticism*. Lincoln: U of Nebraska P, 2000.

Adereth, M. *Aragon, the Resistance Poems: "Le Crève-coeur," "Les Yeux d'Elsa" and "La Diane française."* London: Grant and Cutler, 1985.

_____. *Elsa Triolet and Louis Aragon: An Introduction to Their Interwoven Lives and Works*. Lewiston, NY: Mellen, 1994.

Adorno, Theodor W. *Aesthetic Theory*. Trans. Robert Hullot-Kentor. Minneapolis: U of Minnesota P, 1997.

_____. *The Culture Industry: Selected Essays on Mass Culture*. Ed. J. M. Bernstein. London: Routledge, 1971.

_____. "Engagement." *Noten zur Literatur*. Vol. 3. Frankfurt: Suhrkamp, 1963.

_____. *Minima Moralia*. Trans. Edmund Jephcott. London: Verso, 1974.

_____. *Negative Dialectics*. Trans. E. B. Ashton. New York: Seabury P, 1973.

_____. *Notes to Literature*. Trans. Shierry Weber Nicholsen. New York: Columbia UP, 1991.

————, and Max Horkheimer. *Dialectic of Enlightenment*. Trans. Edmund Jephcott. Stanford: Stanford UP, 2002.

Aghacy, Samira. "The Use of Autobiography in Rashid Al-Daif's *Dear Mr. Kawabata*." *Writing the Self*. Ed. Robin Ostle, Ed DeMoor, and Stefan Wild. London: Saqi Books, 1998. 217–28.

Ahearne, Jeremy. *Between Cultural Theory and Policy: The Cultural Policy Thinking of Pierre Bourdieu, Michel de Certeau and Régis Debray*. Warwick, England: Centre for Cultural Policy Studies, U of Warwick, 2004.

————. *Michel de Certeau: Interpretation and Its Other*. Stanford, CA: Stanford UP, 1996.

Ahmad, Aijaz. *In Theory: Classes, Nations, Literatures*. London: Verso, 1992.

Alarcón, Norma. "Chicana Feminism: In the Tracks of 'The' Native Woman." *Living Chicana Theory*. Ed. Carla Trujillo. Berkeley: Third Woman P, 1998. 371–82.

Alber, Charles J. *Embracing the Lie: Ding Ling and the Politics of Literature in the People's Republic of China*. Westport, CT: Praeger, 2004.

————. *Enduring the Revolution: Ding Ling and the Politics of Literature in Guomindang China*. Westport, CT: Praeger, 2002.

Albiac, Gabriel. *Otros mundos*. Edición de J. Marchante, A. Mira, y J. Sánchez Tortosa. Madrid: Páginas de Espuma, 2002.

Alcántara Almánzar, José. *Estudios de poesía dominicana*. Santo Domingo: Editora Alfa y Omega, 1979.

Aldiss, Brian. *Trillion Year Spree: The History of Science Fiction*. New York: Avon, 1986.

Aldritt, Keith. *Modernism in the Second World War*. New York: Peter Lang, 1989.

Alexander, M. Jacqui, and Chandra Talpade Mohanty, eds. *Feminist Genealogies, Colonial Legacies, Democratic Futures*. New York: Routledge, 1997.

Alexandrov, Vladimir E. *Andrei Bely: The Major Symbolist Fiction*. Cambridge, MA: Harvard UP, 1985.

Algren, Nelson. *Nonconformity: Writing on Writing*. New York: Seven Stories P, 1998.

Alkon, Paul. *Origins of Futuristic Fiction*. Athens: U of Georgia P, 1987.

Allen, Paula Gunn. "Bringing Home the Fact: Tradition and Continuity in the Imagination." *Recovering the Word: Essays on Native American Literature*. Ed. Brian Swann and Arnold Krupat. Berkeley: U of California P, 1987. 563–79.

Allesandrini, Anthony, ed. *Frantz Fanon: Critical Perspectives*. New York: Routledge, 1999.

Allison, Jonathan, ed. *Yeats's Political Identities*. Ann Arbor: U of Michigan P, 1995.

Alpatov, A. V. *Aleksei Tolstoi—master istoricheskogo romana*. Moscow: Sovetskii pisatel, 1958.

Althusser, Louis. *The Future Lasts Forever: A Memoir*. Trans. Richard Veasey. New York: New P, 1993.

————. *Lenin and Philosophy and Other Essays*. Trans. Ben Brewster. London: Monthly Review P, 1971.

————, and Etienne Balibar. *Reading Capital*. London: Verso, 1970.

Álvarez Borland, Isabel. *Cuban-American Literature of Exile: From Person to Persona*. Charlottesville: UP of Virginia, 1998.

Alves, Susan. "'Whilst working at my frame': The Poetic Production of Ethel Carnie." *Victorian Poetry* 38.1 (Spring 2000): 77–93.

Amees, Munawar A. *The Kiss of Judas: Affairs of a Brown Sahib*. Kuala Lumpur, Malaysia: Quill, 1989.

Amell, Samuel, ed. *Literature, the Arts, and Democracy: Spain in the Eighties.* London: Associated UP, 1990.

American Indian Quarterly 5 (1979). Special Issue on Leslie Marmon Silko's *Ceremony.*

Amert, Susan. *In a Shattered Mirror: The Later Poetry of Anna Akhmatova.* Stanford: Stanford UP, 1992.

Ames, Russell. *Citizen Thomas More and His Utopia.* Princeton, NJ: Princeton UP, 1949.

Ammons, Elizabeth, ed. *Critical Essays on Harriet Beecher Stowe.* Boston: G. K. Hall, 1980.

Amuta, Chidi. *Towards a Sociology of African Literature.* Oguta, Nigeria: Zim Pan, 1986.

Anderson, Edward. *Hungry Men.* 1935. Norman: U of Oklahoma P, 1993.

Anderson, James M. *The Spanish Civil War: A History and Reference Guide.* Westport, CT: Greenwood, 2003.

Anderson, Perry. *The Origins of Postmodernity.* London: Verso, 1998.

Andrews, William L. *To Tell a Free Story: The First Century of Afro-American Autobiography, 1760–1865.* Urbana: Illinois UP, 1986.

————, ed. *The Oxford Frederick Douglass Reader.* Oxford: Oxford UP, 1996.

Angulo, María-Elena. *Magic Realism: Social Context and Discourse.* New York: Garland, 1995.

Annas, Julia. *An Introduction to Plato's Republic.* Oxford: Clarendon, 1981.

Annenkov, P. V. *The Extraordinary Decade: Literary Memoirs.* Trans. Irwin Titunik. Ann Arbor: U of Michigan P, 1968.

Ansell-Pearson, Keith, et al., eds. *Cultural Readings of Imperialism: Edward Said and the Gravity of History.* New York: St. Martin's, 1997.

Antoine, Régis. *La littérature franco-antillaise.* Paris: Karthala, 1992.

Appignanesi, Lisa, and Sara Maitland. *The Rushdie File.* London: Fourth Estate, 1989.

Aquin, Hubert. *Prochain épisode.* Critical edition. Ed. Jacques Allard et al. Montreal: Bibliothèque québécoise, 1995.

Arac, Jonathan. "The Struggle for the Cultural Heritage: Christina Stead Refunctions Charles Dickens and Mark Twain." *Cultural Critique* 2 (1985–1986): 171–89.

Arcana, Judith. *Grace Paley's Life Stories: A Literary Biography.* Urbana: U of Illinois P, 1993.

Ardis, Ann. *New Women, New Novels: Feminism and Early Modernism.* New Brunswick: Rutgers UP, 1990.

Arias, Arturo, ed. *The Rigoberta Menchú Controversy.* Minneapolis: U of Minnesota P, 2001.

Arnold, A. James. *Modernism and Negritude.* Cambridge, MA: Harvard UP, 1981.

Aronson, Ronald. *Jean-Paul Sartre: Philosophy in the World.* London: New Left Books, 1980.

Arthur, Charles, and Michael J. Dash. *Libète: A Haitian Anthology.* New Jersey: Markus Wiener, 1999.

Arunachalam, M. *An Introduction to the History of Tamil Literature.* Tanjavur, India: Gandhi Vidyalayam, 1974.

Arvin, Newton. *Whitman.* New York: Macmillan, 1938.

Asein, Samuel. *Alex La Guma: The Man and His Work.* Ibadan: New Horn/Heinemann, 1987.

Ashcroft, Bill, and Pal Ahluwalia. *Edward Said: The Paradox of Identity.* New York: Routledge, 1999.

Ashcroft, Bill, Gareth Griffiths, and Helen Tiffin. *The Empire Writes Back: Theory and Practice in Post-Colonial Literatures.* London: Routledge, 1989.

Ashraf, Phyllis Mary. *Introduction to Working-Class Literature in Great Britain. Part 2: Prose.* Berlin: VEB Kongres und Werbedruck Oberlungwitz, 1979.

Aston, Elaine. *Caryl Churchill.* Plymouth, UK: Northcote House, 1997.

Attridge, Derek, and Rosemary Jane Jolly, eds. *Writing South Africa: Literature, Apartheid, and Democracy, 1970–1995.* Cambridge: Cambridge UP, 1998.

Auerbach, Eric. *Mimesis: The Representation of Reality in Western Literature.* Trans. Willard R. Trask. Princeton, NJ: Princeton UP, 1953.

Augenbraum, Harold, and Margarite Fernández-Olmos, eds. *U.S. Latino Literature: A Critical Guide for Students and Teachers.* Westport, CT: Greenwood, 2000.

Austin, Addell. "The Opportunity and Crisis Literary Contests." *CLAJ* 32 (1988): 235–46.

Aviram, Amittai F. "Gender Theory." *The Oxford Companion to Women's Writing in the United States.* Ed. Cathy N. Davidson and Linda Wagner-Martin. New York: Oxford UP, 1995.

Awodiya, Muyiwa P., ed. *Excursions in Drama and Literature: Interviews with Femi Osofisan.* Ibadan: Kraft Books, 1993.

Azicri, Max. *Cuba Today and Tomorrow: Reinventing Socialism.* Gainesville: UP of Florida, 2000.

Azim, Firdous. *The Colonial Rise of the Novel.* London: Routledge, 1993.

Baeza Flores, Alberto. *La poesía dominicana en el siglo XX.* Santiago, República Dominicana: Universidad Católica Madre y Maestra, 1975–1977.

Baines, Jocelyn. *Joseph Conrad: A Critical Biography.* 1960. London: Weidenfield, 1993.

Bair, Deirdre. *Simone de Beauvoir: A Biography.* New York: Simon and Schuster, 1990.

Baker, Carlos. *Ernest Hemingway: A Life Story.* New York: Scribner, 1969.

Baker, Christina. *In a Generous Spirit: A First-Person Biography of Myra Page.* Urbana: U of Illinois P, 1996.

Baker, David Weil. *Divulging Utopia: Radical Humanism in Sixteenth-Century England.* Amherst: U of Massachusetts P, 1999.

Baker, Houston A., Jr. *Afro-American Poetics: Revisions of Harlem and the Black Aesthetic.* Madison: U of Wisconsin P, 1988.

———. *Modernism and the Harlem Renaissance.* Chicago: U of Chicago P, 1987.

Baker, Robert S. *Brave New World: History, Science, and Dystopia.* Boston: Twayne, 1990.

Bakhtin, Mikhail M. *Art and Answerability: Early Philosophical Essays by M. M. Bakhtin.* Ed. Michael Holquist and Vadim Liapunov. Trans. Vadim Liapunov. Austin: U of Texas P, 1990.

———. "The Bildungsroman and Its Significance in the History of Realism." *Speech Genres and Other Late Essays.* Ed. C. Emerson and M. Holquist. Austin: U of Texas P, 1986. 10–59.

———. *The Dialogic Imagination: Four Essays by M. M. Bakhtin.* Ed. Michael Holquist. Trans. Caryl Emerson and Michael Holquist. Austin: U of Texas P, 1981.

———. *Problems of Dostoevsky's Poetics.* Ed. and trans. Caryl Emerson. Minneapolis: U of Minnesota P, 1984.

———. *Rabelais and His World.* Trans. Hélène Iswolsky. Cambridge, MA: MIT P, 1984.

———. *Speech Genres and Other Late Essays.* Ed. Caryl Emerson and Michael Holquist. Trans. Vern W. McGee. Austin: U of Texas P, 1986.

———, and P. N. Medvedev. *The Formal Method in Literary Scholarship: A Critical Introduction to Sociological Poetics.* Trans. Albert J. Wehrle. Cambridge, MA: Harvard UP, 1985.

Baldick, Chris. *In Frankenstein's Shadow: Myth, Monstrosity, and Nineteenth-Century Writing.* Oxford: Clarendon P, 1990.

Baldinger, Kurt. *Introduction aux dictionnaires les plus importants pour l'histoire du français.* Paris: Klincksieck, 1974.

Baldridge, Cates. *Graham Greene's Fictions: The Virtues of Extremity.* Columbia: U of Missouri P, 2000.

Baldwin, James. "Everybody's Protest Novel." *Notes of a Native Son.* Boston: Beacon Press, 1984. 13–23.

Balfour, Lawrie. *The Evidence of Things Not Said: James Baldwin and the Promise of American Democracy.* Ithaca: Cornell UP, 2001.

Ball, Gordon. "Ginsberg and Revolution." *Selected Essays: West Georgia College International Conference on Representing Revolution, 1989.* West Georgia International Conference, 1991. 137–50.

Balutansky, Kathleen. *The Novels of Alex La Guma: The Representation of a Political Conflict.* Boulder, CO: Lynne Rienner, 1990.

————, and Marie-Agnès Sourieau, eds. *Caribbean Creolization: Reflections on the Cultural Dynamics of Language, Literature, and Identity.* Gainesville: U of Florida P, 1998.

Bance, Alan, ed. *Weimar Germany: Writers and Politics.* Edinburgh: Scottish Academic P, 1982.

Banerjee, Maria Nêmcová. *Terminal Paradox: The Novels of Milan Kundera.* New York: Grove Weidenfeld, 1990.

Baraka, Amiri. *The Autobiography of LeRoi Jones/Amiri Baraka.* New York: Freundlich Books, 1984.

————. *Blues People: Negro Music in White America.* New York: William Morrow, 1963.

————. *The LeRoi Jones/Amiri Baraka Reader.* Ed. William J. Harris. New York: Thunder's Mouth P, 1991.

Barański, Zygmunt G., ed. *Pasolini Old and New: Surveys and Studies.* Dublin: Four Courts P, 1999.

Barber, Stephen M., and David L. Clark, eds. *Regarding Sedgwick: Essays on Queer Culture and Critical Theory.* New York: Routledge, 2002.

Barmé, Geremie. *In the Red: On Contemporary Chinese Culture.* New York: Columbia UP, 1999.

Barnard, Ian. "Gloria Anzaldúa Queer Mestisaje." *MELUS* 22 (1997): 35–53.

Barnard, Rita. *The Great Depression and the Culture of Abundance: Kenneth Fearing, Nathanael West, and Mass Culture in the 1930s.* Cambridge: Cambridge UP, 1995.

Barnett, Louise K., and James L. Thorson, eds. *Leslie Marmon Silko: A Collection of Critical Essays.* Albuquerque: U of New Mexico P, 1999.

Barnett, Ursula A. *A Vision of Order: A Study of Black South African Literature in English (1914–1980).* Amherst: U of Massachusetts P, 1983.

Barr, Marlene S. *Lost in Space: Probing Feminist Science Fiction and Beyond.* Chapel Hill: U of North Carolina P, 1993.

Barratt, Andrew, and Barry P. Scherr, eds. and trans. *Maksim Gorky: Selected Letters.* Oxford: Clarendon P, 1997.

Barrett, Michèle, ed. *Virginia Woolf: Women and Writing.* London: Women's P, 1979.

Barroll, J. Leeds. *Politics, Plague, and Shakespeare's Theater: The Stuart Years.* Ithaca: Cornell UP, 1991.

Bart, Philip, Theodore Bassett, William W. Weinstone, and Arthur Zipser, eds. *Highlights of a Fighting History: Sixty Years of the Communist Party, USA*. New York: International Publishers, 1979.

Bartkowski, Frances. *Feminist Utopias*. Lincoln: U of Nebraska P, 1989.

Bartolovich, Crystal, and Neil Lazarus, eds. *Marxism, Modernity, and Postcolonial Studies*. Cambridge: Cambridge UP, 2002.

Bates, Ralph. "Disaster in Finland." *New Republic*, 13 December 1939, 221–25.

Baudin, Antoine. *Le Réalisme socialiste soviétique de la période jdanovienne, 1947–1952. Vol. 1: Les Arts plastiques et leurs institutions*. Bern: Peter Lang, 1997.

————, and Leonid Heller. *Le Réalisme socialiste soviétique de la période jdanovienne, 1947–1952. Vol. 2: Usages à l'intérieur, image à exporter*. Bern: Peter Lang, 1998.

Baudrillard, Jean. *America*. Trans. Chris Turner. London: Verso, 1988.

————. *Cool Memories*. Trans. Chris Turner. London: Verso, 1987.

————. *Fatal Strategies*. Trans. Philip Beitchman and W.G.J. Niesluchowski. Ed. Jim Fleming. New York: Semiotext(e), 1990.

————. *The Illusion of the End*. Trans. Chris Turner. Cambridge: Polity P, 1994.

————. *In the Shadow of the Silent Majorities; or, The End of the Social, and Other Essays*. Trans. Paul Foss, John Johnston, and Paul Patton. New York: Semiotext(e), 1983.

————. *Simulations*. Trans. Paul Foss, Paul Patton, and Philip Beitchman. New York: Semiotext(e), 1983.

————. *Symbolic Exchange and Death*. Trans. Iain Hamilton Grant. London: Sage, 1993.

————. *The Transparency of Evil: Essays on Extreme Phenomena*. Trans. James Benedict. London: Verso, 1993.

Baugh, Albert C., ed. *A Literary History of England*. New York: Appleton-Century-Crofts, 1948.

Baumann, Michael L. *B. Traven: An Introduction*. Albuquerque: U of New Mexico P, 1976.

Baxandall, Lee, and Stefan Morawski, eds. *Karl Marx and Frederick Engels on Literature and Art*. New York: International General, 1973.

Bazin, Nancy Topping, and Marilyn Dallman Seymour, eds. *Conversations with Nadine Gordimer*. Jackson: UP of Mississippi, 1990.

Beach, Christopher. *The Politics of Distinction: Whitman and the Discourses of Nineteenth-Century America*. Athens: U of Georgia P, 1996.

Beal, Fred E. *Proletarian Journey: New England, Gastonia, Moscow*. New York: Hillman-Curl, 1947.

Beardsworth, Richard. *Derrida and the Political*. London: Routledge, 1996.

Beck, John. *Writing the Radical Center: William Carlos Williams, John Dewey, and American Cultural Politics*. Albany: State U of New York P, 2001.

Beck, Kent. "The Odyssey of Joseph Freeman." *Historian* 38.1 (November 1974): 101–20.

Becker, Marc. *Mariátegui and Latin American Marxist Theory*. Athens: Ohio University Center for International Studies, 1993.

Bedford, Sybille. *Aldous Huxley*. New York: Harper and Row, 1974.

Beidler, Philip D. *Rewriting America: Vietnam Authors in Their Generation*. Athens: U of Georgia P, 1991.

Beinart, William. *Twentieth-Century South Africa*. Oxford: Oxford UP, 1994.

Bejoint, Henri. *Modern Lexicography. An Introduction*. Oxford: Oxford UP, 2000.

Belfrage, Cedric. *American Inquisition, 1945–1960*. 1973. New York: Thunder's Mouth P, 1989.

Bell, Bernard. *The Afro-American Novel and Its Tradition.* Amherst: U of Massachusetts P, 1987.

Bell, Daniel. *The Cultural Contradictions of Capitalism.* 1976. New York: Basic Books, 1996.

————. *The End of Ideology: On the Exhaustion of Political Ideas in the Fifties.* 1960. Cambridge, MA: Harvard UP, 1988.

Bell, David. *Ardent Propaganda: Miners' Novels and Class Conflict, 1929–39.* Uppsala: Swedish Science P, 1995.

Belnap, Jeffrey, and Raúl Fernández. *José Martí's "Our America": From National to Hemispheric Cultural Studies.* Durham, NC: Duke UP, 1998.

Belpoliti, Marco, and Robert S.C. Gordon, eds. *The Voice of Memory: Primo Levi—Interviews, 1961–1987.* Cambridge: Polity, 2001.

Belsey, Catherine. "Constructing the Subject, Deconstructing the Text." *Feminisms: An Anthology of Literary Theory and Criticism.* Robyn R. Warhol and Diane Price Herndl, eds. New Brunswick: Rutgers UP, 1991. 657–73.

————. *Critical Practice.* London: Methuen, 1980.

Benhabib, Seyla. *The Reluctant Modernism of Hannah Arendt.* Thousand Oaks, CA: Sage, 1996.

Benjamin, Walter. *The Arcades Project.* Trans. Howard Eiland and Kevin McLaughlin. Cambridge, MA: Belknap P, 1999.

————. *Illuminations.* New York: Harcourt, Brace and World, 1968.

————. *Selected Writings.* Ed. Marcus Bullock and Michael W. Jennings. 4 vols. Cambridge, MA: Belknap P, 1996–2003.

————. *Understanding Brecht.* Trans. Anna Bostock. London: NLB, 1973.

Benman-Gibson, Margaret. *Clifford Odets, American Playwright.* New York: Atheneum, 1982.

Benn, Maurice B. *The Drama of Revolt: A Critical Study of Georg Büchner.* Cambridge: Cambridge UP, 1976.

Bennett, Bruce, and Jennifer Strauss, eds. *The Oxford Literary History of Australia.* Melbourne: Oxford UP, 1998.

Bennett, William. "'To Reclaim a Legacy': Text of Report on Humanities in Education." *Chronicle of Higher Education,* 28 November 1984, 16–21.

Bennington, Geoffrey, and Jacques Derrida. *Jacques Derrida.* Chicago: U of Chicago P, 1991.

Benson, Frederick R. *Writers in Arms: The Literary Impact of the Spanish Civil War.* New York: NYU P, 1967.

Benson, Jackson. *The True Adventures of John Steinbeck, Writer.* New York: Viking, 1984.

Berardinelli, Alfonso. *Franco Fortini.* Florence: Nuova Italia, 1973.

Bercovitch, Sacvan. "The Problem of Ideology in American Literary History." *Critical Inquiry* 12.4 (Summer 1986): 631–53.

————, ed. *The Cambridge History of American Literature.* New York: Cambridge UP, 1994.

————, and Myra Jehlen, eds. *Ideology and Classic American Literature.* New York: Cambridge UP, 1986.

Berg, James, and Chris Freeman, eds. *Conversations with Christopher Isherwood.* Jackson: UP of Mississippi, 2001.

Bergonzi, Bernard. *The Early H.G. Wells.* Manchester: Manchester UP, 1961.

Berke, Nancy. *Women Poets on the Left: Lola Ridge, Genevieve Taggard, Margaret Walker.* Gainesville: UP of Florida, 2001.

Berlin, Isaiah. "Fathers and Children: Turgenev and the Liberal Predicament." *Russian Thinkers*. Ed. Henry Hardy and Aileen Kelly. New York: Viking, 1978. 261–305.

————. *The Hedgehog and the Fox: An Essay on Tolstoy's View of History*. New York: Simon and Schuster, 1970.

————. *Karl Marx: His Life and Environment*. 4th ed. New York: Oxford UP, 1996.

Berlin, James. *Rhetorics, Poetics, and Culture: Refiguring College English Studies*. Urbana, IL: NCTE, 1996.

Bernabé, Jean, Patrick Chamoisieau, and Raphael Confiant. *Eloge de la Créolité* and *In Praise of Creoleness*. Bilingual edition. Paris: Gallimard, 1993.

Bernstein, Richard J., ed. *Habermas and Modernity*. Cambridge, MA: MIT P, 1985.

Berresford Ellis, Peter. *A History of the Irish Working Class*. 1972. London: Pluto P, 1996.

Berry, Faith, ed. *Good Morning Revolution: Uncollected Writings of Social Protest by Langston Hughes*. New York: Citadel P, 1973.

Best, Steven, and Douglas Kellner. *The Postmodern Adventure*. London: Routledge, 2001.

————. *Postmodern Theory: Critical Interrogations*. New York: Guilford P, 1991.

————. *The Postmodern Turn*. New York: Guilford P, 1997.

Bethell, Leslie, ed. *Cuba: A Short History*. New York: Cambridge UP, 1993.

Beverley, John. *Against Literature*. Minneapolis: U of Minnesota P, 1993.

————. "Poetry in the Central American Revolution: Ernesto Cardenal and Roque Dalton." *Journal of the Society of Contemporary Hispanic and Lusophone Revolutionary Literatures* 1 (1984–1985): 295–312.

————, and Marc Zimmerman. *Literature and Politics in the Central American Revolutions*. Austin: U of Texas P, 1990.

Bevilacqua, Winifred Farrant. *Josephine Herbst*. Boston: Twayne, 1985.

Bewes, Timothy. *Reification, or the Anxiety of Late Capitalism*. London: Verso, 2002.

Bhabha, Homi. *The Location of Culture*. London: Routledge, 1994.

————, ed. *Nation and Narration*. London: Routledge, 1994.

Bhaskar, Roy. *Reclaiming Reality: A Critical Introduction to Contemporary Philosophy*. London: Verso, 1989.

Bhatt, Indira, and Indira Nityanandan. *The Fiction of Amitav Ghosh*. New Delhi: Creative Books, 2001.

Biasin, Gian-Paulo. *The Smile of the Gods: A Thematic Study of Cesare Pavese's Works*. Ithaca, NY: Cornell UP, 1968.

Bibby, Michael, ed. *The Vietnam War and Postmodernity*. Amherst: U of Massachusetts P, 1999.

Billington, Michael. *The Life and Works of Harold Pinter*. London: Faber and Faber, 1996.

Binyon, T. J. *Pushkin: A Biography*. New York: Knopf, 2003.

Biondi, Jean-Pierre. *Senghor, ou, la tentation de l'universel*. Paris: Denoël, 1993.

Birbalsingh, Frank. *Passion and Exile: Essays on Caribbean Literature*. London: Hansib, 1988.

Bird, Delys, ed. *Katharine Susannah Prichard: Stories, Journalism and Essays*. St. Lucia: U of Queensland P, 2000.

Bird, Stewart, Dan Georgakas, and Deborah Shaffer, eds. *Solidarity Forever: An Oral History of the IWW*. Chicago: Lake View P, 1985.

Birkett, Jennifer, ed. *Samuel Beckett*. New York: Longman, 1999.

Birnbaum, Marianna D. "History and Human Relationships in the Fiction of Danilo Kiš." *Cross Currents* 8 (1989): 346–60.

Blaazer, David. *The Popular Front and the Progressive Tradition: Socialists, Liberals, and the Quest for Unity, 1884–1939*. Cambridge: Cambridge UP, 1992.

Black, Karen, ed. *A Biobibliographical Handbook of Bulgarian Authors*. Trans. Predrag Matejic. Columbus, OH: Slavica, 1981.

Black, Stanley. *Juan Goytisolo and the Poetics of Contagion: The Evolution of a Radical Aesthetics in the Later Novels*. Liverpool: Liverpool UP, 2001.

Blaeser, Kimberly. *Gerald Vizenor: Writing in the Oral Tradition*. Norman: U of Oklahoma P, 1996.

Blanchard, W. Scott. *Scholar's Bedlam: Menippean Satire in the Renaissance*. London: Associated UP, 1995.

Bliss, Corinne Demas. "Against the Current: A Conversation with Anita Desai." *Massachusetts Review* 29.3 (Fall 1988): 521–37.

Bloch, Ernst. *The Principle of Hope*. 3 vols. Trans. Neville Plaice, Stephen Plaice, and Paul Knight. Cambridge, MA: MIT P, 1995.

———. *Spuren*. Berlin: Suhrkamp, 1959.

Bloom, Alexander. *Prodigal Sons: The New York Intellectuals and Their World*. New York: Oxford UP, 1986.

Bloom, Allan. *The Closing of the American Mind: How Higher Education Has Failed Democracy and Impoverished the Souls of Today's Students*. New York: Simon and Schuster, 1987.

Bloom, Harold. *The Western Canon: The Books and School of the Ages*. New York: Harcourt Brace, 1994.

———, ed. *Elie Wiesel's* Night. Philadelphia: Chelsea House, 2001.

———, ed. *Isabel Allende*. Philadelphia: Chelsea House, 2003.

———, ed. *Literature of the Holocaust*. Philadelphia: Chelsea House, 2004.

Bloom, James D. *Left Letters: The Culture Wars of Mike Gold and Joseph Freeman*. New York: Columbia UP, 1992.

Blotner, Joseph. *Faulkner: A Biography*. 2 vols. New York: Random House, 1974.

Blum, John Morton. *V Was for Victory: Politics and American Culture during World War II*. New York: Harcourt Brace Jovanovich, 1976.

Boal, Augusto. *Theater of the Oppressed*. London: Pluto, 1979.

Bobb, June. *Beating a Restless Drum: The Poetics of Kamau Brathwaite and Derek Walcott*. Trenton, NJ: Africa World P, 1998.

Boehmer, Elleke. *Colonial and Postcolonial Literature*. New York: Oxford UP, 1995.

Bogert, Ralph. *The Writer as Naysayer: Miroslav Krleža and the Aesthetic of Interwar Central Europe*. Columbus, OH: Slavica, 1991.

Boggs, Carl. *Gramsci's Marxism*. Ann Arbor: U of Michigan P, 1976.

Bogues, Anthony. *C.L.R. James and Marxism*. London: Pluto, 1993.

Bolaffi, Guido, Raffaele Bracalenti, Peter Braham, and Sandro Gindro, eds. *Dictionary of Race, Ethnicity and Culture*. London: Sage, 2003.

Bold, Alan. *Hugh MacDiarmid: Christopher Murray Grieve: A Critical Biography*. Rev. ed. London: Paladin, 1990.

———. *Modern Scottish Literature*. London: Longman, 1983.

Boldy, Steven. *The Narrative of Carlos Fuentes: Family, Text, Nation*. Durham: U of Durham, 2002.

Bolloten, Burnett. *The Spanish Civil War*. Chapel Hill: U of North Carolina P, 1991.

Booker, M. Keith. *The African Novel in English*. Portsmouth, NH: Heinemann, 1998.

————. *Dystopian Literature: A Theory and Research Guide*. Westport, CT: Greenwood, 1994.

————. "Mike Gold or James Joyce? The Literature of Politics and the Politics of Literature." *Socialist Cultures East and West: A Post–Cold War Reassessment*. Ed. Dubravka Juraga and M. Keith Booker. Westport, CT: Praeger, 2002. 81–99.

————. *The Modern American Novel of the Left: A Research Guide*. Westport, CT: Greenwood, 1999.

————. *The Modern British Novel of the Left: A Research Guide*. Westport, CT: Greenwood, 1998.

————. *The Post-Utopian Imagination: American Culture in the Long 1950s*. Westport, CT: Greenwood, 2002.

————. *Strange TV: Innovative Television Series from "The Twilight Zone" to "The X-Files."* Westport, CT: Greenwood, 2002.

————. *"Ulysses," Capitalism, and Colonialism: Reading Joyce after the Cold War*. Westport, CT: Greenwood, 2000.

————. *Vargas Llosa among the Postmodernists*. Gainesville: UP of Florida, 1994.

————. "Writing for the Wretched of the Earth: Frantz Fanon and the Radical African Novel." *Rereading Global Socialist Cultures after the Cold War: The Reassessment of a Tradition*. Ed. Dubravka Juraga and M. Keith Booker. Westport, CT: Praeger, 2002. 27–54.

————, ed. *The Chinua Achebe Encyclopedia*. Westport, CT: Greenwood, 2003.

————, ed. *Critical Essays on Salman Rushdie*. New York: G. K. Hall, 1999.

————, and Dubravka Juraga. *Bakhtin, Stalin, and Modern Russian Fiction: Carnival, Dialogism, and History*. Westport, CT: Greenwood P, 1995.

————, and Dubravka Juraga. *The Caribbean Novel in English: An Introduction*. Portsmouth, NH: Heinemann, 2001.

————, and Dubravka Juraga. "The Reds and the Blacks: The Historical Novel in the Soviet Union and Postcolonial Africa." *Socialist Cultures East and West: A Post–Cold War Reassessment*. Ed. Dubravka Juraga and M. Keith Booker. Westport, CT: Praeger, 2002. 11–30.

Boorman, Howard L. "The Literary World of Mao Tse-tung." *China Quarterly* 13 (January–March 1963): 15–38.

Booth, Allyson. *Postcards from the Trenches: Negotiating the Space between Modernism and the First World War*. New York: Oxford UP, 1996.

Borden, Richard C. *The Art of Writing Badly: Valentin Kataev's Mauvism and the Rebirth of Russian Modernism*. Evanston, IL: Northwestern UP, 1999.

Borenstein, Eliot. *Men without Women: Masculinity and Revolution in Russian Fiction, 1917–1929*. Durham, NC: Duke UP, 2000.

Borgeson, Paul W., Jr. *Hacia el hombre nuevo: poesía y pensamiento de Ernesto Cardenal*. London: Tamesis, 1984.

Borras, F. M. *Maxim Gorky the Writer: An Interpretation*. Oxford: Clarendon P, 1967.

Bose, Brinda, ed. *Amitav Ghosh: Critical Perspectives*. New Delhi: Pencraft International, 2003.

Bosi, Alfredo. *História concisa da literatura brasileira*. São Paulo: Cultrix, 2002.

Botting, Fred. *Gothic*. London: Routledge, 1996.

————. *Making Monstrous: "Frankenstein," Criticism, Theory*. Manchester: Manchester UP, 1991.

Boundas, Constantin, and Dorothea Olkowski, eds. *Gilles Deleuze and the Theatre of Philosophy*. London: Routledge, 1994.

Bourdieu, Pierre. *Distinction: A Social Critique of the Judgment of Taste*. London: Routledge, 1984.

————. *La Domination masculine*. Paris: Seuil, 1998.

————. *Language and Symbolic Power*. Cambridge, MA: Harvard UP, 1991.

————. *The Logic of Practice*. Cambridge: Polity, 1990.

————. *The Rules of Art*. Stanford, CA: Stanford UP, 1995.

————. *Sociologie de l'Algérie*. Paris: PUF, 1962.

————, and Loic Wacquant. *An Invitation to Reflexive Sociology*. Cambridge: Polity, 1992.

Bové, Paul A., ed. *Edward Said and the Work of the Critic: Speaking Truth to Power*. Durham, NC: Duke UP, 2000.

Bowles, Samuel, and Herbert Gintis. *Schooling in Capitalist America: Education and the Contradictions of American Economic Life*. New York: Basic Books, 1976.

Boyd, Brian. *Vladimir Nabokov: The American Years*. Princeton, NJ: Princeton UP, 1991.

————. *Vladimir Nabokov: The Russian Years*. Princeton, NJ: Princeton UP, 1990.

Boyle, Nicholas. *Goethe: The Poet and the Age: Revolution and Renunciation, 1790–1803*. Oxford: Clarendon P, 2000.

Bradbrook, Bohuslava R. *Karel Čapek: In Pursuit of Truth, Tolerance and Trust*. Brighton: Sussex Academic P, 1997.

Bradbury, Malcolm. *The Social Content of Modern English Literature*. New York: Schocken, 1971.

Braidotti, Rosi. *Nomadic Subjects: Embodiment and Sexual Difference in Contemporary Feminist Theory*. New York: Columbia UP, 1994.

Bramer, Monte, director. *Paul Monette: The Brink of Summer's End*. Home Box Office, 1997.

Brand, C. P., and Lino Pertile. *Cambridge History of Italian Literature*. Cambridge: Cambridge UP, 1997.

Brannigan, John. *New Historicism and Cultural Materialism*. London: Palgrave Macmillan, 1998.

Brantlinger, Patrick. *Crusoe's Footprints: Cultural Studies in Britain and America*. New York: Routledge, 1990.

Brater, Enoch, ed. *Around the Absurd*. Ann Arbor: U of Michigan P, 1990.

Brecht, Bertolt. *Brecht on Art and Politics*. Ed. Tom Kuhn and Steve Giles. London: Methuen, 2003.

————. *Brecht on Theatre: The Development of an Aesthetic*. Ed. and trans. John Willett. London: Methuen, 1964.

Brennan, Timothy. "The Cuts of Language: The East/West of North/South." *Public Culture* 13.1 (Winter 2001): 39–63.

————. *Salman Rushdie and the Third World: Myths of the Nation*. London: Macmillan, 1989.

Brenner, Johanna. *Women and the Politics of Class*. New York: Monthly Review P, 2000.

Brenner, Phillip, et al. *The Cuba Reader: The Making of a Revolutionary Society*. New York: Grove, 1989.

Breton, André. *Manifestoes of Surrealism*. Trans. Richard Seaver and Helen R. Lane. Ann Arbor: U of Michigan P, 1969.

Brett-Jones, Ann. "Ralph Fox: A Man in His Time." *Bulletin of the Marx Memorial Library* 137 (Spring 2003): 27–41.

Brewer, Gay. *Laughing Like Hell: The Harrowing Satires of Jim Thompson*. San Bernadino: Brownstone, 1996.

Briggs, Susan. *The Home Front: War Years in Britain, 1939–45*. London: Weidenfeld and Nicolson, 1975.

Bristol, Michael D. *Carnival and Theater: Plebaian Culture and the Structure of Authority in Renaissance England*. New York: Methuen, 1985.

Britton, Celia. *Edouard Glissant and Postcolonial Theory: Strategies of Language and Resistance*. Charlottesville: U of Virginia P, 1999.

Brockmann, Stephen. *Literature and German Reunification*. Cambridge: Cambridge UP, 1999.

Brodsky, Joseph. "Catastrophes in the Air." *Less Than One: Selected Essays*. New York: Farrar, Straus and Giroux, 1986. 268–303.

———. "On 'September 1, 1939.'" *Less Than Zero*. New York: Farrar, Straus and Giroux, 1986. 304–56.

Bronner, Stephen Eric. *Of Critical Theory and Its Theorists*. Cambridge, MA: Blackwell, 1994.

Brooke, Stephen. "Gender and Working Class Identity in Britain during the 1950s." *Journal of Social History* 34.4 (Summer 2001): 773–95.

Brooker, Jewel Spears, ed. *Conversations with Denise Levertov*. Jackson: UP of Mississippi, 1998.

Brooker, Peter. *Bertolt Brecht: Dialectics, Poetry, Politics*. London: Croom Helm, 1988.

———. *The Well Wrought Urn*. 1947. San Diego: Harcourt Brace Jovanovich, 1975.

Brooks, Cleanth. *William Faulkner: The Yoknapatawpha Country*. New Haven, CT: Yale UP, 1963.

Brooks, Gwendolyn, ed. *A Broadside Treasury*. Detroit: Broadside P, 1971.

Brotherston, Gordon. *The Emergence of the Latin American Novel*. Cambridge: Cambridge UP, 1977.

Brotherstone, Terry, and Paul Dukes. *The Trotsky Reappraisal*. Edinburgh: Edinburgh UP, 1992.

Browder, Laura. *Rousing the Nation: Radical Culture in Depression America*. Amherst: U of Massachusetts P, 1998.

Brower, Keith H., Earl E. Fitz, and Enrique E. Martinez-Vidal, eds. *Jorge Amado: Critical Essays*. New York: Routledge, 2001.

Brown, Clarence. *Mandelstam*. Cambridge: Cambridge UP, 1973.

Brown, Deming. *The Last Years of Soviet Russian Literature: Prose Fiction, 1975–1991*. Cambridge: Cambridge UP, 1993.

Brown, Edward J. *"Brave New World," "1984" and "We": An Essay on Anti-Utopia (Zamyatin and English Literature)*. Ann Arbor: Ardis, 1976.

———. *Mayakovsky: A Poet in the Revolution*. Princeton, NJ: Princeton UP, 1973.

———. *Russian Literature since the Revolution*. London: Collier-Macmillan, 1969.

Brown, Frederick. *Zola: A Life*. New York: Farrar, Straus and Giroux, 1995.

Brown, Jane K. *Goethe's "Faust": The German Tragedy*. Ithaca: Cornell UP, 1986.

Brown, Lloyd L. *The Young Paul Robeson: "On My Journey Now."* Boulder: Westview, 1997.

Brown, Richard. *James Joyce and Sexuality*. Cambridge: Cambridge UP, 1985.

Brown, Sterling. "The New Negro in Literature (1925–1955)." *The Harlem Renaissance,*

1920–1940: Remembering the Harlem Renaissance. Ed. Cary D. Wintz. New York: Garland, 1996. 203–18.

Brown, Stewart. *The Art of Kamau Brathwaite.* Bridgend, Mid Glamorgen, Wales: Seren, 1995.

———, ed. *All Are Involved: The Art of Martin Carter.* Leeds: Peepal Tree, 2000.

Browning, Gary. *Boris Pilniak: Scythian at a Typewriter.* Ann Arbor, MI: Ardis, 1985.

Bryant-Bertail, Sarah. *Space and Time in Epic Theater: The Brechtian Legacy.* Rochester: Camden House, 2000.

———. "Women, Space, Ideology: *Mutter Courage und ihre Kinder.*" *Brecht Yearbook* 12 (1983): 43–61.

Brydon, Diana, ed. *Testing the Limits: Postcolonial Theories and Canadian Literature.* Special issue of *Essays on Canadian Writing* 56 (Fall 1995).

Buchanan, Ian. *Michel de Certeau: Cultural Theorist.* London: Sage, 2000.

Bucher, Irving H. *Isaac Bashevis Singer and the Eternal Past.* New York: New York UP, 1968.

Buck-Morss, Susan. *The Dialectics of Seeing: Walter Benjamin and the Arcades Project.* Cambridge, MA: MIT P, 1989.

Buckner, Noel, Mary Dore, and Sam Sills. *The Good Fight: The Abraham Lincoln Brigade in the Spanish Civil War.* Film distributed by First Run Features and Kino International, New York, 1984.

Buckridge, Pat. "Katharine Susannah Prichard and the Literary Dynamics of Political Commitment." *Gender, Politics and Fiction: Twentieth Century Australian Women's Novels.* Ed. Carole Ferrier. St. Lucia: U of Queensland P, 1986. 85–100.

Buell, Lawrence. *The Environmental Imagination: Thoreau, Nature Writing, and the Formation of American Culture.* Cambridge: Harvard UP, 1995.

Buford, Bill. "Introduction." *Granta* 3 (1980): 7–16.

Buhle, Paul. *Marxism in the USA: Remapping the American Left.* London: Verso, 1987.

———, ed. *C.L.R. James: The Artist as Revolutionary.* London: Verso, 1988.

———, and Dave Wagner. *A Very Dangerous Citizen: Abraham Lincoln Polonsky and the Hollywood Left.* Berkeley: U of California P, 2001.

Buitenhuis, Peter. *The Great War of Words: Literature as Propaganda, 1914–18 and After.* 1987. London: Batsford, 1989.

Bunting, Basil. *The Rise of the South African Reich.* Harmondsworth: Penguin, 1963.

Bürger, Peter. *Theory of the Avant-Garde.* Trans. Michael Shaw. Minneapolis: U of Minnesota P, 1984.

Burkman, Katherine H., ed. *Myth and Ritual in the Plays of Samuel Beckett.* Madison: Fairleigh Dickinson UP, 1987.

———, and John L. Kundert-Gibbs, eds. *Pinter at Sixty.* Bloomington: Indiana UP, 1993.

Burnham, Clint. *The Jamesonian Unconscious: The Aesthetics of Marxist Theory.* Durham: Duke UP, 1995.

Burns, Tony. "Zamyatin's *We* and Postmodernism." *Utopian Studies* 11.1 (2000): 66–90.

Burton, Richard E. D., and Fred Reno, eds. *French and West Indian: Martinique, Guadeloupe, and French Guiana Today.* Charlottesville: U of Virginia P, 1995. 137–66.

Butler, Judith. *Bodies That Matter: On the Discursive Limits of "Sex."* New York: Routledge, 1993.

————. "Contingent Foundations: Feminism and the Question of 'Postmodernism.'" *Feminists Theorize the Political*. Ed. Judith Butler and Joan W. Scott. New York: Routledge, 1992.

————. *Excitable Speech: A Politics of the Performative*. New York: Routledge, 1997.

————. *Gender Trouble: Feminism and the Subversion of Identity*. New York: Routledge, 1990.

————. *Subjects of Desire: Hegelian Reflections in Twentieth-Century France*. New York: Columbia UP, 1987.

————, and Joan W. Scott, eds. *Feminists Theorize the Political*. New York: Routledge, 1992.

————, Slavoj Zizek, and Ernesto Laclau. *Contingency, Hegemony, Universality: Contemporary Dialogues on the Left*. London: Verso, 2000.

Butler, Marilyn. *Jane Austen and the War of Ideas*. 1975. Oxford: Clarendon P, 1987.

Cady, Joseph. "Immersive and Counterimmersive Writing about AIDS: The Achievement of Paul Monette's *Love Alone*." *Writing AIDS: Gay Literature, Language and Analysis*. Ed. Timothy Murphy and Suzanne Poirier. New York: Columbia UP, 1993. 244–64.

Caesar, Adrian Caesar. *Taking It Like a Man: Suffering, Sexuality and the War Poets*. Manchester: Manchester UP, 1993.

Cain, William E. *F. O. Matthiessen and the Politics of Criticism*. Madison: U of Wisconsin P, 1988.

Cainen, Brian. *Study Guide to Tomasi di Lampedusa's* Il gattopardo. Market Harborough, UK: Troubadour, 2003.

Calder, Angus. *The People's War*. London: Cape, 1969.

Calinescu, Matei. *Five Faces of Modernity*. Durham, NC: Duke UP, 1987.

Callaloo 18.3 (1995). Special Issue on Maryse Condé.

Callan, Richard J. *Miguel Angel Asturias*. Boston: Twayne, 1970.

Callinicos, Alex. *Against Postmodernism: A Marxist Critique*. New York: St. Martin's, 1989.

Calvino, Italo. *The Uses of Literature: Essays*. Trans. P. Creagh. New York: Harcourt, 1986.

Campbell, Ian. *Lewis Grassic Gibbon*. Edinburgh: Scottish Academic P, 1985.

Campbell, James. *Talking at the Gates: A Life of James Baldwin*. New York: Penguin, 1991.

Campbell, Robert. *A'laam al-Adab al-Arabi al-Muaasir; Siyar wa Siyar Dhatiyya*. Beirut: Goethe Institute for Oriental Research, 1996.

Campomanes, Oscar V. "Carlos Bulosan." *Encyclopedia of the American Left*. Ed. Mary Jo Buhle et al. Urbana: U of Illinois P, 1992.

Candido, Antonio. *Formação da literatura brasileira*. 2 vols. São Paulo: Martins, 1959.

Canovan, Margaret. *Hannah Arendt: A Reinterpretation of Her Political Thought*. New York: Cambridge UP, 1992.

Cantor, Milton. *Max Eastman*. New York: Twayne, 1970.

Cantwell, Robert. "A Town and Its Novels." *New Republic* 86 (February 1936): 51–52.

Capozzi, Rocco, and Mario Mignone, eds. *Homage to Moravia*. Stony Brook, NY: Forum Italicum, 1993.

Carby, Hazel. "The Politics of Fiction, Anthropology and the Folk: Zora Neale Hurston." *Zora Neale Hurston's "Their Eyes Were Watching God": A Casebook*. New York: Oxford UP, 2000.

Carey-Webb, Allen, and Stephen Benz, eds. *Teaching and Testimony: Rigoberta Menchú and the North American Classroom*. Albany: SUNY P, 1996.

Cargas, Harry James, ed. *Responses to Elie Wiesel*. New York: Persea, 1978.

Carlisle, Rodney. *The Roots of Black Nationalism.* Port Washington, NY: Kennikat, 1975.

Carnes, Mark, ed. *Novel History: Historians and Novelists Confront America's Past.* New York: Simon and Schuster, 2001.

Carpenter, Humphrey. *A Serious Character: The Life of Ezra Pound.* Boston: Houghton Mifflin, 1988.

Carroll, David. *Chinua Achebe: Novelist, Poet, Critic.* 2nd ed. Houndmills, UK: Macmillan, 1990.

Carter, Angela. "Notes from the Front Line." *Shaking a Leg: Collected Writings.* New York: Penguin, 1998. 36–43.

————. *The Sadeian Woman and the Ideology of Pornography.* New York: Harper Colophon Books, 1978.

Carter, Stephen K. *The Political and Social Thought of F. M. Dostoevsky.* New York: Garland, 1991.

Cascardi, Anthony J., ed. *The Cambridge Companion to Cervantes.* Cambridge: Cambridge UP, 2002.

Case, Sue-Ellen. "Developments in Post-Brechtian Political Theater: The Plays of Heiner Müller." Diss. University of California, Berkeley, 1981.

Casey, Janet Galligani. *Dos Passos and the Ideology of the Feminine.* Cambridge: Cambridge UP, 1998.

Cashmore, Ellis, ed. *Encyclopedia of Race and Ethnic Studies.* New York: Routledge, 2004.

Casillo, Robert. "Fascists of the Final Hour: Pound's Italian Cantos." *Fascism, Aesthetics, and Culture.* Ed. Richard J. Golsan. Hanover: UP of New England, 1992. 98–127.

————. *The Genealogy of Demons: Anti-Semitism, Fascism, and the Myths of Ezra Pound.* Evanston, IL: Northwestern UP, 1988.

Cassill, R. V. "The Killer Inside Me: Fear, Purgation, and the Sophoclean Light." *Tough Guy Writers of the Thirties.* Ed. David Madden. Carbondale: Southern Illinois UP, 1968. 230–38.

Castillo, Debra. "Appropriating the Master's Weapons: Luisa Valenzuela." *Talking Back: Toward a Latin American Feminist Literary Criticism.* Ithaca: Cornell UP, 1992.

Cate, Curtis. *André Malraux: A Biography.* London: Hutchinson, 1995.

Caudwell, Christopher. *Scenes and Actions: Unpublished Manuscripts.* Ed. and introduction, Jean Duparc and David Margolies. New York: Routledge and Kegan Paul, 1986.

Caulfield, Max. *The Easter Rebellion, Dublin 1916.* Dublin: Robert Rinehart, 1963.

Caute, David. *Frantz Fanon.* New York: Viking, 1970.

Cavanagh, Clare. *Osip Mandelstam and the Creation of Modernist Tradition.* Princeton, NJ: Princeton UP, 1995.

Cavell, Richard. *McLuhan in Space: A Cultural Geography.* Toronto: U Toronto P, 2002.

Cazamian, Louis. *The Social Novel in England, 1830–1850.* 1903. Trans. Martin Fido, London: Routledge, 1973.

Ceplair, Larry, and Steven Englund. *The Inquisition in Hollywood.* Berkeley: U of California P, 1983.

Césaire, Aimé. *Discourse on Colonialism.* Trans. Joan Pinkham. New York: Monthly Review P, 1972.

Cesarani, David. *Arthur Koestler: The Homeless Mind.* New York: Free P, 1998.

Cham, Mbye Baboucar. "Ousmane Sembène and the Aesthetics of African Oral Traditions." *African Journal* 13 (1982): 24–40.

Chamberlain, Bobby J. *Jorge Amado*. Boston: Twayne, 1990.

Chandramohan, Balasubramanyam. *A Study in Trans-Ethnicity in Modern Africa: The Writings of Alex La Guma*. Lampeter: Mellen Research UP, 1992.

Chang-Rodríguez, Eugenio. *Poética e ideología en José Carlos Mariátegui*. Madred: José Porrúa Turanzas, 1983.

Chaple, Sergio. *Estudios de narrative cubana*. Havana: Ediciones Unión, 1996.

Chapman, Michael. *Southern African Literatures*. London: Longman, 1997.

Charlton, John. *The Chartists: The First National Workers' Movement*. London: Pluto, 1997.

Chartier, Roger. *The Cultural Origins of the French Revolution*. Durham, NC: Duke UP, 1991.

Chatterjee, Bhabatosh. *Rabindranath Tagore and Modern Sensibility*. Delhi: Oxford UP, 1996.

Chen Yu-Shih. *Realism and Allegory in the Early Fiction of Mao Dun*. Bloomington: Indiana UP, 1986.

Cheng, Vincent. *Joyce, Race, and Empire*. Cambridge: Cambridge UP, 1995.

Chernyshevsky, N. G. *Selected Philosophical Essays*. Moscow: Foreign Languages Publishing House, 1953.

Chilton, Paul, and Crispin Aubrey, eds. *"Nineteen Eighty-Four" in 1984: Autonomy, Control and Communication*. London: Comedia, 1983.

Chin, Frank. "Come All Ye Asian American Writers of the Real and Fake." *The Big Aiiieeeee! An Anthology of Chinese American and Japanese American Literature*. Ed. Frank Chin et al. New York: Penguin, 1991.

———, Jeffery Paul Chan, Lawson Fusao Inada, and Shawn Hsu Wong, eds. *Aiiieeeee! An Anthology of Asian-American Writers*. Washington, DC: Howard UP, 1974.

Chisholm, Anne. *Nancy Cunard: A Biography*. New York: Alfred Knopf, 1979.

Chiwengo, Ngwarsungu. "Gazing through the Screen: Richard Wright's Africa." *Richard Wright's Travel Writings: New Reflections*. Ed. Virginia Whatley Smith. Jackson: UP of Mississippi, 2001.

Choudhury, Bidulata. *Women and Society in the Novels of Anita Desai*. New Delhi: Creative Books, 1995.

Christian, Karen. *Show and Tell: Identity as Performance in U.S. Latina/o Fiction*. Albuquerque: U of New Mexico P, 1997.

Chung, Hilary, et al., eds. *In the Party Spirit: Socialist Realism and Literary Practice in the Soviet Union, East Germany and China*. Atlanta: Rodopi, 1996.

Cicioni, Mirna. *Primo Levi: Bridges of Knowledge*. Oxford: Berg, 1995.

Cioran, Samuel. *The Apocalyptic Symbolism of Andrej Belyj*. The Hague: Mouton, 1973.

Claeys, Gregory, and Lyman Tower Sargent, eds. *The Utopia Reader*. New York: New York UP, 1999.

Clark, John, Charles Critcher, and Richard Johnson, eds. *Working Class Culture: Studies in History and Theory*. London: Hutchinson, 1979.

Clark, Jon, et al. *Culture and Crisis in Britain in the Thirties*. London: Lawrence and Wishart, 1979.

Clark, Katerina. *The Soviet Novel: History as Ritual*. Chicago: U of Chicago P, 1985.

———, and Michael Holquist. *Mikhail Bakhtin*. Cambridge, MA: Harvard UP, 1984.

Clayton, John Jacob. *Saul Bellow: In Defense of Man*. Bloomington: Indiana UP, 1968.

Clements, Barbara Evans. *Bolshevik Feminist: The Life of Aleksandra Kollontai*. Bloomington: Indiana UP, 1979.

Clemit, Pamela. *The Godwinian Novel: The Rational Fiction of Godwin, Brockden Brown, Mary Shelley.* Oxford: Oxford UP, 1993.

Clingman, Stephen. *The Novels of Nadine Gordimer: History from the Inside.* 2nd ed. Amherst: U of Massachusetts P, 1992.

Clum, John M. "'The Time Before the War': AIDS, Memory, and Desire." *American Literature* 62.2 (1990): 648–67.

Clute, John, and Peter Nicholls, eds. *The Encyclopedia of Science Fiction.* 2nd ed. New York: St. Martin's, 1995.

Cmiel, Kenneth. "Whitman the Democrat." *A Historical Guide to Walt Whitman.* Ed. David S. Reynolds. New York: Oxford UP, 2000. 205–33.

Coalition for the Academic Workforce. *Who Is Teaching in U.S. College Classrooms? A Collaborative Study of Undergraduate Faculty, Fall 1999.* American Historical Association Website. 21 March 2003 (http://www.theaha.org/caw).

Cobb, Martha. *Harlem, Haiti and Havana: A Comparative Critical Study of Langston Hughes, Jacques Roumain and Nicolás Guillén.* Washington, DC: Three Continents P, 1979.

Cobban, Alfred. *The Social Interpretation of the French Revolution.* Cambridge: Cambridge UP, 1964.

Coetzee, A. J., Tim Couzens, and Stephen Gray. "South African Literatures to World War II." *European-Language Writing in Sub-Saharan Africa.* Vol. 1. Ed. Albert Gerard. Budapest: Akadēmiai Kaidō, 1986. 173–213.

Coetzee, A. J., and Michael Wade. "White South African Literature after World War II." *European-Language Writing in Sub-Saharan Africa.* Vol. 1. Ed. Albert Gerard. Budapest: Akadēmiai Kaidō. 1986. 217–50.

Cohen, Joseph. "The Three Roles of Siegfried Sassoon." *Tulane Studies in English* 7 (1957): 169–85.

Cohen, Mitchell. *The Wager of Lucien Goldmann.* Princeton, NJ: Princeton UP, 1994.

Cohen, Robert. "The Political Aesthetics of Holocaust Literature: Peter Weiss's 'The Investigation' and Its Critics." *History and Memory* 10.2 (1998): 43–67.

————. *Understanding Peter Weiss.* Trans. Martha Humphreys. Columbia: U of South Carolina P, 1993.

Cohen, Susan D. *Women and Discourse in the Fiction of Marguerite Duras: Love, Legends, Language.* Oxford: Macmillan, 1993.

Cohen, Tom, ed. *Jacques Derrida and the Humanities: A Critical Reader.* Cambridge: Cambridge UP, 2001.

Cohen-Solal, Anne, and Henriette Nizan. *Paul Nizan, Communist Impossible.* Paris: Grasset, 1980.

Cohn, Ruby. "Sarah Kane: Architect of the Theater." *Cycnos* 18.1 (2001): 39–49.

Coiner, Constance. *Better Red: The Writing and Resistance of Tillie Olsen and Meridel LeSueur.* New York: Oxford UP, 1995.

Coleman, Stephen, and Paddy O'Sullivan, eds. *William Morris and "News from Nowhere": A Vision for Our Time.* Bideford, UK: Green Books, 1990.

Collins, Jim. *Uncommon Cultures: Popular Culture and Post-Modernism.* New York: Routledge, 1989.

Colmer, John. *Coleridge: Critic of Society.* Oxford: Clarendon P, 1959.

Condé, Maryse. "*Créolité* without Creole Language?" *Caribbean Creolization: Reflections on the Cultural Dynamics of Language, Literature and Identity*. Ed. Kathleen Balutansky and Marie-Agnès Sourieau. Gainesville: UP of Florida, 1998.

————, and Madeleine Cottenet-Hage, eds. *Penser la créolité*. Paris: Karthala, 1995.

Conn, Peter. *Literature in America*. Cambridge: Cambridge UP, 1989.

Connor, Steven. *Postmodernist Culture: An Introduction to Theories of the Contemporary*. 2nd ed. Oxford: Blackwell, 1997.

Connors, Robert. "Rhetoric in the Modern University: The Creation of an Underclass." *The Politics of Writing Instruction: Postsecondary*. Ed. Richard Bullock and John Trimbur. Portsmouth, NH: Boynton/Cook, 1991. 55–84.

Conroy, Jack. *The Disinherited*. 1933. Columbia: U of Missouri P, 1991.

Constantine, Stephen. "*Love on the Dole* and Its Reception in the 1930s." *Literature and History* 8.2 (1982): 232–47.

Conway, Christopher. "Of Subjects and Cowboys: Frontier and History in Pedro Mir's 'Countersong to Walt Whitman.'" *Walt Whitman Quarterly Review* 15.4 (Spring 1998): 161–71.

Coogan, Tim Pat. *1916: The Easter Rising*. Cassell: London, 2001.

Cook, Sylvia Jenkins. *From Tobacco Road to Route 66: The Southern Poor White in Fiction*. Chapel Hill: U North Carolina P, 1976.

————. "Gastonia: The Literary Reverberations of the Strike." *Southern Literary Journal* 7.1 (1974): 49–66.

Cooke, Brett. *Human Nature in Dystopia: Zamyatin's "We."* Evanston, IL: Northwestern UP, 2002.

Cooke, John. *The Novels of Nadine Gordimer: Private Lives/Public Landscapes*. Baton Rouge: Louisiana State UP, 1985.

Cooke, Paul, and Andrew Plowman, eds. *German Writers and the Politics of Culture: Dealing with the Stasi*. Basingstoke: Palgrave, 2003.

Cooney, Terry A. *The Rise of the New York Intellectuals: "Partisan Review" and Its Circle*. Madison: U of Wisconsin P, 1986.

Cooper, Stephen. *The Politics of Ernest Hemingway*. Ann Arbor, MI: UMI Research, 1987.

Cooper, Wayne F. *Claude McKay: Rebel Sojourner in the Harlem Renaissance*. Baton Rouge: Louisiana UP, 1987.

————, ed. *The Passion of Claude McKay*. New York: Schocken Books, 1973.

Cordell, Dennis D. "Ousmane Sembène's *God's Bits of Wood*." *African Novels in the Classroom*. Ed. Margaret Jean Hay. Boulder, CO: Lynne Rienner, 2000.

Cordones-Cook, Juana María. *Poética de transgression en la novelística de Luisa Valenzuela*. New York: Peter Lang, 1991.

————, ed. Special issue of *Letras Femeninas* 27.1 (Spring 2001).

Cornejo Polar, Antonio. *Escribir en el aire*. Lima: Horizonte, 1994.

Cornevin, Robert. *Littératures d'Afrique noire de langue française*. Paris: PU de France, 1976.

Cornwell, Neil, ed. *The Gothic-Fantastic in Nineteenth-Century Russian Literature*. Amsterdam: Rodopi, 1999.

————. *Reference Guide to Russian Literature*. Chicago: Fitzroy Dearborn, 1998.

————. *The Routledge Companion to Russian Literature*. London: Routledge, 2001.

————. *The Society Tale in Russian Literature: From Odoevskii to Tolstoi*. Amsterdam: Rodopi, 1998.

Cortiel, Jeanne. *Demand My Writing: Joanna Russ/Feminism/Science Fiction*. Liverpool: Liverpool UP, 1999.

Cousin, Geraldine. *Churchill: The Playwright*. London: Methuen, 1989.

Coutinho, Afranio. *A literatura no Brasil*. 2nd ed. 6 vols. Rio de Janeiro: Editorial Sul Americana, 1968–1971.

Cowasjee, Saros. *Studies in Indian and Anglo-Indian Fiction*. New Delhi: HarperCollins, 1993.

Cox, Jeffrey N., and Larry J. Reynolds, eds. *New Historical Literary Study: Essays on Reproducing Texts, Representing History*. Princeton, NJ: Princeton UP, 1993.

Craig, Cairns, ed. *The History of Scottish Literature*. 4 vols. Aberdeen: Aberdeen UP, 1986–1987.

Craig, David. *Marxists on Literature: An Anthology*. Harmondsworth: Penguin, 1975.

Craig, Terrence. *Racial Attitudes in English-Canadian Fiction, 1905–1980*. Waterloo, ON: Wilfrid Laurier UP, 1987.

Creelman, David. *Setting in the East: Maritime Realist Fiction*. Montréal: McGill-Queen's UP, 2003.

Crick, Bernard. *George Orwell: A Life*. Boston: Little Brown, 1980.

Croft, Andy. *Comrade Heart: A Life of Randall Swingler*. Manchester: Manchester UP, 2003.

————. *Red Letter Days: British Fiction in the 1930s*. London: Lawrence and Wishart, 1990.

————, ed. *A Weapon in the Struggle: The Cultural History of the Communist Party in Britain*. London: Pluto, 1998.

Cronin, Richard. *The Politics of Romantic Poetry: In Search of the Pure Commonwealth*. London: Palgrave Macmillan, 2000.

Crowley, Martin. *Duras, Writing and the Ethical: Making the Broken Whole*. Oxford: Clarendon P, 2000.

Cruz, Anne J., and Carroll B. Johnson, eds. *Cervantes and His Postmodern Constituencies*. Hispanic Issues, vol. 17. New York: Garland, 1999.

Cryle, Peter M. *Thematics of Commitment: The Tower and the Plain*. Princeton, NJ: Princeton UP, 1984.

Cuddihy, Michael, ed. *Czesław Miłosz: A Special Issue. Ironwood* 18. Tucson, AZ: Ironwood, 1981.

Cudjoe, Selwyn. *V. S. Naipaul: A Materialist Reading*. Amherst: U of Massachusetts P, 1988.

————, and William E. Cain, eds. *C.L.R. James: His Intellectual Legacies*. Amherst: U of Massachusetts P, 1995.

Culler, Jonathan. *Flaubert: The Uses of Uncertainty*. Ithaca, NY: Cornell UP, 1974.

————. *On Deconstruction: Theory and Criticism after Structuralism*. London: Routledge, 1983.

Cullingford, Elizabeth Butler. *Yeats, Ireland and Fascism*. London: Macmillan, 1981.

Cunard, Nancy, ed. *Negro: An Anthology*. 1934. New York: Continuum, 1996.

Cundy, Catherine. *Salman Rushdie*. Manchester: Manchester UP, 1996.

Cunningham, Charles. "Rethinking the Politics of *The Grapes of Wrath*." *Cultural Logic* 5 (2002). http://eserver.org/clogic/2002/cunningham.html.

Curran, Stewart, ed. *The Cambridge Companion to British Romanticism*. Cambridge: Cambridge UP, 1993.

Currie, Barbara. "Diverging Attitudes in Literary Criticism: The 'Plenzdorf Debate' in the Early 1970s in East and West Germany." *Neophilologus* 79.2 (April 1995): 283–94.

Curtis, J.A.E. *Bulgakov's Last Decade: The Writer as Hero*. New York: Cambridge UP, 1987.

Czigány, Lóránt. *The Oxford History of Hungarian Literature: From the Earliest Times to the Present*. Oxford: Oxford UP, 1986.

Dabydeen, David, and Nan Wilson-Tagoe. *A Reader's Guide to West Indian and Black British Literature.* Rev. ed. London: Hansib, 1997.

Daly, Catherine, et al. "Readings: Lola Ridge." *How2* 1.7 (Fall 2002). http://www.scc.rutgers. edu/however/v1_8_2002/current/index.shtm.

Daniel, Cletus E. *Bitter Harvest: A History of California Farmworkers, 1870–1941.* Ithaca: Cornell UP, 1981.

Daniel, Jamie Owen, and Tom Moylan, eds. *Not Yet: Reconsidering Ernst Bloch.* London: Verso, 1997.

Dash, J. Michael. *Edouard Glissant.* New York: Cambridge UP, 1995.

————. *Haiti and the United States: National Stereotypes and the Literary Imagination.* 2nd ed. New York: St. Martin's, 1997.

————. *Literature and Ideology in Haiti, 1915–61.* London: Macmillan, 1981.

————. *The Other America: Caribbean Literature in a New World.* Charlottesville: UP of Virginia, 1998.

Da Silva, A. J. Simoes. *The Luxury of Nationalist Despair: George Lamming's Fiction as Decolonizing Project.* Atlanta, GA: Rodopi, 2000.

Davenport-Hines, Richard. *Gothic: Four Hundred Years of Excess, Horror, Evil and Ruin.* New York: North Point, 1998.

Davey, Frank. *Canadian Literary Power.* Edmonton: NeWest P, 1994.

Davidson, Basil. *Black Star: A View of the Life and Times of Kwame Nkrumah.* London: Allen Lane, 1973.

Davies, Carole Boyce, and Elaine Savory Fido. *Out of the Kumbla: Caribbean Women and Literature.* Trenton, NJ: Africa World P, 1990.

Davies, Ioan. *Writers in Prison.* Oxford: Basil Blackwell, 1990.

Davis, Charles T., and Henry Louis Gates Jr. *The Slave's Narrative.* Oxford: Oxford UP, 1985.

Davis, Geoffrey V. *Voices of Justice and Reason: Apartheid and Beyond in South African Literature.* Amsterdam: Rodopi, 2003.

Davis, Jack. *A Boy's Life.* Broome, Western Australia: Magabala Books, 1991.

Davis, Lennard. *Factual Fictions: The Origins of the English Novel.* New York: Columbia UP, 1983.

Dawahare, Anthony. *Nationalism, Marxism, and African American Literature between the Wars: A New Pandora's Box.* Jackson: UP of Mississippi, 2003.

————. "'That Joyous Certainty': History and Utopia in Tillie Olsen's Depression-Era Literature." *Twentieth Century Literature* 44.3 (Fall 1998): 261–75.

Dawes, Greg. *Aesthetics and Revolution: Nicaraguan Poetry, 1979–90.* Minneapolis: U of Minnesota P, 1993.

Day, Aidan. *Romanticism.* London: Routledge, 1996.

Day Lewis, Sean. *C. Day Lewis: An English Literary Life.* London: Weidenfeld and Nicolson, 1980.

Dean, Misao. *Practising Femininity: Domestic Realism and the Performance of Gender in Early Canadian Fiction.* Toronto: U of Toronto P, 1998.

Deane, Seamus. *A Short History of Irish Literature.* London: Hutchinson, 1986.

————. "Yeats and the Idea of Revolution." *Yeats's Political Identities.* Ed. Jonathan Allison. Ann Arbor: U of Michigan P, 1995. 133–44.

Dearborn, Mary V. *Love in the Promised Land: The Story of Anzia Yezierska and John Dewey.* New York: Free P, 1988.

_____. *Mailer: A Biography*. Boston: Houghton Mifflin, 1999.

Debord, Guy. *Comments on the Society of the Spectacle*. Trans. Malcolm Imrie. London: Verso, 1990.

_____. *Panegyric*. Trans. James Brook. London: Verso, 1991.

_____. *The Society of the Spectacle*. Trans. Donald Nicholson-Smith. New York: Zone Books, 1994.

De Costa, René. *The Poetry of Pablo Neruda*. Cambridge: Harvard UP, 1979.

Deery, Jane. *Aldous Huxley and the Mysticism of Science*. New York: St. Martin's, 1996.

DeLamotte, Eugenia. *Perils of the Night: A Feminist Study of Nineteenth-Century Gothic*. New York: Oxford UP, 1989.

Delany, Samuel R. *Jewel-Hinged Jaw: Notes on the Language of Science Fiction*. New York: Berkley, 1977.

_____. *The Motion of Light in Water*. 1988. New York: Kasak, 1993.

_____. "Racism and Science Fiction." *Dark Matter: A Century of Speculative Fiction from the African Diaspora*. Ed. Sheree R. Thomas. New York: Warner Books, 2000.

_____. *Silent Interviews: On Language, Race, Sex, Science Fiction, and Some Comics*. Hanover, NH: Wesleyan UP, 1994.

_____. *Starboard Wine: More Notes on the Language of Science Fiction*. Pleasantville, NY: Dragon P, 1984.

_____. *Times Square Red, Times Square Blue*. New York: New York UP, 1999.

Deloria, Vine, Jr. *Spirit and Reason: The Vine Deloria, Jr. Reader*. Golden, CO: Fulcrum, 1999.

Denning, Michael. *The Cultural Front: The Laboring of American Culture in the Twentieth Century*. New York: Verso, 1996.

_____. *Culture in the Age of Three Worlds*. London: Verso, 2004.

Depestre, René. *Bonjour et adieu à la Négritude*. Paris: Seghers, 1980.

De Santis, Christopher. *Langston Hughes and the Chicago Defender: Essays on Race, Politics, and Culture, 1942–62*. Chicago: U of Illinois P, 1995.

Deutscher, Isaac. *The Prophet Armed: Trotsky, 1879–1921*. New York: Oxford UP, 1954.

_____. *The Prophet Disarmed: Trotsky, 1921–1929*. New York: Oxford UP, 1959.

_____. *The Prophet Exiled: Trotsky, 1929–1940*. New York: Oxford UP, 1963.

De Veaux, Alexis. *Warrior Poet: A Biography of Audre Lorde*. New York: W. W. Norton, 2004.

De Vera, Arleen. "Without Parallel: The Local 7 Deportation Cases, 1949–1955." *Amerasia Journal* 20.2 (1994): 1–25.

Dhawan, R. K. *The Novels of Amitav Ghosh*. New Delhi: Prestige Books, 1999.

_____, ed. *The Novels of Mulk Raj Anand*. New Delhi: Prestige, 1992.

Díaz, Gwendolyn, ed. *Luisa Valenzuela sin máscara*. Buenos Aires: Feminista, 2002.

Dick, Bernard F. *Hellman in Hollywood*. Rutherford, NJ: Fairleigh Dickinson UP, 1982.

Dickson, Keith A. *Towards Utopia: A Study of Brecht*. Oxford: Clarendon P, 1978.

Dickstein, Morris. "Hallucinating the Past: *Jews without Money* Revisited." *Grand Street* 9.2 (Winter 1989): 155–68.

Diemert, Brian. *Graham Greene's Thrillers and the 1930's*. Montreal: McGill-Queen's UP, 1996.

Diggins, John Patrick. *The Rise and Fall of the American Left*. New York: Norton, 1992.

Dimock, Edward, et al., eds. *The Literatures of India: An Introduction*. Chicago: U of Chicago P, 1974.

Dinega, Alyssa W. "Bearing the Standard: Transformative Ritual in Gorky's *Mother* and the Legacy of Tolstoy." *Slavic and East European Journal* 42.1 (1998): 76–101.

Dirlik, Arif. *The Postcolonial Aura: Third World Criticism in the Age of Global Capitalism.* Boulder, CO: Westview P, 1997.

———, Paul Healy, and Nick Knight, eds. *Critical Perspectives on Mao Zedong's Thought.* Atlantic Highlands, NJ: Humanities P, 1997.

Disch, Thomas. *The Dreams Our Stuff Is Made Of: How Science Fiction Conquered the World.* New York: Simon and Schuster, 1998.

Djwa, Sandra. *The Politics of the Imagination: A Life of F. R. Scott.* Toronto: McClelland and Stewart, 1987.

Dobrenko, Evgeny. *The Making of the State Reader: Social and Aesthetic Contexts of the Reception of Soviet Literature.* Trans. Jesse M. Savage. Stanford, CA: Stanford UP, 1997.

———. *The Making of the State Writer: Social and Aesthetic Origins of Soviet Literary Culture.* Trans. Jesse M. Savage. Stanford, CA: Stanford UP, 2002.

———. *Metafora vlasti: Literatura stalinskoi epokhi v istoricheskom osveshchenii.* Munich: Otto Sagner, 1993.

Doctorow, E. L. *Reporting the Universe.* Cambridge, MA: Harvard UP, 2003.

Dollimore, Jonathan, and Alan Sinfield, eds. *Political Shakespeare.* Ithaca: Cornell UP, 1985.

Dolman, Everett Carl. "Military, Democracy, and the State in Robert A. Heinlein's *Starship Troopers*." *Political Science Fiction.* Ed. Donald M. Hassler and Clyde Wilcox. Columbia: U of South Carolina P, 1997. 196–213.

Domínguez, Jorge. *Cuba: Order and Revolution.* Cambridge, MA: Belknap P, 1978.

Donohue, H. E. *Conversations with Nelson Algren.* New York: Hill and Wang, 1964.

Doody, Margaret Anne. *The True Story of the Novel.* New Brunswick, NJ: Rutgers UP, 1996.

Dosse, François. *Michel de Certeau: le marcheur blessé.* Paris: La Découverte, 2002.

Dotti, Ugo. *Storia degli intellettuali in Italia.* 3 vols. Rome: Editori Riuniti, 1997, 1998, 1999.

Douglas, Ann. "The Failure of the New York Intellectuals." *Raritan* (Spring 1998): 1–23.

———. *The Feminization of American Culture.* New York: Knopf, 1977.

———. Introduction to *Studs Lonigan: A Trilogy* by James T. Farrell. New York: Penguin, 2001.

Dove, Richard. *A Biography of Ernst Toller: He Was a German.* London: Libris, 1990.

Dowell, Richard. Introduction to *An Amateur Laborer* by Theodore Dreiser. Ed. Richard W. Dowell, James L. W. West III, and Neda Westlake. Philadelphia; U of Pennsylvania P, 1984.

Dowling, William C. *Jameson, Althusser, Marx: An Introduction to the Political Unconscious.* Ithaca: Cornell UP, 1984.

Downs, Brian W. *Ibsen: The Intellectual Background.* New York: Octagon, 1969.

Drake, William. *The First Wave: Women Poets in America, 1915–1945.* New York: Macmillan, 1987.

Draper, Theodore. *American Communism and Soviet Russia.* New York: Viking, 1960.

———. "Gastonia Revisited." *Social Research* 38 (1971): 3–29.

———. *Roots of American Communism.* New York: Viking, 1957.

Drees, Hajo. *A Comprehensive Interpretation of the Life and Work of Christa Wolf, 20th-Century German Writer.* Lewiston, Queenston: Lampeter, 2002.

Dreiser, Theodore. *Dreiser's Russian Diary.* Ed. T. P. Riggio and James L. W. West III. Philadelphia: U of Pennsylvania P, 1996.

_____. *Newspaper Days*. Ed. T. D. Nostwich. Philadelphia: U of Pennsylvania P, 1992.

Drew, Bettina. *Nelson Algren*. Austin: U of Texas P, 1989.

Drinnon, Richard. *Rebel in Paradise: A Biography of Emma Goldman*. Chicago: U of Chicago P, 1961.

Drozd, Andrew M. *Chernyshevskii's "What Is to Be Done?" A Reevaluation*. Evanston, IL: Northwestern UP, 2001.

D'Souza, Dinesh. *Illiberal Education: The Politics of Race and Sex on Campus*. New York: Free P, 1991.

Dubofsky, Melvyn. *We Shall Be All: A History of the Industrial Workers of the World*. Ed. Joseph Anthony McCartin. Updated ed. Urbana: U of Illinois P, 1988.

Du Bois, W.E.B. "The Color Line Belts the World." *Collier's Weekly*, 20 October 1906.

_____. *The Souls of Black Folk: Essays and Sketches*. 1903. London: Penguin, 1996.

_____. *The World and Africa*. New York: International Publishers, 1946.

Dubson, Michael, ed. *Ghosts in the Classroom: Stories of College Adjunct Faculty—and the Price We All Pay*. Boston: Camel's Back Books, 2001.

Duchatelet, B. *Romain Rolland tel qu'en lui-même*. Paris: Albin Michel, 2002.

Dudley, Edward. *The Endless Text: "Don Quixote" and the Hermeneutics of Romance*. Albany: SUNY P, 1997.

Duff, David. *Romance and Revolution: Shelley and the Politics of a Genre*. Cambridge: Cambridge UP, 1994.

Duke, David C. *John Reed*. Boston: Twayne, 1987.

Dunaway, David King. *Huxley in Hollywood*. New York: Harper and Row, 1989.

Dunham, Vera S. *In Stalin's Time: Middleclass Values in Soviet Fiction*. Enlarged and updated ed. Durham, NC: Duke UP, 1990.

Dunlop, John B., Richard Haugh, and Alexis Klimoff, eds. *Aleksandr Solzhenitsyn: Critical Essays and Documentary Materials*. 2nd ed. New York: Collier, 1975.

Dunlop, John B., Richard Haugh, and Michael Nicholson, eds. *Solzhenitsyn in Exile: Critical Essays and Documentary Materials*. Stanford: Hoover Institution P, 1985.

Durán, Javier. *José Revueltas: una poética de la disidencia*. Xalapa: Universidad Veracruzana, 2002.

Durfee, Thea Margaret. "*Cement* and *How the Steel Was Tempered*: Variations on the New Soviet Woman." *A Plot of Her Own: The Female Protagonist in Russian Literature*. Ed. Sona Stephan Hoisington. Evanston, IL: Northwestern UP, 1995. 89–101.

During, Simon, ed. *The Cultural Studies Reader*. London: Routledge, 1993.

Dutt, Krishna, and Andrew Robinson. *Rabindranath Tagore: The Myriad-Minded Man*. New York: St. Martin's, 1996.

Dutt, R. Palme. *The Internationale*. London: Lawrence and Wishart, 1964.

Duvenage, Pieter. *Habermas and Aesthetics: The Limits of Communicative Reason*. London: Polity P, 2003.

Dworkin, Dennis. *Cultural Marxism in Postwar Britain: History, the New Left and the Origins of Cultural Studies*. Durham, NC: Duke UP, 1997.

_____, and Leslie G. Roman, eds. *Views beyond the Border Country: Raymond Williams and Cultural Politics*. London: Routledge, 1993.

Dyer, Geoff. *Ways of Telling: The Work of John Berger*. London: Pluto, 1986.

Dyment, Clifford. *C. Day Lewis*. London: Longmans, Green, 1955.

Eagleton, Mary. *Feminist Literary Theory: A Reader*. 2nd ed. Cambridge, MA: Blackwell, 1996.

Eagleton, Terry. *After Theory*. New York: Basic Books, 2003.

————. *Against the Grain: Selected Essays*. London: Verso, 1986.

————. *Criticism and Ideology: A Study in Marxist Literary Theory*. London: NLB, 1976.

————. *Exiles and Emigres: Studies in Modern Literature*. New York: Schocken, 1970.

————. *Figures of Dissent: Critical Essays on Fish, Spivak, Zizek and Others*. London: Verso, 2003.

————. *The Function of Criticism: From the Spectator to Post-Structuralism*. London: Verso, 1984.

————. *The Idea of Culture*. Oxford: Blackwell, 2000.

————. *Ideology: An Introduction*. London: Verso, 1991.

————. *The Ideology of the Aesthetic*. Oxford: Blackwell, 1990.

————. *The Illusions of Postmodernism*. Oxford: Blackwell, 1996.

————. *Literary Theory: An Introduction*. 1983. 2nd ed. Minneapolis: U of Minnesota P, 1996.

————. *Marxism and Literary Criticism*. London: Routledge, 2002.

————. "Nature and Violence: The Prefaces of Edward Bond." *Critical Quarterly* 26.1–2 (1984): 127–35.

————. *The Significance of Theory*. Oxford: Blackwell, 1989.

————. *Walter Benjamin; or, Towards a Revolutionary Criticism*. London: Verso, 1981.

————, ed. *Raymond Williams: Critical Perspectives*. Boston: Northeastern UP, 1989.

Eagleton, Terry, and Drew Milne, eds. *Marxist Literary Theory: A Reader*. Oxford: Blackwell, 1996.

Easson, Angus. *Elizabeth Gaskell*. London: Routledge, 1979.

Eastman, Max. *Artists in Uniform: A Study of Literature and Bureaucratism*. New York: Alfred A. Knopf, 1934.

Ebert, Teresa L. "Left of Desire." *Cultural Logic* 3.1 (Fall 1999–Spring 2000), http://eserver. org/clogic/3-1%262/ebert.html.

————. *Ludic Feminism and After*. Ann Arbor: U of Michigan P, 1996.

Ecksteins, Modris. *Rites of Spring: The Great War and the Birth of the Modern Age*. Boston: Houghton Mifflin, 1989.

Edwards, Paul. *Wyndham Lewis: Painter and Writer*. New Haven and London: Yale UP, 2000.

Edwards, Thomas R. *Imagination and Power: A Study of Poetry on Public Themes*. London: Chatto and Windus, 1971.

Ehrenpreis, Irvin. *Swift: The Man, His Works, and the Age*. 3 vols. London: Methuen, 1962–1983.

Ehrlich, Robert. *Norman Mailer: The Radical as Hipster*. Metuchen, NJ: Scarecrow P, 1978.

Eisner, Douglas. "Liberating Narrative: AIDS and the Limits of Melodrama in Monette and Weir." *College Literature* 24.1 (1997): 213–26.

Eke, Norbert Otto. *Heiner Müller: Apokalypse und Utopie*. Paderborn: Ferdinand Schöningh, 1989.

Ekwe-Ekwe, Herbert. *The Biafra War: Nigeria and the Aftermath*. Lewiston, NY: Mellen, 1990.

Eliot, Gregory. *Perry Anderson: The Merciless Laboratory of History*. Minneapolis: U of Minnesota P, 1999.

Eliot, T. S. *Notes Towards the Definition of Culture*. New York: Harcourt, Brace and Company, 1949.

Elistratova, Anne. "Jack Conroy: American Worker-Writer." *International Literature* 1 (May 1934): 112–18.

Elliott, Robert C. *The Shape of Utopia*. Chicago: Chicago UP, 1970.

Ellis, Keith. *Critical Approaches to Rubén Darío*. Toronto: U of Toronto P, 1974.

————. *Cuba's Nicolás Guillén: Poetry and Ideology*. Toronto: U of Toronto P, 1985.

Ellison, Fred P. *Brazil's New Novel: Four Northeastern Masters; José Lins do Rego, Jorge Amado, Graciliano Ramos, Rachel de Queiroz*. Berkeley: U of California P, 1954.

Ellmann, Mary. *Thinking about Women*. London: Virago, 1979.

Ellmann, Richard. *The Consciousness of Joyce*. Oxford: Oxford UP, 1977.

Elsie, Robert. *History of Albanian Literature*. New York: Columbia UP, 1995.

Emmel, Hildegard. *History of the German Novel*. Trans. Ellen Summerfield. Detroit: Wayne State UP, 1984.

Engels, Friedrich. *The Origin of the Family, Private Property, and the State*. 1884. New York: International Publishers, 1972.

Ensor, Robert. *The Novels of Peter Abrahams and the Rise of Nationalism in Africa*. Essen: Verlag Die Blaue Eule, 1992.

Epps, Brad. *Significant Violence: Oppression and Resistance in the Narratives of Juan Goytisolo, 1970–1990*. Oxford: Oxford UP, 1996.

Ericson, Edward E., Jr. *Solzhenitsyn and the Modern World*. Washington: Regnery Gateway, 1993.

Erisman, Fred. "Robert A. Heinlein's Primers of Politics." *Extrapolation* 38.2 (Summer 1997): 94–101.

Erlich, Victor. *Gogol*. New Haven, CT: Yale UP, 1969.

————. *Modernism and Revolution: Russian Literature in Transition*. Cambridge, MA: Harvard UP, 1994.

Ermath, Elizabeth Deeds. *The English Novel in History, 1840–1895*. London: Routledge, 1997.

Ermolaev, Herman. *Mikhail Sholokhov and His Art*. Princeton, NJ: Princeton UP, 1982.

————. *Soviet Literary Theories, 1917–1934: The Genesis of Socialist Realism*. Berkeley: U of California P, 1963.

Escalante, Evodio. *José Revueltas: una literatura del "lado moridor."* Mexico: Era, 1979.

Esslin, Martin. *Pinter: The Playwright*. 5th ed. London: Methuen, 1992.

————. *The Theatre of the Absurd*. 3rd ed. New York: Vintage-Random House, 2004.

Estrin, Mark W. *Lillian Hellman: Plays, Films, Memoirs: A Reference Guide*. Boston: G. K. Hall, 1980.

Esty, Jed. *A Shrinking Island: Modernism and National Culture in England*. Princeton, NJ: Princeton UP, 2004.

Ettin, Andrew Vogel. *Betrayals of the Body Politic: The Literary Commitments of Nadine Gordimer*. Charlottesville: U of Virginia P, 1993.

Evangelista, Susan. *Carlos Bulosan and His Poetry: A Biography and Anthology*. Quezon City, Philippines: Ateneo de Manila UP, 1985.

Evans, J. Martin. *Milton's Imperial Epic: "Paradise Lost" and the Discourse of Colonialism*. Ithaca, NY: Cornell UP, 1996.

Evers, Lawrence J. "Words and Place: A Reading of *House Made of Dawn*." *Critical Essays on Native American Literature*. Ed. Andrew Wiget. Boston: G. K. Hall, 1985. 211–30.

Ezenwa-Ohaeto. *Chinua Achebe: A Biography*. Bloomington: Indiana UP, 1997.

Fabre, Genevieve, and Michel Feith. *Jean Toomer and the Harlem Renaissance*. New Brunswick, NJ: Rutgers UP, 2001.

Fabre, Michel. "Jack Conroy as Editor." *New Letters* 39.2 (Winter 1972): 115–37.

————. *The Unfinished Quest of Richard Wright.* Urbana: U of Illinois P, 1993.

————, and Robert Skinner, eds. *Conversations with Chester Himes.* Jackson: UP of Mississippi, 1995.

Falk, Candace. *Love, Anarchy, and Emma Goldman.* New York: Holt, Rinehart, and Winston, 1984.

Fallaize, Elizabeth, ed. *Simone de Beauvoir: A Critical Reader.* New York: Routledge, 1998.

Fanger, Donald. *The Creation of Nikolai Gogol.* Cambridge, MA: Harvard UP, 1979.

Fanon, Frantz. *Black Skin, White Masks.* 1952. New York: Grove, 1982.

————. *The Wretched of the Earth.* 1963. New York: Grove, 1968.

Faris, Wendy B. *Ordinary Enchantments: Magical Realism and the Remystification of Narrative.* Nashville, TN: Vanderbilt UP, 2004.

Farnsworth, Beatrice. *Aleksandra Kollontai: Socialism, Feminism, and the Bolshevik Revolution.* Stanford, CA: Stanford UP, 1980.

Farrell, James T. *A Note on Literary Criticism.* New York: Vanguard, 1936.

Fast, Howard. *Being Red.* Boston: Houghton Mifflin, 1990.

Feal, Rosemary Geisdorfer, and Yvette E. Miller, eds. *Isabel Allende Today: An Anthology of Essays.* Pittsburgh, PA: Latin American Literary Review P, 2002.

Featherstone, Simon. *War Poetry.* London: Routledge, 1995.

Feder, Lillian. *Naipaul's Truth: The Making of a Writer.* New York: Rowman and Littlefield, 2001.

Fehervary, Helen. *Anna Seghers: The Mythic Dimension.* Ann Arbor: U of Michigan P, 2001.

Feiler, Lily. *Marina Tsvetaeva: The Double Beat of Heaven and Hell.* Durham: Duke UP, 1994.

Fernández Liria, Carlos. *Sin vigilancia y sin castigo: Una discusión con Michel Foucault.* Madrid: Libertarias/Prodhufi, 1992.

Fernández Retamar, Roberto. *Caliban and Other Essays.* Trans. Edward Baker. Minneapolis: U of Minnesota P, 1989.

Ferraro, Thomas. *Ethnic Passages: Literary Immigrants in Twentieth Century America.* Chicago: U of Chicago P, 1993.

Ferrier, Carole, ed. *Gender, Politics and Fiction: Twentieth Century Australian Women's Novels.* St. Lucia: U of Queensland P, 1986.

Fetterley, Judith. *The Resisting Reader: A Feminist Approach to American Fiction.* Bloomington: Indiana UP, 1978. 101–53.

Feuerwerker, Yi-tsi. *Ding Ling's Fiction: Ideology and Narrative in Modern Chinese Literature.* Cambridge, MA: Harvard UP, 1982.

Fickert, Kurt F. "Literature as Documentation: Plenzdorf's *Die neuen Leiden des jungen W.*" *International Fiction Review* 12.1 (Winter 1985): 69–75.

Filreis, Alan. *Modernism from Right to Left: Wallace Stevens, the Thirties, and Literary Radicalism.* New York: Cambridge UP, 1994.

Finello, Dominick L. *Cervantes: Essays on Social and Literary Polemics.* Rochester, NY: Tamesis, 1998.

Finn, Patrick. *Literacy with an Attitude: Educating Working-Class Children in Their Own Self-Interest.* Albany: SUNY P, 1999.

Firchow, Peter Edgerly. *The End of Utopia: A Study of Aldous Huxley's* Brave New World. Lewisburg, PA: Bucknell UP, 1984.

————. *Envisioning Africa: Racism and Imperialism in Conrad's* Heart of Darkness. Lexington: UP of Kentucky, 1999.

Fischer, Gerhard, ed. *Debating Enzensberger: "Great Migration" and "Civil War."* Tübingen: Stauffenburg, 1996.

Fish, Stanley Eugene. *How Milton Works.* Cambridge, MA: Harvard Belknap, 2001.

Fishbein, Leslie. *Rebels in Bohemia: The Radicals of "The Masses," 1911–1917.* Chapel Hill: North Carolina UP, 1982.

Fisher, D. J. *Romain Rolland and the Politics of Intellectual Engagement.* Berkeley: California UP, 1979.

Fiske, John. *Understanding Popular Culture.* London: Routledge, 1991.

Fitting, Peter. "The Modern Anglo-American SF Novel: Utopian Longing and Capitalist Cooptation." *Science Fiction Studies* 6.1 (1979): 59–76.

Fitzpatrick, Sheila. *The Russian Revolution: 1917–1932.* Oxford: Oxford UP, 1984.

Fiut, Aleksander. *The Eternal Moment: The Poetry of Czeslaw Milosz.* Trans. Theodosia S. Robertson. Berkeley: U of California P, 1990.

Flaxman, Gregory, ed. *The Brain Is the Screen: Deleuze and the Philosophy of Cinema.* Minneapolis: U of Minnesota P, 2000.

Fleenor, Juliann E., ed. *The Female Gothic.* Montreal: Eden, 1983.

Fleishman, Avrom. *Conrad's Politics: Community and Anarchy in the Fiction of Joseph Conrad.* Baltimore, MD: Johns Hopkins UP, 1967.

Fletcher, M. D., ed. *Reading Rushdie: Perspectives on the Fiction of Salman Rushdie.* Amsterdam, Netherlands: Rodopi, 1995.

Flores, Ángel. "Magical Realism in Spanish American Fiction." *Hispanía* 38.2 (May 1955): 187–92.

Flores, Lauro. Introduction to *The Floating Borderlands: Twenty-five Years of U.S. Hispanic Literature.* Seattle: U of Washington P, 1998. 3–11.

Flower, J. E. *Literature and the Left in France.* London: Macmillan, 1983.

————. *Writers and Politics in Modern France (1909–1961).* London: Hodder and Stoughton, 1977.

Flynn, Thomas R. *Sartre, Foucault and Historical Reason.* Chicago: U of Chicago P, 1997.

Foley, Barbara. "From Communism to Brotherhood: The Drafts of *Invisible Man*." *Left of the Color Line: Race, Radicalism, and Twentieth-Century Literature of the United States.* Ed. Bill Mullen and James Smethurst. Chapel Hill: U of North Carolina P, 2003. 163–82.

————. "'In the Land of Cotton': Economics and Violence in Jean Toomer's *Cane*." *African American Review* 32 (Summer 1998): 181–98.

————. Introduction to *Moscow Yankee* by Myra Page. Urbana: U of Illinois P, 1995.

————. "Jean Toomer's Sparta." *American Literature* 67 (December 1995): 747–75.

————. "Race and Class in Radical African-American Fiction of the Depression Years." *Nature, Society, and Thought* 3.3 (1990): 305–24.

————. *Radical Representations: Politics and Form in U.S. Proletarian Fiction, 1929–1941.* Durham, NC: Duke UP, 1993.

————. "Ralph Ellison as Proletarian Journalist." *Science and Society* 62 (Winter 1998–1999): 537–56.

————. "Reading Redness: Politics and Audience in Ralph Ellison's Proletarian Short Fiction." *Journal of Narrative Theory* 29 (Fall 1999): 323–39.

————. "The Rhetoric of Anticommunism in Invisible Man." *College English* 59 (September 1997): 530–47.

————. *Spectres of 1919: Class and Nation in the Making of the New Negro.* Urbana: U of Illinois P, 2003.

Folsom, Michael Brewster. "The Book of Poverty." Review of *Jews without Money* by Michael Gold. *Nation,* 28 February 1966, 242–45.

————. "The Education of Mike Gold." *Proletarian Writers of the Thirties.* Ed. David Madden. Carbondale: Southern Illinois UP, 1968. 222–51.

————. "The Pariah of American Letters." Introduction to *Mike Gold: A Literary Anthology.* Ed. Michael Brewster Folsom. New York: International Publishers, 1972. 7–20.

Foner, Philip S. *The Industrial Workers of the World, 1905–1917.* New York: International Publishers, 1965.

Fonkoua, Romuald Blaise. *Essai sur une mesure du monde au XXe siècle: Edouard Glissant.* Paris: Honoré Champion, 2002.

Foot, Paul. *Red Shelley.* London: Bookmarks, 1984.

Forcione, Alban K. *Cervantes and the Humanist Vision: A Study of Four Exemplary Novels.* Princeton, NJ: Princeton UP, 1982.

Forgàcs, David. "Franco Fortini." *Writers and Society in Contemporary Italy.* Ed. M. Caesar and P. Hainswroth. Leamington Spa: Berg, 1984. 84–116.

Fortini, Franco. *Insistenze: cinquanta scritti 1976–1984.* Milan: Garzanti, 1985.

————. *Nuovi saggi italiani.* Milan: Garzanti, 1987.

————. *Saggi ed epigrammi.* Ed. Luca Lenzini. Milan: Mondadori, 2003.

Foster, David William. "Bibliografía del indigenismo hispanoamericano." *Revista iberoamericana* 50.127 (1984): 587–620 (special issue on indigenismo).

Foster, Edward Halsey. *Understanding the Beats.* Columbia: U of South Carolina P, 1992.

Foster, R. F. *W. B. Yeats: A Life. Vol. 2: The Arch-Poet.* London: Oxford UP, 2003.

Foster, William Z. *History of the Three Internationals: The World Socialist and Communist Movements from 1848 to the Present.* New York: International Publishers, 1955.

Foucault, Michel. *The Care of the Self.* (Vol. 3 of *The History of Sexuality.*) Trans. Robert Hurley. New York: Vintage-Random House, 1988.

————. *Discipline and Punish: The Birth of the Prison.* Trans. Alan Sheridan. New York: Vintage-Random House, 1979.

————. *The History of Sexuality, Volume 1: An Introduction.* Trans. Robert Hurley. New York: Vintage-Random House, 1980.

————. *Language, Counter-Memory, Practice: Selected Essays and Interviews.* Ed. Donald F. Bouchard. Ithaca: Cornell UP, 1977.

————. *Madness and Civilization.* Trans. Richard Howard. New York: Random House, 1965.

————. *The Order of Things.* Trans. Alan Sheridan. New York: Pantheon, 1970.

————. *Power.* Ed. James D. Faubion. New York: Free P, 2000.

————. "Theatrum Philosophicum." *Language, Counter-Memory, Practice.* Trans. Donald F. Bouchard and Sherry Simon. Ithaca, NY: Cornell UP, 1977.

————. *The Use of Pleasure.* (Vol. 2 of *The History of Sexuality.*) Trans. Robert Hurley. New York: Vintage-Random House, 1986.

Fowler, Carolyn. *A Knot in the Thread: The Life and Work of Jacques Roumain*. Washington, DC: Howard UP, 1976.

Fowler, Douglas. *Understanding E. L. Doctorow*. Columbia: South Carolina UP, 1992.

Fox, Pamela. *Class Fictions*. Durham: Duke UP, 1994.

Fox, Ralph. *The Novel and the People*. 1937. Intro. Jeremy Hawthorn. London: Lawrence and Wishart, 1979.

Frail, David. *The Early Politics and Poetics of William Carlos Williams*. Ann Arbor, MI: UMI P, 1987.

Fraiman, Susan. *Unbecoming Women: British Women Writers and the Novel of Development*. New York: Columbia UP, 1993.

Francis, R. A. *Romain Rolland*. Oxford: Berg, 1999.

Franco, Jean. *César Vallejo: The Dialectics of Poetry and Silence*. Cambridge: Cambridge UP, 1976.

Frank, Joseph. *Dostoevsky*. 5 vols. Princeton: Princeton UP, 1976–2002.

Franklin, H. Bruce. Introduction. *Prison Writing in Twentieth-Century America*. Ed. H. Bruce Franklin. New York: Penguin, 1998.

―――. *Prison Literature in America: The Victim as Criminal and Artist*. Exp. edition. New York: Oxford UP, 1989.

―――. *Robert A. Heinlein: America as Science Fiction*. New York: Oxford UP, 1980.

Fraser, Robert. *The Novels of Ayi Kwei Armah: A Study in Polemical Fiction*. London: Heinemann, 1980.

Frederick, Karl R. *George Eliot: Voice of a Century*. New York: W. W. Norton, 1995.

Freeborn, Richard. *The Russian Revolutionary Novel: Turgenev to Pasternak*. Cambridge: Cambridge UP, 1982. 39–52.

Freedman, Carl. *Critical Theory and Science Fiction*. Hanover, NH: Wesleyan UP, 2000.

French, Marilyn. *The Book as World*. Cambridge, MA: Harvard UP, 1975.

Friedberg, Maurice. "New Editions of Soviet Belles-Lettres: A Study in Politics and Palimpsests." *American Slavic and East European Review* 8 (1954): 72–88.

Frohock, Wilbur M. *André Malraux and the Tragic Imagination*. Stanford: Stanford UP, 1967.

Frow, Ruth, and Edmund Frow. "Ethel Carnie: Writer, Feminist and Socialist." *The Rise of Socialist Fiction, 1880–1914*. Ed. H. Gustav Klaus. Brighton: Harvester, 1987. 251–56.

Frye, Northrop. *Anatomy of Criticism*. Princeton, NJ: Princeton UP, 1957.

Fuchs, Barbara. *Passing for Spain: Cervantes and the Fictions of Identity*. Urbana: U of Illinois P, 2003.

Fuchs, Daniel. *Saul Bellow: Vision and Revision*. Durham, NC: Duke UP, 1984.

Fuegi, John. *Bertolt Brecht: Chaos, According to Plan*. Cambridge: Cambridge UP, 1987.

Fuentes, Carlos. "Juan Goytisolo or the Novel as Exile." *Review of Contemporary Fiction* 4 (1984): 72–76.

Fuller, Jean Overton. *Shelley: A Biography*. London: Cape, 1968.

Fundación Rigoberta Menchú Tum. http://www.frmt.org. Accessed 5 April 2004.

Fuss, Diana. *Essentially Speaking: Feminism, Nature, and Difference*. London: Routledge, 1989.

Fussell, Paul. *The Great War and Modern Memory*. New York: Oxford UP, 1975.

Gainor, J. Ellen. *Imperialism and Theatre: Essays on World Theatre, Drama, and Performance*. London: Routledge, 1995.

Gálik, Marián. *Mao Tun and Modern Chinese Literary Criticism*. Wiesbaden: F. Steiner, 1969.

Gallagher, Catherine. *The Industrial Reform of English Fiction: Social Discourse and Narrative Form, 1832–1867.* Chicago: U of Chicago P, 1985.

———, and Stephen Greenblatt. *Practicing New Historicism.* Chicago: U of Chicago P, 2001.

Gamble, Sarah. *The Fiction of Angela Carter.* New York: Palgrave Macmillan, 2002.

Gandhi, Leela. *Postcolonial Theory: A Critical Introduction.* New York: Columbia UP, 1998.

Garber, Eric. "A Spectacle in Color: The Lesbian and Gay Subculture of Jazz Age Harlem." *Hidden from History.* Ed. Martin B. Duberman et al. New York: NAL, 1989. 318–31.

Gardiner, Allan. "Striking Images: Ralph De Boissière's Australian Socialist Realism." *Rereading Global Socialist Cultures after the Cold War.* Ed. Dubravka Juraga and M. Keith Booker. Westport, CT: Praeger, 2002.

Garner, Stanton B. "Post-Brechtian Anatomies: Weiss, Bond and the Politics of Embodiment." *Theater Journal* 42.2 (1990): 145–64.

Garrard, John Gordon, and Carol Garrard. *Inside the Soviet Writers' Union.* New York: Free P, 1990.

Gasché, Rodolphe. *Inventions of Difference: On Jacques Derrida.* Cambridge: Harvard UP, 1994.

Gates, Henry Louis, Jr. *Figures in Black: Words, Signs, and the "Racial" Self.* New York: Oxford UP, 1987.

———. *Loose Canons: Notes on the Culture Wars.* New York: Oxford UP, 1992.

———, and K. A. Appiah, eds. *Toni Morrison: Critical Perspectives Past and Present.* New York: Amistad, 1993.

———, and Nellie McKay, eds. *The Norton Anthology of African American Literature.* New York: Norton, 2004.

Gatón Arce, Freddy. *Estos días de tíbar—la poesía soprendida.* Santo Domingo: Taller, 1983.

Gatt-Rutter, John. "Calvino Ludens: Literary Play and Its Political Implications." *Journal of European Studies* 5 (1975).

———. *Writers and Politics in Modern Italy.* London: Hodder and Stoughton, 1978.

Gayle, Addison, Jr., ed. *The Black Aesthetic.* New York: Doubleday, 1971.

———. *Claude McKay: The Black Poet at War.* Detroit: Broadside P, 1972.

———. *The Way of the World: The Black Novel in America.* Garden City, NY: Doubleday, 1975.

Geiss, Imanuel. *The Pan-African Movement.* Trans. Ann Keep. London: Methuen, 1974.

Gelfand, Elissa D. *Imagination in Confinement: Women's Writings from French Prisons.* Ithaca, NY: Cornell UP, 1983.

Gelpi, Albert. *Living in Time: The Poetry of C. Day Lewis.* New York: Oxford UP, 1998.

———, ed. *Denise Levertov: Selected Criticism.* Ann Arbor: U of Michigan P, 1993.

Geogeghan, Vincent. *Ernst Bloch.* New York: Routledge, 1996.

George, Paul S. "Beat Politics: New Left and Hippie Beginnings in the Postwar Counterculture." *Cultural Politics: Radical Movements in Modern History.* Ed. Jerold M. Starr. New York: Praeger, 1985.

George Orwell and "Nineteen Eighty-Four": The Man and the Book. Washington, DC: Library of Congress, 1985.

Gernsback, Hugo. "A New Sort of Magazine." *Amazing Stories* 1 (1926): 3.

Ghosh, Amitav. "The Diaspora in Indian Culture." *Public Culture* 2.1 (1989): 75–77.

Giard, Luce, ed. *Michel de Certeau*. Paris: Centre Georges Pompidou, 1987.

Giard, Luce, Hervé Martin, and Jacques Revel. *Histoire, mystique et politique: Michel de Certeau*. Grenoble: Jérome Millon, 1991.

Gibbs, Donald A. *A Bibliography of Studies and Translations of Modern Chinese Literature, 1918–1942*. Cambridge, MA: East Asian Research Center, Harvard University, 1975.

Gibbs, James. *Wole Soyinka*. New York: Grove P, 1986.

Gibbs, James, and Bernth Lindfors, eds. *Research on Wole Soyinka*. Trenton: Africa World P, 1993.

Gibson, Andrew. *Joyce's Revenge: History, Politics and Aesthetics in "Ulysses."* Oxford: Oxford UP, 2002.

Gibson, Ian. *The Assassination of Federico García Lorca*. New York: Penguin, 1983.

———. *Federico García Lorca: A Life*. New York: Pantheon, 1989.

Gibson, Nigel. *Fanon: The Postcolonial Imagination*. Malden, MA: Blackwell, 2003.

———, ed. *Rethinking Fanon: The Continuing Dialogue*. Amherst, NY: Humanity Books, 1999.

Gies, David T., ed. *The Cambridge Companion to Modern Spanish Culture*. Cambridge: Cambridge UP, 1999.

Gifford, Douglas. *Neil Gunn and Lewis Grassic Gibbon*. Edinburgh: Oliver and Boyd, 1983.

Gifford, Douglas, et al., eds. *Scottish Literature in English and Scots*. Edinburgh: Edinburgh UP, 2003.

Gikandi, Simon. *Ngugi wa Thiong'o*. New York: Cambridge UP, 2001.

———. *Reading Chinua Achebe: Language and Ideology in Fiction*. Portsmouth, NH: Heinemann, 1991.

———. *Writing in Limbo: Modernism and Caribbean Literature*. Ithaca, NY: Cornell UP, 1992.

Gilbert, Helen. *Sightlines: Race, Gender and Nation in Contemporary Australian Theatre*. Ann Arbor: U of Michigan P, 1998.

Gilbert, James. *Writers and Partisans: A History of Literary Radicalism in America*. 1968. New York: Columbia UP, 1992.

Gilbert, Sandra M., and Susan Gubar. *The Madwoman in the Attic: The Woman Writer and the Nineteenth Century Literary Imagination*. New Haven, CT: Yale UP, 1979.

Giles, James Richard. *Claude McKay*. Boston: Twayne, 1976.

Giles, Steve. "From Althusser to Brecht: Formalism, Materialism and *The Threepenny Opera*." *New Ways in Germanistik*. Ed. Richard Sheppard. Oxford: Berg, 1990.

———. "Rewriting Brecht: *Die Dreigroschenoper*, 1928–1931." *Literaturwissenschaftliches Jahrbuch* 30 (1989): 249–79.

Gillen, Francis, and Stephen H. Gale, eds. *The Pinter Review: Collected Essays 2001 and 2002*. Tampa, FL: U of Tampa P, 2002.

Gillen, Paul. *Faithful to the Earth: A Jack Lindsay Compendium*. Sydney: Collins/Angus and Robertson, 1993.

Gilmour, David. *The Last Leopard: A Life of Giuseppe di Lampedusa*. New York: Pantheon, 1988.

Gilroy, Paul. *The Black Atlantic: Double Consciousness and Modernity*. Cambridge, MA: Harvard UP, 1993.

————, Lawrence Grossberg, and Angela McRobbie, eds. *Without Guarantees: In Honour of Stuart Hall*. London: Verso, 2000.

Gilyard, Keith. *Liberation Memories: The Rhetoric and Poetics of John Oliver Killens*. Detroit: Wayne State UP, 2003.

Gimenez, Martha. "The Mode of Reproduction in Transition: A Marxist-Feminist Analysis of the Effects of Reproductive Technologies." *Gender and Society* 5.3 (Fall 1991): 334–50.

Ginsberg, Allen, and David Carter, eds. *Spontaneous Mind: Selected Interviews, 1958–1996*. New York: HarperCollins, 2001.

Gish, Nancy K. *Hugh MacDiarmid: The Man and His Work*. London: Macmillan, 1984.

Glen, Duncan. *Hugh MacDiarmid and the Scottish Renaissance*. Edinburgh: W.R. Chambers, 1964.

Glissant, Edouard. *Caribbean Discourse: Selected Essays*. Trans. J. Michael Dash. Charlottesville: UP of Virginia, 1989.

————. *Poetics of Relation*. Trans. Betsy Wing. Ann Arbor: U of Michigan P, 1997.

————. *Traité du tout-monde*. Paris: Gallimard, 1997.

Glotfelty, Cheryl, and Harold Fromm, eds. *The Ecocriticism Reader: Landmarks in Literary Ecology*. Athens: Georgia UP, 1996.

Goddu, Teresa A. *Gothic America: Narrative, History, and Nation*. New York: Columbia UP, 1997.

Goetz-Stakiewicz, Marketa, and Phyllis Carey, eds. *Critical Esays on Vaclav Havel*. New York: G.K. Hall, 1999.

Göksu, Saime, and Edward Timms. *Romantic Communist: The Life and Work of Nazım Hikmet*. London: Hurst, 1999.

Gold, Michael. *Change the World!* New York: International Publishers, 1936.

————. *The Hollow Men*. New York: International Publishers, 1941.

————. *Jews without Money*. 1930. New York: Carroll and Graf, 1984.

Goldberg, Jonathan. *James I and the Politics of Literature*. Baltimore: Johns Hopkins UP, 1983.

Goldblatt, Howard. "Sex and Society: The Fiction of Li Ang." *Worlds Apart: Recent Chinese Writing and Its Audience*. Ed. Howard Goldblatt. Armonk, NY: M. E. Sharpe, 1990. 150–65.

————, ed. *Chinese Literature for the 1980s: The Fourth Congress of Writers and Artists*. Armonk, NY: M. E. Sharpe, 1982.

Goldgar, Bertrand A. *Walpole and the Wits: The Relation of Politics to Literature, 1722–1742*. Lincoln: U of Nebraska P, 1976.

Goldman, Emma. *Anarchism and Other Essays*. New York: Dover, 1969.

————. *Living My Life: An Autobiography of Emma Goldman*. Salt Lake City, UT: Peregrine Smith Book, 1982.

Goldman, Jane. *The Feminist Aesthetics of Virginia Woolf*. Cambridge: Cambridge UP, 1998.

Goldman, Merle. *Literary Dissent in Communist China*. Cambridge, MA: Harvard UP, 1967.

————. *Sowing the Seeds of Democracy in China: Political Reform in the Deng Xiaoping Era*. Cambridge, MA: Harvard UP, 1994.

Goldmann, Lucien. *The Human Sciences and Philosophy*. Trans. Hayden V. White and Robert Anchor. London, 1964.

————. *Marxisme et sciences humaines*. Paris: NRF and Gallimard, 1970.

————. *Recherches dialectiques*. Paris: NRF and Gallimard, 1959.

————. *Structures mentales et création culturelle*. Paris: Anthropos, 1970.

Golstein, Vladimir. *Lermontov's Narratives of Heroism*. Evanston, IL: Northwestern UP, 2000.

González, Manuel Pedro, and Ivan Schulman. *Martí, Darío y el modernismo*. Madrid: Editorial Gredos, S.A., 1969.

González, Mike, and David Treece. "Roque Dalton: Speaking Aloud." *The Gathering of Voices: The Twentieth-Century Poetry of Latin America*. London: Verso, 1992. 298–305.

González Echeverría, Roberto. *Alejo Carpentier: The Pilgrim at Home*. Ithaca, NY: Cornell UP, 1977.

———, and Klaus Muller-Bergh. *Alejo Carpentier: Bibliographical Guide*. Westport, CT: Greenwood, 1983.

Gordimer, Nadine. *The Essential Gesture: Writing Politics and Places*. Ed. Stephen Clingman. New York: Knopf, 1988.

———. "A Writer in South Africa." *London Magazine* (May 1965): 21–28.

———, et al. *What Happened to "Burger's Daughter"; or, How South African Censorship Works*. Johannesburg: Taurus, 1980.

Gordon, Lewis. *Frantz Fanon and the Crisis of European Man*. Cambridge, MA: Blackwell, 1995.

———, ed. *Fanon: A Critical Reader*. Cambridge, MA: Blackwell, 1996.

Gordon, Robert S. C. *Primo Levi's Ordinary Virtues: From Testimony to Ethics*. Oxford: Oxford UP, 2001.

Gorky, Maxim, et al. *Soviet Writers' Congress, 1934: The Debate on Socialist Realism and Modernism in the Soviet Union*. London: Lawrence and Wishart, 1977.

Görner, Rüdiger, ed. *Politics in Literature*. Munich: Iudicium, 2004.

Gossett, Thomas F. *Race: The History of an Idea in America*. Dallas: Southern Methodist UP, 1963.

Goudet, J. *Dante et la politique*. Paris: Aubier, 1959.

Gould, Karen. *Writing in the Feminine: Feminism and Experimental Writing in Quebec*. Carbondale: Southern Illinois UP, 1990.

Gracia, Jorge J. E. *Hispanic/Latino Identity: A Philosophical Perspective*. Oxford: Blackwell, 2000.

Graff, Gerald. *Beyond the Culture Wars: How Teaching the Conflicts Can Revitalize American Education*. New York: Norton, 1992.

———. *Professing Literature: An Institutional History*. Chicago: U of Chicago P, 1979.

Graham, Helen, and Paul Preston, eds. *The Popular Front in Europe*. New York: St. Martin's, 1987.

Graham, Maryemma. *Conversations with Margaret Walker*. Jackson: UP of Mississippi, 2002.

———, ed. *Fields Watered with Blood: Critical Essays on Margaret Walker*. Athens: U of Georgia P, 2001.

Gramsci, Antonio. *An Antonio Gramsci Reader*. Ed. David Forgacs. New York: Schocken Books, 1988.

———. *Letters from Prison*. Ed. and trans. Lynne Lawner. New York: Farrar, Straus and Giroux, 1973.

———. *Prison Notebooks*. 2 vols. Ed. and trans. Joseph A. Buttigieg. New York: Columbia UP, 1992, 1996.

Gray, Chris Hables. *Cyborg Citizen: Politics in the Posthuman Age*. New York: Routledge, 2002.

———, ed., with Heidi J. Figueroa-Sarriera and Steven Mentor. *The Cyborg Handbook*. New York: Routledge, 1995.

Gray, Richard. *The Life of William Faulkner: A Critical Biography*. Oxford: Blackwell, 1994.

Gray, Stephen. *Southern African Literature: An Introduction*. Cape Town: David Philip, 1979.

Greeman, Richard. "Victor Serge: The Making of a Novelist (1890–1928)." Diss. Columbia University, 1968.

Green, Richard Firth. *A Crisis of Truth: Literature and Law in Ricardian England*. Philadelphia: U of Pennsylvania P, 1999.

Greenblatt, Stephen. *Shakespearean Negotiations: The Circulation of Social Energy in Renaissance England*. Berkeley: U of California P, 1988.

Greene, Gayle, and Coppelia Kahn, eds. *Making a Difference: Feminist Literary Criticism*. London: Methuen, 1985.

Greene, Gayle Jacoba. *Doris Lessing: The Poetics of Change*. Ann Arbor: U of Michigan P, 1994.

Gregerson, Linda K. *Powers of Desire: Specularity and the Subject of the Tudor State*. Ann Arbor: U of Michigan P, 1992.

Grenier, Yvon. "Cambio de piel: disposiciones y posiciones políticas de Carlos Fuentes." *Foro Hispánico* 22 (2002): 121–35.

Griffiths, Gareth. "Femi Osofisan." *African Writers*. Ed. C. Brian Cox. New York: Scribner's, 1997. 619–29.

Grimm, Reinhold, and Jost Hermand, eds. *Our Faust? Roots and Ramifications of a Modern German Myth*. Madison: U of Wisconsin P, 1987.

Grossberg, Lawrence. "The Formations of Cultural Studies: An American in Birmingham." *Relocating Cultural Studies: Developments in Theory and Research*. Ed. Valda Blundell et al. New York: Routledge, 1993. 21–66.

———, Cary Nelson, and Paula Treichler, eds. *Cultural Studies*. New York: Routledge, 1992.

Grosswiler, Paul. *The Method Is the Message: Rethinking McLuhan through Critical Theory*. Montreal: Black Rose, 1998.

Groys, Boris. *The Total Art of Stalinism: Avant-Garde, Aesthetic Dictatorship, and Beyond*. Trans. Charles Rougle. Princeton, NJ: Princeton UP, 1992.

Guberman, Ross Mitchell, ed. *Julia Kristeva Interviews*. New York: Columbia UP, 1996.

Gugelberger, Georg M., ed. *Marxism and African Literature*. London: James Currey, 1985.

———. *The Real Thing: Testimonial Discourse in Latin America*. Durham: Duke UP, 1996.

———, and Michael Kearney, eds. "Voices of the Voiceless: Testimonial Literature in Latin America." Two-part special issue of *Latin American Perspectives* 18.3–4 (1991).

Guillemin, Henri. Preface to *Germinal* by Émile Zola. Paris: Garnier Flammarion, 1968. 9–23.

Guillory, John. *Cultural Capital: The Problem of Literary Canon Formation*. Chicago: U of Chicago P, 1993.

Guin, John Pollard. *Shelley's Political Thought*. Paris: Mouton, 1969.

Gunn, Giles. *F. O. Matthiessen: The Critical Achievement*. Seattle: U of Washington P, 1975.

Günther, Hans. *Die Verstaatlichung der Literatur: Entstehung und Funktionsweise des sozialistisch-realistischen Kanons in der Sowjetischen Literatur der 30 er Jahre*. Stuttgart: J.B. Metzler, 1984.

———, ed. *The Culture of the Stalin Period*. New York: St. Martin's, 1990.

———, and Evgeny Dobrenko, eds. *Sotsrealicheskii kanon*. St. Petersburg: Akademicheskii proekt, 2000.

Guthke, Karl. *B. Traven: The Life behind the Legends.* Chicago: Lawrence Hill, 1991.

Gutman, Stanley T. *Mankind in Barbary: The Individual and Society in the Novels of Norman Mailer.* Hanover, NH: UP of New England, 1975.

Gutting, Gary, ed. *The Cambridge Companion to Foucault.* Cambridge: Cambridge UP, 1994.

Guttman, Sondra. "Working Towards 'Unity in Diversity': Rape and the Reconciliation of Color and Comrade in Agnes Smedley's *Daughter of Earth.*" *Studies in the Novel* 32.4 (Winter 2000): 488–514.

Guy, John, ed. *The Reign of Elizabeth I: Court and Culture in the Last Decade.* Cambridge UP, 1995.

Guy, Josephine M. *The Victorian Social-Problem Novel: The Market, the Individual, and Communal Life.* London: Macmillan, 1996.

Guyon, Bernard. *La Pensée politique et sociale de Balzac.* Paris: Armand Colin, 1967.

Habermas, Jürgen. *The Philosophical Discourse of Modernity.* Trans. Frederick Lawrence. Cambridge, MA: MIT P, 1987.

———. *The Structural Transformation of the Public Sphere: An Inquiry into a Category of Bourgeois Society.* Trans. Thomas Burger. Cambridge, MA: MIT P, 1989.

———. *The Theory of Communicative Action.* Trans. Thomas McCarthy. 2 vols. Boston: Beacon P, 1984, 1987.

Haddon, Rosemary. "From Pulp to Politics: Aspects of Topicality in Fiction by Li Ang." *Modern Chinese Literature and Culture* 13.1 (2001): 36–72.

Hadfield, Andrew. *Shakespeare, Spenser, and the Matter of Britain.* New York: Macmillan, 2004.

Hadjor, Kofi Buenor. *Nkrumah and Ghana: The Dilemma of Post-Colonial Power.* London: Kegan Paul International, 1988.

Hagedorn, Jessica, ed. *Charlie Chan Is Dead: An Anthology of Contemporary Asian American Fiction.* New York: Penguin, 1993.

Haigh, Sam. *Mapping a Tradition: Francophone Women's Writing from Guadeloupe.* Leeds: Maney, 2000.

Haight, Amanda. *Anna Akhmatova: A Poetic Pilgrimage.* New York: Oxford UP, 1976.

Haight, Gordon S. *George Eliot: A Biography.* New York: Oxford UP, 1968.

Hall, Catherine, Keith McClelland, and Jane Rendall. *Defining the Victorian Nation: Class, Race, Gender and the Reform Act of 1867.* Cambridge: Cambridge UP, 2000.

Hall, Joan Wylie, ed. *Conversations with Audre Lorde.* Jackson: UP of Mississippi, 2004.

Hall, Stuart. "Cultural Studies and Its Theoretical Legacies." *Cultural Studies.* Ed. Lawrence Grossberg, Cary Nelson, and Paula Treichler. New York: Routledge, 1992. 277–85.

———. "Encoding/Decoding." *Culture, Media, Language: Working Papers in Cultural Studies, 1972–79.* London: Hutchinson, 1980. 128–38.

———. "Notes on Deconstructing 'The Popular.'" *People's History and Socialist Theory.* Ed. R. Samuel. London: Routledge and Kegan Paul, 1981. 227–40.

———. "The Problem of Ideology: Marxism without Guarantees." *Stuart Hall: Critical Dialogues in Cultural Studies.* Ed. David Morley and Kuan-Hsing Chen. New York: Routledge, 1996. 25–46.

Hall, Stuart, et al. *Critical Dialogues in Cultural Studies.* New York: Routledge, 1996.

———. *Policing the Crisis: Mugging, the State, and Law and Order.* London: Macmillan, 1978.

Halliday, Mark. "Damned Good Poet: Kenneth Fearing." *Michigan Quarterly Review* 40.2 (Spring 2001): 384–411.

Hamilton, Iain. *Koestler: A Biography*. London: Macmillan, 1982.

Haney, David P. *The Challenge of Coleridge: Ethics and Interpretation in Romanticism and Modern Philosophy*. University Park: Pennsylvania State UP, 2001.

Hannaford, Ivan. *Race: The History of an Idea in the West*. Baltimore: Johns Hopkins UP, 1996.

Hansen, Miriam. "Alexander Kluge, Cinema and the Public Sphere: The Construction Site of Counter-History." *Discourse: Journal for Theoretical Studies in Media and Culture* 6 (Fall 1983): 53–74.

————. "Unstable Mixtures, Dilated Spheres: Negt and Kluge's *The Public Sphere and Experience*, Twenty Years Later." *Public Culture* 5.2 (Winter 1993): 179–212.

————, ed. Special Issue on Alexander Kluge. *New German Critique: An Interdisciplinary Journal of German Studies* 49 (Winter 1990).

Hapke, Laura. *Daughters of the Great Depression: Women, Work, and Fiction in the American 1930s*. Athens: U of Georgia P, 1995.

————. *Labor's Text: The Worker in American Fiction*. Rutgers UP, 2001.

Haraway, Donna J. "A Cyborg Manifesto: Science, Technology, and Socialist-Feminism in the Late Twentieth Century." 1985. Rev. *Simians, Cyborgs, and Women: The Reinvention of Nature*. New York: Routledge, 1991. 149–81.

————. *Modest_Witness@Second_Millennium.FemaleMan©_Meets_OncoMouse™: Feminism and Technoscience*. New York: Routledge, 1997.

————. *Primate Visions: Gender, Race, and Nature in the World of Modern Science*. New York: Routledge, 1989.

Harding, Neil. *Leninism*. Durham, NC: Duke UP, 1996.

Harding, Walter. *The Days of Henry Thoreau*. Princeton, NJ: Princeton UP, 1982.

————, and Michael Meyer. *The New Thoreau Handbook*. New York: New York UP, 1980.

Hardt, Michael. *Gilles Deleuze: An Apprenticeship in Philosophy*. Minneapolis: U of Minnesota P, 1993.

————, and Antonio Negri. *Labor of Dionysus: Critique of the State-Form*. Minneapolis: U of Minnesota P, 1994.

————. *Empire*. Cambridge: MA: Harvard UP, 2000.

Hardt, Michael, and Kathi Weeks, eds. *The Jameson Reader*. Oxford: Blackwell, 2000.

Harlow, Barbara. *Barred: Women, Writing and Political Detention*. Hanover, NH: Wesleyan UP, 1992.

————. *Resistance Literature*. New York: Methuen, 1987.

Harman, Barbara Leah. *The Feminine Political Novel in Victorian England*. Charlottesville: UP of Virginia, 1998.

Harman, Claire. *Sylvia Townsend Warner: A Biography*. London: Chatto and Windus, 1989.

Harris, Greg. "Compulsory Masculinity, Britain, and the Great War: The Literary-Historical Work of Pat Barker." *Critique* 39 (Summer 1998): 290–305.

Harris, Jane Gary. *Osip Mandelstam*. Boston: Twayne, 1988.

Harris, Margaret, ed. *The Magic Phrase: Critical Essays on Christina Stead*. St. Lucia: U of Queensland P, 2000.

Harris, Michael T. *Outsiders and Insiders: Perspectives of Third World Culture in British and Post-colonial Fiction*. New York: Peter Lang, 1992.

Harris, Sharon M. *Rebecca Harding Davis and American Realism*. Philadelphia: U of Pennsylvania P, 1991.

Harrison, J. *Salman Rushdie*. New York: Twayne, 1992.

Harrisson, Tom. *Living through the Blitz*. London: Penguin, 1990.

Harron, Mary. "I'm a Socialist, Damn It! How Can You Expect Me to Be Interested in Fairies?" *Guardian*, 25 September 1984, 10.

Harss, Luis, and Barbara Dohmann. *Into the Mainstream: Conversations with Latin American Writers*. New York: Harper and Row, 1968.

Harter, Carol C., and James R. Thompson. *E. L. Doctorow*. Boston: Twayne, 1990.

Harvey, David. *The Condition of Postmodernity: An Enquiry into the Origins of Cultural Change*. Cambridge, MA: Blackwell, 1990.

————. *Justice, Nature and the Geography of Difference*. Malden, MA: Blackwell, 1996.

————. *The Limits of Capital*. 1982. New ed. New York: Verso, 1999.

————. *The New Imperialism*. Oxford: Oxford UP, 2003.

————. *Paris, Capital of Modernity*. New York: Routledge, 2003.

————. *Spaces of Capital: Towards a Critical Geography*. New York: Routledge, 2001.

————. *Spaces of Hope*. Berkeley: U of California P, 2000.

————. *The Urban Experience*. Oxford: Basil Blackwell, 1989.

Haslett, Moyra. *Marxist Literary and Cultural Theories*. Basingstoke: Macmillan, 2000.

————. "Terry Eagleton." *The Edinburgh Encyclopedia of Modern Criticism and Theory*. Ed. Julian Wolfreys. Edinburgh: Edinburgh UP, 2002.

Hassan, Ihab. "Postmodernism." *New Literary History* 3 (1971): 5–30.

Hawkesworth, Celia. "Yugoslav Literature of the Second World War." *Journal of European Studies* 16 (1986): 217–26.

Hawthorn, Jeremy, ed. *The British Working-Class Novel in the Twentieth Century*. London: Edward Arnold, 1984.

Hay, John, and Brenda Walker, eds. *Katharine Susannah Prichard: Centenary Essays*. Nedlands: U of Western Australia Centre for Studies in Australian Literature, 1984.

Hay, Malcolm, and Philip Roberts. *Bond: A Study of His Plays*. London, 1980.

Haydar, P., and A. Haydar. "Yusef Habshi al-Ashqar: *The Shadow and the Echo*." *Banipal* 4 (Spring 1999): 30–36.

Hayne, David M. *"Les Anciens Canadiens." The Oxford Companion to Canadian Literature*. Ed. Eugene Benson and William Toye. 2nd ed. Toronto: Oxford UP, 1997. 33–34.

Hayward, Helen. *The Enigma of V. S. Naipaul: Sources and Contexts*. New York: Palgrave Macmillan, 2002.

Head, Dominic. *Nadine Gordimer*. Cambridge: Cambridge UP, 1994.

Heaney, Seamus. "Yeats as an Example?" *Preoccupations: Selected Prose, 1968–1978*. London: Faber and Faber, 1980. 98–114.

Heath, Stephen. *Madame Bovary*. Cambridge: Cambridge UP, 1992.

————. *The Sexual Fix*. London: Macmillan, 1982.

Heavilin, Barbara, ed. *The Critical Response to John Steinbeck's* The Grapes of Wrath. Westport, CT: Greenwood, 2000.

Hebdige, Dick. *Subculture: The Meaning of Style*. London: Methuen, 1979.

Heble, Ajay, Donna Palmateer Pennee, and J. R. (Tim) Struthers, eds. *New Contexts of Canadian Criticism*. Peterborough, ON: Broadview P, 1997.

Hedrick, Joan D. *Harriet Beecher Stowe: A Life*. Oxford: Oxford UP, 1994.

Heilbut, Anthony. *Thomas Mann: Eros and Literature*. London: Macmillan, 1996.

Heller, Deborah. "Faith, Optimism and the Place of the Personal." *Studies in American Jewish Literature* 22 (2003): 79–91.

Heller, Leonid. "L'Esthétique réaliste socialiste est-elle possible? A propos de l'ouvrage de Régine Robin, *Le Réalisme socialiste: Une esthétique impossible.*" *Revue des études slaves* 61.3 (1989): 293–305.

————. "A World of Prettiness: Socialist Realism and Its Aesthetic Categories." *Socialist Realism without Shores*. Ed. Thomas Lahusen and Evgeny Dobrenko. Durham, NC: Duke UP, 1997. 687–714.

Hellman, John. *American Myth and the Legacy of Vietnam*. New York: Columbia UP, 1986.

Hemingway, Andrew. *Artists on the Left: American Artists and the Communist Movement, 1926–1956*. New Haven, CT: Yale UP, 2002.

Hemingway, Ernest. *For Whom the Bell Tolls*. New York: Charles Scribner's Sons, 1940.

————. "Who Murdered the Vets?" *New Masses* 16 (September 1935): 9–10.

Hemmings, F.W.J. (Frederick William John). *The Life and Times of Émile Zola*. New York: Scribner, 1977.

Hendershot, Cyndy. "Rolling toward the Horizon on Empty: Jim Thompson's West Texas Crime Fiction." *Bad Boys and Bad Girls in the Badlands*. Ed. Steve Glassman and Maurice J. O'Sullivan. Bowling Green: Popular P, 2001. 177–89.

Henderson, Harry B. *Versions of the Past: The Historical Imagination in American Fiction*. New York: Oxford UP, 1974.

Henderson, Mae G. "Toni Morrison's *Beloved*: Re-Membering the Body as Historical Text." *Comparative American Identities: Race, Sex, and Nationality in the Modern Text*. Ed. Hortense J. Spillers. New York: Routledge, 1991. 62–86.

Henighan, Stephen. *Assuming the Light: The Parisian Literary Apprenticeship of Miguel Angel Asturias*. Oxford: Legenda, 1999.

Henn, Katherine. *Rabindranath Tagore: A Bibliography*. Metuchen, NJ: Scarecrow, 1985.

Henrikson, Louise Levitas. *Anzia Yezierska: A Writer's Life*. Brunswick, NJ: Rutgers UP, 1988.

Henriquez Ureña Max. *Panorama histórico de la literature cubana*. Havana: Edición revolucionaria, 1967.

Henry, Nancy. *George Eliot and the British Empire*. Cambridge: Cambridge UP, 2002.

Henry, Paget, and Paul Buhle, eds. *C.L.R. James's Caribbean*. Durham, NC: Duke UP, 1992.

Herbst, Josephine. *The Starched Blue Sky of Spain*. 1991. Boston: Northeastern UP, 1999.

Hermand, Jost, and Marc Silberman, eds. *Rethinking Peter Weiss*. New York: Peter Lang, 2000.

Hewison, Robert. *In Anger: British Writing in the Cold War, 1945–60*. New York: Oxford UP, 1981.

————. *Too Much: Art and Society in the Sixties, 1960–75*. New York: Oxford UP, 1987.

————. *Under Siege: Literary Life in London, 1939–45*. New York: Oxford UP, 1977.

Hewith, Nicholas. *Literature and the Right in Postwar France*. Washington, DC: Berg, 1996.

Hibberd, Dominic. *Owen the Poet*. Athens: U of Georgia P, 1986.

Hicks, Granville. *John Reed: The Making of a Revolutionary*. New York: Macmillan, 1937.

Higgins, John. *Raymond Williams: Literature, Marxism and Cultural Materialism*. London: Routledge, 1999.

Higonnet, Patrice. *Goodness beyond Virtue: Jacobins during the French Revolution*. Cambridge, MA: Harvard UP, 1998.

Higuera, Henry. *Eros and Empire: Politics and Christianity in* Don Quixote. Lanham, MD: Rowman and Littlefield, 1995.

Hikmet, Nazim. *Poems of Nazim Hikmet.* Trans. Randy Blasing and Mutlu Konuk. New York: Persea Books, 2002.

Hill, Leslie. *Marguerite Duras: Apocalyptic Desires.* London: Routledge, 1993.

Hill, Patricia Liggins, ed. *Call and Response: The Riverside Anthology of the African American Literary Tradition.* Boston: Houghton Mifflin, 1998.

Hillegas, Mark. *The Future as Nightmare: H. G. Wells and the Anti-Utopians.* Carbondale: Southern Illinois UP, 1974.

Hinchman, Lewis P., and Sandra K. Hinchman. *Hannah Arendt: Critical Essays.* Albany: SUNY P, 1994.

Hingley, Ronald. *Russian Writers and Society in the Nineteenth Century.* 2nd rev. ed. London: Weidenfeld and Nicolson, 1977.

Hinton, Stephen, ed. *Kurt Weill: "The Threepenny Opera."* Cambridge: Cambridge UP, 1990.

Hirsh, Jerrold. *Portrait of America: A Cultural History of the Federal Writers' Project.* Chapel Hill: U of North Carolina P, 2003.

Hitchcock, Peter. *Dialogics of the Oppressed.* Minneapolis: U of Minnesota P, 1993.

————. "Passing: Henry Green and Working-Class Identity." *Modern Fiction Studies* 40.1 (Spring 1994): 1–31.

————. "What Is Prior? Working-Class Masculinity in Pat Barker's Trilogy." *Genders* 35 (2002). (Online publisher: www.genders.org.)

————. "'Work Has the Smell of Vinegar': Sensing Class in John Berger's Trilogy." *Modern Fiction Studies* 47.1 (Spring 2001): 12–42.

————. *Working-Class Fiction in Theory and Practice: A Reading of Alan Sillitoe.* Ann Arbor, MI: UMI, 1989.

Hobday, Charles. *Edgell Rickword: A Poet at War.* Manchester: Carcanet, 1989.

Hoberek, Andrew. "Cold War Culture to Fifties Culture." *Minnesota Review* 55–57 (2002): 143–52.

Hobsbawm, Eric. *The Age of Extremes: A History of the World, 1914–1991.* New York: Pantheon, 1994.

Hodge, Bob, and Vijay Mishra. *Dark Side of the Dream: Australian Literature and the Postcolonial Mind.* Sydney: Allen and Unwin, 1991.

Hoffmann, Léon-François. *Le Roman haïtien.* Sherbrooke: Naaman, 1982.

Hogan, Patrick, and Lalita Pandit, eds. *Rabindranath Tagore: Universality and Tradition.* Cranbury, NJ: Fairleigh Dickinson UP, 2003.

Hoggart, Richard. *The Uses of Literacy.* Harmondsworth: Penguin, 1957.

Holmes, John Clellon. "This Is the Beat Generation." *New York Times Magazine*, 16 November 1952, SM 10–13.

Holmes, Richard. *Shelley: The Pursuit.* London: Penguin, 1987.

Holroyd, Michael. *Bernard Shaw.* 4 vols. London: Chatto and Windus, 1988–1992.

Holt, Alix, ed. *Alexandra Kollontai: Selected Writings with an Introduction and Commentaries by Alix Holt.* New York: Norton, 1977.

Holub, Robert C. *Jürgen Habermas: Critic in the Public Sphere.* London: Routledge, 1991.

Homberger, Eric. *American Writers and Radical Politics: Equivocal Commitments, 1900–39.* New York: St. Martin's P, 1989.

Homer, Sean. *Fredric Jameson: Marxism, Hermeneutics, Postmodernism*. New York: Routledge, 1998.

Honan, Park. *Shakespeare: A Life*. Oxford UP, 1998.

Honey, Maureen. *Creating Rosie the Riveter: Class, Gender and Propaganda during World War II*. Amherst: U of Massachusetts P, 1984.

Hooker, James T. *Black Revolutionary: George Padmore's Path from Communism to Pan-Africanism*. London: Mall P, 1967.

Horkheimer, Max, and Adorno, Theodor W. *Dialectic of Enlightenment: Philosophical Fragments*. Trans. Edmund Jephcott. Stanford, CA: Stanford UP, 2002.

Horne, Gerald. *Black and Red: W.E.B. Du Bois and the Afro-American Response to the Cold War, 1944–1963*. Albany: SUNY P, 1986.

_____. "The Red and the Black: The Communist Party and African Americans in Historical Perspective." *New Studies in the Politics and Culture of U.S. Communism*. Ed. Michael E. Brown et al. New York: Monthly Review P, 1993. 199–238.

Horno Delgado, Asunción. *Breaking Boundaries: Latina Writing and Critical Readings*. Amherst: U of Massachusetts P, 1989.

Horowitz, Irving Louis, and Jaime Suchlicki, eds. *Cuban Communism, 1959–2003*. 11th ed. New Brunswick, NJ: Transaction P, 2003.

Horsley, Lee. *Fictions of Power in English Literature: 1900–1950*. London: Longman, 1995.

Horvath, Brooke, ed. "Introduction to Danilo Kiš." Special issue of *The Review of Contemporary Fiction* 15.1 (1994).

Hosking, Geoffrey A., and George F. Cushing, eds. *Perspectives on Literature and Society in Eastern and Western Europe*. New York: St. Martin's, 1989.

Hovet, Theodore R. *The Master Narrative: Harriet Beecher Stowe's Subversive Story of Master and Slave in "Uncle Tom's Cabin" and "Dred."* New York: UP of America, 1989.

Howard, Jean E. *The Stage and Social Struggle in Early Modern England*. London: Routledge, 1994.

Howe, Irving. "Black Boys and Native Sons." *Richard Wright's "Native Son": A Critical Handbook*. Ed. Richard Abcarian. Belmont, CA: Wadsworth, 1970. 135–42.

_____. "The New York Intellectuals." *Selected Writings: 1950–1990*. New York: Harcourt Brace Jovanovich, 1990.

_____. "Turgenev: The Politics of Hesitation." *Politics and the Novel*. Ed. Irving Howe. New York: Horizon P, 1957. 129–33.

_____, ed. *Orwell's "Nineteen Eighty-Four": Text, Sources, Criticism*. New York: Harcourt, Brace and World, 1963.

Howells, Christina, ed. *The Cambridge Companion to Sartre*. Cambridge: Cambridge UP, 1992.

Howes, Marjorie. *Yeats's Nations: Gender, Class, and Irishness*. Cambridge UP, 1996.

Hsia, C. T. *A History of Modern Chinese Fiction*. New Haven, CT: Yale UP, 1961.

Hsia, T. A. *The Gate of Darkness: Studies on the Leftist Literary Movement in China*. Seattle: U of Washington P, 1968.

Hudson, Wayne. *The Marxist Philosophy of Ernst Bloch*. New York: St. Martin's, 1982.

Huggins, Nathan Irvin. *Harlem Renaissance*. New York: Oxford UP, 1971.

Hughes, Langston. *The Big Sea: An Autobiography*. 1940. New York: Thunder's Mouth, 1986.

Hulme, Peter, and William Sherman, eds. *The Tempest and Its Travels*. Philadelphia: U of Pennsylvania P, 2000.

Hunt, Hugh. *Sean O'Casey*. Dublin: Gill and Macmillan, 1998.

Hunt, Lynn. *The Family Romance of the French Revolution*. Berkeley: U of California P, 1992.

Huot, Claire. *China's New Cultural Scene: A Handbook of Changes*. Durham, NC: Duke UP, 2000.

Hutcheon, Linda. *A Poetics of Postmodernism: History, Theory, Fiction*. New York: Routledge, 1988.

————. *The Politics of Postmodernism*. New York: Routledge, 1989.

Hutchinson, Earl Ofari. *Blacks and Reds: Race and Class in Conflict: 1919–1990*. East Lansing: Michigan State UP, 1994.

Hutchinson, George. *The Harlem Renaissance in Black and White*. Cambridge, MA: Belknap-Harvard UP, 1995.

Hutchinson, Peter. *Stefan Heym: The Perpetual Dissident*. Cambridge: Cambridge UP, 1992.

Huxley, Aldous. *Brave New World Revisited*. 1958. *"Brave New World" and "Brave New World Revisited."* New York: Harper and Row, 1965.

Huxley, Laura Archera. *This Timeless Moment*. New York: Farrar, Straus and Giroux, 1968.

Huyssen, Andreas. *After the Great Divide: Modernism, Mass Culture, Postmodernism*. Bloomington: Indiana UP, 1986.

Hynes, Samuel. *The Auden Generation: Literature and Politics in England in the 1930s*. New York: Viking, 1977.

————. *The Edwardian Turn of Mind*. Princeton, NJ: Princeton UP, 1968.

————. *A War Imagined: The First World War and English Culture*. New York: Collier, 1990.

Iakimenko, Lev Grigor'evich. *Tvorchestvo M. A. Sholokhova*. Moscow: Sovetskii Pisatel, 1970.

Ilie, Paul. *Literature and Inner Exile: Authoritarian Spain, 1939–1975*. Baltimore: Johns Hopkins UP, 1980.

Ingermanson, Birgitta. "The Political Function of Domestic Objects in the Fiction of Aleksandra Kollontai." *Slavic Review* (Spring 1989): 71–82.

Ingersoll, Earl, ed. *Margaret Atwood: Conversations*. Willowdale, ON: Firefly, 1990.

Inglis, Fred. *Raymond Williams*. London: Routledge, 1995.

Ingwersen, Faith, and Niels Ingwersen. *Quests for a Promised Land: The Works of Martin Andersen Nexø*. Westport, CT: Greenwood, 1984.

Innes, C. L. *Chinua Achebe*. New York: Cambridge UP, 1990.

————. *A History of Black and Asian Writing in Britain, 1700–2000*. Cambridge: Cambridge UP, 2002.

Innes, Christopher. "The Political Spectrum of Edward Bond: From Rationalism to Rhapsody." *Modern Drama* 25.2 (1982): 189–206.

Instituto de Literatura y Lingüística. *Diccionario de la literatura cubana*. Havana: Editorial Letras Cubanas. Vol. 1, 1980. Vol. 2, 1984.

Irele, Abiola. *The African Experience in Literature and Ideology*. London: Heinemann, 1981.

————, ed. *Aimé Césaire: Cahier d'un retour au pays natal*. Ibadan: New Horn Press Limited, 1994.

Irons, Peter. *Justice at War: The Story of the Japanese American Internment Cases*. New York: Oxford UP, 1983.

Isaacs, Neil David. *Grace Paley: A Study of the Short Fiction*. Boston: Twayne, 1990.

Isherwood, Christopher. *The Berlin Stories*. 1935. New York: New Directions, 1954.

————. *Christopher and His Kind*. New York: Farrar, Straus and Giroux, 1976.

Isserman, Maurice. *If I Had a Hammer: The Death of the Old Left and the Birth of the New Left*. Middletown, CT: Wesleyan UP, 1982.

————. *Which Side Were You On? The American Communist Party during the Second World War*. Middletown, CT: Wesleyan UP, 1982.

Jackson, Gabriel. *The Spanish Republic and the Civil War, 1931–1939*. Princeton, NJ: Princeton UP, 1965.

Jackson, Julian. *The Popular Front in France: Defending Democracy, 1934–38*. Cambridge: Cambridge UP, 1988.

Jackson, Lawrence. *Ralph Ellison: Emergence of Genius*. New York: John Wiley and Sons, 2002.

Jacobus, Mary. *Reading Woman: Essays in Feminist Criticism*. New York: Columbia UP, 1986.

Jacoby, Russell. *The Last Intellectuals: American Culture in the Age of Academe*. New York: Basic Books, 1987.

Jagose, Annamarie. *Queer Theory: An Introduction*. New York: New York UP, 1997.

Jaimes, M. Annette, ed. *The State of Native America: Genocide, Colonization, and Resistance*. Boston: South End P, 1992.

Jain, Jasbir. "Anita Desai." *Indian English Novelists*. Ed. Madhusudhan Prasad. New Delhi: Sterling Publishers, 1982. 23–50.

James, C.L.R. *The Black Jacobins: Toussaint L'Ouverture and the San Domingo Revolution*. 1938. New York: Vintage-Random House, 1989.

————. "George Padmore: Black Revolutionary." *At the Rendezvous of Victory: Selected Writings*. Vol. 3. London: Allison and Busby, 1984. 251–63.

————. *Nkrumah and the Ghana Revolution*. London: Allison and Busby, 1977.

James, C. Vaughan. *Soviet Socialist Realism: Origins and Theory*. New York: St. Martin's, 1973.

James, Winston. "Dimensions and Main Currents of Caribbean Radicalism in America: Hubert Harrison, the African Blood Brotherhood, and the UNIA." *Holding Aloft the Banner of Ethiopia: Caribbean Radicalism in Early Twentieth-Century America*. New York: Verso, 1998. 122–84.

Jameson, Fredric. *Brecht and Method*. London: Verso, 1998.

————. *The Cultural Turn: Selected Writings on the Postmodern, 1983–1998*. London: Verso, 1998.

————. *Fables of Aggression: Wyndham Lewis, the Modernist as Fascist*. Berkeley: U of California P, 1979.

————. "Generic Discontinuities in SF: Brian Aldiss' *Starship*." *Science Fiction Studies* 1.2 (1973): 57–68.

————. *The Geopolitical Aesthetic: Cinema and Space in the World System*. Bloomington: Indiana UP, 1992.

————. *Late Marxism: Adorno; or, The Persistence of the Dialectic*. London: Verso, 1990.

————. *Marxism and Form: Twentieth-Century Dialectical Theories of Literature*. Princeton, NJ: Princeton UP, 1971.

————. "On Cultural Studies." *The Identity in Question*. Ed. John Rajchman. New York: Routledge, 1995. 251–95.

————. *The Political Unconscious: Narrative as a Socially Symbolic Act*. Ithaca, NY: Cornell UP, 1981.

————. "The Politics of Utopia." *New Left Review* 25 (2004): 35–54.

————. *Postmodernism; or, The Cultural Logic of Late Capitalism*. Durham, NC: Duke UP, 1991.

————. *The Prison-House of Language: A Critical Account of Structuralism and Poststructuralism*. Princeton, NJ: Princeton UP, 1972.

————. "Progress versus Utopia; or, Can We Imagine the Future?" *Science Fiction Studies* 9.2 (1982): 147–58.

————. *Sartre: The Origins of a Style.* New Haven, CT: Yale UP, 1961.

————. "Science Fiction as a Spatial Genre: Generic Discontinuities and the Problem of Figuration in Vonda McIntyre's *The Exile Waiting*." *Science Fiction Studies* 14 (1987): 44–59.

————. *Signatures of the Visible.* New York: Routledge, 1992.

————. *A Singular Modernity: Essay on the Ontology of the Present.* London: Verso, 2002.

————. "Postmodernism and Consumer Society." *The Anti-Aesthetic: Essays on Postmodern Culture.* Ed. Hal Foster. Port Townshend, WA: Bay P, 1983. 111–26.

————. "The Space of Science Fiction: Narrative in A. E. Van Vogt." *Polygraph* 2/3 (1989): 52–65.

————. "World-Reduction in Le Guin: The Emergence of Utopian Narrative." *Science Fiction Studies* 2 (1975): 221–30.

JanMohamed, Abdul R. *Manichean Aesthetics: The Politics of Literature in Colonial Africa.* Amherst: U of Massachusetts P, 1983.

Jappe, Anselm. *Guy Debord.* Trans. Donald Nicholson-Smith. Berkeley: U of California P, 1999.

Jarvis, Simon. *Adorno: A Critical Introduction.* New York: Routledge, 1998.

Jay, Gregory S. *American Literature and the Culture Wars.* Ithaca, NY: Cornell UP, 1997.

Jay, Martin. *The Dialectical Imagination: A History of the Frankfurt School and the Institute of Social Research, 1923–1950.* London: Heinemann, 1973.

Jeffords, Susan. *The Remasculinization of America: Gender and the Vietnam War.* Bloomington: Indiana UP, 1989.

Jensen, Peter Alberg. *Nature as Code: The Achievement of Boris Pilnjak, 1915–1924.* Copenhagen: Rosenkilde and Bagger, 1979.

Jewinski, Ed. *Michael Ondaatje: Express Yourself Beautifully.* Toronto: ECW Press, 1994.

Jeyifo, Biodun. *Ngugi wa Thiong'o.* London: Pluto, 1990.

Johnson, Carroll B. *Cervantes and the Material World.* Urbana: U of Illinois P, 2000.

Johnson, Kent, ed. *A Nation of Poets: Writings from the Poetry Workshops of Nicaragua.* Los Angeles: West End P, 1985.

Johnson, Roy. "Victor Serge as Revolutionary Novelist: The First Trilogy." *Literature and History* 5.1 (1979): 58–86.

Jones, Eldred Durosimi. *The Writing of Wole Soyinka.* London: Heinemann, 1973.

Jones, Gareth Stedman. *Languages of Class.* Cambridge, UK: Cambridge UP, 1983.

Jordan, Barry, and Rikki Morgan-Tamosunas. *Contemporary Spanish Cultural Studies.* London: Arnold, 2000.

Josephs, Allen. *"For Whom the Bell Tolls": Ernest Hemingway's Undiscovered Country.* New York: Twayne, 1994.

The Journal of the Sylvia Townsend Warner Society, 2000– .

Jrade, Cathy Login. *Rubén Darío and the Romantic Search for Unity: The Modernist Recourse to Esoteric Tradition.* Austin: U of Texas P, 1983.

Jumonville, Neil. *Critical Crossings: The New York Intellectuals in Postwar America.* Berkeley: U of California P, 1991.

Juraga, Dubravka. "Miroslav Krleža's *Zastave*: Socialism, Yugoslavia, and the Historical Novel." *South Atlantic Review* 62.4 (Fall 1997): 32–56.

————. "'The Mirror of Us All': *Midnight's Children* and the Twentieth-Century Bildungsroman." *Critical Essays on Salman Rushdie*. Ed. M. Keith Booker. New York: G. K. Hall, 1999. 169–87.

————, and M. Keith Booker. "Literature, Power, and Oppression in Stalinist Russia and Catholic Ireland: Danilo Kiš's Use of Joyce in *A Tomb for Boris Davidovich*." *South Atlantic Review* 58.4 (November 1993): 39–58.

Kadić, Ante. "Miroslav Krleža." *Dictionary of Literary Biography: South Slavic Writers before World War II*. Detroit: Gale Research Inc., 1995.

Kafka, Phillipa. *"Saddling la Gringa": Gatekeeping in Literature by Contemporary Latina Writers*. Westport, CT: Greenwood, 2000.

Kalb, Jonathan. *The Theater of Heiner Müller*. Rev. and enlarged edition. New York: Limelight Editions, 2001.

Kampf, Louis, and Paul Lauter, eds. *The Politics of Literature*. New York: Pantheon, 1972.

Kamuf, Peggy. "Writing Like a Woman." *Women and Language in Literature and Society*. Ed. Sally McConnell-Ginet et al. New York: Praeger, 1980.

Kane, Martin, ed. *Socialism and the Literary Imagination: Essays on East German Writers*. New York: Berg, 1991.

Kanellos, Nicolás, ed. *The Hispanic Literary Companion*. Detroit: Visible Ink P, 1997.

Kaplan, Amy, and Donald Pease, eds. *Cultures of American Imperialism*. Durham, NC: Duke UP, 1993.

Kaplan, Carey, and Ellen Cronan Rose, eds. *Doris Lessing: The Alchemy of Survival*. Columbus: Ohio UP, 1988.

Kaplan, Carter. *Critical Synoptics: Menippean Satire and the Analysis of Intellectual Mythology*. Madison: Fairleigh Dickinson UP, 2000.

Karlinsky, Simon. *Marina Tsvetaeva: The Woman, Her World, and Her Poetry*. Cambridge: Cambridge UP, 1985.

Katsavos, Anna. "Angela Carter." *Modern British Women Writers: An A-to-Z Guide*. Ed. Vicki K. Janik and Del Ivan Janik. Westport, CT: Greenwood, 2002. 63–71.

Katz, Eliot. "Radical Eyes: Political Poetics and the Work of Allen Ginsberg." Diss. Rutgers University, May 2000.

Kaufmann, Vincent. *Guy Debord*. Paris: Fayard, 2001.

Kay, Sarah. *Zizek: A Critical Introduction*. Cambridge: Polity, 2003.

Keach, William. *Arbitrary Power: Romanticism, Language, Politics*. Princeton, NJ: Princeton UP, 2004.

Keating, AnaLouise. *Women Reading Women Writing: Self-Invention in Paula Gunn Allen, Gloria Anzaldúa, and Audre Lorde*. Philadelphia: Temple UP, 1996.

Keating, P. J. *The Working Classes in Victorian Fiction*. London: Allen and Unwin, 1971.

Keller, Betty. *Pauline*. Vancouver: Douglas and McIntyre, 1981.

Kellner, Douglas. "Ernst Bloch, Utopia, and Ideology Critique." *Not Yet: Reconsidering Ernst Bloch*. Ed. Jamie Owen Daniel and Tom Moylan. London: Verso, 1997. 80–95.

————. *Jean Baudrillard: From Marxism to Postmodernism and Beyond*. Stanford, CA: Stanford UP, 1989.

————, ed. *Baudrillard: A Critical Reader*. Oxford: Blackwell, 1994.

————. *Postmodernism/Jameson/Critique*. Washington, DC: Maisonneuve P, 1989.

Kelly, Aileen M. *Toward Another Shore: Russian Thinkers between Necessity and Chance*. New Haven: Yale UP, 1998.

Kelly, Gary. *Revolutionary Feminism: The Mind and Career of Mary Wollstonecraft.* 2nd ed. Basingstoke: Macmillan, 1996.

Kelly, Laurence. *Lermontov: Tragedy in the Caucasus.* New York: George Braziller, 1978.

Kemp-Welsh, A. *Stalin and the Literary Intelligentsia, 1928–1939.* Hong Kong: Macmillan, 1991.

Kennedy, Valerie. *Edward Said: A Critical Introduction.* Malden, MA: Polity, 2000.

Kenner, Hugh. *The Pound Era.* Berkeley: U of California P, 1971.

Kenny, Michael. *The First New Left: British Intellectuals after Stalin.* London: Lawrence and Wishart, 1995.

Kermode, Frank. *Forms of Attention.* Chicago: U of Chicago P, 1985.

Kern, Gary, ed. *Zamyatin's "We": A Collection of Critical Essays.* Ann Arbor, MI: Ardis, 1988.

Kershner, R. Brandon. *Joyce, Bakhtin, and Popular Literature.* Chapel Hill: U of North Carolina P, 1989.

Kertzer, Jonathan. *Worrying the Nation: Imagining a National Literature in English Canada.* Toronto: U of Toronto P, 1998.

Kesteloot, Lilyan. *Anthologie négro-africaine: Panorama critique des prosateurs, poètes et dramaturges noirs du XXe siècle.* Vanve, France: EDICEF, 1993.

_____. *Black Writers in French: A Literary History of Negritude.* Philadelphia: Temple UP, 1974.

Kestner, Joseph. *Protest and Reform: The British Social Narrative by Women, 1827–1867.* London: Methuen, 1985.

Keys, Roger. *The Reluctant Modernist: Andrei Bely and the Development of Russian Fiction, 1902–1914.* New York: Oxford UP, 1996.

Kiberd, Declan. *Inventing Ireland: The Literature of the Modern Nation.* London: Jonathan Cape, 1995.

Killam, G. D. *An Introduction to the Writings of Ngugi.* London: Heinemann, 1980.

_____. *The Writings of Chinua Achebe.* London: Heinemann, 1977.

Killens, John Oliver. "The Half Ain't Never Been Told." *Contemporary Authors: Autobiography Series.* Vol. 2. Ed. Adele Sarkissian. Detroit: Gale, 1985.

Kim Chung-ryol. "Mao Tse-tung's Views of Revolutionary Literature." *Journal of Asiatic Studies* 24.1 (1981): 69–84.

Kim, Elaine. *Asian-American Literature: An Introduction to the Writings and Their Social Context.* Philadelphia: Temple UP, 1982.

Kimball, Roger. *Tenured Radicals: How Politics Has Corrupted Higher Education.* New York: HarperCollins, 1990.

Kimyongür, Angela. *Socialist Realism in Louis Aragon's "Le monde réel."* Hull, UK: U of Hull P, 1995.

King, Bruce, ed. *The Later Fiction of Nadine Gordimer.* New York: St. Martin's, 1993.

_____. *West Indian Literature.* 2nd ed. Carbondale: Southern Illinois UP, 1995.

Kinkley, Jeffrey C. *The Odyssey of Shen Congwen.* Stanford, CA: Stanford UP, 1987.

Kinnamon, Keneth. *The Emergence of Richard Wright: A Study in Literature and Society.* Urbana: U of Illinois P, 1972.

Kirk, Eugene P. *Menippean Satire: An Annotated Catalogue of Texts and Criticism.* New York: Garland, 1980.

Kirk, John. "Recovered Perspectives: Gender, Class, and Memory in Pat Barker's Writing." *Contemporary Literature* 40 (Winter 1999): 603–26.

Kirkup, Gill, Linda Janes, Kath Woodward, and Fiona Hovenden, eds. *The Gendered Cyborg: A Reader*. New York: Routledge, 2000.

Kishimoto, Jorge Luis. "Vallejo y la Bohemia de Trujillo." *Intensidad y altura de César Vallejo*. Ed. Ricardo Gónzalez Vigil. Lima: Editorial Pontificia Universidad Católica del Perú, 1993. 33–58.

Klaus, H. Gustav. "Harold Heslop: Miner Novelist." *The Literature of Labour: Two Hundred Years of Working-Class Writing*. Ed. H. Gustav Klaus. New York: St. Martin's, 1985. 89–105.

————, ed. *The Literature of Labour: Two Hundred Years of Working-Class Writing*. New York: St. Martin's, 1985.

————. *The Socialist Novel in Britain: Towards the Recovery of a Tradition*. London: Harvester, 1982.

Klein, Kathleen Gregory. *Diversity and Detective Fiction*. Bowling Green, OH: Bowling Green State U Popular P, 1999.

Klein, Marcus. *Foreigners: The Making of American Literature, 1900–1940*. Chicago: U of Chicago P, 1981.

Klima, Ivan. *Karel Čapek: Life and Works*. Trans. Norma Comrada. North Haven: Catbird P, 2002.

Kluge, Alexander. *Chronik der Gefühle*. Vol. 1: "Basisgeschichten"; vol. 2: "Lebensläufe." Frankfurt am Main: Suhrkamp Verlag, 2000.

————. *Die Wächter des Sarkophags: 10 Jahre Tschernobyl*. Hamburg: Rotbuch, 1996.

————. *Gelegenheitsarbeit einer Sklavin: Zur realistischen Methode*. Frankfurt am Main: Suhrkamp Verlag, 1975.

————. *In Gefahr und grösster Not bringt der Mittelweg den Tod: Texte zu Kino, Film, Politik*. Berlin: Vorwerk 8, 2002.

————. *Schlachtbeschreibung*. Frankfurt am Main: Suhrkamp Verlag, 1964, 1978, 1983.

Kluge, Alexander, and Oskar Negt. *Geschichte und Eigensinn*. Vols. 1–3. Frankfurt am Main: Suhrkamp Verlag, 1981.

————. *Öffentlichkeit und Erfahrung: Zur Organisationsanalyse von bürgerlicher und proletarischer Öffentlichkeit*. Frankfurt am Main: Suhrkamp Verlag, 1972.

Knight, Damon. *The Futurians*. New York: John Day, 1977.

Knight, Diana. *Barthes and Utopia: Space, Travel, Writing*. Oxford: Clarendon P, 1997.

Knight, Stephen. *Crime Fiction, 1800–2000: Detection, Death, Diversity*. New York: Palgrave Macmillan, 2004.

Knowlson, James. *Damned to Fame: The Life of Samuel Beckett*. New York: Simon and Schuster, 1996.

Koestler, Cynthia. *Stranger on the Square*. Ed. Harold Harris. London: Hutchinson, 1984.

Kolbas, E. Dean. *Critical Theory and the Literary Canon*. Boulder, CO: Westview P, 2001.

Konkle, Maureen. *Writing Indian Nations: Native Intellectuals and the Politics of Historiography, 1827–1863*. Chapel Hill: U of North Carolina P, 2004.

Konzett, Delia C. *Ethnic Modernisms: Anzia Yezierska, Zora Neale Hurston, Jean Rhys, and the Aesthetics of Dislocation*. New York: Palgrave Macmillan, 2002.

Kornbluh, Joyce, ed. *Rebel Voices: An IWW Anthology*. Ann Arbor: U of Michigan P, 1972.

Kovel, Joel. *Red-Hunting in the Promised Land*. New York: Basic Books, 1994.

Kowallis, Jon Eugene von. *The Lyrical Lu Xun: A Study of His Classical Style Verse*. Honolulu: U of Hawaii P, 1996.

————. *The Subtle Revolution: Poets of the "Old Schools" in Late-Qing and Early Republican China*. Berkeley: Institute of East Asian Studies, U of California, 2004.

Kraemaer, Michael, and Hana Wirth-Nesher. *Cambridge Companion to Jewish-American Literature*. Cambridge: Cambridge UP, 2003.

Kramer, Hilton. "Political Romance." *Commentary* 80 (October 1975): 76–80.

Kraus, Karl. *Half Truths and One-and-a-Half Truths: Selected Aphorisms*. Ed. and trans. Harry Zohn. New York: Carcanet P, 1986.

————. *The Last Days of Mankind*. Abr. and ed. Frederick Ungar. Trans. Alexander Gode and Sue Ellen Wright. New York: Frederick Ungar, 1974.

Krause, David. *Sean O'Casey: The Man and His Work*. New York: Macmillan, 1960.

————, and Robert G. Lowery, eds. *Sean O'Casey: Centenary Essays*. Totowa, NJ: Barnes and Noble, 1980.

Kremer, Lillian S. *Women's Holocaust Writing*. Lincoln: U of Nebraska P, 1999.

————, ed. *Holocaust Literature: An Encyclopedia of Writers and Their Work*. New York: Routledge, 2003.

Kristal, Efrain. *Temptation of the Word: The Novels of Mario Vargas Llosa*. Nashville: Vanderbilt UP, 1999.

Kristeva, Julia. *Hannah Arendt*. New York: Columbia UP, 2001.

————. *Powers of Horror: An Essay in Abjection*. Trans. Leon S. Roudiez. New York: Columbia UP, 1982.

————. *Revolution in Poetic Language*. Trans. Margaret Waller. New York: Columbia UP, 1984.

————. "Women's Time." Trans. Alice Jardine and Harry Blake. *Feminisms: An Anthology of Literary Theory and Criticism*. Ed. Robyn R. Warhol and Diane Price Herndl. New Brunswick, NJ: Rutgers UP, 1991. 860–77.

Kritzer, Amelia Howe. *The Plays of Caryl Churchill: Theatre of Empowerment*. London, Basingstoke: Macmillan, 1991.

Krtalić, Ivan. *Krleža, za i protiv (1914–1927)*. 2 vols. Zagreb: Komunist, 1988.

Krupat, Arnold. *The Voice in the Margin: Native American Literature and the Canon*. Berkeley: U of California P, 1989.

Kumar, Krishan. *Utopia and Anti-Utopia in Modern Times*. Oxford: Basil Blackwell, 1987.

Kuortti, Joel. *Place of the Sacred: The Rhetoric of the "Satanic Verses" Affair*. New York: Peter Lang, 1997.

Kurzke, Hermann. *Thomas Mann: Life as a Work of Art: A Biography*. Trans. Leslie Willson. Princeton, NJ: Princeton UP, 2002.

Kurzweil, Edith, and William Phillips, eds. *Writers and Politics: A* Partisan Review *Reader*. Boston: Routledge, 1983.

LaBahn, Kathleen J. *Anna Seghers's Exile Literature: The Mexican Years*. Bern: Peter Lang, 1986.

Labanyi, Jo. *Myth and History in the Contemporary Spanish Novel*. Cambridge: Cambridge UP, 1989.

————. *National Identity in Modern Spain*. London: U of London, 1994.

————, and Helen Graham, eds. *Spanish Cultural Studies*. New York: Oxford UP, 1995.

Labor, Earle. *Jack London*. New York: Twayne, 1974.

LaCapra, Dominick. *Madame Bovary on Trial*. Ithaca: Cornell UP, 1982.

Laclau, Ernesto, and Chantal Mouffe. *Hegemony and Socialist Strategy: Towards a Radical Democratic Politics*. London: Verso, 1985.

Lacouture, Jean. *Malraux, une vie dans le siècle*. Paris: Seuil, 1976.

Laguna, Elpidio. "Social Genesis and Historical Understanding in the Works of Pedro Mir." *Revista canadiense de estudios hispánicos* 15.2 (Invierno 1991): 235–50.

Lahusen, Thomas. *How Life Writes the Book: Real Socialism and Socialist Realism in Stalin's Russia*. Ithaca, NY: Cornell UP, 1997.

———, and Evgeny Dobrenko, eds. *Socialist Realism without Shores*. Durham, NC: Duke UP, 1997.

Lalić, Ivan V. "Some Notes on Yugoslav Literature: A Historical Approach." *North Dakota Quarterly* 61.1 (1993): 12–17.

Lamming, George. *The Pleasures of Exile*. 1960. Ann Arbor: U of Michigan P, 1992.

Landau, Sidney. *Dictionaries: The Art and Craft of English Lexicography*. 2nd ed. Cambridge: Cambridge UP, 2001.

Landrum, Larry. "The Shattered Modernism of Momaday's *House Made of Dawn*." *Modern Fiction Studies* 42 (1996): 763–86.

Landry, Donna, and Gerald McLean, eds. *The Spivak Reader*. London: Routledge, 1995.

Landsberg, Melvin. *Dos Passos' Path to "U.S.A.": A Critical Biography, 1912–1936*. Boulder, CO: Associated UP, 1972.

Langer, Elinor. *Josephine Herbst: The Story She Could Never Tell*. Boston: Little Brown, 1984.

Langer, Lawrence. *The Holocaust and the Literary Imagination*. New Haven: Yale UP, 1975.

Lara Martínez, Rafael. *En la humedad del secreto: Antología poética de Roque Dalton*. San Salvador: Concultura, 1994.

———, and Dennis L. Seager. *Otros Roques: La poética múltiple de Roque Dalton*. New Orleans: UP of the South, 1999.

Larbalestier, Justine. *The Battle of the Sexes in Science Fiction*. Middletown, CT: Wesleyan UP, 2002.

Larrat, Jean-Claude. *André Malraux*. Paris: Librairie Générale Française, 2001.

Larsen, Neil. *Determinations: Essays on Theory, Nation and Narrative in the Americas*. London and New York: Verso, 2001.

———. *Reading North by South*. Minneapolis: Minnesota UP, 1990.

Lasić, Stanko. *Sukob na književnoj ljevici, 1928–1952*. Zagreb: Liber, 1970.

Lassner, Phyllis. *British Women Writers of World War II: Battlegrounds of Their Own*. New York: St. Martin's, 1998.

Laurence, Dan H., ed. *Bernard Shaw: Collected Letters*. London: Reinhardt, 1965–1998.

Lauter, Paul. "American Proletarianism." *The Columbia History of the American Novel*. Ed. Emory Elliott et al. New York: Columbia UP, 1991. 331–56.

———. *Canons and Contexts*. Oxford: Oxford UP, 1991.

Lavers, Annette. *Roland Barthes: Structuralism and After*. Cambridge, MA: Harvard UP, 1982.

Lawrie, Steven W. *Erich Fried: A Writer without a Country*. New York: Lang, 1996.

Laybourn, Keith. *The General Strike: Day by Day*. Stroud, UK: Sutton, 1996.

———. *The General Strike of 1926*. Manchester: Manchester UP, 1993.

Layman, Richard. *Shadow Man: The Life of Dashiell Hammett*. New York: Manley, 1981.

Layton, Susan. *Russian Literature and Empire: Conquest of the Caucasus from Pushkin to Tolstoy*. Cambridge: Cambridge UP, 1994.

Lazarus, Neil. *Resistance in Postcolonial African Fiction*. New Haven: Yale UP, 1990.

Lazo, Raimundo. *La literatura Cubana, esquema histórico (desde sus orígenes hasta 1966)*. Havana: Editora Universitaria, 1967.

Leach, Robert. "*Mother Courage and Her Children.*" *The Cambridge Companion to Brecht.* Ed. Peter Thomson and Glendyr Sacks. Cambridge: Cambridge UP, 1994.

Leatherbarrow, W. J., ed. *Dostoevsky's* The Devils: *A Critical Companion.* Evanston, IL: Northwestern UP, 1999.

Lederer, Katherine. *Lillian Hellman.* Boston: Twayne, 1979.

Lee, Hermione. *Philip Roth.* London: Methuen, 1982.

Lee, Leo Ou-fan. *The Romantic Generation of Modern Chinese Writers.* Cambridge, MA: Harvard UP, 1973.

———. *Voices from the Iron House: A Study of Lu Xun.* Bloomington: Indiana UP, 1987.

———, ed. *Lu Xun and His Legacy.* Berkeley: U of California P, 1985.

Lee, Robert A., ed. *Loosening the Seams: Interpretations of Gerald Vizenor.* Bowling Green, KY: Popular P, 2000.

Leeming, David. *James Baldwin.* New York: Knopf, 1994.

Lefanu, Sarah. *In the Chinks of the World Machine: Feminism and Science Fiction.* London: Women's P, 1988. 173–99.

Lefebvre, Henri. *Alfred de Musset: Dramaturge.* Paris: L'Arche, 1955.

———. *The French Revolution: From Its Origins to 1793.* Trans. Elizabeth Moss Evanson. New York: Columbia UP, 1962.

———. *The French Revolution: From 1793 to 1799.* Trans. John Hall Stewart and James Fruguglietti. New York: Columbia UP, 1964.

———. *Introduction to Modernity.* Trans. John Moore. London: Verso, 1995.

———. *The Production of Space.* Trans. Donald Nicholson-Smith. Oxford: Blackwell, 1991.

———. *Rabelais.* Paris: Les Éditeurs français réunis, 1955.

Le Guin, Ursula K. *Dancing at the Edge of the World.* New York: Grove, 1989.

Lehman, Paul R. *The Development of the Black Psyche in the Writings of John Oliver Killens (1916–1987).* Lewiston, NY: Edwin Mellon, 2003.

Lehmann, John. *New Writing in Europe.* Harmondsworth: Penguin, 1940.

———, T. A. Jackson, and C. Day Lewis, eds. *Ralph Fox: A Writer in Arms.* London: Lawrence and Wishart, 1937.

Leigh, Nigel. *Radical Fictions and the Novels of Norman Mailer.* New York: St. Martin's, 1990.

Lemire, Maurice. "*Les Anciens Canadiens.*" *Dictionnaire des oeuvres littéraires du Québec.* Vol 1. Montreal: Fides, 1978. 16–24.

Lenin, Vladimir Ilyich. "The Collapse of the Second International." *Collected Works.* Vol. 21. Moscow: Progress Publishers, 1980. 207–59.

———. *Collected Works of V. I. Lenin.* New York: International Publishers, 1927.

———. "Opportunism, and the Collapse of the Second International." *Collected Works.* Vol. 21. Moscow: Progress Publishers, 1980. 438–53.

Lenzini, Luca. *Il poeta di nome Fortini: saggi e proposte di lettura.* Lecce: P. Manni, 1999.

Leonard, Tom, ed. *Radical Renfrew: Poetry from the French Revolution to the First World War.* Edinburgh: Polygon, 1990.

LeSeur, Geta. *Ten Is the Age of Darkness: The Black Bildungsroman.* Columbia: U of Missouri P, 1995.

Lessing, Doris. "The Small Personal Voice." 1957. *A Small Personal Voice: Essays, Reviews, Interviews.* Ed. Paul Schleuter. New York: Vintage, 1975. 3–21.

Levenson, Leah, and Jerry H. Natterstad. *Granville Hicks: The Intellectual in Mass Society.* Philadelphia: Temple UP, 1993.

Levenson, Michael, ed. *The Cambridge Companion to Modernism*. Cambridge: Cambridge UP, 1999.

————. "Does *The Waste Land* Have a Politics?" *Modernism/Modernity* 6.3 (1999): 1–13.

Levenstain, Harvey A. "*The Worker*: Cleveland, Chicago, and New York, 1922–1924; *Daily Worker*: Chicago and New York, 1924–1958." *The American Radical Press, 1880–1960, Volume 1*. Ed. Joseph R. Conlin. Westport, CT: Greenwood, 1974. 224–43.

Levin, Dan. *Stormy Petrel: The Life and Work of Maxim Gorky*. New York: Appleton-Century, 1965.

Levine, George, and U. C. Knoepflmacher, eds. *The Endurance of Frankenstein: Essays on Mary Shelley's Novel*. Berkeley: U of California P, 1982.

Levine, Lawrence W. *The Opening of the American Mind: Canons, Culture, and History*. Boston: Beacon P, 1996.

Levine, Linda Gould. Introduction to *Reivindicación del Conde don Julián*. Madrid: Cátedra, 1985. 25–44.

————. *Isabel Allende*. New York: Twayne, 2002.

Levine, Robert S. *Martin Delany, Frederick Douglass, and the Politics of Representative Identity*. Chapel Hill: North Carolina UP, 1997.

Levitt, Marcus C. *Russian Literary Politics and the Pushkin Celebration of 1880*. Ithaca, NY: Cornell UP, 1989.

Levy, Bernard-Henri. *Sartre: The Philosopher of the Twentieth Century*. Trans. Andrew Brown. Cambridge: Polity P, 2003.

Lewis, David Levering. *W.E.B. Du Bois: Biography of a Race*. New York: Henry Holt, 1993.

————. *When Harlem Was in Vogue*. 1970. New York: Oxford UP, 1981.

Lewis, Jane. *Women in England, 1870–1950*. Bloomington: Indiana UP, 1984.

Lewis, Richard W. B. *The Picaresque Saint*. Philadelphia: Lippincott, 1959.

Lewis, Wyndham. *Left Wings over Europe*. London: Cape, 1936.

————. *The Revenge for Love*. Ed. Reed Way Dasenbrock. Santa Rosa, CA: Black Sparrow P, 1991.

————. *The Revenge for Love*. Intro. Paul Edwards. London: Penguin, 2004.

Li, David Leiwei. *Imagining the Nation: Asian American Literature and Cultural Consent*. Stanford, CA: Stanford UP, 1998.

Liano, Dante. "La génesis de *Rigoberta, La nieta de los mayas*." *La memoria popular y sus transformaciones*. Ed. Martin Lienhard. Madrid: Iberoamericana, 2000. 209–19.

Libert, Florence. "An Interview with Anita Desai." *World Literature Written in English* 30.1 (1990): 47–55.

Libretti, Tim. "First and Third Worlds in U.S. Literature: Rethinking Carlos Bulosan." *MELUS* 23.4 (Winter 1998): 135–55.

Li Dian. "Ideology and Conflicts in Bei Dao's Poetry." *Modern Chinese Literature* 9.2 (1996): 369–85.

Lie, Nadia, and Theo D'haen, eds. *Constellation Caliban: Figurations and Character*. Amsterdam: Rodopi, 1977.

Lieb, Michael. *Milton and the Culture of Violence*. Ithaca: Cornell UP, 1994.

Lienhard, Martin. *La voz y su huella*. Hanover, NH: Ediciones del Norte, 1990.

Light, Alison. *Forever England: Femininity, Literature and Conservatism between the Wars*. London: Routledge, 1991.

Lindemann, Marilee. *Willa Cather: Queering America*. New York: Columbia UP, 1999.

Lingeman, Richard. *Theodore Dreiser*. 2 vols. New York: Putnam, 1990.

Lisella, Julia, et al. "Readings: Genevieve Taggard." *How2* 2.1 (Spring 2003). http://www.scc. rutgers.edu/however/vl_2_2003/current/index.shtm.

A Litany for Survival: The Life and Work of Audre Lorde. Dir. Ada Gay Griffin and Michelle Parkerson. Third World Newsreel, 1996.

Liu, James J. Y. *Chinese Theories of Literature*. Chicago: U of Chicago P, 1975.

Liu, Wu-chi. *An Introduction to Chinese Literature*. Bloomington: Indiana UP, 1966.

————, and Irving Lo, eds. *Sunflower Splendor: Three Thousand Years of Chinese Poetry*. Bloomington: Indiana UP, 1975.

Lloyd, David. *Anomalous States: Irish Writing and the Post-colonial Moment*. Dublin: The Lilliput P, 1993.

Lock, F. P. *Swift's Tory Politics*. London: Duckworth, 1983.

Locke, Don. *A Fantasy of Reason: The Life and Thought of William Godwin*. London: Routledge and Kegan Paul, 1980.

Lodge, Tom. *Black Politics in South Africa*. London: Longman, 1983.

Logan, George. *The Meaning of More's Utopia*. Princeton, NJ: Princeton UP, 1983.

London, Jack. *Jack London, American Rebel: A Collection of His Social Writings*. New York: Citadel, 1947.

London, Joan. *Jack London and His Daughters*. San Bernadino, CA: Borego P, 1995.

Long, Terry. *Granville Hicks*. Boston: Twayne, 1981.

————. "Interview with Granville Hicks." *Antioch Review* 33 (Summer 1935): 93–102.

Longinović, Tomislav. "Danilo Kiš." *Dictionary of Literary Biography: South Slavic Writers since World War II*. Detroit: Gale Research Inc., 1997.

López, Alfred. *Posts and Pasts: A Theory of Postcolonialism*. New York: SU of New York P, 2001.

López Ortega, Ramón. "The Language of the Working-Class Novel of the 1930s." *The Socialist Novel in Britain: Towards the Recovery of a Tradition*. Ed. H. Gustav Klaus. New York: St. Martin's, 1982. 122–44.

Lord, George deF., et al., eds. *Poems on Affairs of State: Augustan Satirical Verse, 1660–1714*. 7 vols. New Haven: Yale UP, 1963–1975.

Lovell, Terry. *Consuming Fiction*. London: Verso, 1987.

Loving, Jerome. *Walt Whitman: The Song of Himself*. Berkeley: U of California P, 1999.

Lowe, Lisa. *Immigrant Acts*. Durham, NC: Duke UP, 1996.

Löwenthal, Leo. *Literature and the Image of Man*. New Brunswick: Transaction Books, 1986.

Lucas, John. *The Radical Twenties: Writing, Politics, and Culture*. New Brunswick: Rutgers UP, 1999.

Ludington, C. Townsend. *John Dos Passos: A Twentieth-Century Odyssey*. New York: E.P. Dutton, 1980.

Lukács, Georg. *The Destruction of Reason*. 2 vols. Trans. Peter Palmer. Atlantic Highlands, NJ: Humanities P, 1981.

————. *Die Eigenart des Äesthetischen*. 2 vols. Berlin: Aufbau-Verlag, 1987.

————. *Essays on Realism*. Ed. Rodney Livingstone. Cambridge, MA: MIT P, 1981.

————. *Existentialisme ou marxisme?* Trans. E. Kelemen. Paris: Nagel, 1948.

————. *Heidelberger Ästhetik (1916–1918)*. Ed. György Márkus and Frank Benseler. Darmstadt: Luchterhand, 1975.

————. *Heidelberger Philosophie der Kunst (1912–1914)*. Ed. György Márkus and Frank Benseler. Darmstadt: Luchterhand, 1974.

————. *The Historical Novel*. Trans. Hannah Mitchell and Stanley Mitchell. Lincoln: U of Nebraska P, 1983.

————. *History and Class Consciousness: Studies in Marxist Dialectics*. Trans. Rodney Livingstone. Cambridge, MA: MIT P, 1971.

————. *The Ontology of Social Being*. Trans. David Fernbach. London: Merlin, 1980.

————. *Realism in Our Time: Literature and the Class Struggle*. Trans. John Mander and Necke Mander. New York: Harper and Row, 1964.

————. *Soul and Form*. Trans. Anna Bostock. Cambridge, MA: MIT P, 1974.

————. *Studies in European Realism: A Sociological Survey of the Writings of Balzac, Stendhal, Tolstoy, Gorky, and Others*. Trans. Edith Bone. New York: Fertig Howard, 2002.

————. *The Theory of the Novel*. 1920. Trans. Anna Bostock. Cambridge, MA: MIT P, 1971.

————. *The Young Hegel: Studies in the Relation between Dialectics and Economics*. Trans. Rodney Livingstone. Cambridge, MA: MIT P, 1975.

Luker, Nicholas. *From Furmanov to Sholokhov*. Ann Arbor, MI: Ardis, 1988.

Lumpkin, Katharine Du Pre. *The Making of a Southerner*. 1946. Athens: U of Georgia P, 1992.

Lundquist, James. *Chester Himes*. New York: Ungar, 1976.

————. *Jack London: Adventures, Ideas, and Fiction*. New York: Ungar, 1987.

Lunn, Eugene. *Marxism and Modernism: An Historical Study of Lukács, Brecht, Benjamin, and Adorno*. Berkeley: U of California P, 1982.

Luperini, Romano. *La lotta mentale: Per un profilo di Franco Fortini*. Rome: Editori Riuniti, 1986.

Lu Tonglin. "*Red Sorghum*: Limits of Transgression." *Politics, Ideology, and Literary Discourse in Modern China: Theoretical Interventions and Cultural Critique*. Ed. Liu Kang and Tang Xiaobing. Durham, NC: Duke UP, 1993. 188–208.

Lutz, William, ed. *Beyond "Nineteen Eighty-Four": Doublespeak in a Post-Orwellian Age*. Urbana, IL: National Council of Teachers of English, 1989.

Lutze, Peter. *Alexander Kluge: The Last Modernist*. Wayne State UP, 1998.

Lycett, Andrew. *Rudyard Kipling*. London: Weidenfeld and Nicolson, 1999.

Lyell, William A. *Lu Hsün's Vision of Reality*. Berkeley: U of California P, 1976.

Lynn, Richard John. *Chinese Literature: A Draft Bibliography in Western European Languages*. Canberra: Australian National UP, 1979.

Lyon, James K. *Bertolt Brecht in America*. Princton, NJ: Princeton UP, 1980.

Lyotard, Jean-François. *The Postmodern Condition: A Report on Knowledge*. Trans. Geoff Bennington and Brian Massumi. Minneapolis: U of Minnesota P, 1984.

MacCabe, Colin. *James Joyce and the Revolution of the Word*. London: Macmillan, 1978.

MacDiarmid, Hugh. *Collected Works*. Gen. ed. Alan Riach. Manchester: Carcanet, 1992–ongoing.

Macdonald, Andrew. *Howard Fast: A Critical Companion*. Westport, CT: Greenwood, 1996.

Macey, David. *The Lives of Michel Foucault: A Biography*. New York: Vintage-Random House, 1993.

Macherey, Pierre. *In a Materialist Way: Selected Essays*. Ed. Warren Montag. London: Verso, 1998.

————. *The Object of Literature*. Cambridge: Cambridge UP, 1995.

————. *A Theory of Literary Production*. Trans. Geoffrey Wall. London: Routledge and Kegan Paul, 1978.

_____, and Etienne Balibar. "On Literature as an Ideological Form." Trans. I. McCleod, J. Whitehead, and A. Wordsworth. *Oxford Literary Review* 3 (1978): 4–12.

MacKinnon, Janice R., and Stephan R. MacKinnon. *Agnes Smedley: The Life and Times of an American Radical*. Berkeley: U of California P, 1988.

Madden, David, ed. *Nathanael West: The Cheaters and the Cheated: A Collection of Critical Essays*. De Land, FL: Everett Edwards, 1973.

Madiebo, Alexander A. *The Nigerian Revolution and the Biafran War*. Enugu, Nigeria: Fourth Dimension Publishers, 1980.

Madsen, Axel. *André Malraux: A Biography*. New York: William Morrow, 1976.

Magnarelli, Sharon. *Reflections/Refractions: Reading Luisa Valenzuela*. New York: Peter Lang, 1988.

Maguire, Robert A. *Exploring Gogol*. Stanford, CA: Stanford UP, 1994.

_____. *Red Virgin Soil: Soviet Literature in the 1920s*. Princeton, NJ: Princeton UP, 1968.

Mahoney, Daniel J. *Aleksandr Solzhenitsyn: The Ascent from Ideology*. Lanham, MD: Rowman and Littlefield, 2001.

Major, Robert. *The American Dream in Nineteenth-Century Quebec: Ideologies and Utopia in Antoine Gérin-Lajoie's "Jean Rivard."* Toronto: U of Toronto P, 1996.

Makin, Michael. *Marina Tsvetaeva: Poetics of Appropriation*. Oxford: Clarendon, 1993.

Malay, Rosario S. "*Mga Ibong Mandaragit* and the Second Propaganda Movement." *General Education Journal* 17 (1969–1970): 107–17.

Malia, Martin. *Russia under Western Eyes: From the Bronze Horseman to the Lenin Mausoleum*. Cambridge, MA: Belknap-Harvard UP, 2000.

Malin, Irvin. *Critical Views of Isaac Bashevis Singer*. New York: New York UP, 1972.

Malmstad, John E., ed. *Andrey Bely: The Spirit of Symbolism*. Ithaca, NY: Cornell UP, 1987.

Mandel, Ernest. *Delightful Murder: A Social History of the Crime Story*. Minneapolis: U of Minnesota P, 1984.

_____. *Late Capitalism*. Trans. Joris De Bres. London: NLB, 1975.

Mandel'shtam, Osip. *Sobranie sochinenii* [collected works]. Ed. Pavel Nerler et al. 4 vols. Moscow: Art-Biznes-Tsentr, 1993–1997.

Manganiello, Dominic. *Joyce's Politics*. London: Routledge and Kegan Paul, 1980.

Mangione, Jerre. *The Dream and the Deal: The Federal Writers' Project, 1935–1943*. Philadelphia: U of Pennsylvania P, 1983.

Manuel, Frank E., and Fritzie P. Manuel. *Utopian Thought in the Western World*. Cambridge, MA: Harvard UP, 1979.

Mao Zedong. "Talk to Music Workers." *Mao Tse-tung Unrehearsed*. Ed. Stuart R. Schram. Harmondsworth: Penguin, 1974. 84–90.

Marable, Manning. *W.E.B. Du Bois: Black Radical Democrat*. Boston: Twayne, 1986.

Maravall, José Antonio. *Utopia and Counterutopia in the "Quixote."* Trans. Robert W. Felkel. Detroit: Wayne State UP, 1991.

Marchand, Philip. *Marshall McLuhan: The Medium and the Messenger: A Biography*. Toronto: Vintage Canada, 1998.

Marcus, Jane. *Art and Anger: Reading Like a Woman*. Columbus: Ohio State UP, 1988.

_____. *Hearts of Darkness: White Women Write Race*. New Brunswick, NJ: Rutgers UP, 2004.

_____. *Virginia Woolf and the Languages of Patriarchy*. Bloomington: Indiana UP, 1987.

Margolies, David. *The Function of Literature: A Study of Christopher Caudwell's Aesthetics*. New York: International Publishers, 1969.

————. *Novel and Society in Elizabethan England*. Totowa, NJ: Barnes and Noble, 1985.

————, ed. *Writing the Revolution: Cultural Criticism from "Left Review."* Chicago: Pluto, 1998.

Margolies, Edward, and Michel Fabre. *The Several Lives of Chester Himes*. Jackson: UP of Mississippi, 1997.

Mariani, Paul. *William Carlos Williams: A New World Naked*. New York: McGraw-Hill, 1981.

Mariátegui, José Carlos. *Seven Interpretive Essays on Peruvian Reality*. Trans. Marjori Urquidi. Austin: U of Texas P, 1989.

Markov, Vladimir. *Russian Futurism: A History*. Berkeley: U of California P, 1968.

Markovitz, Irving Leonard. *Léopold Sédar Senghor and the Politics of Negritude*. New York: Atheneum, 1969.

Marling, William. *American Roman Noir: Hammett, Cain, and Chandler*. Athens: U of Georgia P, 1998.

Márquez, Alexis. *La obra narrative de Alejo Carpentier*. Caracas: Ediciones de la Biblioteca de la Universidad Central de Venezuela, 1970.

Marsh, Alec. *Money and Modernity: Pound, Williams, and the Spirit of Jefferson*. Tuscaloosa: U of Alabama P, 1998.

Marshall, Bill. *Victor Serge: The Uses of Dissent*. Oxford: Berg, 1992.

Marshall, Peter. *William Godwin*. New Haven, CT: Yale UP, 1984.

Martin, Carol, ed. *A Sourcebook of Feminist Theatre and Performance: On and Beyond the Stage*. London: Routledge, 1996.

Martin, Gerald. *Journeys through the Labyrinth: Latin American Fiction in the Twentieth Century*. London: Verso, 1989.

Martin, Jay. *Nathanael West: The Art of His Life*. New York: Farrar, Straus and Giroux, 1970.

Martin, Robert A. "Hemingway's *For Whom the Bell Tolls*: Fact into Fiction." *Studies in American Fiction* 15.2 (Spring 1987): 219–25.

Martin, Robert K., and Eric Savoy, eds. *American Gothic: New Interventions in a National Narrative*. Iowa City: U of Iowa P, 1998.

Marx, Karl. *Capital: A Critique of Political Economy*. Vol. 1. Trans. Samuel Moore and Edward Aveling. Ed. Frederick Engels. New York: International Publishers, 1967.

————. *A Contribution to the Critique of Political Economy*. Trans. S. W. Ryazanskaya. Ed. Maurice Dobb. New York: International Publishers, 1970.

————. *Economic and Philosophical Manuscripts of 1844*. Trans. Martin Milligan. Amherst, NY: Prometheus Books, 1988.

————. *Grundrisse: Foundations of the Critique of Political Economy*. Trans. Martin Nicolaus. Harmondsworth: Penguin, 1973.

————. *Karl Marx: Early Writings*. Trans. and ed. T. B. Bottomore. New York: McGraw-Hill, 1964.

————, and Friedrich Engels. *The Marx-Engels Reader*. 2nd ed. Ed. Robert Tucker. New York: W. W. Norton, 1978.

Marzani, Carl. *The Open Marxism of Antonio Gramsci*. New York: Cameron Associates, 1957.

Mason, Anne L. "The Artist and Politics in Günter Grass' *Aus dem Tagebuch einer Schnecke*." *Germanic Review* 51 (1976): 105–20.

Massumi, Brian. *A User's Guide to "Capitalism and Schizophrenia": Deviations from Deleuze and Guattari*. Cambridge, MA: MIT P, 1992.

Mathewson, Rufus W., Jr. *The Positive Hero in Russian Literature*. Stanford, CA: Stanford UP, 1975. 205–9.

Matich, Olga, and Michael Heim, eds. *The Third Wave: Russian Literature in Emigration*. Ann Arbor, MI: Ardis, 1984.

Matthiessen, F. O. *American Renaissance: Art and Expression in the Age of Emerson and Whitman*. New York: Oxford UP, 1941.

————. *The Responsibilities of the Critic: Essays and Reviews*. Ed. John Rackliffe. New York: Oxford UP, 1952.

Matvejević, Predrag. "Danilo Kiš: *Encyclopedia of the Dead*." *Cross Currents* 7 (1988): 337–49.

Maxwell, William J. *New Negro, Old Left*. New York: Columbia UP, 1999.

McAfee, Noëlle. *Julia Kristeva*. London: Routledge, 2004.

McBranty, John. *Imperial Subjects, Imperial Space: Rudyard Kipling's Fiction of the Native-Born*. Columbus: Ohio UP, 2002.

McCabe, Richard A. *Spenser's Monstrous Regiment: Elizabethan Ireland and the Poetics of Difference*. Oxford: Oxford UP, 2002.

McCaffery, Larry, ed. *Storming the Reality Studio: A Casebook of Cyberpunk and Postmodern Fiction*. Durham, NC: Duke UP, 1991.

McCarthy, Thomas. *The Critical Theory of Jürgen Habermas*. Cambridge, MA: MIT P, 1978.

McCauley, Michael J. *Jim Thompson: Sleep with the Devil*. New York: Mysterious P, 1991.

McConnell, Frank. *The Science Fiction of H. G. Wells*. Oxford: Oxford UP, 1981.

McConnell, Gary Scott. "Joseph Freeman: A Personal Odyssey from Romance to Revolution." Diss. University of North Carolina, 1985.

McCracken, Ellen. *New Latina Narrative: The Feminine Space of Postmodern Ethnicity*. Tucson: U of Arizona P, 1999.

McCulloch, Margery Palmer, ed. *Modernism and Nationalism: Literature and Society in Scotland, 1918–1939: Source Documents for the Scottish Renaissance*. Glasgow: Association for Scottish Literary Studies, 2004.

McCulloch, Margery Palmer, and Sarah M. Dunnigan, eds. *Lewis Grassic Gibbon: A Centenary Celebration*. Glasgow: Association for Scottish Literary Studies, 2003.

McDonald, Ronan. *Tragedy and Irish Literature: Synge, O'Casey, Beckett*. New York: Palgrave, 2002.

McDonough, Tom, ed. *Guy Debord and the Situationist International*. Cambridge, MA: MIT P, 2002.

McDougall, Bonnie S. "Bei Dao's Poetry: Revelation and Communication." *Modern Chinese Literature* 1.2 (1985): 225–52.

————. *Mao Zedong's "Talks at the Yan'an Conference on Literature and Art": A Translation of the 1943 Text with Commentary*. Ann Arbor: Michigan Papers in Chinese Studies, no. 39, 1980.

————, and Kam Louie. *The Literature of China in the Twentieth Century*. New York: Columbia UP, 1997.

McFarlane, James, ed. *The Cambridge Companion to Ibsen*. Cambridge: Cambridge UP, 1994.

McGee, Patrick. *Paperspace*. Lincoln: U of Nebraska P, 1988.

McGilligan, Patrick, and Paul Buhle. *Tender Comrades: A Backstory of the Hollywood Blacklist*. New York: St. Martin's, 1997.

McGowan, John. *Hannah Arendt: An Introduction*. Minneapolis: U of Minnesota P, 1998.

McGowan, Moray, and Ricarda Schmidt, eds. *From High Priests to Desecrators: Contemporary Austrian Writers*. Sheffield: Sheffield Academic P, 1993.

McHale, Brian. *Constructing Postmodernism*. London: Routledge, 1992.

————. *Postmodernist Fiction*. New York: Methuen, 1987.

McIntosh, William A. "Handel, Walpole and Gay: The Aims of *The Beggar's Opera*." *Eighteenth Century Studies* 7 (1974): 415–33.

McKay, Nellie Y., and Kathryn Earle, eds. *Approaches to Teaching the Novels of Toni Morrison*. New York: MLA, 1997.

McKenzie, Kermit E. *Comintern and World Revolution, 1928–1943*. New York: Columbia UP, 1964.

McKeon, Michael. *The Origins of the English Novel, 1600–1740*. Baltimore: Johns Hopkins UP, 1987.

McLaren, John. *Writing in Hope and Fear: Literature as Politics in Postwar Australia*. Cambridge: Cambridge UP, 1996.

McLaughlin, M. L. *Italo Calvino*. Edinburgh: Edinburgh UP, 1997.

McLellan, David. *Ideology*. Milton Keynes, UK: Open UP, 1986.

McLeod, John. "A Night at 'the Cosmopolitan': Axes of Transnational Encounter in the 1930s and 1940s." *Interventions: International Journal of Postcolonial Studies* 4.1 (2002): 53–67.

McMillan, Pauline. "Kevin Gilbert and 'Living Black.'" *Journal of Australian Studies* 45 (June 1995): 1–14.

McRobbie, Angela. "Post-Marxism and Cultural Studies: A Post-Script." *Cultural Studies*. Ed. Lawrence Grossberg, Cary Nelson, and Paula Treichler. New York: Routledge, 1992. 719–30.

Medeiros-Lichem, María Teresa, and Gladys M. Varona-Lacey, eds. *Reading the Feminine Voice in Latin American Women's Fiction: From Teresa de la Parra to Elena Poniatowska and Luisa Valenzuela*. Latin America Series, vol. 2. New York: Peter Lang, 2003.

Medovoi, Leerom. "Cold War American Culture as the Age of Three Worlds." *Minnesota Review* 55–57 (2002): 167–86.

Meier, Paul. *William Morris: The Marxist Dreamer*. Trans. Frank Gubb. 2 vols. Brighton: Harvester P, 1978.

Meisel, Martin. *Shaw and the Nineteenth Century Theater*. Westport, CT: Greenwood, 1976.

Meissner, Boris. *The Communist Party of the Soviet Union: Party Leadership, Organization, and Ideology*. Westport, CT: Greenwood, 1976.

Mejía, Marisol. "Politics in the Poetry and Prose of César Vallejo." Diss. Florida State University, 1998.

Melling, Philip L. *Vietnam in American Literature*. Boston: Twayne, 1990.

Mendelson, Edward. *Early Auden*. New York: Farrar, Straus and Giroux, 1981.

————. *Late Auden*. New York: Farrar, Straus and Giroux, 1999.

Mendelson, Maurice. *Life and Work of Walt Whitman: A Soviet View*. Trans. Andrew Broomfield. Moscow: Progress Publishers, 1976.

Mercer, Kobena. "Black Art and the Burden of Representation." *Third Text* 10 (Spring 1990): 61–78.

Merlin-Kajman, Hélène. *L'Excentricité académique: littérature, institution, société*. Paris: Les Belles Lettres, 2001.

Merrill, Robert. *Norman Mailer Revisited*. New York: Twayne, 1992.

Meszaros, Istvan. *Beyond Capital*. New York: Monthly Review P, 1995.

Meyer, Adam. "Faith and the 'Black Thing': Political Action and Self-Questioning in Grace Paley's Short Fiction." *Studies in Short Fiction* 31 (1994): 79–89.

Meyer, Michael. *Henrik Ibsen*. 3 vols. London: Rupert Hart-Davis, 1971.

————. *Several More Lives to Live: Thoreau's Political Reputation in America*. Westport, CT: Greenwood, 1977.

Meyers, Jeffrey. *Hemingway: A Biography*. New York: Harper and Row, 1985.

————. *Joseph Conrad: A Biography*. 1991. New York: Cooper Square P, 2001.

Mezo, Richard E. *A Study of B. Traven's Fiction: The Journey to Solipaz*. Lewiston, NY: E. Mellen, 1993.

Michaels, Walter Benn. *The Gold Standard and the Logic of Capitalism: American Literature at the Turn of the Century*. Berkeley: U of California P, 1987.

————. *Our America: Nativism, Modernism, and Pluralism*. Durham: Duke UP, 1995.

Michelet, Jules. *History of the French Revolution*. Trans. Charles Cocks. Chicago: Chicago UP, 1967.

Miles, Peter. "The Painter's Bible and the British Workman: Robert Tressell's Literary Activism." *The British Working-Class Novel in the Twentieth Century*. Ed. Jeremy Hawthorn. London: Edward Arnold, 1984. 1–18.

Miller, Christopher. *Theories of Africans: Francophone Literature and Anthropology in Africa*. Chicago: U of Chicago P, 1990.

Miller, J. Hillis. *Charles Dickens: The World of His Novels*. Cambridge, MA: Harvard UP, 1958.

Miller, Nina. *Making Love Modern: The Intimate Public Worlds of New York's Literary Women*. New York: Oxford UP, 1998.

Miller, Richard. *Analyzing Marx*. Princeton: Princeton UP, 1984.

Millett, Kate. *Sexual Politics*. London: Virago, 1977.

Milliken, Stephen F. *Chester Himes: A Critical Appraisal*. Columbia: U of Missouri P, 1976.

Milne, Lesley. *"The Master and Margarita": A Comedy of Victory*. Birmingham, UK: Birmingham Slavonic Monographs, 1977.

Milosz, Czeslaw. *The History of Polish Literature*. Berkeley: U of California P, 1983.

————. *Native Realm: A Search for Self-Definition*. Trans. Catherine S. Leach. Garden City, NY: Doubleday, 1968.

————. *Nobel Lecture*. New York: Farrar, Straus and Giroux, 1981.

————. *The Witness of Poetry*. Cambridge, MA: Harvard UP, 1983.

Minden, Michael, ed. *Thomas Mann*. New York: Longman, 1995.

Minow-Pinkney, Makiko. *Virginia Woolf and the Problem of the Subject*. New Brunswick: Rutgers UP, 1987.

Minter, David. *William Faulkner: His Life and Work*. Baltimore: Johns Hopkins UP, 1980.

Misurella, Fred. *Understanding Milan Kundera: Public Events, Private Affairs*. Columbia: U of South Carolina P, 1993.

Mitchell, Don. *The Lie of the Land: Migrant Workers and the California Landscape*. Minneapolis: U of Minnesota P, 1996.

Moers, Ellen. *Literary Women*. London: Women's P, 1978.

Mohanty, Chandra Talpade. *Feminism without Borders: Decolonizing Theory, Practicing Solidarity*. Durham: Duke UP, 2003.

————. "Transnational Pedagogy: Doing Political Work in Women's Studies: An Interview with Chandra Talpade Mohanty." *Atlantis* 26.2 (Spring/Summer 2002): 66–77.

————, Ann Russo, and Lourdes Torres, eds. *Third World Women and the Politics of Feminism*. Bloomington: Indiana UP, 1991.

Mohanty, Satya. *Literary Theory and the Claims of History: Postmodernism, Objectivity, Multicultural Politics*. Ithaca: Cornell UP, 1997.

Moi, Toril. *Sexual/Textual Politics*. London: Methuen, 1985.

————. *Simone de Beauvoir: The Making of an Intellectual Woman*. Oxford: Blackwell, 1994.

————, ed. *The Kristeva Reader*. New York: Columbia UP, 1986.

Mollier, Jean-Yves. *Pierre Larousse et son temps*. Paris: Larousse, 1995.

Monet-Viera, Molly. "Post-Boom Magical Realism: Appropriations and Transformation of a Genre." *Revista de estudios hispánicos* 38.1 (January 2004): 95–117.

Mongia, Padmini, ed. *Contemporary Postcolonial Theory: A Reader*. London: Arnold, 1996.

Monsiváis, Carlos. *Amor Perdido*. México: Biblioteca Era, 1978.

Montefiore, Janet. *Men and Women Writers of the 1930s: The Dangerous Flood of History*. London and New York: Routledge, 1996.

Montero, Oscar. *José Martí: An Introduction*. New York: Palgrave, 2004.

Montrose, Louis Adrian. "The Elizabethan Subject and the Spenserian Text." *Literary Theory/Renaissance Texts*. Ed. Patricia Parker and David Quint. Baltimore: Johns Hopkins UP, 1986. 303–40.

Moody, David, ed. *Cambridge Companion to T. S. Eliot*. Cambridge: Cambridge UP, 1994.

Moody, Richard. *Lillian Hellman, Playwright*. New York: Pegasus, 1972.

Moorcraft, Jean. *Siegfried Sassoon: The Making of a War Poet. A Biography, 1886–1918*. New York: Routledge, 1999.

Moore-Gilbert, B. J. *Kipling and "Orientalism."* New York: St. Martin's, 1986.

Moore-Gilbert, Bart. *Postcolonial Theory: Contexts, Practices, Politics*. London: Verso, 1997.

Mootry, Maria K. "Bitches, Whores, and Woman Haters: Archetypes and Typologies in the Art of Richard Wright." *Richard Wright: A Collection of Critical Essays*. Ed. Richard Macksey and Frank E. Moorer. Englewood Cliffs: Prentice-Hall, 1984. 117–28.

Moraga, Cherrie, and Gloria Anzaldúa, eds. *This Bridge Called My Back: Writings by Radical Women of Color*. Watertown, MA: Persephone P, 1981.

Moraña, Mabel, ed. *Indigenismo hacia el final del milenio*. Pittsburgh: Instituto Internacional de Literatura, 1998.

Moravia, Alberto. *Man as an End*. Trans. Bernard Wall. London: Secker and Warburg, 1965.

————, and Alain Elkann. *Vita di Moravia*. Rome: Bompiani, 1990.

Moretti, Franco. "'A Useless Longing for Myself': The Crisis of the European Bildungsroman, 1898–1914." *Studies in Historical Change*. Ed. Ralph Cohen. Charlottesville: U of Virginia P, 1992. 43–59.

————. *The Way of the World: The Bildungsroman in European Culture*. London: Verso, 1987.

Morgan, Arthur. *Edward Bellamy*. New York: Columbia UP, 1944.

Morgan, Edwin. *Crossing the Border: Essays on Scottish Literature*. Manchester: Carcanet, 1990.

Moriarty, Michael. *Roland Barthes*. Cambridge: Polity, 1991.

Morley, David. *The "Nationwide" Audience: Structure and Decoding*. London: BFI, 1980.

————, ed. *Stuart Hall: Critical Dialogues in Cultural Studies*. London: Routledge, 1996.

————, and Kuan-Hsing Chen, eds. *Stuart Hall: Critical Dialogues in Cultural Studies*. New York: Routledge, 1996.

Morris, Christopher D. *Models of Misrepresentation: On the Fiction of E. L. Doctorow*. Jackson: UP of Mississippi, 1991.

Morris, Margaret. *The General Strike*. London: Journeyman Press, 1976.

Morrison, Toni. *The Nobel Lecture in Literature, 1993*. New York: Alfred A. Knopf, 1997.

_____. *Playing in the Dark: Whiteness and the Literary Imagination.* New York: Vintage, 1992.

_____. "Site of Memory." *Inventing the Truth: The Art and Craft of Memoir.* Rev. ed. Ed. William Zinsser. Boston: Houghton Mifflin, 1998. 183–200.

Morton, Stephen. *Gayatri Chakravorty Spivak.* London: Routledge, 2002.

Morton, Tim, ed. *A Routledge Literary Sourcebook on Mary Shelley's "Frankenstein."* London: Routledge, 2002.

Moses, Wilson. *The Golden Age of Black Nationalism: 1850–1925.* Oxford: Oxford UP, 1988.

Moskowitz, Sam. "How Science Fiction Got Its Name." *The Prentice Hall Anthology of Science Fiction and Fantasy.* Ed. Garyn G. Roberts. Upper Saddle River, NJ: Prentice Hall, 2003. 1127–35.

_____. *The Immortal Storm.* Atlanta: Atlanta Science Fiction Organization P, 1954.

Moylan, Tom. *Demand the Impossible: Science Fiction and the Utopian Imagination.* New York: Methuen, 1986.

_____. *Scraps of the Untainted Sky: Science Fiction, Utopia, Dystopia.* Boulder, CO: Westview P, 2001.

_____, and Raffaella Baccolini, eds. *Dark Horizons: Science Fiction and the Dystopian Imagination.* London: Routledge, 2003.

Możejko, Edward. *Between Anxiety and Hope: The Poetry and Writing of Czesław Miłosz.* Edmonton: U of Alberta P, 1988.

Mudrooroo. *Writing from the Fringe: A Study of Modern Aboriginal Literature.* Melbourne, Victoria: Hyland House, 1990.

Mufti, Aamir R. "Reading the Rushdie Affair: 'Islam,' Cultural Politics, Form." *Critical Essays on Salman Rushdie.* Ed. M. Keith Booker. New York: G. K. Hall, 1999. 51–77.

Mugglestone, Lynda, ed. *Hidden Histories. The Making of the Oxford English Dictionary.* New Haven, CT: Yale UP, 2005.

_____. *Lexicography and the OED: Pioneers in the Untrodden Forest.* Oxford: Oxford UP, 2002.

Mulford, Wendy. *This Narrow Place: Sylvia Townsend Warner and Valentine Ackland: Life, Letters and Politics.* London: Pandora P, 1998.

Mulhern, Francis, ed. *Contemporary Marxist Literary Criticism.* Harlow: Longman, 1992.

Mullen, Bill, and Sherry Lee Linkon, eds. *Radical Revisions: Rereadings of 1930s Culture.* Urbana: U of Illinois P, 1996.

Mullen, R. D., et al., eds. *On Philip K. Dick.* Terre Haute, IN: SF-TH, 1992.

Muller, Gilbert H. *Chester Himes.* Boston: Twayne, 1989.

Muller, Harro. "'In solche Not kann nicht die Natur bringen': Stichworte zu Alexander Kluges Schlachtbeschreibung." *Merkur: Deutsche-Zeitschrift-fur-europaisches-Denken* 36.9 (September 1982): 888–97.

Mullin, Katherine. *James Joyce, Sexuality and Social Purity.* Cambridge: Cambridge UP, 2003.

Mulvey, Laura. *Fetishism and Curiosity.* Bloomington: Indiana UP, 1996.

_____. "Some Thoughts on Theories of Fetishism in the Context of Contemporary Culture." *October* 65 (1993): 3–20.

_____. *Visual and Other Pleasures.* Bloomington: Indiana UP, 1989.

Munro, Ian S. *Leslie Mitchell: Lewis Grassic Gibbon.* Edinburgh: Oliver and Boyd, 1966.

Munton, Alan. "Ralph Bates." Obituary. *Independent,* 7 December 2000, sec. 2: 6.

_____. "Ralph Bates." *Seven Writers of the English Left: A Bibliography of Literature and Pol-*

itics, 1916–1980. Ed. Alan Munton and Alan Young. New York: Garland, 1981. 83–115.

———, ed. "Edgell Rickword: A Celebration." *PN Review* 6.1 (1979): i–xxxii. Contributions by William Empson, E. P. Thompson, and C. Hill.

Murphy, David. *Sembène: Imagining Alternatives in Film and Fiction*. Trenton, NJ: Africa World P, 2001.

Murphy, James F. *The Proletarian Moment: The Controversy over Leftism in Literature*. Urbana: U of Illinois P, 1991.

Mustafa, Fawzia. *V. S. Naipaul*. Cambridge: Cambridge UP, 1995.

Myers, Tony. *Slavoj Zizek*. London: Routledge, 2003.

Nabokov, Vladimir. *Lectures on Russian Literature*. London: Weidenfeld and Nicolson, 1982.

———. *Nikolai Gogol*. Norfolk, CT: New Directions, 1944.

Nadel, Ira, ed. The Cambridge Companion to Ezra Pound. Cambridge: Cambridge UP, 1999.

Naess, Harald S., ed. *A History of Norwegian Literature*. Lincoln: U of Nebraska P, 1993.

Nägele, Rainer. "Brecht's Theatre of Cruelty." *Reading after Freud: Essays on Goethe, Holderlin, Habermas, Nietzsche, Brecht, Celan, and Freud*. New York: Columbia UP, 1987.

Naiman, Eric. "Andrej Platonov and the Inadmissibility of Desire." *Russian Literature* 23 (1988): 319–66.

Nair, Supriya. *Caliban's Curse: George Lamming and the Revisioning of History*. Ann Arbor: U of Michigan P, 1996.

Nash, Roderick. *Wilderness and the American Mind*. 3rd ed. New Haven, CT: Yale UP, 1982.

Nasta, Susheila. *Home Truths: Fictions of the South Asian Diaspora in Britain*. Basingstoke: Palgrave, 2002.

Nathan, Leonard, and Arthur Quinn. *The Poet's Work: An Introduction to Czeslaw Milosz*. Cambridge, MA: Harvard UP, 1991.

Naylor, Paul. *Poetic Investigations: Singing the Holes in History*. Evanston, IL: Northwestern UP, 1999.

Neal, Larry. *Visions of a Liberated Future: Black Arts Movement Writings*. Ed. Michael Schwartz. New York: Thunder's Mouth P, 1989.

———, and LeRoi Jones. *Black Fire: An Anthology of Afro-American Writing*. New York: William Morrow, 1968.

Negri, Antonio. *Insurgencies: Constituent Power and the Modern State*. 1992. Trans. M. Boscagli. Minneapolis: U of Minnesota P, 1999.

———. *Il Lavoro di Giobbe*. Milan: SugarCo, 1990.

———. *Lenta ginestra: Saggio sull'ontologia di Giacomo Leopardi*. Milan: SugarCo, 1987.

———. *Marx beyond Marx: Lessons on the "Grundrisse."* 1979. Trans. H. Cleaver et al. New York: Autonomedia, 1991.

———. *Revolution Retrieved: Selected Writings*. Trans. E. Emery. London: Red Notes, 1988.

———. *The Savage Anomaly: The Power of Spinoza's Metaphysics and Politics*. 1981. Trans. M. Hardt. Minneapolis: U of Minnesota P, 1991.

Negrín, Edith, ed. *Nocturno en que todo se oye: José Revueltas ante la crítica*. Mexico: Era/UNAM, 1999.

Nelson, Cary. *Repression and Recovery: Modern American Poetry and the Politics of Cultural Memory, 1910–1945*. Madison: U of Wisconsin P, 1989.

———, and Stephen Watt. *Academic Keywords: A Devil's Dictionary for Higher Education*. New York: Routledge, 1999.

Nelson, Deborah. *Pursuing Privacy in Cold War America*. New York: Columbia UP, 2002.

Neuman, Shirley, and Smaro Kamboureli, eds. *A Mazing Space: Writing Canadian, Women Writing*. Edmonton: Longspoon/NeWest P, 1986.

Newman, Judie. "History and Letters: Anita Desai's *Baumgartner's Bombay*." *World Literature Written in English* 30.1 (1990): 37–46.

———. Introduction to *Dred: A Tale of the Great Dismal Swamp* by Harriet Beecher Stowe. Edinburgh: Edinburgh UP, 1998.

———. *Nadine Gordimer*. London: Routledge, 1988.

———. "Napalm and After: The Politics of Grace Paley's Short Fiction." *Yearbook of English Studies* 31 (2001): 1–9.

———, ed. *Nadine Gordimer's "Burger's Daughter": A Casebook*. Oxford: Oxford UP, 2003.

Ng, Sheung-Yuen Daisy. "Feminism in the Chinese Context: Li Ang's *The Butcher's Wife*." *Gender Politics in Modern China: Writing and Feminism*. Ed. Tani E. Barlow. Durham, NC: Duke UP, 1993. 266–89.

———. "Li Ang's Experiments with the Epistolary Form." *Modern Chinese Literature* 3.1–2 (1987): 91–106.

Ngandu Nkashama, Pius. *Littératures africaines (de 1930 à nos jours)*. Paris: Silex, 1984.

Ngara, Emmanuel. *Art and Ideology in the African Novel: A Study of the Influence of Marxism on African Writing*. London: Heinemann, 1985.

Ngũgĩ wa Thiong'o. *Barrel of a Pen: Resistance to Repression in Neo-colonial Kenya*. London: Heinemann, 1983.

———. *Decolonising the Mind: The Politics of Language in African Literature*. London: James Currey, 1986.

———. *Detained: A Prison Diary*. London: Heinemann, 1981.

———. *Moving the Centre: Struggle for Cultural Freedoms*. London: James Currey, 1993.

———. *Penpoints, Gunpoints and Dreams: Towards a Critical Theory of the Arts and the State of Africa*. New York: Oxford UP, 1998.

Nicholls, Peter. *Modernisms: A Literary Guide*. Berkeley: U of California P, 1995.

———. *Politics, Economics and Writing: A Study of Ezra Pound's "Cantos."* London: Macmillan, 1984.

Nichols, Geraldine Cleary. *Miguel Hernández*. Boston: Twayne, 1978.

Ni Chreachain, Firinne. "Festus Iyayi's *Heroes*: Two Novels in One?" *Research in African Literatures* 22.1 (1991): 43–53.

Nienhauser, William H. *The Indiana Companion to Traditional Chinese Literature*. 2 vols. Bloomington: Indiana UP, 1986.

Nixon, Rob. *London Calling: V. S. Naipaul, Postcolonial Mandarin*. New York: Oxford UP, 1992.

Nkrumah, Kwame. The *Autobiography of Kwame Nkrumah*. London: Panaf, 1973.

———. *Neo-colonialism: The Last Stage of Imperialism*. London: Nelson, 1965.

Noble, Yvonne, ed. *Twentieth-Century Interpretations of* The Beggar's Opera. Englewood Cliffs, NJ: Prentice-Hall, 1975.

Nokes, David. *John Gay: A Profession of Friendship*. New York: Oxford UP, 1995.

Nolan, Emer. *James Joyce and Nationalism*. London: Routledge, 1995.

Norris, Christopher, ed. *Inside the Myth: Orwell, Views from the Left*. London: Lawrence and Wishart, 1984.

North, Joseph. *New Masses: An Anthology of the Rebel Thirties.* New York: International Publishers, 1969.

North, Michael. *The Political Aesthetic of Yeats, Eliot, and Pound.* Cambridge: Cambridge UP, 1991.

Norton, Ann. *Paradoxical Feminism: The Novels of Rebecca West.* Lanham, MD: International Scholars Publications, 2000.

Norval, Aletta J. *Deconstructing Apartheid Discourse.* London: Verso, 1996.

Novák, Arne. *Czech Literature.* Trans. Peter Kussi. Ann Arbor: Michigan Slavic Publications, 1986.

Ntuli, D. B., and C. F. Swanepoel. *South African Literature in African Languages: A Concise Historical Perspective.* Pretoria: Acacia, 1993.

O'Brien, Conor Cruise. "Passion and Cunning: An Essay on the Politics of W. B. Yeats." *Passion and Cunning and Other Essays.* London: Weidenfeld and Nicolson, 1988. 8–61.

O'Brien, Geoffrey. *Hardboiled America: Lurid Paperbacks and the Masters of Noir.* 1981. Exp. ed. New York: Da Capo, 1997.

O'Brien, Sharon. *Willa Cather: The Emerging Voice.* New York: Oxford UP, 1987.

Ochshorn, Kathleen G. *The Heart's Essential Landscape: Bernard Malamud's Hero.* New York: Lang, 1990.

O'Connor, Alan. *Raymond Williams: Writing, Culture, Politics.* Oxford: Basil Blackwell, 1989.

O'Connor, Garry. *Sean O'Casey: A Life.* New York: Atheneum, 1988.

O'Daly, William. *Pablo Neruda.* Port Townsend, WA: Copper Canyon P, 1984.

Odendaal, Andre, and Roger Field, eds. *Liberation Chabalala: The World of Alex La Guma.* Bellville: Mayibuye Books, 1993.

Ogede, Ode. *Achebe and the Politics of Representation.* Trenton, NJ: Africa World P, 2001.

———. *Ayi Kwei Armah, Radical Iconoclast: Pitting Imaginary Worlds Against the Actual.* Athens: Ohio UP, 2000.

Ogungbesan, Kolawole. *The Writing of Peter Abrahams.* London: Hodder and Stoughton, 1979.

Ohmann, Richard. *English in America: A Radical View of the Profession.* New York: Oxford UP, 1976.

———. *Politics and Letters.* Middletown, CT: Wesleyan UP, 1988.

———. *The Politics of Knowledge: The Commercialization of the University, the Professions, and Print Culture.* Middletown, CT: Wesleyan UP, 2003.

———. *Selling Culture: Magazines, Markets, and Class at the Turn of the Century.* London: Verso, 1996.

———. *Shaw: The Style and the Man.* Middletown, CT: Wesleyan UP, 1962.

O'Keeffe, Paul. *Some Sort of Genius: A Life of Wyndham Lewis.* London: Cape, 2000.

Olander, Joseph, and Martin Harry Greenberg, eds. *Ursula K. Le Guin.* New York: Taplinger, 1979.

Oliver, Kelly, ed. *The Portable Kristeva.* Updated ed. New York: Columbia UP, 2002.

Olivera, Otto. "Indices de la poesía soprendida y entre las soledades." *Revista Interamericana de bibliografia* 39.3 (1989): 334–54.

Ollman, Bertell. *Alienation: Marx's Conception of Man in a Capitalist Society.* 2nd ed. Cambridge: Cambridge UP, 1977.

Omi, Michael, and Howard Winant. *Racial Formation in the United States.* New York: Routledge, 1986.

O'Neil, Paul. "The Only Rebellion Around." *Life* 47 (November 1959): 115–30.

O'Neill, Michael. *Percy Bysshe Shelley: A Literary Life*. London: Macmillan, 1989.

O'Neill, William L. *The Last Romantic: A Life of Max Eastman*. New York: Oxford UP, 1978.

Oodgeroo. *Stradbroke Dreamtime*. Sydney: Angus and Robertson, 1972.

O'Prey, Paul. *A Reader's Guide to Graham Greene*. New York: Thames and Hudson, 1988.

Orel, Harold. *The Historical Novel from Scott to Sabatini*. New York: St. Martin's, 1995.

Ormerod, Beverley. *An Introduction to the French Caribbean Novel*. London: Heinemann, 1985.

Orr, Leonard. *W. B. Yeats and Postmodernism*. Syracuse, NY: Syracuse UP, 1991.

Ortega, Ramon Lopez. "The Language of the Working-Class Novel of the 1930s." *The Socialist Novel in Britain*. Ed. H. Gustav Klaus. London: Harvester, 1982. 122–43.

Ortiz Cofer, Judith. "The Myth of the Latin Woman: I Just Met a Girl Named María." *Borícuas*. Ed. Roberto Santiago. New York: Ballantine Books, 1995. 102–8.

Orwin, Donna Tussig. "Tolstoy as Artist and Public Figure." Introduction to *The Cambridge Companion to Tolstoy*. Ed. Donna Tussig Orwin. Cambridge: Cambridge UP, 2002. 49–62.

Osborne, Peter, and Stella Standford. *Philosophies of Race and Ethnicity*. London: Continuum, 2002.

Oster, Daniel. *Histoire de l'Académie française*. Paris: Vialetay, 1970.

Ostrom, Hans. *A Langston Hughes Encyclopedia*. Westport, CT: Greenwood, 2002.

Ottaneli, Fraser M. *The Communist Party of the United States: From the Depression to World War*. New Brunswick, NJ: Rutgers UP, 1991.

Ouditt, Sharon. *Fighting Forces, Writing Women: Identity and Ideology in the First World War*. New York: Routledge, 1994.

Owen, Harold. *Journey from Obscurity: Memoirs of the Owen Family*. Vol. 1. London: Oxford UP, 1963.

Owen, Wilfred. *Collected Letters*. Ed. Harold Owen and John Bell. London: Oxford UP, 1967.

Padmore, George. *How Britain Rules Africa*. London: Wishart Books, 1936.

———. *The Life and Struggles of Negro Toilers*. London: International Council of Trade and Industrial Unions, 1931.

———. *Pan-Africanism or Communism? The Coming Struggle for Africa*. London: Dennis Dobson, 1956.

Padura Fuentes, Leonardo. *Un camino de medio siglo: Carpentier y la narrative de lo real maravilloso*. Havana: Editorial Letras Cubanas, 1994.

Palavestra, Predrag. *Posleratna srpska knjizevnost, 1945–1970*. Beograd: Prosveta, 1972.

Paley, Grace. *Just as I Thought*. New York: Farrar, Straus and Giroux, 1998.

Panshin, Alexei. *Heinlein in Dimension*. Chicago: Advent, 1968.

Paoli, Roberto. *Mapas anatómicos de César Vallejo*. Firenze: D'Anna, 1981.

Papastergiadis, Nikos. *Modernity as Exile: The Stranger in John Berger's Writing*. Manchester: Manchester UP, 1993.

Paperno, Irina. *Chernyshevsky and the Age of Realism*. Stanford, CA: Stanford UP, 1988.

Paquet, Sandra Pouchet. *The Novels of George Lamming*. London: Heinemann, 1982.

Parini, Jay. *John Steinbeck: A Biography*. New York: Henry Holt, 1995.

Paris, Renzo. *Alberto Moravia*. Florence: Nuova Italia, 1991.

Parkes, Stuart, and John J. White, eds. *The Gruppe 47 Fifty Years On: A Re-appraisal of Its Literary and Political Significance*. Amsterdam: Rodopi, 1999.

Parkinson Zamora, Lois, and Wendy B. Faris, eds. *Magical Realism: Theory, History, Community*. Durham, NC: Duke UP, 1995.

Parr, James A. *"Don Quixote": An Anatomy of Subversive Discourse*. Newark, DE: Juan de la Cuesta, 1988.

Parrinder, Patrick, ed. *Learning from Other Worlds: Estrangement, Cognition, and the Politics of Science Fiction and Utopia*. Durham, NC: Duke UP, 2001.

Parry, Benita. *Conrad and Imperialism: Ideological Boundaries and Visionary Frontiers*. London: Macmillan, 1983.

———. *Postcolonial Studies: A Materialist Critique*. London, Routledge, 2004.

Patai, Daphne. *The Orwell Mystique: A Study in Male Ideology*. Amherst: U of Massachusetts P, 1984.

———, ed. *Looking Backward 1988–1888: Essays on Edward Bellamy*. Amherst: U of Massachusetts P, 1988.

Patrick, Josephine. "Remembering Carlos: Interview with Josephine Patrick." By Odette Taverna. *Katipunan* (April 1989): 13–14.

Patteson, Richard F. "Robert Antoni: The Voyage In." *Caribbean Passages: Critical Perspectives on New Fiction from the West Indies*. Boulder: Lynne Rienner, 1998. 143–73.

Patton, Venetria K., and Maureen Honey, eds. Introduction. *Double-Take: A Revisionist Harlem Renaissance Anthology*. New Brunswick: Rutgers UP, 2001.

Pawling, Christopher. *Christopher Caudwell: Towards a Dialectical Theory of Literature*. Basingstoke: Macmillan, 1989.

Paxton, Nancy L. *George Eliot and Herbert Spencer: Feminism, Evolutionism, and the Reconstruction of Gender*. Princeton, NJ: Princeton UP, 1991.

Payne, Michael. *Reading Knowledge: An Introduction to Barthes, Foucault and Althusser*. Oxford: Blackwell, 1997.

Paynter, Maria Nicolai. *Ignazio Silone: Beyond the Tragic Vision*. Toronto: U of Toronto P, 2000.

Peacock, D. Keith. *Harold Pinter and the New British Theatre*. Westport, CT: Greenwood, 1997.

Peck, David. "The Tradition of American Revolutionary Literature: The Monthly *New Masses*, 1926–1933." *Science and Society* 42 (Winter 1978–1979).

Pell, Mike. *S.S. Utah*. New York: International P, 1933.

Pells, Richard H. *Radical Vision and American Dreams: Culture and Social Thought in the Depression Years*. New York: Harper and Row, 1973.

Pendelton, Robert. *Graham Greene's Conradian Masterplot: The Arabesque of Influence*. New York: St. Martin's, 1996.

Penkower, Monty Noam. *The Federal Writers' Project: A Study in Government Patronage of the Arts*. Urbana: U of Illinois P, 1977.

Pereira, N.G.O. *The Thought and Teachings of N. G. Černyševskij*. The Hague: Mouton, 1975.

Pérez, Janet, and Wendell Aycock, eds. *The Spanish Civil War in Literature*. Lubbock: Texas Tech UP, 1990.

Pérez, Luis A., Jr. *Cuba: Between Reform and Revolution*. 2nd ed. New York: Oxford UP, 1995.

Pérez Firmat, Gustavo. *Life on the Hyphen: The Cuban-American Way*. Austin: U of Texas P, 1994.

Perriam, Chris, et al. *A New History of Spanish Writing, 1939 to the 1990s*. Oxford: Oxford UP, 2000.

Perry, Jeffrey B., ed. *A Hubert Harrison Reader*. Westport: Wesleyan UP, 2001.

Perryman, Sally Anne. "Vladimir Voinovich: The Evolution of a Satirical Soviet Writer." Ph.D. diss., Vanderbilt U, 1981.

Petelin, Viktor. *Zhizn Alekseia Tolstago: Krasnyi Graf.* Moscow: Tsentropoligraf, 2001.

Peters, Sally. *Bernard Shaw: The Ascent of the Superman*. New Haven, CT: Yale UP, 1996.

Peterson, Nancy J., ed. *Toni Morrison: Critical and Theoretical Approaches*. Baltimore: Johns Hopkins UP, 1997.

Peterson, Thomas E. *Alberto Moravia*. New York: Twayne, 1996.

————. *The Ethical Muse of Franco Fortini*. Gainesville: U of Florida P, 1997.

Petro, Peter. *A History of Slovak Literature*. Montreal: McGill-Queens UP, 1995.

————, ed. *Critical Essays on Milan Kundera*. New York: G. K. Hall, 1999.

Petty, Sheila. *A Call to Action: The Films of Ousmane Sembène*. Westport, CT: Greenwood, 1996.

Pfaelzer, Jean. *Parlor Radical: Rebecca Harding Davis and the Origins of American Social Realism*. Pittsburgh: U of Pittsburgh P, 1996.

Pfaff, Françoise. *The Cinema of Ousmane Sembène, A Pioneer of African Film*. Westport, CT: Greenwood, 1984.

————. *Conversations with Maryse Condé*. Lincoln: U of Nebraska P, 1997.

Phillips, Gordon. *The General Strike: The Politics of Industrial Conflict*. London: Weidenfeld and Nicolson, 1976.

Phillips, Michael, and Trevor Phillips, eds. *Windrush: The Irresistible Rise of Multi-racial Britain*. London: HarperCollins, 1998.

Phillips, William. *A Partisan View: Five Decades of the Literary Life*. New York: Stein and Day, 1983.

Philp, Mark. *Godwin's Political Justice*. London: Duckworth, 1986.

Piscator, Erwin. *The Political Theatre: A History, 1914–1929*. Trans. Hugh Rorrison. New York: Avon, 1978.

Pizer, Donald. *American Literary Naturalism: Recent and Uncollected Essays*. Bethesda, MD: Academic P, 2002.

————. *Dos Passos' "U.S.A.": A Critical Study*. Charlottesville: UP of Virginia, 1988.

————. *Twentieth-Century American Literary Naturalism: An Interpretation*. Carbondale: Southern Illinois UP, 1992.

Plain, Gill. *Women's Fiction of the Second World War*. Edinburgh: Edinburgh UP, 1996.

Plato. *The Republic*. Trans. H.D.P. Lee. 2nd rev. ed. Harmondsworth: Penguin, 1987.

Podhoretz, Norman. "The Know-Nothing Bohemians." *Partisan Review* 25 (Spring 1958): 305–18.

Pohl, Frederik. *The Way the Future Was*. New York: Ballantine, 1978.

Poliak, L. M. *Aleksei Tolstoi—khudozhnik*. Moscow: Nauka, 1964.

Polito, Robert. *Savage Art: A Biography of Jim Thompson*. New York: Knopf, 1995.

Pollock, Sheldon, ed. *Literary Cultures in History: Reconstructions from South Asia*. Berkeley: U of California P, 2003.

Pomper, Philip. *Lenin, Trotsky, and Stalin: The Intelligentsia and Power*. New York: Columbia UP, 1990.

Pope, Randolph. *Understanding Juan Goytisolo*. Columbia, SC: U of South Carolina P, 1995.

Popovic Karic, Pol. *Carlos Fuentes: perspectivas críticas*. Mexico City: Siglo XXI, 2002.

Porter, Dennis. *The Pursuit of Crime: Art and Ideology in Detective Fiction*. New Haven, CT: Yale UP, 1981.

Porter, Robert. *Four Contemporary Russian Writers*. Oxford: Berg, 1989.

Portuondo, José Antonio. *Bosquejo histórico de las letras cubanas*. Havana: Editora del Ministerio de Educación, 1962.

Posel, Deborah. *The Making of Apartheid*. Oxford: Oxford UP, 1991.

Prawer, S. S. *Karl Marx and World Literature*. Oxford: Oxford UP, 1976.

Preda, Roxana. *Ezra Pound's (Post)modern Poetics and Politics*. New York: Peter Lang, 2001.

Preece, Julian. *The Life and Work of Günter Grass: Literature, History, Politics*. 2nd ed. Basingstoke: Palgrave, 2004.

Prescott, Lynda. "Past and Present Darkness: Sources for V. S. Naipaul's *A Bend in the River*." *Modern Fiction Studies* 30.3 (1984): 547–59.

Preston, Paul. *The Coming of the Spanish Civil War*. London: Macmillan, 1978.

Priestman, Martin, ed. *The Cambridge Companion to Crime Fiction*. Cambridge: Cambridge UP, 2003.

Prieto, René. "The Literature of Indigenismo." *Cambridge History of Latin American Literature*. Vol. 2. Ed. Roberto González Echeverría and Enrique Pupo Walker. Cambridge: Cambridge UP, 1996. 138–63.

————. *Miguel Angel Asturias's Archeology of Return*. Cambridge: Cambridge UP, 1993.

Pringle, David. *Science Fiction: The 100 Best Novels: An English-Language Selection, 1949–1984*. London: Xanadu, 1985.

Printz, Jessica Kimball. "Tracing the Fault Lines of the Radical Female Subject: Grace Lumpkin's *The Wedding*." In *Radical Revisions: Rereading 1930s Culture*. Ed. Bill Mullen and Sherry Lee Linkon. Urbana: U of Southern Illinois P, 1996. 167–86.

Procter, James. *Dwelling Places: Postwar Black British Writing*. Manchester: Manchester UP, 2003.

————, ed. *Writing Black Britain, 1948–1998: An Interdisciplinary Anthology*. Manchester: Manchester UP, 2000.

Proffer, Ellendea. *Bulgakov: Life and Work*. Ann Arbor, MI: Ardis, 1984.

Prusek, Jaroslav. *The Lyrical and the Epic*. Bloomington: Indiana UP, 1985.

Pruvost, Jean. *Les Dictionnaires de langue française*. Paris: Honoré Champion, 2001.

Punter, David. *Gothic Pathologies: The Text, the Body, and the Law*. New York: St. Martin's, 1998.

Purdy, Anthony. *A Certain Difficulty of Being: Essays on the Quebec Novel*. Montreal: McGill UP, 1990.

Pyman, Avril. *A History of Russian Symbolism*. Cambridge: Cambridge UP, 1994.

Pyros, John. *Mike Gold: Dean of American Proletarian Writers*. New York: Dramatika P, 1979.

Quah, Sy Ren. *Gao Xingjian and Transcultural Chinese Theatre*. Honolulu: U of Hawaii P, 2004.

Quémada, Bernard, ed. *Les Préfaces du Dictionnaire de l'Académie française*. Paris: Honoré Champion, 1997.

Quigley, Austin E. *The Pinter Problem*. Princeton, NJ: Princeton UP, 1975.

Quint, David. *Cervantes's Novel of Modern Times: A New Reading of "Don Quijote."* Princeton, NJ: Princeton UP, 2003.

Rabasa, José. "Pre-Columbian Pasts and Mexican Presents in Mexican History." *Colonialism Past and Present*. Ed. Alvaro Felix Bolaños and Gustavo Verdesio. Albany: SUNY P, 2002. 51–78.

Rabellato, Dan. "Sarah Kane: An Appreciation." *New Theatre Quarterly* 15 (1999): 280–81.

Rabillard, Sheila, ed. *Essays on Caryl Churchill: Contemporary Representations.* Winnipeg: Blizzard, 1997.

Rabinowitz, Paula. "Ending Difference/Different Endings: Class, Closure, and Collectivity in Women's Proletarian Fiction." *Genders* 8 (Summer 1990): 62–77.

————. *Labor and Desire: Women's Revolutionary Fiction in Depression America.* Chapel Hill: U of North Carolina P, 1991.

Rajan, P. K. *Mulk Raj Anand: A Revaluation.* New Delhi: Arnold, 1994.

Rama, Angel. *La ciudad letrada.* Hanover, NH: Ediciones del Norte, 1984.

Ramblada-Minero, María de la Cinta. *Isabel Allende's Writing of the Self: Trespassing the Boundaries of Fiction and Autobiography.* Lewiston, NY: E. Mellen P, 2003.

Ramchand, Kenneth. "An Interview with Ralph de Boissière: Back to *Kangaroos.*" *CRNLE Reviews Journal* 1 (1994): 7–32.

Ramos, Julio. *Divergent Modernities: Culture and Politics in Nineteenth-Century Latin America.* Trans. John D. Blanco. Durham, NC: Duke UP, 2001.

Rampersad, Arnold. *The Life of Langston Hughes.* 2 vols. New York: Oxford UP, 1986, 1988.

————, ed. *Richard Wright: A Collection of Critical Essays.* Englewood Cliffs: Prentice Hall, 1995.

Rance, Nicholas. *The Historical Novel and Popular Politics in Nineteenth-Century England.* New York: Barnes and Noble, 1975.

Rancière, Jacques. *The Flesh of Words: The Politics of Writing.* Stanford, CA: Stanford UP, 2004.

Randall, Don. *Kipling's Imperial Boy: Adolescence and Cultural Hybridity.* London: Palgrave, 2000.

Randall, Dudley. *Black Poetry: A Supplement to Anthologies Which Exclude Black Poets.* Broadside Press, 1969.

Randall, Francis B. *Chernyshevskii.* New York: Twayne, 1967.

Ransom, John Crowe. *The New Criticism.* Norfolk, CT: New Directions, 1941.

Ransome, Paul. *Antonio Gramsci: A New Introduction.* Hempstead, UK: Harvester Wheatsheaf, 1992.

Raskin, Jonah. *My Search for B. Traven.* New York: Methuen, 1980.

Rattenbury, Arnold. "Poems by Randall Swingler." *The 1930s: A Challenge to Orthodoxy.* Ed. John Lucas. Hassocks, UK: Harvester, 1978.

Ravenscroft, Arthur. "The Nigerian Civil War in Nigerian Literature." *Commonwealth Literature and the Modern World.* Ed. Hena Maes-Jelinek. Bruxelles: Librairie Marcel Didier, 1975. 105–13.

Rawson, Claude, ed. *Jonathan Swift: A Collection of Critical Essays.* Englewood Cliffs, NJ: Prentice Hall, 1995.

Re, Lucia. *Calvino and the Age of Neo-realism: Fables of Estrangement.* Stanford, CA: Stanford UP, 1990.

Rea, Michael. *World without Design: The Ontological Consequence of Naturalism.* New York: Oxford UP, 2002.

Rebay, Luciano. *Alberto Moravia.* New York: Columbia UP, 1970.

Redfern, W. D. *Paul Nizan: Committed Literature in a Conspiratorial World.* Princeton, NJ: Princeton UP, 1972.

Redfield, Marc. *The Politics of Aesthetics: Nationalism, Gender, Romanticism.* Stanford, CA: Stanford UP, 2003.

Redman, Tim. *Ezra Pound and Italian Fascism.* Cambridge: Cambridge UP, 1991.

Reed, John. *Ten Days That Shook the World*. New York: Penguin, 1977.

Reed, T. J. *Thomas Mann: The Uses of Tradition*. Oxford: Clarendon P, 1974, 1996.

Reed, T. V. "Unimagined Existence and the Fiction of the Real: Postmodernist Realism in *Let Us Now Praise Famous Men*." *Representation* 24 (Fall 1988): 156–76.

Reeder, Roberta. *Anna Akhmatova: Poet and Prophet*. New York: St. Martin's, 1994.

Reeves, Nigel. *Heinrich Heine: Poetry and Politics*. London: Libris, 1994.

Regan, Stephen, ed. *The Eagleton Reader*. Oxford: Blackwell, 1998.

Reid, Donald. "Metaphor and Management: The Paternal in *Germinal*." *French Historical Studies* 17 (1992): 979–1,000.

Reid, H. J. *Writing without Taboos: The New East German Literature*. New York: Oxford UP, 1990.

Reid, James H. *Heinrich Böll: A German for His Time*. Oxford: Wolff, 1988.

Reid, Robert, ed. *Problems of Russian Romanticism*. Brookfield, VT: Gower, 1986.

Reinelt, Janelle. *After Brecht: British Epic Theater*. Ann Arbor: U of Michigan P, 1994.

Reiss, Frank. *The Word and the Stone*. Oxford: Oxford UP, 1972.

Reiss, Timothy J., ed. *For the Geography of a Soul: Emerging Perspectives on Kamau Brathwaite*. Trenton, NJ: Africa World P, 2001.

Relihan, Joel C. *Ancient Menippean Satire*. Baltimore: Johns Hopkins UP, 1993.

Renshaw, Patrick. *The General Strike*. London: Eyre Methuen, 1975.

————. *The Wobblies: A History of the IWW and Syndicalism in the United States*. Updated ed. Chicago: Ivan R. Dee, 1999.

Resch, Margit. *Understanding Christa Wolf: Coming Home to a Foreign Land*. Columbia: U of South Carolina P, 1997.

Rétif, André. *Pierre Larousse et son oeuvre*. Paris: Larousse, 1975.

Rey, Alain. *Émile Littré: l'humaniste et les mots*. Paris: Gallimard, 1970.

Reynolds, David S. *Beneath the American Renaissance: The Subversive Imagination in the Age of Emerson and Melville*. Cambridge, MA: Harvard UP, 1988.

————. *George Lippard*. Boston: Twayne, 1982.

————. *Walt Whitman's America: A Cultural Biography*. New York: Knopf, 1995.

————, ed. *George Lippard, Prophet of Protest: Writings of an American Radical, 1822–1854*. New York: Peter Lang, 1986.

Reynolds, Michael S. *The Young Hemingway*. New York: Basil Blackwell, 1986.

Riach, Alan. "The Idea of Order and 'On a Raised Beach': The Language of Location and the Politics of Music." *Terranglian Territories*. Ed. Susanne Hagemann. Frankfurt-am-Main: Peter Lang, 2000. 613–29.

————. *The Poetry of Hugh MacDiarmid*. Glasgow: Association for Scottish Literary Studies, 1999.

————. *Representing Scotland in Literature, Popular Culture and Iconography*. London: Palgrave Macmillan, 2004.

Rice, Alan J., and Martin Crawford, eds. *Liberating Sojourn: Frederick Douglass and Transatlantic Reform*. Athens: U of Georgia P, 1999.

Rich, Adrienne. "Compulsory Heterosexuality and Lesbian Existence." *Blood, Bread, and Poetry: Selected Prose, 1979–85*. New York: Norton, 1986. 23–75.

Richards, Sandra L. *Ancient Songs Set Ablaze: The Theatre of Femi Osofisan*. Washington: Howard UP, 1996.

Richardson, Al, ed. *Victor Serge: The Century of the Unexpected*. Special issue of *Revolutionary History* 5.3 (1994).

Richter, David H. *Falling into Theory: Conflicting Views on Reading Literature*. 2nd ed. New York: Bedford-St. Martin's, 2000.

Ricks, Christopher. *T. S. Eliot and Prejudice*. Los Angeles: U of California P, 1988.

Riddel, Joseph N. *C. Day Lewis*. New York: Twayne, 1971.

Rideout, Walter B. *The Radical Novel in the United States, 1900–1954*. Cambridge: Harvard UP, 1956.

Ripp, Victor. "*A Hero of Our Time* and the Historicism of the 1830s: The Problem of the Whole and the Parts." *Modern Language Notes* 92 (1977): 969–86.

————. *Turgenev's Russia: From "Notes of a Hunter" to "Fathers and Sons."* Ithaca, NY: Cornell UP, 1982.

Riquelme Rojas, Sonia, and Edna Aguirre Rehbein, eds. *Critical Approaches to Isabel Allende*. New York: Peter Lang, 1991.

Robb, Graham. *Balzac: A Life*. New York: Norton, 1994.

Robbins, Bruce. "Feeling Global: John Berger and Experience." *Postmodernism and Politics*. Ed. Jonathan Arac. Minneapolis: U of Minnesota P, 1986. 145–61.

Roberts, Adam. *Fredric Jameson*. New York: Routledge, 2000.

Roberts, David. "'Marat/Sade' or the Birth of Post-modernism from the Spirit of the Avant-garde." *New German Critique* 38 (1986): 112–30.

Roberts, Nora Ruth. *Three Radical Women Writers: Class and Gender in Meridel Le Sueur, Tillie Olsen, and Josephine Herbst*. New York: Garland, 1996.

Roberts, Philip. *The Royal Court Theatre and the Modern Stage*. Cambridge: Cambridge UP, 1999.

Roberts, Robin. *A New Species: Gender and Science in Science Fiction*. Urbana: U of Illinois P, 1993.

Roberts, Stephen G. H. "Unamuno and the Restoration Political Project: A Reevaluation." *Spain's 1898 Crisis: Regenerationism, Modernism, Post-Colonialism*. Ed. J. Harrison and A. Hoyle. Manchester: Manchester UP, 2000. 68–80.

————. "Unamuno, Spanishness and the Ideal Patria: An Intellectual's View." *Journal of the Institute of Romance Studies* 8 (2000): 125–36.

Robertson, Ritchie, ed. *The Cambridge Companion to Thomas Mann*. Cambridge: Cambridge UP, 2002.

Robeson, Paul. *Here I Stand*. 1958. Preface by Lloyd L. Brown. Introduction by Sterling Stuckey. Boston: Beacon, 1988.

Robin, Régine. *Socialist Realism: An Impossible Aesthetic*. Stanford: Stanford UP, 1992.

Robinson, Ione. *A Wall to Paint On*. New York: Dutton, 1946.

Robinson, Kim Stanley. *The Novels of Philip K. Dick*. Ann Arbor: UMI Research P, 1984.

Robinson, Lillian S. *In the Canon's Mouth: Dispatches from the Culture Wars*. Bloomington: Indiana UP, 1997.

————. *Sex, Class, and Culture*. Bloomington: Indiana UP, 1978.

Rocha, João Cezar de Castro, ed. "Brazil 2001—A Revisionary History of Brazilian Literature and Culture." Special issue of *Portuguese Literary and Cultural Studies* 4–5 (Spring/Fall 2000).

Rockmore, Tom. *Irrationalism: Lukács and the Marxist View of Reason*. Philadelphia: Temple UP, 1992.

————. *Marx after Marxism: The Philosophy of Karl Marx*. Oxford: Blackwell, 2002.

Rodden, John. *The Politics of Literary Reputation: The Making and Claiming of "St. George" Orwell*. New York: Oxford UP, 1989.

Rodríguez-Luis, Julio. *Re-Reading José Martí: One Hundred Years Later.* Albany: SUNY P, 1999.

Roe, Sue, ed. *The Cambridge Companion to Virginia Woolf.* Cambridge: Cambridge UP, 2000.

Roeder, George H. *The Censored War: American Visual Experience during World War Two.* New Haven: Yale UP, 1993.

Roemer, Kenneth M. *The Obsolete Necessity: America in Utopian Writings, 1888–1900.* Kent, OH: Kent State UP, 1976.

———. *Utopian Audiences: How Readers Locate Nowhere.* Amherst: U of Massachusetts P, 2003.

Rohlehr, Gordon. *Cultural Resistance and the Guyana State.* Havana: Casa de las Americas, 1984.

Rojek, Chris. *Stuart Hall.* London: Polity P, 2003.

Rollyson, Carl. *Rebecca West: A Life.* New York: Scribner, 1996.

Romero, Christiane Zehl. *Anna Seghers: Eine Biographie.* 2 vols. Berlin: Aufbau, 2000, 2003.

Roopnaraine, Rupert. *Web of October: Rereading Martin Carter.* Leeds: Peepal Tree, 1987.

Rose, Jane Atterbridge. *Rebecca Harding Davis.* New York: Twayne, 1993.

Rose, Mark. *Alien Encounters: Anatomy of Science Fiction.* Cambridge, MA: Harvard UP, 1981.

Rosemont, Franklin, ed. *Apparitions of Things to Come: Edward Bellamy's Tales of Mystery and Imagination.* Chicago: Charles H. Kerr Co., 1990.

Rosen, Robert C. *John Dos Passos: Politics and the Writer.* Lincoln: U of Nebraska P, 1981.

Rosenberg, Dorothy. Afterword to *The Seventh Cross* by Anna Seghers. New York: Monthly Review P, 1987. 347–81.

Rosenfeld, Alvin. *A Double Dying: Reflections on Holocaust Literature.* Bloomington: Indiana UP, 1980.

Rosenfeld, Alvin H., and Irving Greenberg, eds. *Confronting the Holocaust: The Impact of Elie Wiesel.* Bloomington: Indiana UP, 1978.

Rosenfelt, Deborah. Afterword to *Daughter of the Hills* by Myra Page. New York: Feminist P, 1986. 247–68.

———. "From the Thirties: Tillie Olsen and the Radical Tradition." *Feminist Studies* 7 (Fall 1981): 371–406.

Rosenstone, Robert A. *Crusade of the Left: The Lincoln Battalion in the Spanish Civil War.* New York: Pegasus, 1969.

———. *Romantic Revolutionary: A Biography of John Reed.* New York: Alfred A. Knopf, 1975.

Ross, Andrew. *Strange Weather: Culture, Science and Technology in the Age of Limits.* London: Verso, 1991.

Ross, Kristin. *Fast Cars, Clean Bodies: Decolonization and the Reordering of French Culture.* Cambridge, MA: MIT P, 1995.

Ross, Marlon B. "White Fantasies of Desire: Baldwin and the Racial Identities of Sexuality." *James Baldwin Now.* Ed. Dwight A. McBride. New York: New York UP, 1999. 13–55.

Rothe, Wolfgang. *Der politische Goethe. Dichter und Staatsdiener im deutschen Spätabsolutismus.* Göttingen: Vandenhoeck and Ruprecht, 1998.

Rotker, Susana. *The American Chronicles of José Martí: Journalism and Modernity in Spanish America.* Trans. Jennifer French and Katherine Semler. Hanover, NH: UP of New England, 2000.

Rowley, Hazel. *Christina Stead: A Biography*. Port Melbourne, Victoria: William Heinemann Australia, 1993.

Royle, Trevor. *The Mainstream Companion to Scottish Literature*. Edinburgh: Mainstream, 1993.

Rubinstein, Harry R. "Political Regression in New Mexico: The Destruction of the National Miners' Union in Gallup." *Labor in New Mexico: Union, Strikes, and Social History since 1881*. Ed. Robert Kern. Albuquerque, NM: U of New Mexico Press, 1983. 91–140.

Rubenstein, Roberta. *The Novelistic Vision of Doris Lessing: Breaking the Forms of Consciousness*. Urbana: U of Illinois P, 1979.

Rudé, George. *The French Revolution*. New York: Grove, 1988.

Rühle, J. "Italy between Black and Red." Trans. J. Steinberg. *Literature and Revolution*. London: Pall Mall, 1969.

Rumble, Patrick Allen, and Bart Testa. *Pier Paolo Pasolini: Contemporary Perspectives*. Toronto: U of Toronto P, 1996.

Ruppert, Peter. *Reader in a Strange Land: The Activity of Reading Literary Utopias*. Athens: U of Georgia P, 1986.

Rushdie, Salman. *Imaginary Homelands: Essays and Criticism, 1981–1991*. London: Granta, 1991.

Rushdy, Ashraf. "Daughters Signifyin(g) History: The Example of Toni Morrison's *Beloved*." *American Literature* 64.3 (1992): 567–97.

————. *Neo-Slave Narratives: Studies in the Social Logic of a Literary Form*. Oxford: Oxford UP, 1999.

Russ, Joanna. *To Write Like a Woman: Essays in Feminism and Science Fiction*. Bloomington: Indiana UP, 1995.

Russell, Robert. *Valentin Kataev*. Boston: Twayne, 1981.

Ryan-Hayes, Karen. *Contemporary Russian Satire: A Genre Study*. Cambridge: Cambridge UP, 1995.

Sadiq, Muhammad. *A History of Urdu Literature*. Delhi: Oxford UP, 1984.

Said, Edward. *Beginnings: Intention and Method*. New York: Basic Books, 1975.

————. *Covering Islam: How the Media and the Experts Determine How We See the Rest of the World*. New York: Vintage-Random House, 1997.

————. *Culture and Imperialism*. New York: Vintage-Random House, 1994.

————. *The Edward Said Reader*. Ed. Moustafa Bayoumi and Andrew Rubin. New York: Vintage-Random House, 2000.

————. *The End of the Peace Process: Oslo and After*. New York: Pantheon, 2000.

————. *Joseph Conrad and the Fiction of Autobiography*. Cambridge, MA: Harvard UP, 1966.

————. *Orientalism*. New York: Vintage-Random House, 1978.

————. *Out of Place: A Memoir*. New York: Knopf, 1999.

————. *Peace and Its Discontents: Essays on Palestine in the Middle East Peace Process*. New York: Vintage-Random House, 1995.

————. *The Politics of Dispossession: The Struggle for Palestinian Self-Determination, 1969–1994*. New York: Pantheon, 1994.

————. *Representations of the Intellectual*. New York: Pantheon, 1994.

————. "Swift's Tory Anarchy." *The World, the Text, and the Critic*. Cambridge, MA: Harvard UP, 1983. 54–71.

————. *The World, the Text, and the Critic*. Cambridge, MA: Harvard UP, 1983.

————. "Yeats and Decolonization." *Culture and Imperialism*. New York: Knopf, 1993. 220–38.

St. Clair, William. *The Godwins and the Shelleys: The Biography of a Family*. London: Faber and Faber, 1989.

Sakelliou-Schulz, Liana. *Denise Levertov: An Annotated Primary and Secondary Bibliography*. New York: Garland, 1988.

Salih, Sara. *Judith Butler*. London: Routledge, 2002.

————, and Judith Butler, eds. *The Judith Butler Reader*. Oxford: Blackwell, 2002.

Sallis, James. *Chester Himes: A Life*. New York: Walker and Co., 2001.

————, ed. *Ash of Stars: On the Writing of Samuel R. Delany*. Jackson: UP of Mississippi, 1996.

Salmon, Richard J. "Two Operas for Beggars: A Political Reading." *Theoria* 57 (1981): 63–81.

Sánchez-Eppler, Karen. *Touching Liberty: Abolition, Feminism and the Politics of the Body*. Berkeley: U of California P, 1993.

Sander, Reinhard W. *The Trinidad Awakening: West Indian Literature of the Nineteen-Thirties*. Westport, CT: Greenwood, 1988.

Sanders, Andrew. *Charles Dickens*. Oxford: Oxford UP, 2003.

Sandhu, Sukhdev. *London Calling: How Black and Asian Writers Imagined a City*. New York: HarperCollins, 2003.

Sandler, Stephanie. *Commemorating Pushkin: Russia's Myth of a National Poet*. Stanford, CA: Stanford UP, 2004.

San Juan, E., Jr. *Ang Sining ng Tula*. Quezon City: Alemar-Phoenix Publishing House, 1975.

————. *Beyond Postcolonial Theory*. New York: St. Martin's, 1998.

————. *Carlos Bulosan and the Imagination of the Class Struggle*. Quezon City, Philippines: U of the Philippines P, 1972.

————. *From Exile to Diaspora: Versions of the Filipino Experience in the United States*. Boulder, CO: Westview P, 1998.

————. *Hegemony and Strategies of Transgression: Essays in Cultural Studies and Comparative Literature*. Albany: SUNY P, 1995.

————. *Introduction to Modern Pilipino Literature*. New York: Twayne, 1974.

————. *Only by Struggle: Reflections on Philippine Culture, Politics and Society*. Quezon City: Giraffe Books, 2002.

————. *The Philippine Temptation*. Philadelphia, PA: Temple UP, 1996.

————. *Racism and Cultural Studies: Critiques of Multiculturalist Ideology and the Politics of Difference*. Durham, NC: Duke UP, 2002.

————. *Reading the West/Writing the East*. New York: Peter Lang, 1992.

————. *Toward a People's Literature*. Quezon City: U of the Philippines P, 1984.

————. *Writing and National Liberation*. Quezon City: U of the Philippines P, 1991.

Santora, Patricia B. "The Life of Kenneth Flexner Fearing." *CLA Journal* 32 (March 1989): 309–22.

Sargent, Lyman Tower. "The Three Faces of Utopianism Revisited." *Utopian Studies* 5.1 (1994): 1–37.

Saro-Wiwa, Ken. *On a Darkling Plain: An Account of the Nigerian Civil War*. London: Saros International, 1989.

Sartre, Jean-Paul. *Basic Writings*. Ed. Stephen Priest. London: Routledge, 2001.

————. *Oeuvres romanesques*. Paris: Gallimard, 1981. 1,461–1,534.

Saul, Nigel. *Richard II*. New Haven, CT: Yale UP, 1997.

Saunders, Frances Stonor. *The Cultural Cold War: The CIA and the World of Arts and Letters*. New York: New P, 1999.

Saunders, Graham. *Love Me or Kill Me: Sarah Kane and the Theatre of Extremes*. Manchester: Manchester UP, 2002.

Sawyer, Dana. *Aldous Huxley: A Biography*. New York: Crossroad Publishing, 2002.

Saydaawi, Rafif. *Al-Nadhra al-Riwaaiyya Ila al-Harb al-Lubnaaniyya, 1975–1995*. Beirut: Dar al-Farabi, 2003.

Sayers, Sean. *Plato's "Republic": An Introduction*. Edinburgh: Edinburgh UP, 1999.

Scammell, Michael. *Solzhenitsyn: A Biography*. New York: Norton, 1984.

Schaer, Roland, Gregory Claeys, and Lyman Tower Sargent, eds. *Utopia: The Search for the Ideal Society in the Western World*. New York: Oxford UP, 2000.

Schapiro, Leonard. *Turgenev: His Life and Times*. New York: Random House, 1978.

Schaub, Thomas Hill. *American Fiction in the Cold War*. Madison: U of Wisconsin P, 1991.

Scheckner, Peter, ed. *An Anthology of Chartist Poetry: Poetry of the British Working Class, 1830s–1850s*. Rutherford, NJ: Fairleigh Dickinson UP, 1989.

Schell, Eileen. *Gypsy Academics and Mother-Teachers: Gender, Contingent Labor, and Writing Instruction*. Portsmouth, NH: Boynton/Cook, 1998.

Scherr, Barry P. *Maxim Gorky*. Boston: G. K. Hall, 1988.

————. "Shadow Narratives and the Novel: The Role of Rybin in Gorky's *Mother*." *Twentieth-Century Russian Literature: Selected Papers from the Fifth World Congress of Central and East European Studies*. Ed. Karen L. Ryan and Barry P. Scherr. London: Macmillan, 2000. 25–41.

Schirmer, Daniel B., and Stephen Rosskamm Shalom, eds. *The Philippines Reader: A History of Colonialism, Neocolonialism, Dictatorship, and Resistance*. Boston, MA: South End P, 1987.

Schleuning, Neala. *America: Song We Sang without Knowing: The Life and Ideas of Meridel LeSueur*. Mankato, MN: Little Red Hen P, 1983.

Schmitt, Hans-Jürgen. *Die Expressionismusdebatte*. Frankfurt am Main: Suhrkamp, 1973.

Schneider, Karen. *Loving Arms: Women's Writing of World War II*. Lexington: UP of Kentucky, 1996.

Schocket, Eric. " 'Discovering Some New Race': Rebecca Harding Davis's 'Life in the Iron Mills' and the Literary Emergence of Working-Class Whiteness." *PMLA* 115.1 (January 2000): 46–59.

Schom, Alan. *Émile Zola: A Biography*. New York: Holt, 1988.

Schoolfield, George C., ed. *A History of Finland's Literature*. Lincoln: U of Nebraska P, 2002.

Schram, Stuart R. *Mao Tse-tung*. Harmondsworth: Penguin, 1966.

Schrecker, Ellen. *No Ivory Tower*. New York: Oxford UP, 1986.

Schuchard, Ronald. "Burbank with a Baedeker, Eliot with a Cigar: American Intellectuals, Anti-Semitism, and the Idea of Culture." *Modernism/Modernity* 10.1 (2003): 1–26.

Schulte, Christane, and Winfried Siebers, eds. *Kluges Fernsehen: Alexander Kluges Kulturmagazine*. Frankfurt am Main: Suhrkamp, 2002.

Schulz, Genia. *Heiner Müller*. Stuttgart: Metzler, 1980.

Schumacher, Michael. *Dharma Lion*. New York: St. Martin's, 1992.

Schuyler, George S. *Black and Conservative: The Autobiography of George S. Schuyler*. New Rochelle: Arlington House, 1966.

Schwartz, Lawrence. *Creating Faulkner's Reputation: The Politics of Modern Literary Criticism*. Knoxville: U of Tennessee P, 1988.

Schwarz, Bill. "George Padmore." *West Indian Intellectuals in Britain*. Ed. Bill Schwarz. Manchester: Manchester UP, 2004. 132–52.

Schwarz, Roberto. *Misplaced Ideas: Essays on Brazilian Culture*. London: Verso, 1992.

Schweik, Susan. *A Gulf So Deeply Cut: American Women Poets and the Second World War*. Madison: U of Wisconsin P, 1991.

Schweitzer, Viktoria. *Tsvetaeva*. Ed. Angela Livingstone. Trans. Robert Chandler and H. T. Willetts. London: HarperCollins, 1992.

Scott, Bonnie Kime. *Joyce and Feminism*. Bloomington: Indiana UP, 1984.

————. *Refiguring Modernism*. 2 vols. Bloomington: Indiana UP, 1995.

Scott, H. G., ed. *Problems of Soviet Literature: Reports and Speeches at the First Soviet Writers' Congress*. 1935. Westport, CT: Greenwood, 1979.

Scriven, Michael. *Paul Nizan: Communist Novelist*. London: MacMillan, 1988.

Scruggs, Charles. "'My Chosen World': Jean Toomer's Articles in the *New York Call*." *Arizona Quarterly* 51 (Summer 1995): 103–26.

————, and Lee Van DeMarr. *Jean Toomer and the Terrors of American History*. Philadelphia: U of Pennsylvania P, 1998.

Sealy, Clifford. "*Crown Jewel:* A Note on Ralph de Boissière." *Voices* 2.3 (March 1973): 1–3.

Seaton, James. "Henry James's *The Princess Casamassima:* Revolution and the Preservation of Culture." *The Moral of the Story: Literature and Public Ethics*. Ed. Henry T. Edmondson. Lanham, MD: Lexington Books, 2000. 15–25.

————. "Milan Kundera vs. Richard Rorty." *South Carolina Review* 29.1 (Fall 1996): 211–17.

————. "On Politics and Literature: The Case of *O Pioneers!*" *Perspectives in Political Science* 28.3 (1999): 142–46.

————. "Was Hemingway an Intellectual?" *The Hemingway Review* 10.1 (Fall 1990): 52–56.

Sedgwick, Eve Kosofsky. *Between Men: English Literature and Male Homosocial Desire*. New York: Columbia UP, 1985.

————. *A Dialogue on Love*. Boston: Beacon, 1999.

————. *Epistemology of the Closet*. Berkeley: U of California P, 1990.

————. *Tendencies*. Durham, NC: Duke UP, 1993.

————. *Touching Feeling: Affect, Pedagogy, Performativity*. Durham, NC: Duke UP, 2003.

Seed, David. "Take-Over Bids: The Power Fantasies of Frederik Pohl and Cyril Kornbluth." *Foundation* 59 (Fall 1993): 42–58.

Seguin, Jean-Pierre. "La langue française aux XVIIe et XVIII siècles." *Nouvelle histoire de la langue française*. Ed. Jacques Chaurand. Paris: Seuil, 1999.

Seifrid, Thomas. *Andrei Platonov: Uncertainties of Spirit*. Cambridge: Cambridge UP, 1992.

Seigneurie, Ken. "The Importance of Being Kawabata: The Narratee in Today's Literature of Commitment." *Journal of Narrative Theory* 31.1 (Winter 2004): 111–30.

Sekora, John, and Darwin T. Turner, eds. *The Art of the Slave Narrative: Original Essays in Criticism and Theory*. Macomb: Western Illinois UP, 1982.

Sekyi-Otu, Ato. *Fanon's Dialectic of Experience*. Cambridge, MA: Harvard UP, 1996.

Sellar, Tom. "Truth and Dare: Sarah Kane's *Blasted.*" *Theater* 27.1 (1997): 29–34.

Semanov, S. N. *Tikhii Don—literature i istoria.* Moscow: Sovremennik, 1977.

———. *V mire "Tikhogo Dona."* Moscow: Sovremennik, 1987.

Sembène, Ousmane. "Film-makers and African Culture" (uncredited interview with Sembène). *Africa* 71 (1977): 80.

———. "Man Is Culture." The Sixth Annual Hans Wolff Memorial Lecture (March 1975). Bloomington: African Studies Program, Indiana University, 1979.

Semmel, Bernard. *George Eliot and the Politics of National Inheritance.* New York: Oxford UP, 1994.

Sen, Sukumar. *History of Bengali Literature.* New Delhi: Sahitya Akademi, 1960.

Sequoya-Magdaleno, Jana. "Telling the *différance*: Representations of Identity in the Discourse of Indianness." *The Ethnic Canon: Histories, Institutions, and Interventions.* Ed. David Palumbo-Liu. Minneapolis: U of Minnesota P, 1995. 88–116.

Shabecoff, Philip. *A Fierce Green Fire: The American Environmental Movement.* New York: Farrar, Straus and Giroux, 1993.

Shane, A. M. *The Life and Works of Evgenij Zamjatin.* U of California P, 1968.

Sharistanian, Janet. "Tess Slesinger's Hollywood Sketches." *Michigan Quarterly Review* 18.3 (Summer 1979): 429–54.

Sharma, E. K., ed. *Perspectives on Mulk Raj Anand.* Atlantic Highlands, NJ: Humanities P, 1982.

Sharpe, Tony. *Vladimir Nabokov.* London: Edward Arnold, 1991.

Sharrock, Roger. *Saints, Sinners, and Comedians: The Novels of Graham Greene.* Notre Dame: U of Notre Dame P, 1984.

Shaw, Bradley A., and N. Vera-Godwin, eds. *Critical Perspectives on Gabriel García Márquez.* Lincoln: U of Nebraska P, 1986.

Shaw, Donald Leslie. *Alejo Carpentier.* Boston: Twayne, 1985.

Shaw, Gisela. "Ideal and Reality in the Works of Ulrich Plenzdorf." *GermanLife and Letters* 35.1 (October 1981): 84–97.

Shek, Ben-Z. "*Bonheur d'occasion.*" *The Oxford Companion to Canadian Literature.* Ed. Eugene Benson and William Toye. 2nd ed. Toronto: Oxford UP, 1997. 130–31.

———. "La critique gauchiste (et gauche?) de *Bonheur d'occasion.*" *Colloque international "Gabrielle Roy."* Ed. André Fauchon. Saint-Boniface, Presses universitaires de Saint-Boniface, 1996. 55–68.

———. *French-Canadian and Québécois Novels.* Toronto: Oxford UP, 1991.

———. "In the Beginning Was the Conquest." *Keeping Canada Together.* Ed. N. Penner. Toronto: Amethyst, 1978. 12–24.

———. *Social Realism in the French-Canadian Novel.* Montreal: Harvest House, 1977.

Shelley, Mary Wollstonecraft. *Frankenstein: Complete, Authoritative Text with Biographical, Historical, and Cultural Contexts, Critical History, and Essays from Contemporary Critical Perspectives.* Ed. Johanna M. Smith. Basingstoke: Macmillan, 2000.

Shepherd-Barr, Kirsten. *Ibsen and Early Modernist Theatre, 1890–1900.* Westport, CT: Greenwood P, 1997.

Shepler, Michael. "Hollywood Red: The Life of Abraham Polonsky." *Political Affairs* 82.8 (2003): 14–17.

Sheppard, Tresidder Alfred. *The Art and Practice of Historical Fiction.* London: Humphrey Toulmin, 1930.

Sheridan, Susan. *Christina Stead.* Great Britain: Harvester Wheatsheaf, 1988.

Sherry, Norman. *The Life of Graham Greene.* Vol. 1, 1904–1939; vol. 2, 1940–1955. New York: Penguin, 1989, 1995.

Sherry, Vincent. *The Great War and the Language of Modernism.* New York: Oxford UP, 2003.

Shiach, Morag. *Discourse on Popular Culture.* Palo Alto, CA: Stanford UP, 1989.

Shields, Rob. *Lefebvre, Love and Struggle: Spatial Dialectics.* London: Routledge, 1999.

Shoaf, R. Allen. *The Poem as Green Girdle:* Commercium *in* Sir Gawain and the Green Knight. Gainesville: UP of Florida, 1984.

Shoemaker, Adam, ed. *Oodgeroo: A Tribute.* St. Lucia: U of Queensland P, 1994.

Showalter, Elaine. *A Literature of Their Own: British Women Novelists from Bronte to Lessing.* Princeton, NJ: Princeton UP, 1977.

———, ed. *The New Feminist Criticism: Essays on Women, Literature and Theory.* New York: Pantheon, 1985.

Shulman, Alix Kates, ed. *Red Emma Speaks: An Emma Goldman Reader.* New York: Schocken, 1983.

Sicherman, Carol. *Ngugi wa Thiong'o: The Making of a Rebel.* London: Hans Zell, 1990.

Siefken, Hinrich, and J. H. Reid, eds. *"Lektüre—ein anarchischer Akt": A Nottingham Symposium with Hans Magnus Enzensberger.* Nottingham: U of Nottingham, 1990.

Siegel, Ben, ed. *Critical Essays on Nathanael West.* New York: G. K. Hall, 1994.

Silet, Charles L. P., ed. *The Critical Response to Chester Himes.* Westport, CT: Greenwood, 1999.

Sillens, Samuel. Review of *Native Son. Richard Wright's "Native Son": A Critical Handbook.* Ed. Richard Abcarian. Belmont: Wadsworth, 1970. 49–52.

Silver, Victoria. *Imperfect Sense: The Predicament of Milton's Irony.* Princeton, NJ: Princeton UP, 2001.

Silverstein, Marc. *Harold Pinter and the Language of Cultural Power.* Lewisburg, PA: Bucknell UP, 1993.

Simons, Margaret. *Beauvoir and "The Second Sex": Feminism, Race, and the Origins of Existentialism.* Lanham, MD: Rowman and Littlefield, 1999.

Sinclair, Alison. *Uncovering the Mind: Unamuno, the Unknown and the Vicissitudes of the Self.* Manchester: Manchester UP, 2002.

Sinclair, Andrew. *Jack: A Biography of Jack London.* New York: Harper and Row, 1977.

Sinfield, Alan. *Literature in Protestant England, 1560–1660.* Totowa, NJ: Barnes and Noble, 1983.

———. *Literature, Politics and Culture in Postwar Britain.* Berkeley: U of California P, 1989.

Singal, Daniel. *William Faulkner: The Making of a Modernist.* Chapel Hill: U of North Carolina P, 1997.

Sinha, Krishna Nandan. *Mulk Raj Anand.* New York: Twayne, 1972.

Sirois, Antoine. *"Bonheur d'occasion." Dictionnaire des oeuvres littéraires du Québec,* vol. 3. Montréal: Fides, 1982. 127–36.

Sivanandan, A. *Communities of Resistance.* London: Verso, 1990.

Skinner, Quentin. "Sir Thomas More's *Utopia* and the Language of Renaissance Humanism." *The Languages of Political Theory in Early-Modern Europe.* Ed. Anthony Pagden. Cambridge: Cambridge UP, 1987.

Skinner, Robert E. *Two Guns from Harlem: The Detective Fiction of Chester Himes.* Bowling Green, OH: Bowling Green State U Popular P, 1989.

Sklodowska, Elzbieta. *Testimonio hispanoamericano*. New York: Peter Lang, 1992.

_____, and Ben Heller, eds. *Roberto Fernández Retamar y los estudios latinoamericanos*. Pittsburgh: Instituto Internacional de Literatura Iberoamericana, 2000.

Skloot, Robert. *The Darkness We Carry: The Drama of the Holocaust*. Madison: U of Wisconsin P, 1988.

Slochower, Harry. *Mythopoesis: Myth Patterns in Literary Classics*. Detroit: Wayne State UP, 1973.

Slotkin, Richard. *The Fatal Environment: The Myth of the Frontier in the Age of Industrialization, 1800–1890*. Norman: U of Oklahoma P, 1998.

Slusser, George Edgar, and T. A. Shippey, eds. *Fiction 2000: Cyberpunk and the Future of Narrative*. Athens: U of Georgia P, 1992.

Smart, Patricia. "*Prochain episode*" and "*Hubert Aquin*." *Oxford Companion to Canadian Literature*. 2nd ed. Ed. Eugene Benson and William Toye. Toronto: Oxford UP, 1997. 58–60 and 970–71.

_____. *Writing in the Father's House: The Emergence of the Feminine in the Quebec Literary Tradition*. Toronto: U of Toronto P, 1991.

Smit, Johannes A., Johan van Wyk, and Jean-Philippe Wade, eds. *Rethinking South African Literary History*. Durban: Y Press, 1996.

Smith, Bernard, ed. *Culture and History*. Sydney: Hale and Iremonger, 1984.

Smith, David. *Lewis Jones*. Cardiff: U of Wales P, 1982.

Smith, Eric D. "Johnny Domingo's Epic Nightmare of History." *Ariel* 31 (2000): 103–15.

Smith, Erin. *Hard-Boiled: Working-Class Readers and Pulp Magazines*. Philadelphia: Temple UP, 2000.

Smith, Grover, ed. *The Letters of Aldous Huxley*. New York: Harper and Row, 1969.

Smith, Harold. *War and Social Change: British Society in the Second World War*. Manchester: Manchester UP, 1986.

Smith, Jon. "John Dos Passos, Anglo-Saxon." *Modern Fiction Studies* 44 (Summer 1998): 282–305.

Smith, Rowland, ed. *Critical Essays on Nadine Gordimer*. Boston: G. K. Hall, 1990.

Smyth, Gerry. *Decolonisation and Criticism: The Construction of Irish Literature*. London: Pluto P, 1998.

Smythe, Karen, ed. Special Michael Ondaatje issue of *Essays on Canadian Writing* 53 (Summer 1994).

Snee, Carole. "Working-Class Literature or Proletarian Writing?" *Culture and Crisis in Britain in the Thirties*. Ed. Jon Clark, Margot Heinemann, David Margolies, and Carole Snee. London: Lawrence and Wishart, 1979. 165–91.

Sollors, Werner. *Amiri Baraka/LeRoi Jones: The Quest for a "Populist Modernism."* New York: Columbia UP, 1978.

Solomon, Martha. *Emma Goldman*. Boston: G. K. Hall, 1987.

Solomon, Maynard, ed. *Marxism and Art: Essays Classic and Contemporary*. New York: Knopf, 1973.

Sommer, Doris. *Foundational Fictions: The National Romances of Latin America*. Berkeley: U of California P, 1991.

_____. "History and Romanticism in Mir's *Cuando amaban las tierras comuneras*." *Revista de Estudios Hispánicos* 6 (1979): 219–48.

_____. *Proceed with Caution When Engaged by Minority Writing in the Americas*. Cambridge: Harvard UP, 1999.

Sovetskii Entsiklopediiski Slovar. Moscow: Sovetskaia Entsiklopedia, 1989.

Sowinska, Suzanne. "Writing across the Color Line: White Women Writers and the 'Negro Question' in the Gastonia Novels." *Radical Revisions: Rereading 1930s Culture.* Ed. Bill Mullen and Sherry Lee Linkon. Urbana: U of Illinois P, 1996. 120–43.

Speirs, Ronald. *Bertolt Brecht.* London: Macmillan, 1987.

Spencer, Jane. *The Rise of the Woman Novelist: From Aphra Behn to Jane Austen.* Oxford: Blackwell, 1986.

Spencer, Jenny S. *Dramatic Strategies in the Plays of Edward Bond.* Cambridge: Cambridge UP, 1992.

Spivak, Gayatri Chakravorty. "Can the Subaltern Speak?" *Marxism and the Interpretation of Culture.* Ed. Cary Nelson and Lawrence Grossberg. Urbana: U of Illinois P, 1988. 271–313.

————. *A Critique of Postcolonial Reason: Toward a History of the Vanishing Present.* Cambridge, MA: Harvard UP, 1999.

————. *Death of a Discipline.* New York: Columbia UP, 2003.

————. *In Other Worlds: Essays in Cultural Politics.* London: Methuen, 1987.

————. *Outside in the Teaching Machine.* London: Routledge, 1993.

————. *The Postcolonial Critic.* London: Routledge, 1990.

Spleth, Janice S. *Léopold Sédar Senghor.* Boston: Twayne, 1985.

Sprague, Claire, and Virginia Tiger. *Critical Essays on Doris Lessing.* Boston: G.K. Hall, 1986.

Sprinker, Michael, ed. *Edward Said: A Critical Reader.* Oxford and Cambridge: Blackwell, 1992.

————. *Ghostly Demarcations: A Symposium on Jacques Derrida's "Specters of Marx."* London: Verso, 1999.

Stainton, Leslie. *Lorca: A Dream of Life.* New York: Farrar, Straus and Giroux, 1999.

Stape, J. H., ed. *The Cambridge Companion to Joseph Conrad.* New York: Cambridge UP, 1996.

Starkey, Paul. "Crisis and Memory in Rashid Al-Daif's *Dear Mr. Kawabata*: An Essay in Narrative Disorder." *Crisis and Memory: The Representation of Space in Modern Levantine Narrative.* Ed. Ken Seigneurie. Wiesbaden: Reichert, 2003. 115–30.

Staub, Michael E. *Voices of Persuasion: Politics of Representation in 1930s America.* New York: Cambridge UP, 1994.

Stead, Christina. "The Writers Take Sides." *Left Review* 1.11 (August 1935): 453–63, 469–75.

Stecher-Hansen, Marianne, ed. *Danish Writers from the Reformation to Decadence: Dictionary of Literary Biography, Vol. 300.* Detroit: Thomson Gale, 2004.

Steele, James. *Paul Nizan, un révolutionnaire conformiste?* Paris: Presses de la Fondation Nationale des Sciences Politiques, 1987.

Steinbeck, John. *A Life in Letters.* Ed. Elaine Steinbeck and Robert Wallsten. New York: Viking, 1975.

————. *Working Days: The Journals of "The Grapes of Wrath."* Ed. Robert DeMott. New York: Viking, 1989.

Steiner, George. *In Bluebeard's Castle.* New York: Atheneum, 1971.

————. *Language and Silence: Essays on Language, Literature, and the Inhuman.* New York: Atheneum, 1967.

Steiner, Peter. *The Deserts of Bohemia: Czech Fiction and Its Social Context.* Ithaca, NY: Cornell UP, 2000.

Steinweg, Reiner. *Das Lehrstück: Brechts Theorie einer politisch-ästhetischen Erziehung*. 2nd ed. Stuttgart: Metzler, 1976.

Stephan, Alexander. *Anna Seghers: Das siebte Kreuz—Welt und Wirkung eines Romans*. Berlin: Aufbau Taschenbuch, 1997.

————. *"Communazis": FBI Surveillance of German Emigré Writers*. Trans. Jan van Heurck. New Haven, CT: Yale UP, 2000.

Stern, Frederick. *F. O. Matthiessen: Christian Socialist as Critic*. Chapel Hill: U of North Carolina P, 1981.

Sternhell, Zeev, Mario Sznajder, and Maia Asheri. *The Birth of Fascist Ideology*. Princeton: Princeton UP, 1994.

Sternlicht, Sanford. *Siegfried Sassoon*. New York: Twayne, 1993.

Stetz, Margaret. "Rebecca West's Criticism: Alliance, Tradition, and Modernism." *Rereading Modernism: New Directions in Feminist Criticism*. Ed. Lisa Rado. New York: Garland, 1994. 41–66.

Stoll, David. *Rigoberta Menchú and the Story of All Poor Guatemalans*. Boulder: Westview P, 1999.

Stone, Lawrence. *The Crisis of the Aristocracy, 1558–1641*. Oxford: Clarendon Press, 1965.

Stoneman, Patsy. *Elizabeth Gaskell*. Hemel Hempstead: Harvester Wheatsheaf/Prentice Hall, 1987.

Stott, William. *Documentary Expression and Thirties America*. Chicago: U of Chicago P, 1973.

Strohm, Paul. *Social Chaucer*. Cambridge, MA: Harvard UP, 1989.

Strong-Boag, Veronica, and Carole Gerson. *Paddling Her Own Canoe: Times and Texts of E. Pauline Johnson (Tekahionwake)*. Toronto: U of Toronto P, 2000.

Sturm, Terry. "Christina Stead's New Realism: *The Man Who Loved Children* and *Cotters' England*." *Cunning Exiles*. Ed. Don Anderson and Stephen Knight. Sydney: Angus and Robertson, 1974. 9–35.

Suárez, Juan, and Millicent Manglis. "Cinema, Gender, and the Topography of Enigmas: A Conversation with Laura Mulvey." *Cinefocus* 3 (1995): 2–8.

Suggs, Jon-Christian. Introduction to *Marching! Marching!* by Clara Weatherwax. Detroit: Omnigraphics, 1990. iii–xliv.

————. "*Iron City*: Race and Revolutionary Romanticism Behind Bars." *Legal Studies Forum* 25 (2001): 449–59.

————. "*Marching! Marching!* and the Idea of the Proletarian Novel." *The Novel and the American Left: Critical Essays on Depression-Era Fiction*. Ed. Janet Galligani Casey. Iowa City: U of Iowa P, 2004. 151–71.

————. "The Proletarian Novel." *Dictionary of Literary Biography*. Vol. 9, pt. 3. Ed. James J. Martine. Detroit: Gale Research, 1981. 231–45.

Suleiman, Susan. *Authoritarian Fictions: The Ideological Novel as a Literary Genre*. New York: Columbia UP, 1983. 102–18.

Suleri, Sara. "Woman Skin Deep: Feminism and the Postcolonial Condition." *Critical Inquiry* 18.4 (1992): 756–69.

Sullivan, Nikki. *A Critical Introduction to Queer Theory*. New York: New York UP, 2003.

Sullivan, Robert. *Christopher Caudwell*. London: Croom Helm, 1987.

Summerfield, Penny. *Women Workers in the Second World War*. London: Routledge, 1984.

Summers, Claude J. *Christopher Isherwood*. New York: Ungar, 1980.

Sundquist, Eric J., ed. *Frederick Douglass: New Literary and Historical Essays*. New York: Cambridge UP, 1990.

Suny, Ronald Grigor. *The Soviet Experiment: Russia, the USSR, and the Successor States*. New York: Oxford UP, 1998.

Surette, Leon. *Pound in Purgatory: From Economic Radicalism to Fascism and Anti-Semitism*. Urbana: U of Illinois P, 1999.

Sutin, Lawrence. *Divine Invasions: A Life of Philip K. Dick*. New York: Harmony Books, 1989.

Suvin, Darko. *Metamorphoses of Science Fiction: On the Poetics and History of a Literary Genre*. New Haven: Yale UP, 1979.

————. *Positions and Presuppositions in Science Fiction*. Kent, OH: Kent State UP, 1988.

————. *To Brecht and Beyond*. New York: Barnes and Noble, 1984.

Swanson, Philip. "California Dreaming: Mixture, Muddle and Meaning in Isabel Allende's North American Narratives." *Journal of Iberian and Latin American Studies* 9.1 (2003): 57–67.

————. *The New Novel in Latin America: Politics and Popular Culture after the Boom*. Manchester: Manchester UP, 1995.

Sweezy, Paul M., and Leo Huberman, eds. *F. O. Matthiessen (1902–1950): A Collective Portrait*. New York: Monthly Review Press, 1951.

Symons, Julian. *Bloody Murder: From the Detective Story to the Crime Novel*. New York: Viking, 1985.

Szarycz, Ireneusz. *Poetics of Valentin Kataev's Prose of the 1960s and 1970s*. New York: Peter Lang, 1989.

Talalay, Kathryn. *Composition in Black and White: The Life of Philippa Schuyler*. New York: Oxford UP, 1995.

Tam, Kwok-kan, ed. *The Soul of Chaos: Critical Perspectives on Gao Xingjian*. Hong Kong: The Chinese UP, 2001.

Tassie, James S. "Philippe Aubert de Gaspé." *Our Living Tradition: Second and Third Series*. Ed. Robert L. MacDougall. Toronto: U of Toronto P, 1959. 55–72.

Tate, Trudi. *Modernism, History and the First World War*. Manchester: Manchester UP, 1998.

Taylor, A.J.P. *English History 1914–1945*. Oxford: Oxford UP, 1992.

Taylor, Jacqueline. *Grace Paley: Illuminating the Dark Lives*. Austin: U of Texas P, 1990.

Taylor, Ronald, ed. *Aesthetics and Politics*. London: NLB, 1977.

Taylor, Yuval, ed. *I Was Born a Slave: An Anthology of Classic Slave Narratives*. 2 vols. Edinburgh: Payback, 1999.

Teitelboim, Volodia. *Neruda: An Intimate Biography*. Austin: U of Texas P, 1991.

Templeton, Joan. *Ibsen's Women*. Cambridge: Cambridge UP, 1997.

Teraoka, Arlene Akiko. *The Silence of Entropy or Universal Discourse: The Postmodernist Poetics of Heiner Müller*. New York: Peter Lang, 1985.

Teres, Harvey M. *Renewing the Left: Politics, Imagination, and the New York Intellectuals*. New York: Oxford UP, 1996.

Terras, Victor. *A History of Russian Literature*. New Haven: Yale UP, 1991.

————. *Vladimir Mayakovsky*. Boston: Twayne, 1983.

Tertz, Abram. *On Socialist Realism*. Trans. George Dennis. Intro. Czeslaw Milosz. New York: Pantheon, 1960.

Thadal, Roland. *Jacques Roumain: l'unité d'une oeuvre*. Port-au-Prince: Editions des Antilles, 1997.

Thatcher, Ian D. *Trotsky.* London: Routledge, 2003.

Thomas, David Wayne. *Cultivating Victorians: Liberal Culture and the Aesthetic.* Philadelphia: U of Pennsylvania P, 2003.

Thompson, Doug. *Cesare Pavese: A Study of the Major Novels and Poems.* Cambridge: Cambridge UP, 1982.

Thompson, E. P. *The Making of the English Working Class.* New York: Vintage-Random House, 1966.

Thompson, Ewa M. *Imperial Knowledge: Russian Literature and Colonialism.* Westport, CT: Greenwood, 2000.

Thompson, John B., and David Held, eds. *Habermas: Critical Debates.* Cambridge, MA: MIT P, 1982.

Thomson, Ian. *Primo Levi.* London: Hutchinson, 2002.

Thomson, Peter. *Shakespeare's Professional Career.* Cambridge: Cambridge UP, 1992.

————, and Glendyr Sacks, eds. *The Cambridge Companion to Brecht.* Cambridge: Cambridge UP, 1994.

Thoreau, Henry David. *Walden and Other Writings.* New York: Random House, 1981.

————. *The Writings of Henry David Thoreau.* Boston: Houghton Mifflin, 1906.

Thornberry, Robert S. *Les Ecrits de Paul Nizan (1905–1940): Portrait d'une époque: Bibliographie commentée suivie de textes retrouvés.* Paris: Honoré Champion, 2001.

Thorson, Connie Capers, and James L. Thorson. "Gomorrah on the Puerco: A Critical Study of Philip Stevenson's Proletarian Epic *The Seed.*" *Labor in New Mexico: Union, Strikes, and Social History since 1881.* Ed. Robert Kern. Albuquerque: U of New Mexico P, 1983. 183–270.

Throssell, Ric. *Wild Weeds and Wind Flowers: The Life and Letters of Katharine Susannah Prichard.* Sydney: Angus and Robertson, 1975.

Thurston, Robert W. *Life and Terror in Stalin's Russia, 1934–1941.* New Haven, CT: Yale UP, 1996.

Tierney-Tello, Mary Beth. *Allegories of Transgression and Transformation: Experimental Fiction by Women Writing under Dictatorship.* Albany: SUNY P, 1996.

Tillery, Tyrone. *Claude McKay: A Black Poet's Struggle for Identity.* Amherst: U of Massachusetts P, 1992.

Timms, Edward. *Karl Kraus: Apocalyptic Satirist.* Vol. 1: *Culture and Catastrophe in Habsburg Vienna.* New Haven, CT: Yale UP, 1986. Vol. 2: *The German-Jewish Dilemma between the World Wars.* New Haven, CT: Yale UP, 2004.

Todd, William Mills, III. *Fiction and Society in the Age of Pushkin: Ideology, Institutions, and Narrative.* Cambridge, MA: Harvard UP, 1986.

————, ed. *Literature and Society in Imperial Russia, 1800–1914.* Stanford: Stanford UP, 1978.

Todorov, Tzvetan. *Mikhail Bakhtin: The Dialogical Principle.* Trans. Wlad Godzich. Minneapolis: U of Minnesota P, 1984.

Tokarczyk, Michelle M. *E. L. Doctorow's Skeptical Commitment.* New York: Peter Lang, 2000.

Tolstoy, Leo. *I Cannot Be Silent: Writings on Politics, Art and Religion by Leo Tolstoy.* Bristol, UK: Bristol P, 1989.

Tompkins, Jane. *Sensational Designs: The Cultural Work of American Fiction.* New York: Oxford UP, 1985.

Torres-Rioseco, Arturo. *New World Literature: Tradition and Revolt in Latin America.* Berkeley: U of California P, 1949.

Torres-Saillant, Silvio. *Caribbean Poetics: Toward an Aesthetic of West Indian Literature.* Cambridge: Cambridge UP, 1997.

Toye, William E., ed. *The Oxford Companion to Canadian Literature.* New York: Oxford UP, 1997.

Trenner, Richard, ed. *E. L. Doctorow: Essays and Conversations.* Princeton, NJ: Ontario Review P, 1983.

Trilling, Lionel. *The Liberal Imagination: Essays on Literature and Society.* 1950. New York: HBJ, 1979.

Trotsky, Leon. *Literature and Revolution.* Trans. Rose Strunsky. Ann Arbor: U of Michigan P, 1960.

Troupe, Quincy, ed. *James Baldwin: The Legacy.* New York: Simon and Schuster, 1989.

Tucker, Jeffrey Allen. *A Sense of Wonder: Samuel R. Delany, Race, Identity, and Difference.* Hanover, NH: Wesleyan UP, 2004.

Tucker, Robert C. *Stalin in Power: The Revolution from Above, 1928–1941.* New York: Norton, 1990.

———, ed. *The Lenin Anthology.* New York: Norton, 1975.

Tudor, J. M. "Soups and Snails and Political Tales . . . Günter Grass and the Revisionist Debate in 'Was Erfurt außerdem bedeutet' and *Der Butt.*" *Oxford German Studies* 18 (1988): 132–50.

Tumarkin, Nina. *Lenin Lives! The Lenin Cult in Soviet Russia.* Enlarged ed. Cambridge, MA: Harvard UP, 1997.

Turgenev, Ivan. *The Essential Turgenev.* Ed. Elizabeth Cheresh Allen. Evanston, IL: Northwestern UP, 1994.

Turgut, Erhan, ed. *Nazim Hikmet: Biographie et Poèmes* (Turkish, English, and French parallel texts). Paris: Turquoise, 2002.

Turner, Graeme. *British Cultural Studies: An Introduction.* 2nd ed. London: Routledge, 1996.

Turner, James. *One Flesh: Paradisal Marriage and Sexual Relations in the Age of Milton.* Oxford: Clarendon P, 1987.

Turner, Stephen P., ed. *The Cambridge Companion to Weber.* New York: Cambridge UP, 2000.

Tylee, Claire. *The Great War and Women's Consciousness: Images of Militarism and Womanhood in Women's Writings, 1914–64.* Iowa City: Iowa UP, 1990.

Udenta, Udenta O. *Revolutionary Aesthetics and the African Literary Process.* Enugu, Nigeria: Fourth Dimension, 1993.

Ugarte, Michael. *Trilogy of Treason: An Intertextual Study of Juan Goytisolo.* Columbia, MO: U of Missouri P, 1982.

Ungar, Steven. *Roland Barthes: The Professor of Desire.* Lincoln: U of Nebraska P, 1983.

Urgo, Joseph R. "Proletarian Literature and Feminism: The Gastonia Novels and Feminist Protest." *Minnesota Review* 24 (1984): 64–84.

Vaillant, Janet. *Black, French, and African: A Life of Léopold Sédar Senghor.* Cambridge, MA: Harvard UP, 1990.

Valdés, María Elena de, and Mario J. Valdés, eds. *Approaches to Teaching García Márquez's "One Hundred Years of Solitude."* New York: Modern Language Association, 1990.

Van Crevel, Maghiel. "Underground Poetry in the 1960s and 1970s." *Modern Chinese Literature* 9.2 (1996): 169–219.

Van Delden, Maarten. *Carlos Fuentes, Mexico, and Modernity.* Nashville, TN: Vanderbilt UP, 1998.

Vanden, Harry E. *National Marxism in Latin America: José Carlos Mariátegui's Thought and Politics.* Boulder: Lynne Rienner, 1986.

Van Laan, Thomas F. "Generic Complexity in Ibsen's *An Enemy of the People.*" *Comparative Drama* 20 (Summer 1986): 95–114.

Van Toorn, Penny. "Indigenous Texts and Narratives." *The Cambridge Companion to Australian Literature.* Ed. Elizabeth Webby. Cambridge: Cambridge UP, 2000. 19–49.

Van Watson, William. *Pier Paolo Pasolini and the Theatre of the Word.* Ann Arbor, MI: UMI Research P, 1989.

Vaverka, Ronald D. *Commitment as Art: A Marxist Critique of a Selection of Alan Sillitoe's Political Fiction.* Stockholm: Almqvist and Wiksell, 1978.

Veeser, H. Aram. *Edward Said.* New York: Routledge, 2005.

———, ed. *The New Historicism.* New York: Routledge, 1989.

Veitch, Jonathan. *American Superrealism: Nathanael West and the Politics of Representation in the 1930s.* Madison: U of Wisconsin P, 1997.

Vicinus, Martha. "Chartist Fiction and the Development of a Class-Based Literature." *The Socialist Novel in Britain.* Ed. H. Gustav Klaus. London: Harvester, 1982. 7–25.

———. *The Industrial Muse: A Study of Nineteenth-Century British Working-Class Literature.* London: Croom Helm, 1974.

Vieira, Nelson H. "Testimonial Fiction and Historical Allegory: Racial and Political Repression in Jorge Amado's Brazil." *Latin American Literary Review* 17.34 (July–December 1989): 6–23.

Villa, Dana, ed. *Cambridge Companion to Hannah Arendt.* New York: Cambridge UP, 2002.

Vizenor, Gerald. *Shadow Distance.* Hanover, NH: Wesleyan UP, 1994.

———, and Robert A. Lee. *Postindian Conversations.* Lincoln: U of Nebraska P, 1999.

Vogel, Lise. *Marxism and the Oppression of Women: Toward a Unitary Theory.* New Brunswick, NJ: Rutgers UP, 1983.

Volkogonov, Dmitri. *Trotsky: The Eternal Revolutionary.* London: HarperCollins, 1996.

Vološinov, V. N. *Freudianism: A Critical Sketch.* Ed. I. R. Titunik and Neil R. Bruss. Trans. I. R. Titunik. Bloomington: Indiana UP, 1987.

———. *Marxism and the Philosophy of Language.* Trans. Ladislav Matejka and I. R. Titunik. Cambridge, MA: Harvard UP, 1986.

Wade, Jean-Philippe. "Song of the City and Mine Boy: The 'Marxist' Novels of Peter Abrahams." *Research in African Literatures* 21.3 (1990): 89–101.

Wade, Michael. *Peter Abrahams.* London: Evans, 1972.

Wade, Stephen. *The Imagination in Transit: The Fiction of Philip Roth.* Sheffield: Sheffield UP, 1996.

———. *Jewish American Literature since 1945: An Introduction.* Edinburgh: Edinburgh UP, 1999.

Wagner, Linda, ed. *Denise Levertov: In Her Own Province.* New York: New Directions, 1979.

Wagner-Martin, Linda. *Critical Essays on Denise Levertov.* Boston: G. K. Hall, 1990.

Wald, Alan M. *Exiles from a Future Time: The Forging of the Mid-Twentieth-Century Literary Left.* Chapel Hill: U of North Carolina P, 2002.

———. *James T. Farrell: The Revolutionary Socialist Years.* New York: New York UP, 1978.

———. *The New York Intellectuals: The Rise and Decline of the Anti-Stalinist Left from the 1930s to the 1980s.* Chapel Hill: U of North Carolina P, 1987.

————. "Science Fiction and Fantasy." *Encyclopedia of the American Left*. Ed. Mari Jo Buhle et al. New York: Oxford UP, 1997. 724–26.

Walker, Alice. *In Search of Our Mother's Gardens: Womanist Prose*. New York: Harcourt, 1983.

Walker, Julia M., ed. *Milton and the Idea of Woman*. Urbana: U of Illinois P, 1988.

Walker, Margaret. *How I Wrote "Jubilee" and Other Essays on Life and Literature*. Ed. Maryemma Graham. New York: Feminist P, CUNY, 1990.

————. *On Being Female, Black and Free: Essays 1932–1992*. Ed. Maryemma Graham. Knoxville: U of Tennessee P, 1997.

Walker, Marshall. *Scottish Literature since 1707*. Harlow: Longman, 1996.

Wallace, Ian, ed. *Anna Seghers in Perspective*. Amsterdam: Rodopi, 1998.

————. *Christa Wolf in Perspective*. Amsterdam: Rodopi, 1994.

Walters, Ronald. *American Reformers, 1815–1860*. New York: Hill and Wang, 1978.

Wang, David Der-wei. *Fin-de-Siècle Splendor: Repressed Modernities of Late Qing Fiction, 1849–1911*. Stanford, CA: Stanford UP, 1997.

Wang Dewei. *Fictional Realism in Twentieth-Century China: Mao Dun, Lao She, Shen Cong-wen*. New York: Columbia UP, 1992.

Wang Hsueh-wen. "Mao Tse-tung's Thought on Literature and Art and the Maoist Struggle between the Two Lines in Literature and Art." *Issues and Studies* 10 (June 1974): 46–56.

Wang Jing. *High Culture Fever: Politics, Aesthetics, and Ideology in Deng's China*. Berkeley: U of California P, 1997.

Warhol, Robyn R., and Diane Price Herndl, eds. *Feminisms: An Anthology of Literary Theory and Criticism*. New Brunswick, NJ: Rutgers UP, 1991.

Warme, Lars, ed. *A History of Swedish Literature*. Lincoln: U of Nebraska P, 1996.

Warwick, Jack. *The Long Journey: Literary Themes of French Canada*. Toronto: U of Toronto P, 1968.

Washington, Robert E. *The Ideologies of African American Literature: From the Harlem Renaissance to the Black Nationalist Revolt*. Lanham, MD: Rowman and Littlefield, 2001.

Wasiolek, Edward, ed. *Critical Essays on Tolstoy*. Boston: G. K. Hall, 1986.

Wasserstein, Bernard. *Britain and the Jews of Europe, 1930–1945*. Oxford: Clarendon P, 1996.

Watson, Burton. *Early Chinese Literature*. New York: Columbia UP, 1962.

Watson, George. *Politics and Literature in Modern Britain*. Totowa, NJ: Rowman and Little-field, 1977.

Watson, Roderick. *The Literature of Scotland*. London: Macmillan, 1986.

Watson, Steven. *The Birth of the Beat Generation*. New York: Pantheon, 1995.

Watt, Donald. *Aldous Huxley, the Critical Heritage*. London: Routledge and Kegan Paul, 1975.

Watt, Ian. *The Rise of the Novel: Studies in Defoe, Richardson, and Fielding*. Berkeley: U of California P, 1957.

Watt, Stephen, Eileen Morgan, and Shakir Mustafa, eds. *A Century of Irish Drama: Widen-ing the Stage*. Bloomington: Indiana UP, 2000.

Weales, Gerald. *Odets the Playwright*. London: Methuen, 1985.

Weaver, Jace. *That the People Might Live: Native American Literatures and Native American Community*. New York: Oxford UP, 1997.

Webb, Constance. *Richard Wright: A Biography*. New York: G.P. Putnam's Sons, 1968.

Webby, Elizabeth, ed. *The Cambridge Companion to Australian Literature*. Cambridge: Cambridge UP, 2000.

Weber, Edgard. *L'Univers romanesque de Rachid el-Daif et la guerre du Liban*. Paris: L'Harmattan, 2001.

Weber, Max. *Economy and Society: An Outline of Interpretive Sociology.* 1968. 3 vols. Ed. and trans. Guenther Roth and Claus Wittich. Berkeley: U of California P, 1978.

————. *From Max Weber: Essays in Sociology.* Trans. H. H. Gerth and C. W. Mills. Oxford: Oxford UP, 1946.

————. *General Economic History.* New Brunswick, NJ: Transaction, 1961; New York: Collier Books, 1981.

————. *The Methodology of the Social Sciences.* Ed. and trans. E. A. Shils and H. A. Finch. New York: Free P, 1949.

————. *Political Writings.* Ed. Peter Lassman and Ronald Speirs. Cambridge: Cambridge UP, 1994.

————. *The Protestant Ethic and the Spirit of Capitalism.* 1904–1905. Trans. Talcott Parsons. New York: Scribner's, 1958.

Webster, Roger. "*Love on the Dole* and the Aesthetic of Contradiction." *The British Working-Class Novel in the Twentieth Century.* Ed. Jeremy Hawthorn. London: Edward Arnold, 1984. 49–62.

Wegner, Phillip E. *Imaginary Communities: Utopia, the Nation, and the Spatial Histories of Modernity.* Berkeley: U of California P, 2002.

————. "The Last Bomb: Historicizing History in Terry Bisson's *Fire on the Mountain* and Gibson and Sterling's *The Difference Engine*." *Comparatist* 23 (1999): 141–51.

————. "Soldierboys for Peace: Cognitive Mapping, Space, and Science Fiction as World Bank Literature." *World Bank Literature.* Ed. Amitava Kumar. Minneapolis: U of Minnesota P, 2003. 280–96.

Weil, Irwin. *Gorky: His Literary Development and Influence on Soviet Intellectual Life.* New York: Random House, 1966.

Weimann, Robert. *Shakespeare and the Popular Tradition in the Theater: Studies in the Social Dimension of Dramatic Form and Function.* Ed. Robert Schwartz. Baltimore: Johns Hopkins UP, 1978.

Weinstein, Cindy, ed. *The Cambridge Companion to Harriet Beecher Stowe.* Cambridge: Cambridge UP, 2005.

Weintraub, Stanley. *Journey to Heartbreak.* London: Routledge and Kegan Paul, 1971.

Weisbord, Vera Buch. *A Radical Life.* Bloomington: Indiana UP, 1977.

Weisenburger, Steven. *Fables of Subversion: Satire and the American Novel, 1930–1980.* Athens: U of Georgia P, 1995.

Weiss, Timothy. *On the Margins: The Art of Exile in V. S. Naipaul.* Amherst: U of Massachusetts P, 1992.

Weissman, Susan. *Victor Serge: The Course Is Set on Hope.* London: Verso, 2001.

————, ed. *The Ideas of Victor Serge: A Life as a Work of Art.* Glasgow: Critique, 1997.

Wellek, Renée. *American Criticism, 1900–1950.* Vol. 6 of *A History of Modern Criticism: 1750–1950.* London: Jonathan Cape, 1986.

————, and Austin Warren. *Theory of Literature.* 3rd ed. San Diego: Harcourt Brace Jovanovich, 1977.

Wendt, Albert. "An Interview with Festus Iyayi." *Landfall* 44.4 (1990): 412–22.

West, Rebecca. *The Young Rebecca: Writings of Rebecca West, 1911–1917.* Ed. Jane Marcus. New York: Viking, 1982.

Westfahl, Gary. *The Mechanics of Wonder: The Creation of the Idea of Science Fiction*. Liverpool: Liverpool UP, 1998.

Wetzsteon, Ross. *Republic of Dreams: Greenwich Village: The American Bohemia, 1910–1960*. New York: Simon and Schuster, 2001.

Wexler, Alice. *Emma Goldman: An Intimate Life*. New York: Pantheon, 1984.

Whale, John C. *Imagination under Pressure, 1789–1832: Aesthetics, Politics, Utility*. Cambridge: Cambridge UP, 2000.

Wheat, Edward M. "The Post-Modern Detective: The Aesthetic Politics of Dashiell Hammett's 'Continental Op.'" *Midwest Quarterly* 36.3 (Spring 1995): 237–50.

Whisnant, David E. *Rascally Signs in Sacred Places: The Politics of Culture in Nicaragua*. Chapel Hill: U of North Carolina P, 1995.

White, Donna R. *Dancing with Dragons: Ursula K. Le Guin and the Critics*. Columbia, SC: Camden House, 1999.

White, George Abbott. "Ideology and Literature: *American Renaissance* and F. O. Matthiessen." *Literature and Revolution*," special issue of *TriQuarterly* 23/24 (Winter/Spring 1972): 430–500.

White, N. P. *A Companion to Plato's "Republic."* Oxford: Blackwell, 1979.

Whitehead, Anne. "Open to Suggestion: Hypnosis and History in Pat Barker's *Regeneration*." *Modern Fiction Studies* 44 (Fall 1998): 674–95.

Whyte, William. *The Organization Man*. New York: Simon and Schuster, 1956.

Wiggershaus, Rolf. *The Frankfurt School: Its History, Theories, and Political Significance*. Trans. Michael Robertson. Cambridge, MA: MIT P, 1994.

Wilford, Hugh. *The New York Intellectuals: From Vanguard to Institution*. Manchester: Manchester UP, 1995.

Willett, John, ed. *Brecht on Theatre*. London: Methuen, 1964.

Williams, Beryl. *Lenin*. New York: Longman, 2000.

Williams, James S. *The Erotics of Passage: Pleasure, Politics, and Form in the Later Work of Marguerite Duras*. New York: St. Martin's, 1997.

Williams, Lorna V. *Self and Society in the Poetry of Nicolás Guillén*. Baltimore: Johns Hopkins UP, 1982.

Williams, Patricia J. *The Alchemy of Race and Rights*. Cambridge, MA: Harvard UP, 1991.

Williams, Paul. *Only Apparently Real: The World of Philip K. Dick*. New York: Arbor House, 1986.

Williams, Raymond. *The Country and the City*. New York: Oxford UP, 1971.

———. *Culture and Society: 1780–1950*. New York: Columbia UP, 1958.

———. "The Industrial Novels: *Mary Barton* and *North and South*." *Culture and Society, 1780–1950*. London: Chatto and Windus, 1958.

———. *Keywords: A Vocabulary of Culture and Society*. Rev. ed. New York: Oxford UP, 1983.

———. "Literature and Sociology: In Memory of Lucien Goldmann." *New Left Review* 67 (May/June 1971): 3–18.

———. *Marxism and Literature*. Oxford: Oxford UP, 1977.

———. *The Politics of Modernism: Against the New Conformists*. London: Verso, 1989.

Williams, Raymond Leslie. *Gabriel García Márquez*. Boston: Twayne, 1984.

———. *Mario Vargas Llosa*. New York: Ungar, 1986.

Williams, Trevor. *Joyce's Politics*. Gainesville: UP of Florida, 1997.

Williamson, Joel. *William Faulkner and Southern History*. New York: Oxford UP, 1993.

Willmott, Glenn. *Unreal Country: Modernity in the Canadian Novel in English*. Montréal: McGill-Queen's UP, 2002.

Wilson, A. N. *Tolstoy*. New York: W. W. Norton, 1988.

Wilson, Diana de Armas. *Cervantes, the Novel, and the New World*. Oxford and New York: Oxford UP, 2000.

Wilson, Sharon Rose. *Margaret Atwood's Fairy-Tale Sexual Politics*. Jackson: UP of Mississippi, 1993.

Wimsatt, William K. *The Verbal Icon*. Lexington: UP of Kentucky, 1954.

Winks, Robin, ed. *Detective Fiction: A Collection of Critical Essays*. Englewood Cliffs, NJ: Prentice-Hall, 1980.

Winton, Calhoun. *John Gay and the London Theatre*. Lexington: UP of Kentucky, 1993.

Wirth, Andrzej. "The *Lehrstück* as Performance." *Drama Review* 43.4 (1999): 113–21.

Wise, Christopher. "The Garden Trampled: The Liquidation of African Culture in V. S. Naipaul's *A Bend in the River*." *College Literature* 23 (October 1996): 58–72.

Wismann, Heinz, ed. *Walter Benjamin et Paris*. Paris: Cerf, 1986.

Witte, Bernd. *Walter Benjamin: An Intellectual Biography*. Detroit: Wayne State UP, 1991.

————, Theo Buck, Hans-Dietrich Dahnke, and Regine Otto, eds. *Goethe-Handbuch*. 5 vols. Stuttgart: Metzler, 1996–1998.

Wixon, Douglas. Introduction to *The Disinherited* by Jack Conroy. Columbia: U of Missouri P, 1991. ii–xxvi.

————. *Worker-Writer in America: Jack Conroy and the Tradition of Midwestern Literary Radicalism, 1898–1990*. Urbana: U of Illinois P, 1994.

Woehrlin, William F. *Chernyshevskii: The Man and the Journalist*. Cambridge, MA: Harvard UP, 1971.

Wolfe, Jesse. "'Ambivalent Man': Ellison's Rejection of Communism." *African American Review* 34 (Winter 2000): 621–38.

Wolin, Richard. *Walter Benjamin: An Aesthetics of Redemption*. New York: Columbia UP, 1982.

Wollstonecraft, Mary, and William Godwin. *A Short Residence in Sweden; Memoirs of the Author of* "The Rights of Woman." 1796. 1798. Ed. Richard Holmes. London: Penguin, 1987.

Woloch, Isser. *The New Regime: Transformations of the French Civic Order, 1789–1820s*. New York: W. W. Norton, 1994.

Womack, Craig C. *Red on Red: Native American Literary Separatism*. Minneapolis: U of Minnesota P, 1999.

Wong, Sau-ling Cynthia. *Reading Asian American Literature: From Necessity to Extravagance*. Princeton, NJ: Princeton UP, 1993.

Wood, Ellen Meiksins. *Democracy against Capitalism*. Cambridge: Cambridge UP, 1995.

————. *The Retreat from Class: A New True Socialism*. London: Verso, 1986.

Woodard, Charles L. *Ancestral Voice: Conversations with N. Scott Momaday*. Lincoln: U of Nebraska P, 1989.

Woodring, Carl R. *Politics in the Poetry of Coleridge*. Madison: U of Wisconsin P, 1961.

Woolf, Virginia. "Dorothy Richardson." *Women and Writing*. Ed. Michele Barrett. New York: Harcourt Brace, 1979.

————. *A Room of One's Own*. New York: Harcourt Brace, 1929.

————. *The Virginia Woolf Reader*. New York: Harcourt, 1984.

Woroszylski, Wiktor. *The Life of Mayakovsky*. Trans. Boleslav Taborski. New York: Orion, 1970.

Worth, Katharine J. "Edward Bond." *Essays on Contemporary British Drama*. Ed. Hedwig Bock and Albert Wertheim. Munich: Hueber, 1981. 205–22.

Worthen, W. B. *Modern Drama and the Rhetoric of Theater*. Berkeley: U of California P, 1992.

Wren, Robert M. *Achebe's World: The Historical and Cultural Context of the Novels of Chinua Achebe*. Washington, DC: Three Continents P, 1980.

Wright, A. Colin. *Mikhail Bulgakov: Life and Interpretations*. Toronto: U of Toronto P, 1978.

Wright, Derek. *Ayi Kwei Armah's Africa: The Sources of His Fiction*. London: Hans Zell, 1989.

———. *Wole Soyinka Revisited*. New York: Twayne, 1993.

———, ed. *Critical Perspectives on Ayi Kwei Armah*. Washington, DC: Three Continents P, 1992.

Wright, Elizabeth, and Edmund Wright, eds. *The Zizek Reader*. Oxford: Blackwell, 1999.

Wright, Richard. *The Color Curtain*. Jackson: UP of Mississippi, 1994.

———. *Native Son*. 1940. New York: Harper and Row, 1989.

———. *12 Million Black Voices*. New York: Thunder's Mouth P, 1988.

Wright, William. *Lillian Hellman: The Image, the Woman*. New York: Simon and Schuster, 1986.

Wyatt, David, ed. *New Essays on* The Grapes of Wrath. Cambridge: Cambridge UP, 1990.

Yale French Studies 65 (1983). Special issue entitled "The Language of Difference: Writing in Québéc(ois)."

Yang, Philip Q. *Ethnic Studies: Issues and Approaches*. New York: State U of New York P, 2000.

Yarborough, Richard. Afterword to *Blood on the Forge* by William Attaway. New York: Monthly Review P, 1987. 295–315.

Yarbro-Bejarano, Yvonne. "Gloria Anzaldúa's *Borderlands/La Frontera*: Cultural Studies, 'Difference,' and the Non-Unitary Subject." *Cultural Critique* 28 (1994): 5–28.

Yeats, William Butler. *Essays and Introductions*. New York: Collier Books, 1961.

———. *Explorations*. New York: Collier Books, 1962.

Yedlin, Tovah. *Maxim Gorky: A Political Biography*. Westport, CT: Praeger, 1999.

Yeh, Michelle. "Shapes of Darkness: Symbols in Li Ang's Dark Night." *Modern Chinese Women Writers: Critical Appraisals*. Ed. Michael S. Duke. Armonk, NY: M. E. Sharpe, 1989. 78–95.

Yelin, Louise. "Problems of Gordimer's Poetics: Dialogue in *Burger's Daughter*." *Feminism, Bakhtin and the Dialogic*. Ed. Dale M. Bauer and Susan Jaret McKinstry. Albany: SUNY P, 1991. 219–38.

Young, Alan. "Edgell Rickword." *Seven Writers of the English Left: A Bibliography of Literature and Politics, 1916–1980*. Ed. Alan Munton and Alan Young. New York: Garland, 1981. 25–81.

Young, D. F. *Beyond the Sunset: A Study of James Leslie Mitchell*. Aberdeen: Impulse Books, 1973.

Young, Robert J. C. *Colonial Desire: Hybridity in Theory, Culture, and Race*. London: Routledge, 1995.

———. *Postcolonialism: An Historical Introduction*. Oxford: Blackwell, 2001.

———. *White Mythologies: Writing History and the West*. London: Routledge, 1990.

Young-Bruehl, Elizabeth. *Hannah Arendt: For Love of the World*. New Haven: Yale UP, 1982.

Yousaf, Nahem. *Alex La Guma: Politics and Resistance*. Portsmouth, NH: Heinemann, 2001.

Zaborowska, Magdalena. *How We Found America: Reading Gender through East European Immigrant Narratives*. Chapel Hill: U of North Carolina P, 1995.

Zha Jianying. *China Pop: How Soap Operas, Tabloids, and Bestsellers Are Transforming a Culture.* New York: New P, 1995.

Zhao, Henry Y. H. *Towards a Modern Zen Theatre: Gao Xingjian and Chinese Theatre Experimentalism.* London: School of Oriental and African Studies, 2000.

Zheutlin, Barbara, and David Talbot. *Creative Differences: Profiles of Hollywood Dissidents.* Boston: South End P, 1978.

Zimmerman, Bonnie. "What Has Never Been: An Overview of Lesbian Feminist Criticism." *The New Feminist Criticism: Essays on Women, Literature and Theory.* Ed. Elaine Showalter. New York: Pantheon, 1985. 200–224.

———, and Toni A. H. McNaron, eds. *The New Lesbian Studies.* New York: Feminist P, 1996.

Zita, Jacquelyn N. "Anzaldúan Body." *Body Talk: Philosophical Reflections on Sex and Gender.* New York: Columbia UP, 1998. 165–83.

Zizek, Slavoj. *The Indivisible Remainder: An Essay on Schelling and Related Matters.* London: Verso, 1996.

———. *Looking Awry: An Introduction to Jacques Lacan through Popular Culture.* Cambridge, MA: MIT P, 1991.

———. *The Metastases of Enjoyment.* London: Verso, 1994.

———. *The Sublime Object of Ideology.* London: Verso, 1991.

———. *Tarrying with the Negative: Kant, Hegel, and the Critique of Ideology.* Durham, NC: Duke UP, 1993.

———. *Welcome to the Desert of the Real.* London: Verso, 2001.

———, ed. *Revolution at the Gates.* London: Verso, 2002.

Zogbaum, Heidi. *B. Traven: A Vision of Mexico.* Wilmington, DE: SR Books, 1997.

Zogović, Radovan. *Na poprištu.* Beograd: Kultura, 1947.

Zohn, Harry, ed. *In These Great Times: A Karl Kraus Reader.* Trans. Joseph Fabry, Max Knight, Karl F. Ross, and Harry Zohn. Montreal: Engendra P, 1976.

Zuck, Virpi, ed. *Dictionary of Scandinavian Literature.* Westport, CT: Greenwood, 1990.

Zurier, Rebecca. *Art for the Masses: A Radical Magazine and Its Graphics, 1911–1917.* Philadelphia: Temple UP, 1988.

Zweig, Michael. *The Working Class Majority: America's Best Kept Secret.* Ithaca, NY: Cornell UP, 2000.

Zwerdling, Alex. *Virginia Woolf and the Real World.* Berkeley: U of California P, 1986.

○○○ *Index* ○○○

Note: Page numbers in **bold** type refer to main entries in encyclopedia.

Delany and, 192; detective fiction and, 198; Doctorow and, 207; Fuentes and, 275–76; Haraway and, 331–32; Harvey on, 335; historical novel and, 353–54; history of concept, 569–70; Jameson on, 382–83, 570–72; in literature, 570; ludic, 576; Marxism and, 24, 467–68, 570, 575–78; modernism versus, 574–77; nature of, 572–78; as oppositional, 574–78; and pastiche, 571–72; popular culture and, 576; poststructuralism and, 569–70; Rushdie and, 631; Russ and, 620; and schizophrenia, 571; South Asian literature, 683; television and, 572; Vietnam War and, 738, 739–40

Poststructuralism: Barthes and, 67; French feminism and, 259, 286; hegemony as concept for, 338–39; Joyce and, 393; Kristeva and, 405; Marxism and, 467–68; New Historicism and, 513; postcolonial studies and, 566, 567; postmodernism and, 569–70

Poud, 551

Poulin, Jacques, 127

Pound, Ezra, 32, 132–33, 182, 229, 230, 369, 392, 483, 484, 488, **579**, 612, 706, 759, 760, 773

Poveda, José Manuel, 172

Power: cultural studies and, 177; Foucault on, 263. *See also* Hegemony

Powhatan, 503

Prado, Adélia, 95

Praed, Rosa, 54

Prakrits, 678–79

Pratolini, Vasco, 374

Pravda (newspaper), 396, 657, 694

Preda, Marin, 226

Premchand (pseudonym of Dhanpat Rai), 681

Présence africaine (magazine), 19, 138, 649

Pretty Shield, 503

Preview (magazine), 641

Prévost d'Exiles, Antoine-François, 269

Prica, Ognjen, 776

Price, Richard, 761

Price-Mars, Jean, 138, 616

Prichard, Katharine Susannah, 54–55, **580**

Priestley, Joseph, 161, 761

Primo de Rivera, Miguel, 725

Pringle, Thomas, 675

Prison literature, **580–82**

Pritchett, V. S., 768

Prochain Épisode (Next Episode) (Aquin), 582–83

Profession, academic, 38–39, 239–42, 291, 529–30. *See also* English departments

Proletarian fiction, American, **583–91**; aesthetics of, 590–91; form and content in, 588–89; gender and race in, 589–90; legacy of, 591; nature of, 585–87. *See also* Proletarian literature

Proletarian literature: American literature (after 1900), 31; Attaway and, 50–51; Burke and, 118; Communist Party USA and, 165; Conroy's *The Disinherited* and, 169; Cultural Revolution and, 454; Davis and, 188; Ellison and, 231; Gastonia Mill strike and, 281; Gold and, 307, 388; Iyayi and, 375; John Reed Clubs and, 389; Lenin and, 422; Lumpkin and, 442; magazines for, 40; *New Masses* and, 515; Olsen's *Yonnondio* as, 530; Popular Front and, 557; Smedley and, 664–65; Weatherwax and, 749; Wright's *Native Son* as, 13, 504–6. *See also* British working-class and socialist literature; Proletarian fiction, American; Socialist realism

Proletkult, 584, 588, 624

Propaganda, 404, 405, 765

Propp, Vladimir, 671

Prose fiction, in Renaissance England, 235–36

Prosser, Gabriel, 328

Protazanov, Jakov, 683, 717

Proudhon, Pierre-Joseph, 736

Proust, Marcel, 517

Provincetown Players, 709

Prudencio, Joe, 115

Prus, Bolesław, 224

Psychoanalysis, 404, 406, 780

Public Interest (magazine), 544

Public sphere, 237, 327

Puerto Ricans, 415

Puig, Manuel, 582

Pulitzer Prize: Norman Mailer, 448; N. Scott Momaday, 492; Toni Morrison, 77, 495

Pushkin, Aleksandr Sergeevich, 423, **591–92**, 620, 621

Pynchon, Thomas, 32, 192, 197, 198, 477, 570, 639, 768

Quadrant (magazine), 55

Quebec, 125–28, 582–83, 641

Queer theory, 282, 644–45

Quiet Revolution (Quebec), 125

Quintero, Héctor, 174

Quintilianus, 94

Quinto Sol, 415

Qu Yuan, 153

○○○ *Notes on Contributors* ○○○

Jeremy Ahearne is Senior Lecturer in French Studies at the University of Warwick, UK.

Charles J. Alber teaches in the Department of Languages, Literatures, and Cultures at the University of South Carolina.

Angela Albright is a member of the English faculty at Northwest Arkansas Community College, Bentonville, Arkansas.

Elizabeth Cheresh Allen is Professor of Russian and Comparative Literature at Bryn Mawr College.

Jeff Allred is a doctoral candidate at the University of Pennsylvania. His dissertation examines American photographic documentary books of the 1930s.

Lori Bailey is a doctoral candidate in English at the University of Arkansas.

David Weil Baker is Associate Professor of Renaissance Literature at Rutgers University, Newark.

Cates Baldridge is Associate Professor of English at Middlebury College, Middlebury, Vermont.

Lawrie Balfour is Assistant Professor of Politics at the University of Virginia. She is the author of *The Evidence of Things Not Said: James Baldwin and the Promise of American Democracy.*

Stephen M. Barber is Associate Professor in the Department of English at the University of Rhode Island. With David L. Clark, he is coeditor and contributor to *Regarding Sedgwick: Essays on Queer Culture and Critical Theory.*

David Barnett is Lecturer in Drama at University College Dublin and specializes in contemporary German theater.

Frank Beardow is Reader in Russian and Comparative Literary Studies at the School of Social and International Studies, the University of Sunderland.

John Beck teaches in the School of English Literature, Language, and Linguistics at the University of Newcastle.

Kathleen Bell teaches in the School of Humanities at De Montfort University, UK.

Steven M. Bell teaches Spanish in the Department of Foreign Languages at the University of Arkansas.

Nancy Berke teaches at Hunter College, City University of New York.

Celeste-Marie Bernier teaches in the School of American and Canadian Studies at the University of Nottingham.

James D. Bloom teaches in the Department of English at Muhlenberg College, Allentown, Pennsylvania.

Kristin Bluemel is Associate Professor of English at Monmouth University and author of *George Orwell and the Radical Eccentrics: Intermodernism in Literary London* (2004).

M. Keith Booker is Professor of English at the University of Arkansas, Fayetteville.

Gavin Bowd teaches in the School of Modern Languages at the University of St. Andrews, Scotland.

Yomi Braester teaches in the Department of Comparative Literature at the University of Washington.

Robert H. Brinkmeyer Jr. is Professor and Chair of the Department of English at the University of Arkansas.

Paul Buhle teaches in the Department of American Civilization at Brown University.

Zofia Burr is Assistant Professor of English at Cornell University.

Jeffrey Arellano Cabusao is a graduate student in English at the University of Michigan, Ann Arbor.

William E. Cain is Professor of English and American Studies at Wellesley College.

Sergio Chaple is a retired full professor and now official researcher at the Instituto de Literatura y Lingüísticas de la Academia de Ciencias de Cuba. A short-story writer and one of his country's leading critics, he is internationally recognized as a specialist on novelist Alejo Carpentier.

Nancy Cho is Associate Professor of English at Carleton College.

Renny Christopher is Professor of English at California State University, Channel Islands.

David L. Clark is Professor in the Department of English and Cultural Studies at McMaster University, where he is also Associate Member of the Health Studies Programme. With Stephen M. Barber, he is coeditor and contributor to *Regarding Sedgwick: Essays on Queer Culture and Critical Theory*.

Alina Clej teaches in the Program in Comparative Literature at the University of Michigan.

Stephen Clingman is Professor of English at the University of Massachusetts.

Steve Cloutier received his Ph.D. in twentieth-century left-wing British literature from the University of Leicester (UK). He currently teaches at St. Mary's University in Halifax, Canada.

Debra Rae Cohen is Assistant Professor of English at the University of Arkansas and the author of *Remapping the Home Front: Locating Citizenship in British Women's Great War Fiction*.

Robert Cohen teaches in the Department of Germanic Languages and Literature at New York University.

Ed Comentale is Assistant Professor of English at Indiana University. He is the author of *Modernism, Cultural Production, and the British Avant-Garde*.

Kathy Comfort is Assistant Professor of French at the University of Arkansas, Fayetteville. Her primary research interests are the nineteenth- and twentieth-century French novel and the interrelationship between literature and medicine.

Neil Cornwell (University of Bristol) has written widely on Russian and comparative literature, and is currently completing a general survey of "The Absurd in Literature."

Mark E. Cory is Professor Emeritus of German at the University of Arkansas.

Andy Croft is a freelance writer, poet, and political activist; author of *Red Letter Days*, a study of British leftist fiction in the 1930s; and editor of *A Weapon in the Struggle*, a cultural history of the Communist Party in Britain.

Charles Cunningham teaches American literature and culture at Eastern Michigan University.

Macdonald Daly teaches at the University of Nottingham.

John E. Davidson teaches in the Department of Germanic Languages and Literature at Ohio State University.

Anthony Dawahare teaches in the Department of English at California State University, Northridge.

Mikhal Dekel teaches English and Comparative Literature at the City College of New York and is currently completing her dissertation on gender and Jewish nationality at Columbia University.

Andrew M. Drozd is Associate Professor of Russian at the University of Alabama.

Osman Durrani teaches in the School of European Culture at the University of Kent.

Dennis Dworkin teaches history at the University of Nevada, Reno, and is the author of *Cultural Marxism in Postwar Britain: History, the New Left, and the Origins of Cultural Studies*. He is currently working on a book on contemporary debates on class.

Joy Dworkin is a Professor of English at Missouri Southern State University, where she teaches world literature and creative-writing courses.

Arlene (Amy) Elder is Professor of English at the University of Cincinnati.

Keith Ellis is Professor Emeritus of Spanish and Portuguese at the University of Toronto.

Joseph Entin teaches in the English Department at Brooklyn College.

Alice Entwistle is a Senior Lecturer in English at the University of the West of England, Bristol (UK). She has written on various aspects of Anglo-American poetics, most recently coauthoring *A History of Twentieth-Century British Women's Poetry* with Jane Dowson.

Brad Epps is Professor of Romance Languages and Literatures at Harvard University.

Edward E. Ericson Jr. is Professor of English, Emeritus, at Calvin College. He has written two books on Aleksandr Solzhenitsyn and, with that author's cooperation, has abridged *The Gulag Archipelago*.

Michael Eskin teaches German and Comparative Literature at Columbia University and is the author of *Nabokov's Version of Pushkin's Eugene Onegin: Between Version and Fiction* (1994) and *Ethics and Dialogue in the Works of Levinas, Bakhtin, Mandel'shtam, and Celan* (2000).

Helen Fehervary is Professor of Germanic Languages and Literature at the Ohio State University.

Alexandra Fitts is Associate Professor of Spanish and Women's Studies in the Department of Foreign Languages and Literatures at the University of Alaska Fairbanks.

Deborah Fleming is Professor of English at Ashland University. She is the author of *"A man who does not exist": The Irish Peasant in W. B. Yeats and J. M. Synge* and has edited two collections of essays on Yeats.

John E. Flower is Professor of French in the School of European Culture and Languages at the University of Kent.

Barbara Foley is Professor of English at Rutgers University, Newark.

Richard Francis is Professor of French Eighteenth-Century Studies at the University of Nottingham. His works include several studies of eighteenth-century literature and the works of Romain Rolland.

Carl Freedman is Professor of English at Louisiana State University and the author of several books and dozens of articles, with a particular concentration on science fiction.

Chris Freeman is Associate Professor of English at St. John's University in Minnesota, where he teaches courses in gender and sexuality, film studies, literature, linguistics, and creative writing. He is currently writing a biography of Paul Monette called *Becoming Paul Monette*.

John Gatt-Rutter is Vaccari Professor in Italian Studies and Program Coordinator for the Italian Studies and European Studies School of Historical and European Studies at La Trobe University in Melbourne, Australia.

Dan Georgakas has written extensively on American labor, film, and ethnicity. He was the longtime editor of *Cineaste* and is the coeditor of *Solidarity Forever: An Oral History of the IWW.*

James Gibbs, who has lectured at universities in Ghana, Malawi, and Nigeria, is currently teaching at the University of the West of England, Bristol.

Steve Giles is Professor of German Studies and Critical Theory at the University of Nottingham. He has published widely on the work of Bertolt Brecht.

Paul A. Gillen is a member of the Faculty of Humanities and Social Sciences at the University of Technology, Sydney, Australia.

Martha E. Gimenez, originally from Argentina, is Professor of Sociology at the University of Colorado, Boulder. She is the author of numerous articles and book chapters on Marxist-feminism, population theory, the politics of racial and ethnic construction, and inequality.

Saime Göksu, who grew up in Turkey, studied natural science in Ankara, where she became a Lecturer in Physics. She coauthored *Romantic Communist: The Life and Work of Nazim Hikmet* (1999) with her husband Edward Timms.

Howard Goldblatt, Research Professor of Chinese at the University of Notre Dame, has translated more than thirty book-length works from China, Taiwan, and Hong Kong, and written or edited a half dozen more. *Notes of a Desolate Man* by the Taiwanese novelist Chu Tien-wen (co-transalted with Sylvia Li-chun Lin) was chosen as Translation of the Year for 1999 by the American Literary Translators Association.

Mayte Gómez is Lecturer in Spanish at the University of Nottingham.

Josh Gosciak teaches Media Studies at City College of New York. His forthcoming book is tentatively titled *Between Diaspora and Internationalism: Claude McKay and the Making of a Black Public Intellectual.*

Sondra Guttman is an Assistant Professor of English at Ithaca College.

Sam Haigh is Senior Lecturer in French Studies at the University of Warwick.

Larry Hanley is Professor of English at the City College of the City University of New York.

Laura Hapke has written a number of books on working-class history and fiction, the most recent *Labor's Text: The Worker in American Fiction* (Rutgers University Press, 2001). Her newest book, *Sweatshop: History of an American Idea*, will appear next year.

Brian Hardman is completing a doctoral degree in English at the University of Arkansas.

Matthew Hart is Assistant Professor in the Department of English at the University of Illinois at Urbana-Champaign.

Timothy Harte teaches Russian at Bryn Mawr University.

Adnan Haydar is Professor of Comparative Literature at the University of Arkansas.

Donghui He teaches at the University of Tennessee.

Cyndy Hendershot is Associate Professor of English at Arkansas State University.

Ian Higgins is Senior Lecturer in English Literature at the Australian National University in Canberra, Australia.

Peter Hitchcock is Associate Professor of English at the City University of New York.

Andrew Hoberek is Assistant Professor of English at the University of Missouri.

Veronica Hollinger is Associate Professor of Cultural Studies at Trent University in Ontario and coeditor of *Science Fiction Studies*.

Robert C. Holub is Professor of German and Dean of the Undergraduate Division of the College of Letters and Science at the University of California at Berkeley.

Yvonne Howell is Associate Professor of Russian at the University of Richmond.

Christina Howells is Professor of Medieval and Modern Languages at the University of Oxford.

Peter Hutchinson is Director of Studies in Modern Languages at Trinity Hall, Cambridge, and Reader in Modern German Studies at the University of Cambridge.

Farhad B. Idris is Assistant Professor of English at Frostburg State University in Frostburg, Maryland.

Faith Ingwersen is widely published as a scholar and translator of Scandinavian literature, sometimes in collaboration with her husband, Niels Ingwersen.

Niels Ingwersen taught in the Department of Scandinavian Studies at the University of Wisconsin at Madison. He recently retired.

Norma Jenckes teaches dramatic literature and playwriting at the University of Cincinnati. She is the founding and continuing editor of the scholarly journal *American Drama* and has published widely on modern drama.

A. Yemisi Jimoh is Associate Professor of English at the University of Arkansas.

José Luís Jobim is the Chair of Theory of Literature at the Universidade do Estado do Rio de Janeiro and Universidade Federal Fluminense (Brazil).

Bruce G. Johnson teaches in the Department of English at the University of Rhode Island.

Dubravka Juraga is a Research Associate with the Center for Technology in Government, state of New York.

Jonathan Kalb is Professor and Chair of the Department of Theatre at Hunter College of the City University of New York.

Kasongo M. Kapanga teaches in the Department of Modern Languages and Literatures at the University of Richmond.

Carter Kaplan is Associate Professor of English at Belmont Technical College, St. Clairsville, Ohio.

Eleanor Kaufman is Assistant Professor of English at the University of Virginia.

AnaLouise Keating is Associate Professor of women's studies at Texas Woman's University. She has published several books on women-of-color theorizing.

Douglas Kellner is the George F. Kneller Chair in the Philosophy of Education at UCLA.

R. Brandon Kershner is Professor of English at the University of Florida.

Nyla Ali Khan is a doctoral student at the University of Oklahoma and is at work on a dissertation entitled "Transporting the Subject: The Fiction of Nationality in an Era of Transnationalism."

Nick Knight teaches in the School of International Business and Asian Studies at Griffith University, Australia.

E. Dean Kolbas received his doctorate from Cambridge University. His publications include *Critical Theory and the Literary Canon*.

Delia C. Konzett is Assistant Professor of English at the University of New Hampshire.

Joel Kovel is Professor of Social Studies at Bard College; the editor of *Capitalism, Nature, Socialism*; and author, most recently, of *The Enemy of Nature*.

Jon Eugene von Kowallis teaches at the University of New South Wales, Sydney.

Joseph G. Kronick teaches in the Department of English at Louisiana State University.

Thomas Lahusen is Canada Research Chair in History, Arts, and Culture at the University of Toronto, where he teaches Russian/Soviet and East-European cultural history, comparative literature, and film.

Carmen Lamas is a Graduate Student at the University of Pennsylvania.

Kenneth Lantz is a Professor of Russian in the Department of Slavic Languages and Literatures at the University of Toronto.

Neil Larsen is Associate Professor of Spanish and Classics at the University of California at Davis.

Phyllis Lassner teaches at Northwestern University.

James Laughton is a member of the English Faculty at Northwest Arkansas Community College, Bentonville, Arkansas.

Keith Laybourn teaches history at the University of Huddersfield, UK.

David Leaton is a doctoral student in English at the University of Arkansas.

Mabel Lee is Honorary Associate in the School of Languages and Cultures at the University of Sydney. Her publications include the translations of three titles by Gao Xingjian: his novels *Soul Mountain* (2000) and *One Man's Bible* (2002), and a collection of short stories entitled *Buying a Fishing Rod for My Grandfather* (2004).

Vincent B. Leitch is Paul and Carol Daube Chair in English at the University of Oklahoma. He is the general editor of *The Norton Anthology of Theory and Criticism* and the author of five books, including *American Literary Criticism from the 1930s to the 1980s* and *Theory Matters*.

Madeline G. Levine teaches in the Department of Slavic Languages and Literatures at the University of North Carolina.

Mitchell R. Lewis is Assistant Professor of English at Elmira College, New York.

Tim Libretti is Assistant Professor of English at Northeastern Illinois University.

Sylvia Li-chun Lin teaches East Asian Languages and Literatures at the University of Notre Dame.

Laura Lomas teaches Literature of the Americas and Ethnic American Literature at Rutgers University, Newark.

Devoney Looser teaches in English and Women's and Gender Studies at the University of Missouri at Columbia.

Thomas J. Lynn is Assistant Professor of English at Penn State Berks-Lehigh Valley College. He has published articles on African literature in several journals, including recent issues of the *Cincinnati Romance Review* and the *International Journal of Francophone Studies*.

James MacDonald is Honorary Research Fellow in Drama at the University of Exeter. His principal activity is writing plays, many of them on Russian themes.

David Margolies teaches English at Goldsmiths College, University of London, and has published extensively on popular culture, Renaissance literature, Shakespeare, and Marxist criticism.

Susan Marren is Associate Professor of English at the University of Arkansas in Fayetteville.

Andrew Martin is Associate Professor of Literary Studies and Film Studies at the University of Wisconsin, Milwaukee.

Doug Martin is a research student at Exeter University.

Gerald Martin is the Andrew W. Mellon Professor of Modern Languages at the University of Pittsburgh.

Derek C. Maus is Assistant Professor of English and Communication at SUNY College at Potsdam.

Raymond A. Mazurek is Associate Professor of English at the Berks campus of Penn State University in Reading, Pennsylvania.

R. John McCaw teaches at the University of Wisconsin, Milwaukee.

Tom McDonough teaches in the Department of Art History at Binghamton University, State University of New York.

John McGowan is Professor of English and Comparative Literature at the University of North Carolina, Chapel Hill. He is the author of one book and coeditor of another on Hannah Arendt.

Michael McKeon is Professor of English at Rutgers University, New Brunswick.

John McLeod teaches at the University of Leeds.

Ana de Medeiros teaches French at the University of Kent, Canterbury.

Marisol Mejía has taught Latin American and Latino/a literature at the University of Utah and Auburn University. Her current works-in-progress include essays on the politics in César Vallejo's poetry and prose, and research in Critical Race Studies. Presently, she is an advocate of immigrant rights in North Florida.

Nick Melczarek teaches English at the University of Florida.

Gregory Meyerson teaches English at North Carolina State University.

Magali Cornier Michael is Associate Professor of English at Duquesne University.

Bart Moore-Gilbert is Professor of Postcolonial Studies and English at Goldsmiths' College, University of London. He is the author of *Kipling and "Orientalism"* (1986), *Postcolonial Theory: Contexts, Practices, Politics* (1997), and *Hanif Kureishi* (2001) as well as many articles on colonial and postcolonial literature and theory. He is currently working on a monograph on postcolonial life writing.

Stephen Morton is a lecturer in Anglophone Literature and Culture at Southampton University, UK.

Lynda C. Mugglestone teaches at Pembroke College at Oxford University.

Bill V. Mullen is Professor of English at the University of Texas at San Antonio. He is the author of *Afro-Orientalism and Popular Fronts: Chicago and African American Cultural Politics, 1935–1946*. He is also editor, with James Smethurst, of *Left of the Color Line: Race, Radicalism, and Twentieth Century Literature of the United States*.

Alan Munton is a researcher at the University of Plymouth, UK.

Timothy S. Murphy, Associate Professor of English at the University of Oklahoma, is the author of *Wising Up the Marks: The Amodern William Burroughs*; general editor of the journal *Genre: Forms of Discourse and Culture*; and translator of books, articles, and seminars by Gilles Deleuze and Antonio Negri.

Supriya Nair teaches in the Department of English at Tulane University.

Nick Nesbitt is Assistant Professor of French and Italian at Miami University.

Judith Newman is Professor of American Studies at the University of Nottingham, UK.

Amy Abugo Ongiri teaches in the Department of English at the University of California at Riverside.

Hans Ostrom is Professor of English at the University of Puget Sound. He is the author of *A Langston Hughes Encyclopedia, Langston Hughes: A Study of the Short Fiction*, and *Three to Get Ready* (a novel). With J. David Macey, he's editing an encyclopedia of African American literature.

Craig N. Owens teaches in the Department of English at Drake University.

Stuart Parkes is Emeritus Professor of German Studies at the University of Sunderland. He has published widely on modern German literature and society.

Michael Payne teaches in the Department of English at Bucknell University.

Phyllis Perrakis teaches in the Department of English at the University of Ottawa.

Rachel Peterson is a doctoral candidate in English at the University of Michigan.

Thomas E. Peterson is Professor of Italian in the Department of Romance Languages at the University of Georgia.

Helmut F. Pfanner is a Professor of German at Vanderbilt University. He has published widely in the field of nineteenth- and twentieth-century German, Austrian, and Swiss literature, especially expressionism, exile literature, and contemporary literature, including authors like Alfred Döblin, Oskar Maria Graf, and Karl Jakob Hirsch.

Tony Pinkney is Senior Lecturer in English Literature at Lancaster University, UK.

Yannick Portebois is the Director of the Centre for Nineteenth Century French Studies at the University of Toronto. Her works deal with book history and the cultural history of the French language.

Roxana Preda is Assistant Professor at the John F. Kennedy Institute, Freie Universität, Berlin, Germany.

Julian Preece teaches in the School of European Culture and Languages at the University of Kent, UK.

Fiona Price teaches in the School of English History and Media at University College, Chichester, UK.

Leigh Pryor is a doctoral candidate in English at the University of Arkansas.

Paula Rabinowitz is Professor of English at the University of Minnesota.

Sandy Rankin is a doctoral candidate in English at the University of Arkansas.

Luis Fernando Restrepo is Associate Professor of Spanish and Director of the Comparative Literature Program at the University of Arkansas.

Alan Riach is Head of the Department of Scottish Literature at the University of Glasgow.

Stephen G. H. Roberts is Lecturer in Spanish at the University of Nottingham.

Tom Rockmore teaches in the Department of Philosophy at Duquesne University.

John B. Romeiser is Professor of French at the University of Tennessee, Knoxville. He has published articles and books on André Malraux, the Spanish Civil War, and World War II. He is the editor of the *André Malraux Review*.

Brigid Rooney is a lecturer in Australian Studies at the University of Sydney.

Stephen Ross is Assistant Professor of English at the University of Victoria and author of *Conrad and Empire* (2004).

Karen Ryan is Professor of Slavic Languages and Literatures at the University of Virginia.

Epifanio San Juan Jr. has taught at a number of different universities in the United States and abroad, including the University of Connecticut, Tamkang University in Taiwan, and Washington State University. He has published widely in a number of areas, including postcolonial literature, Philippine literature, and literary theory.

Mark Sandy teaches in the Department of English Studies at the University of Durham, UK.

Dana Sawyer is Associate Professor of Philosophy and Religion at the Maine College of Art, Portland, Maine.

Sean Sayers is Professor of Philosophy in the School of European Culture and Languages at the University of Kent, Canterbury.

Peter Scheckner is Professor of Literature at Ramapo College of New Jersey. He is the author of books on D. H. Lawrence and on Chartist poetry and has just completed an anthology called *The Way We Work: Contemporary Literature from the Workplace*.

Barry P. Scherr is Mandel Family Professor of Russian at Dartmouth College.

Keith W. Schlegel is Professor of English at Frostburg State University, Frostburg, Maryland.

Yaël R. Schlick is Assistant Adjunct Professor of English at Queen's University in Kingston, Ontario. She has published articles on women's travel writing and colonial literature and has recently translated Victor Segalen's *Essay on Exoticism*.

Sabine Schmidt is a doctoral candidate in Comparative Literature at the University of Arkansas, where she also received an M.F.A. in Literary Translation. She holds an M.A. in American Studies and German Studies from Hamburg University.

Dennis L. Seager is Visiting Associate Professor of Spanish and Graduate Advisor in the Department of Spanish and Portuguese at the University of Wisconsin, Milwaukee.

James Seaton teaches in the Department of English at Michigan State University.

Thomas Seifrid is Associate Professor of Slavic Languages and Literatures at the University of Southern California. He is the author of *Andrei Platonov: Uncertainties of Spirit* and numerous articles on Russian literature and culture.

Janet Sharistanian teaches modern literature and feminist theory at the University of Kansas and is writing a biography of Tess Slesinger.

Ben-Z. Shek is Emeritus Professor of French at the University of Toronto. Author of two books and numerous articles, he is known internationally as a specialist on French-Canadian/Québécois literature.

Jackie Shellard did graduate work on the writing of Victor Serge.

Kirsten Shepherd-Barr is Associate Professor of English at North Carolina State University.

R. Allen Shoaf is Alumni Professor of English at the University of Florida.

Charles L. P. Silet is Professor of English at Iowa State University.

Eric D. Smith received his Ph.D. in English from the University of Florida and is the author of articles on James Joyce and Robert Antoni.

Gerry Smyth is Reader in Cultural History at Liverpool John Moores University. He is the author of *Space and the Irish Cultural Imagination* (2001), and his current research interests are in the area of popular music.

Jeff Solomon is a doctoral candidate in English at the University of Southern California.

Robin J. Sowards is a doctoral candidate in English at Cornell University.

Leslie Stainton is a writer and editor in Ann Arbor, Michigan.

Michael E. Staub teaches in the Department of English at Bowling Green State University.

Marianne Stecher-Hansen is Associate Professor of Scandinavian Literature at the University of Washington. She is the editor of two volumes of the *Dictionary of Literary Biography*, both on Danish writers. She has published on H. C. Andersen, Isak Dinesen (Karen Blixen), and Thorkild Hansen.

Dorothy Stephens is Associate Professor of English at the University of Arkansas, Fayetteville, and Vice President of the International Spenser Society.

Sanford Sternlicht is Professor Emeritus of English and Theater at the State University of New York at Oswego.

David M. Stewart is Assistant Professor of English at National Central University, Taiwan.

Patsy Stoneman is a Reader in English at the University of Hull (UK); her major publications are *Elizabeth Gaskell* and *Bronte Transformations: The Cultural Dissemination of "Jane Eyre" and "Wuthering Heights."*

Jon-Christian Suggs is Professor of African American and American Literature at the City University of New York.

Jason G. Summers is Assistant Professor of Spanish in the Department of Modern Foreign Languages at Indiana University–Purdue University at Fort Wayne.

Ireneusz Szarycz is Associate Professor in the Department of Germanic and Slavic Studies at the University of Waterloo in Waterloo, Ontario.

Harvey Teres is Associate Professor of English at Syracuse University.

Sean Teuton is Assistant Professor of English and American Indian Studies at the University of Wisconsin at Madison. He is an enrolled member of the Cherokee Nation.

Peter Thomson is Emeritus Professor of Drama at the University of Exeter, where he taught from 1974 to 2003. He is General Editor of *The Cambridge History of British Theatre* and coeditor of *The Cambridge Companion to Brecht*. His books include *Shakespeare's Theatre*, *Shakespeare's Professional Career*, and *Mother Courage and Her Children*.

Edward Timms is Research Professor in German Studies at the University of Sussex. He is best known for his book *Karl Kraus—Apocalyptic Satirist* (1986). His interest in multiculturalism led him to establish the Sussex Centre for German-Jewish

Studies, and recent publications include *Writing after Hitler: The Work of Jakov Lind* (2000).

Stephen P. Turner teaches in the Department of Philosophy at the University of South Florida.

Andrea Tyndall teaches at Erasmus University in Rotterdam, Holland.

David H. Uzzell Jr. is a doctoral student in Spanish at the University of Connecticut, Storrs.

Maghiel van Crevel is Professor of Chinese Language and Literature at Leiden University.

Maarten van Delden is Associate Professor and Chair in the Department of Hispanic Studies at Rice University.

Álvaro J. Vidal-Bouzon is Lecturer in Spanish at the University of Nottingham.

Jean-Philippe Wade teaches at the University of KwaZulu-Natal, South Africa.

Alan M. Wald is a Professor in the English Department and in the Program in American Culture at the University of Michigan. He is the author of six books on United States literary radicalism, including *The New York Intellectuals* and *Exiles from a Future Time*.

Martha Watson teaches in the Greenspun College of Urban Affairs at the University of Nevada at Las Vegas.

Elizabeth Webby teaches in the English Department at the University of Sydney, Australia.

Phillip E. Wegner is Associate Professor of English at the University of Florida.

Rowland Weston is a Lecturer in History at the University of Waikato in Tauranga, New Zealand.

James S. Williams teaches in the School of European Culture and Languages at the University of Kent at Canterbury, UK.

Miller Williams is University Professor of English at the University of Arkansas.

Glenn Willmott teaches in the Department of English at Queen's University, Kingston, Ontario.

Julian Wolfreys is Professor of English at the University of Florida.

M. Elizabeth "Betsy" Wood is a graduate studen-at-large at the University of Chicago.

Nahem Yousaf teaches in the Department of English and Media Studies at Nottingham Trent University, UK.